Ark of the Covenant

The most electrifying discovery of our time

Jonathan Gray

First printing 1997
Second printing 1997
Third printing 1998
Fourth printing 2000

Copyright © Jonathan Gray 1997
ISBN 0-646-30073-3
Archaeology; History; Religion; Christianity
Designed and printed in Australia for
Jonathan Gray
P.O. Box 3370
Rundle Mall 5000
South Australia

Dedication

To the protector of the golden Ark.
I say to Him, "Thank you for
hiding the truth from those
who think themselves so wise,
and for revealing it to little
children."*

Acknowledgments

Many people have helped in the making of this book, some of them unwittingly. I wish to acknowledge with genuine gratitude especially my dear friends:

Glen and Suzanne Coopman, Darren Hunter, David Perry, Wetton, Kirstine MacGregor, Gavin Pitman, Albert Biddle, Susan Robertson, Gwen Hardy, Alf Mozeley, Graham and Margaretha Tierney, Beverley Barden, John Paige, Sanford Howard, John Seymour, Kevin Robinson, Carolyn Higgins, Arthur Eedle, Jannene Wade, Elizabeth Sparavec, Larry Hartman, Paul Breeze, Vera Latcham, Brian Davies, Shirley Wheeler, Maurice Colville, Peter O'Connor, Ula Cable, Daryl and Vada Kum Yuen, P. Detamore and John Knowles-Gray, who have been most gracious and helpful in so many different ways.

Cover illustration: Geoff Fox (geoff@zombie.serv.com.au)
Book & Cover design: Paul Teague (paul@dynamic-solutions.com.au)

I continually praise God for my dearest wife and best friend Josephine, whose dedication, enthusiasm and encouragement have been an inspiration to me since the inception of this project.

Jonathan Gray

*Matthew 11:25 LB

iii

About the Author

International explorer, archaeologist and author Jonathan Gray has traveled the world to gather data on ancient mysteries. He has penetrated some largely unexplored areas, including parts of the Amazon headwaters. The author has also led expeditions to the bottom of the sea and to remote mountain and desert regions of the world. He lectures internationally.

Other books by Jonathan Gray

Dead Men's Secrets
Curse of the Hatana Gods
Evidence That Shocks
The Ark Conspiracy
Sting of the Scorpion
Forgotten World
Surprise Witness
The Corpse Came Back
Forbidden Islands

Videos by Jonathan Gray

Surprising Discoveries 1 to 6

**Under the noses of the professionals,
an amateur finds the most prized
artifact on earth. Who is this man?
How did it happen?**

TABLE OF CONTENTS

PROLOGUE

Eskin glanced at his wrist watch. Just twenty-three minutes and Alitalia Flight 801 would be touching down. Baggage and immigration clearance should, hopefully, be quick. He could be in Jerusalem by five.

Rabbi Avigdor Eskin looked down at the photograph of the Prime Minister. Then he closed his eyes and reclined in his seat, rehearsing the plan. For this curse to work, he would need ten men. They would stand outside the house of Prime Minister Yitzhak Rabin and pronounce the words of the death sentence.

Eskin fumbled in his jacket. Fine, the letter was still there. A copy would be sent to several synagogues. Rabin had to die. The man was a **rodef**, endangering the lives of others. Not only that, he was a **moser**, the worst form of traitor.

The ancient curse Eskin would invoke was the **pulsa denura**, the "lashes of fire". Powerful, effective and deadly. So deadly, it could never be written down.

Eskin rehearsed it again. This curse had been handed down by word of mouth. It was the worst curse that could ever be issued.

Ten learned rabbis must agree that its use was justified. Of course, Eskin knew it must be done correctly. His helpers would need to fast for three days. They would cast the spell at midnight, in a ceremony lit by black candles.

...."Sir, would you please pull up your seat? We shall soon be landing."

1

The voice of the stewardess jolted him. For an instant, Eskin glared at her, annoyed at the sudden intrusion. He pressed the seat button.

...Was it Eskin I bumped into that morning at the bus station? As the surly, bearded man brushed past me, I was struck with something sinister in his look.

My crew and I departed Jerusalem the next morning. But a few days later, when I picked up a Cairo newspaper, my blood froze!

Israeli Prime Minister Yitzhak Rabin had just died violently!

It would later be revealed that Eskin had pronounced in triumph, "Our prayer has worked." He had then promptly returned to his native Russia, fearing arrest.

Almost any astute observer could see that the secular Israeli government was treading a tightrope. On the one hand it sought a delicate peace process with the potentially hostile Arabs. And on the other hand, it had to contend with Jewish "religious extremists" who wanted to build on the sacred Temple Mount held by those Arabs.

There were Jewish extremists who felt themselves "betrayed" by their government. The government was now blaming "religious extremists" for Rabin's assassination.

As if that were not enough, the authorities would soon have to deal with a third VERY EXPLOSIVE factor: THE ARK OF THE COVENANT discovery.

And that's where this story begins.

In a nutshell, this is how we shall tell it...

Chapters 1 to 3 will touch on the Ark's alleged "special" powers and recount the stories of some modern attempts to locate this lost treasure.

Chapters 4 to 20 trace the background story of the people who built the Ark. The Ark itself will be seen surfacing from time to time during this story, until vanishing for millennia.

Chapters 21 to 45 recount the search by Ronald Wyatt and his team for the lost Ark, interspersed with flash-backs to some earth-shaking events which *only now* can be seen as linked to the Ark EVEN WHILE IT REMAINED HIDDEN FROM SIGHT. The connection will be mind boggling.

2

In chapters 46 and 47, we ask, "Will the Ark play a role in coming events? Will something happen soon?"

The story about to unfold concerns long forgotten voyages, scientific blood tests, events of precision timing, prophecies uncanny in their fulfillment, secret underground passages, acts of intrigue, and fabulous treasures.

The revelations contained have the potential to ignite an explosion in conventional circles.

Meanwhile our excursion into the past offers a feast of hidden delights.

Let's begin...

IMPORTANT

It is ABSOLUTELY VITAL that the chapters be read IN SEQUENCE or the significance of some events will not be understood.

DUE TO RESTRICTIONS BY THE HOST GOVERNMENT, WE ARE UNABLE TO PRESENT ALL COLLECTED DATA ON THIS SUBJECT. FOR MOST PEOPLE, THAT WHICH CAN BE SAID IN THIS BOOK WILL BE MORE THAN ENOUGH. OTHERS WILL HAVE TO WATCH AND WAIT, UNTIL THAT TIME WHEN IT WILL BE MADE PUBLIC

CHAPTER 1

TOO HOT TO HANDLE

"This is a delicate matter," whispered Bob. He glanced around... saw no one following... and spoke again.

"It's too hot for some people."

I stood riveted, before the niche in the cliff face. Some forty feet under me sat the most explosive artifact on earth.

"They told us to seal off the tunnel mouth," breathed Bob. "I made the door to lead down and fixed it here. It's several feet under. Did it myself."

I surveyed the landscape. A good disguise. "We don't deserve to be here," I said finally. " Let's go."

◆◆◆◆◆◆

My mind drifted back... to the moment I first heard that an unknown American had claimed to have located that long sought treasure, the Ark of the Covenant.

"Rubbish!" I cried. "You say this guy Wyatt asserts he's found the most prized artifact on earth? Who is this crazy nut?"

"I know nothing about him," said my friend, calmly. "But you could easily get his address. Why don't you just check it out?"

"Look," I snorted. "If that treasure had been found it would be BIG NEWS. We'd know about it!"

"Well, you know about it now," said Kristine.

"I've heard such things before. There've been so many different claims. Why should I get involved in this one?"

And how come a bunch of amateurs could accomplish something that professional archaeologists had failed to do for so long?

The whole idea was ridiculous.

Furthermore, Wyatt – and his alleged discovery – were on the opposite side of the earth. Why should I bother? I put the matter to rest and got on with other work.

It was months before Ronald Wyatt's name surfaced again. I took a cursory look at what was said and filed it away for the second time.

But I was doomed. That man's claims were again pushed before my eyes – this time by an atheist.

Now I sat up with a jolt. This amateur archaeologist Wyatt was beginning to get on my nerves.

I mulled over the matter for a few days... and even consulted my bank balance. It would cost me quite a few thousand dollars to do something about this. But the whole thing was nagging at me now, like an aching tooth.

By the time I was ready to act, a whole sheaf of papers against this Wyatt guy was coming into my hands. The attack sounded reasonably scientific, Wyatt's opponent dismissing him as a deceitful character... or, at the very best, deluded.

Whatever the truth of the matter, I had to investigate this for myself. This would be my personal quest – and I would disprove the claims of Ron Wyatt.

Perhaps I should state right here that in my heart was an earnest desire to learn the unfettered truth. I could hold on to my money and from an ivory tower glibly repeat the objections of his enemies. Or I could put my money where my mouth was: confront the man personally... investigate the allegations... and assess the so-called "evidence". I opted for the latter course.

Before even beginning to investigate Ron Wyatt's claim, I would have to satisfy myself on two points: first, that no other claim of discovery was actually authentic; and second, that historical records made Wyatt's claimed location plausible.

Wyatt had also made claims to some other important discoveries. He had claimed to have confirmed the remains of an old boat in the mountains of eastern Turkey, as well as chariot parts on the floor of the Red Sea. The fact that he was claiming so much was a problem in my mind. These I would have to check out.

Ever skeptical, I preferred to believe only that which I could see with my own eyes. Therefore, in the course of investigating Ron Wyatt's Ark of the Covenant claim, it was logical that I and my team personally check into the man's other claims.

My skepticism – and my life – was to take a dramatic turn. I would find myself leading, and accompanying, several serious expeditions to each site. I hired professional divers to go down with me to the Red Sea. We did what no others had done. We physically checked out Wyatt's claims... on site.

There were times when it could have cost us our lives. But experience teaches one to be cautious.

In my first trek into the largely unexplored, unmapped headwaters of the Amazon in 1967, where head-shrinking savages fought with blowpipes and poison darts, I had taken the precaution of wearing a bullet-proof vest. That expedition – my first – had been unforgettable. But that's another story.

Now I was entering areas of the Middle East. This is where Ron Wyatt had been doing his work.

In the Turkish province of Agri, we would run into a military convoy and find ourselves abruptly arrested. We were in serious trouble, it seemed. And it was only the intervention of the governor that secured our freedom!

One night, Turkish armored vehicles were to blast holes in our hotel and pepper the walls around our room, in a battle with the Kurds. Within one hundred yards of the hotel, thirteen civilians would be shot dead.

Another day I would have to make a quick escape when a renegade village chief and his henchman lured me into the mountains with sinister intent.

Sleeping amid scorpions, diving among sharks, detouring to avoid terrorist ambushes...we finally checked out Wyatt's claims. This book is the story of one of those claims - and our surprise findings.

◆◆◆◆◆◆

Did the Ark of the Covenant possess some dangerous inate power?

The Ark of the Covenant has been called the most explosive artifact on earth. For 800 years it was the most precious and sacred object in the world... a large, gold plated chest.

Its lid with two attached cherubim was of pure gold - several hundred pounds of pure gold. In monetary terms it might be worth perhaps two to three million dollars.

But its real value was greater than that.

What celebrating, as King David, second King of Israel, first brought it into Jerusalem! The occasion was one of great rejoicing and imposing display, involving priests, princes and national Hebrew leaders.

With solemn joy the vast procession wound its way around the hills and valleys toward the Holy City. Music and singing mingled with excited shouts.

Then suddenly it happened. The cart that bore the golden chest was shaken by the oxen. One of the entourage, a man named Uzzah, thrust out his hand to steady the Ark.

He dropped dead.[1]

What had happened? Was the Ark electrically charged? Could Uzzah have been electrocuted?

Mystery

To those ancient Hebrews, the Ark was a sacred object, clothed in tremendous mystery.

It was seen by precious few. Even when transported, it had to remain covered throughout its journey.

In Solomon's Temple, the Ark was concealed behind a curtain. Even the priests were not permitted access to it.

Only the high priest was allowed into the room in which it stood – and then only once a year. This room – called the Most Holy Place – was a pitch-black, windowless room – though the Ark had its own light, to which we shall make reference later. By law, the high priest had to carry burning incense, which must fill the whole room with a veil of smoke, before he could approach the Mercy Seat of the Ark.

11

Adolf Hitler of Germany, and his Nazis, believed the Ark to be a mystical artifact, which would give them supernatural powers over mankind.

Before World War II, one of the aims of Mussolini of Italy was the capture of the Ark, thought to be in Ethiopia. His Fascist army conquered and held control of Ethiopia from 1936 to 1941, but the Ark eluded him.

An electric battery?

A man named Erich von Danicken caused a sensation in the seventies when he claimed that the Ark of the Covenant was an extraterrestrial artifact.

He asserted that people from outer space had colonized the earth and that God was an ancient astronaut. He tried to prove that the Bible and other ancient records cryptically supported this view.

The Ark, he theorized, was an electrical conductor, to which a loudspeaker could have been attached for communication between Moses, the Hebrew leader, and an extraterrestrial spaceship. Death from touching the Ark was simply from being electrocuted.

Von Danicken speculated that if a replica of the Ark was to be made, it would function as a battery. The Ark, to his mind, had an innate power as a superweapon.

Well, what is the truth? Could the Ark have possessed some dangerous innate power?

One should be aware, of course, that von Danicken provided no evidence to substantiate his theory. As a matter of fact, replicas of the Ark **have** been made, without any such electrical conductivity resulting.

But, more to the point, our original sources of information concerning the Ark – ancient Hebrew texts – refute such an idea. According to the first book of Samuel, Chapter 4, the Ark had no independent power as a superweapon. It was powerless to prevent its own capture by the enemy.

Too dangerous to touch

Nevertheless, the Scriptures describe in fearful detail the swift judgment that befell any who dared to desecrate the Ark. When captured by the Philistines who lived along the Mediterranean coast, it brought disaster to whatever town hosted it. At Bethshemesh, more than seventy Jewish men who lined up to peer into it, died for their irreverence.

The Ark was carried by poles inserted through rings at the base of the Ark.[2] These poles remained permanently in place, so as to avoid any need to touch the Ark itself when it was being set down or lifted up.

So, we may ask, what was the reason for such careful procedure?

To be treated as holy

Apparently, there was nothing inherently dangerous about the physical structure of the Ark. If we are to believe the ancient writings, the true power of the Ark rested only in the Divine Presence. It is related that when God's presence was with the Ark and the Hebrews who possessed it, the Ark was heralded as a wondrous source of divine blessing and protection to the faithful. It brought them victory in battle – and prosperity to the home of a man named Obed-edom while it rested there.

But when the Divine Presence departed, in response to Israel's faithlessness, the Ark was as powerless as any man-made object.

So holy was the Presence over the Ark considered to be – indicated by a radiant light hovering over it – that when the high priest entered the room, he wore metallic pomegranates alternating with bells around the hem of his garment, so that the people outside would know whether he was still alive.[3] A rope was attached to his ankle so that if he should be struck dead, the priests could withdraw his body from within the sacred place without risking their own lives.

We are dealing here with the Supernatural – something that many readers will consider outside accepted natural boundaries. And one might be excused for asking, how could touching or even looking upon an object be an act worthy of death?

•••••••

The Hebrews held that the Creator of the universe was holy and that they were unholy. This entire planet had fallen temporarily

13

under the powers of evil, and in order for the Deity to meet with His chosen people, He had instructed that a special place be kept aside that was not defiled by unholy beings.

The Ark of the Covenant came to be known as God's earthly "Throne", so to speak. Since the Holy One could be approached only in holiness, the Ark, which represented God's Presence, was to be treated as holy.

According to the writings of Moses, "violation of the holy things" that were set apart exclusively for the worship of God was a serious matter.[4] The Lord Himself, it was declared, had spoken thus:

> By those who come near me I will be treated as holy, and before all the people I will be honored.[5]

Since the holy Creator cannot look upon evil, [6] it meant instant destruction to **any** human, except the high priest, who came into contact with this earthly "Throne" of the Lord. God would not permit men to defile His earthly "Throne". This was the one object on earth which they were powerless to defile.

Uzzah's death

Concerning that man Uzzah, who was struck dead as he stretched out his hand to steady the Ark.

I used to wonder if God wasn't a little harsh on Uzzah. After all, he was only trying to help.

Then I discovered that Uzzah's fate was linked to the violation of a most explicit command. Through Moses, God had given special orders concerning the Ark's transportation.

Firstly, none but the appointed priests, descendants of Aaron, were to look upon it uncovered, much less touch it.[7] After the priests had covered the holy chest, the sons of Kohath must lift it by the poles that were placed in rings on each side.

Secondly, while carts and oxen were used to transport other items belonging to the worship tent, this was **not** to be the method of transportation for the Ark. It was to be borne upon the shoulders of the sons of Kohath.[8]

Thus, on this occasion, there had been a direct and inexcusable violation of the divine command.

Certainly, King David and his subjects were performing a glad and willing act in transporting the Ark to Jerusalem. However, their neglect of the divine instruction was unacceptable. In Uzzah's case, such neglect had apparently lessened his sense of the sacredness of God's plain statements. Only a strict heed to His requirements was acceptable.

Be that as it may, it can be seen that, when the golden Ark is revealed in the ancient writings, it is associated with issues of life and death.

That immediately elevates the interest. And human nature being as it is, many adventurers of our day were to join the search for this elusive treasure.

In the next two chapters we track down the most persistent tales that have surfaced in this quest.

CHAPTER 2

LOST... BUT WHERE?

"She just saw it on Israeli television!"

"Who?"

"Hadassah."

"What did she see?"

"She saw a news report on the Ark of the Covenant discovery in Jerusalem."

"What?"

"Yes, they must have got some of the information. And quite a few people have been phoning, asking where it is, and how to get to it."

"That's something no one's allowed to answer. Not yet."

It was July, 1996. We had been revealing snippets of the Ark discovery story in public presentations. It hadn't taken long for the news to get back to Israel.

Just a little earlier, as I was about to step on a plane to California, a lady in Queensland, Australia, had phoned to ask had I seen the SBS News? (SBS is a multi-cultural television network.)

They had announced, she said, that the Israeli government under the new Prime Minister, Mr. Netanyahu, had just placed a freeze on all archaeological digs "at ancient sites".

Perhaps the two events were related? The second of these news items had actually preceded the first. But in archaeological work, one learns to keep an open mind and just wonder.

•••••••

17

Long before I had got involved, there had been speculations that the lost Ark was anywhere from eastern Africa to Ireland on the Atlantic.

Since the Hollywood fantasy *Raiders of the Lost Ark* was first released in 1981, with Harrison Ford in the starring role as Indiana Jones, there had been a proliferation of attempts to find the secret hiding place of this famous treasure.

The real thing had vanished some 2,500 years ago, at least. Its disappearance, according to some people, was THE great mystery.

So what really happened to it?

In my initial quest for the answer, I had stumbled upon some old Jewish documents that hinted at a possible avenue to pursue.

Taken to Mount Nebo?

One Jewish historical work, not known for its accuracy, did possibly reflect a distortion of the truth. The second book of *Maccabees* stated that Jeremiah the prophet (who lived at the time the Babylonians destroyed the Jerusalem Temple in 586 BC), hid the Ark on a mountain far from Jerusalem.

In a letter of the Jews of Jerusalem to those that were in Egypt, the following was given as copied from a writing of Jeremiah:

> The prophet, being warned by God, commanded that the tabernacle and the ark should accompany him, till he came forth to the mountain where Moses went up and saw the inheritance of God. And when Jeremias came thither he found a hollow cave and he carried in thither the tabernacle and the ark and the altar of incense, and so stopped the door. Then some of them that followed him, came up to mark the place but they could not find it. And when Jeremias perceived it, he blamed them saying: the place shall be unknown, till God gather together the congregation of the people and receive them to mercy. And then the Lord will shew these things, and the majesty of the Lord shall appear, and there shall be a cloud as it was also shewed to Moses, and he shewed it when Solomon prayed that the place might be sanctified to the great God.[1]

This document is believed to have been composed during the first century BC, about 500 years after Jeremiah lived. [2]

The *Catholic Encyclopedia* comments that:

According to many commentators, the letter from which the above-cited lines are supposed to have been copied cannot be regarded as possessing Divine authority; for, as a rule, a citation remains in the Bible what it was outside of the inspired writing; the impossibility of dating the original document makes it very difficult to pass a judgment on its historical reliability.[3]

Jeremiah was indeed the prophet at the time of the Ark's disappearance. And one should not be surprised if the Ark was hidden just before the destruction of Jerusalem, to place it beyond the reach of ruthless hands of the coming destroyers.

Turning back to modern times, we find that at least some adventurers took seriously the possibility of a Mount Nebo location (Nebo being the place from which Moses viewed the promised land).

In the 1980s, some men led by Tom Crotser of Winfield, Kansas, claimed to have seen the Ark in a cave inside the modern country of Jordan. The site was under Mount Pisgah, the highest point of the Mount Nebo range.

Late in 1981, they had spent four days on Mount Nebo itself, sleeping rough. Then they switched their search to Mount Pisgah, where they found a spot on the valley floor blocked by a length of tin sheeting. Removing this, they entered a passage and followed it into the bowels of the earth. Then, beyond a wall which they had to break down, was a crypt.

In the crypt was a gold-covered rectangular chest, and beside that, carrying poles. And off to one side were some packages wrapped in cloth, which Crotser assumed to be cherubim that once adorned the Mercy Seat.

They did not touch it, but took colour photographs, then returned to the United States, where they informed the press.

However, Crotser steadfastly refused to release the pictures. He said that God had instructed him to give them only to David Rothschild, the London banker – because Rothschild was a direct descendant of Jesus Christ. And Rothschild had been chosen by God to build the next Jewish Temple, where the Ark would be installed.

With Rothschild declining to take delivery of the photos, Crotser keeps them at home, showing only selected visitors.

One such visitor was Siegfried H. Horn, a well-known archaeologist. In 1982, he took time to closely examine the photographs. In the developing process, they had apparently come out rather badly. Horn's report states:

> All but two showed absolutely nothing. Of the two that registered images, one is fuzzy but does depict a chamber with a yellow box in the centre. The other slide is quite good and gives a clear view of the front of the box.[4]

An accomplished draughtsman, Horn made a sketch from the slide. Portions of the metal overlay on the box had the appearance of brass, rather than gold, and were stamped with a diamond pattern that looked machine-worked. But the most damaging fact was that a nail with a modern style of head could be seen protruding from the upper right hand corner of the front of the box.[5]

Horn decided:

> I do not know what the object is but the pictures convinced me that it is not an ancient artifact but of modern fabrication with machine-produced decorative stripes and an underlying metal sheet.[6]

In one media interview mentioned by Graham Hancock the box was said to be 62 inches long by 37 inches wide by 37 inches high.[7]

Crotser was also interviewed by journalist Vance Farrell.[8] Farrell asked questions such as, "What did you find in the chamber?"

The reply was, "We found the Ark of the Covenant and we found the Mercy Seat."

The Ark of the Covenant and the Mercy Seat were reportedly both sitting flat on the floor of this chamber.

"What size was the Ark?"

"It was 5 feet long by 4 feet wide." That is, 60 inches by 48 inches. (According to another report it was 59 inches long, 47 inches wide and 43 inches high, with the cherubim standing at a height of 108 inches. That's 9 feet!)

According to the Scriptures, these proportions would disqualify it from being the Ark. The biblical Ark of the Covenant was 2½ cubits long by 1½ cubits wide by 1½ cubits high.[9] Even using the longer cubit of 20.6 inches, the Ark's dimensions would be no more than 51½ inches long by 31 inches wide by 31 inches high.

We refer here to the royal Egyptian cubit, which Moses and the Hebrews knew and used – and which was in use as late as the First Temple period.[10]

The interviewer asked the question, "What size is the Mercy Seat in the cave?"

"The same as the Ark," came the reply. "5 feet by 4."

Away down at the end of the interview, the question was asked, "Is there anything else that you figure is significant, that you would like to share with my readers?"

"Yes, the chamber itself was very unique. It was a perfect cube, 7 feet by 7 feet by 7 feet."

Well, we all have a love for sevens, don't we? According to the Bible, God Himself loves sevens. So this made the whole thing sound just great. Except that you cannot get two 5 by 4 foot objects flat on a 7 by 7 foot floor. That is impossible.

Had the claimant tripped himself up when he gave the dimensions?

It has been said, "By thy words thou shalt be justified. And by thy words thou shalt be condemned." [11]

A skeptic by nature, I had come to learn that if we listen carefully and prayerfully to somebody when they make a claim, there will be evidence in their own comments, out of their own mouth, that will show the certainty of a matter, or otherwise.

According to the group leader, the cave they entered was lined on the sides by "ancient tombs that resembled catacombs". Such features suggest that the site may have been a burial spot, probably for monks.

The site is close to the Church of the Franciscan Fathers of Terra Santa. The "Ark" room is directly beneath a building that preserves the remains of an ancient Byzantine church. This room is probably related to the museum storerooms located nearby. Certainly the monks were familiar with this site. Among them have been men with avid archaeological interest, who have explored the whole area. This was not a secret cave sealed since the time of Jeremiah.

The flimsy tin-sheet covering of the entrance would have been designed for easy entrance by the monks.

I would not accuse Crotser of lying when he claimed to have found something. But what was it? The box was the wrong shape and size to be the Ark. What he found is anyone's guess, but it certainly wasn't what Moses built and placed in the Hebrew tabernacle. My guess is that it was a replica of the true Ark.

One explanation put forward is that it was made in Jeremiah's day (a possibility if one can dismiss the "machined" diamond pattern and modern nail seen protruding from it). This theory would have Jeremiah depositing the replica in the cave according to the words of 2 Maccabees.

We might ask why Jeremiah should do this. One might answer, Because he was a man of great integrity and honor toward the Lord, who lived among people, even his own, who were dishonest to the core. Some of them would be watching his every move, wanting to know what he was doing. This would make it likely that SOMEONE would find the Ark and raid it. And that was something he did not want to happen. So he made a replica and took it to Mount Nebo.

Another theory is that in 2 Maccabees the wrong mountain was given. The story became changed in the retelling through the centuries. Yet in it some truth remained. Accordingly, this location was only a guess as to where the prophet Jeremiah had gone. Well might the legends be correct in stating that Jeremiah was responsible for hiding the Ark, although the writers had no accurate knowledge of the location. Hence the various traditions.

But in the case of the Nebo location, this would still contain only a replica, probably fashioned in more recent times.

Taken to Ethiopia?

"Good to see y'mate!" beamed my friend John Seymour, thrusting out his hand.

I had just alighted from a Qantas flight from Melbourne.

"How did it go?"

John had a passion for archaeology and was always on the lookout for something to share with me.

We got into his car and began the journey back home to my wife and son. Josephine, young John-Paul and I lived about an hour from the city. We had come to prefer country living. It was healthy. And private too. A place to relax between seminars and expeditions.

"I have a book here you'll enjoy," offered John. "Picked it up yesterday. You can take all the time you need with it."

"Graham Hancock," I grunted. "Anyway, looks interesting." [12]

"Yeah. I don't know about his theory. Check it out, anyway."

The book was an account of Hancock's travels in Ethiopia in search of the Ark of the Covenant. There was a tradition that the Ark was held in great secrecy by a people who followed a strange mixture of Judaism and Christianity. Hancock was never able to gain access to the building where this "Ark" was supposed to be kept, closely guarded by a monk named Abba Fameray.

According to the story, King Solomon (10th century BC) sired a son by the Queen of Sheba. The son's name was Menelech. When Menelech was in his late teens he traveled to Jerusalem, where he was well treated by Solomon, who asked what gift he would like to take back with him.

"The Ark of the Covenant," was his reply.

This prompted an immediate refusal.

Menelech was displeased with this refusal and later, with several companions, stole the Ark in the dead of night and transported it to Ethiopia, where it has rested in Axum to this very day.

Recent belief has it that the Ark is hidden in that town in the sanctuary chapel of Saint Mary of Zion church.

This is a highly unlikely tale. It would have been a major embarrassment to the priests of Israel if they had found their Ark had been stolen. Doubtless a "holy war" would have been raised by Solomon to regain this priceless treasure. But no, there is no mention of it anywhere else, save in Ethiopia.

An addition to this tale claimed that Menelech had a copy made to replace the original.

Well, why not? Could this have happened? At first, that sounded a plausible idea. But as I continued to probe, a few things bothered me.

The next time John phoned, I put the matter to him.

"John," I began, "suppose someone wanted to make a copy of the Ark. What would they have to do?"

"Easy," coughed John. "**Someone** would have to view it."

"Yet no one except the high priest could access it, right? And even then, he stood before it only once a year."

"Right, mate, and I tell you, if anyone else so much as looked at it, or touched the covering over it, they were struck dead."

"So whoever would have seen it to copy it?"

"Well the high priest wouldn't abuse it. To him it was a life and death situation. He would have no motive," drawled John. "But you're missing the real point here, Jono?"

"OK, spit it out," I said.

John was quick on the draw. "Look, doesn't it say somewhere that the Shekinah glory, the presence of the Lord, left the Mercy Seat of the Ark of the Covenant just before the Babylonians came to destroy Jerusalem?"[13]

"You mean, in 586 BC?"

"Yeah, about then. Now Menelech might have been clever enough to get Solomon to make a copy. He might have been clever enough to switch it and get it down to Sheba. But do you think he would be clever enough to get the Shekinah glory to dwell on a bogus Mercy Seat for over 400 years – or for one second?"

I saw his point. "You're saying, Would one dare to presume that the all-knowing Lord God could be fooled?"

I was aware of this much. The sacred writings recorded that the Divine Presence dwelled constantly above that Mercy Seat.

The bottom line was, did God just "move over" complacently to the fake Ark?

The Lord's requirements for the protection of the Most Holy Place where the Ark was enshrined, to protect the chamber from being defiled, were so precise. He even gave very, very strict requirements as to the high priest's garments when he came into the Divine Presence.

24

No, the Deity would not allow any man to defile His earthly "Throne". He would not permit unsacred hands to carry His Throne away.

John chuckled. "And something else, if I might mention it. The town of Axum wasn't founded until at least the 3rd century BC – and maybe later. That's seven or eight hundred years **after** the alleged theft of the Ark."

"It could have stopped over for a while somewhere else," I thought aloud, playing the devil's advocate.

"I guess so," John responded.

However, there were many other fallacies and anachronisms in the legend. Inaccuracies, too.

It came to mind that, around the world, there were countless cities and churches claiming to possess holy relics. Investigation showed most of these claims to be hollow. Why should Axum be different? Just because its citizens believed their own legends, proved absolutely nothing.

Later I would find it had been recently established that there was no record of the Ark being in Ethiopia until the end of the 13th century.

Harry Atkins, who researched Ethiopian history and lectured for the Ethiopian government at the Menelik School in Addis Ababa, writes:

> At that time there was a dispute over who should be king. One of the claimants to the throne said he was a descendant of King Solomon and the Queen of Sheba. When Ykuna Amlak became king (1274-1285 AD), the legend of the Ark entered Ethiopian history.[14]

It is only fair to say that, of recent days, Graham Hancock has withdrawn his belief that this was the true Ark of the Covenant.

So what do they have in that land which they guard so carefully? Another replica, not taken in Solomon's day, but probably in the time of Jeremiah, or thereabouts?

Conflicting theories

First Jordan, then Ethiopia... where next? The deeper the probe, the more it would become apparent how much confusion existed concerning the fate of the Ark.

To Ireland?

One curious legend had it that, when Solomon's Temple was destroyed in 586 BC, the Ark had been taken to the Irish isles by a Jewish prophet.

Further checking, however, established that this legend had no historical support.

To Rome?

The First Temple had been destroyed in 586 BC. Later, a Second Temple was built in 515 BC, and this was destroyed by the Romans in 70 AD.

According to the Jewish historian, Josephus, who was present at that second destruction of the Temple, the Roman emperor, Vespasian, erected a "peace sanctuary" after the Jewish War to commemorate the destruction of the **Second Temple**.[15]

Josephus says that captured Temple treasures had been taken to Rome and placed in this building.

On the Arch of Titus in Rome, a 7-branched Candlestick and Table of Shewbread are depicted as objects that had been seized from the doomed Temple and taken to Rome.

However, it is doubtful that these dated from the **First Temple** of Jeremiah's time, the Temple that had contained the Ark of the Covenant.

It is known that there were many duplicates of the Table of Shewbread and the Candlestick and other vessels, kept in storage in the Temple treasuries in case the vessels in use were defiled.[16]

The 7-branched Candlestick, depicted as booty on the Arch of Titus, can hardly be an original, say many Jewish scholars, because its octagonal base is shown to have graven images. No Jewish Candlestick ever possessed images, since they were considered a form of idolatry.[17]

And the earliest form of the 7-branched Candlestick (undoubtedly patterned after the Mosaic model) possessed a 3-legged stand, not an octagonal base, according to archaeological evidence.

The Candlestick depicted on the Arch of Titus was very likely a non-Jewish creation made by Herod's craftsmen as a gift to Rome.

One notes Josephus' statement that priests gave to Titus "two lampstands similar to those deposited in the Temple." [18]

On the Arch of Titus in Rome, where all that was captured is portrayed quite vividly, the Ark of the Covenant is not inscribed. THERE IS NO EVIDENCE THAT THE ARK WAS TAKEN TO ROME.

As a matter of fact, **the Ark was never in the Second Temple**.

I investigated carefully to determine whether, after the Jewish captivity in Babylon, when the Second Temple was built, the Ark had been placed in that Temple. Since I was in South Australia at the time, I placed a call to a rabbi there in Adelaide.

"Rabbi David," I asked, "did the Second Temple contain the Ark of the Covenant?"

The rabbi responded, "There was no longer a supernatural Presence. Where the Ark should have been, there was placed a table."

Indeed, the Most Holy Place remained empty. This was much to the astonishment of Pompey, the Roman general, who in 63 BC forced his way into the inner sanctuary of the Second Temple.

And Josephus, familiar with the Temple, and present when the Romans destroyed it, states:

There was nothing at all in the Holy of Holies.[19]

I found confirmation in the Jewish Talmud that the Ark was non-existent in Herod's Temple (the refurbished Second Temple).[20]

Ark of the Covenant disappears

The evidence, then, tends to support the suggestion that the Ark **did** disappear before the destruction of the First Temple.

Biblical sources declare that the Divine Presence in the Temple was always above the Mercy Seat of the Ark. Numerous passages inform us that the Ark emitted a dazzling radiance. According to Talmudic sources, in the days before the Ark of the Covenant disappeared, "The High Priest of Israel entered and left by the light that the Holy Ark issued forth." [21]

This had changed after the Ark vanished. From then on the priest "groped his way in the dark."

27

The last references to the Ark's location end with King Josiah.[22] He placed it back in Solomon's Temple after it had evidently been removed.

Then, less than 50 years later, the Babylonians destroyed the Temple.[23]

Shortly before that, the prophet Ezekiel saw, in a vision, the glory of the Lord leave the Temple.[24] In the subsequent record of the Babylonians carrying off the treasure and vessels of the Temple,[25] the Ark is not mentioned. At this point it vanishes from history. It disappeared, AFTER the time of Josiah, but BEFORE the destruction of the Temple.

•••••••

Now the search takes a new twist. We follow it into the secret passages under the city of Jerusalem... and uncover a fascinating story of intrigue.

CHAPTER 3

INTO DARK TUNNELS

Have you ever thought you'd like to find some remote spot where no human has ever trod? Such places do exist, you know, for anyone prepared to rough it.

Or you may prefer something not quite as ambitious, like exploring an unmapped tunnel that has not been entered for who knows how long?

Jerusalem is a city 4,000 years old. Archaeologists claim that tunnels, cisterns and such like, honeycomb the area beneath the entire city. Many of these remain unexplored.

Under the Temple Mount alone are 32 caves and cisterns. Below the Temple foundation platform itself are great vaults, secret doors and mysterious passages! The entrances to many have been carefully blocked with boards and other obstacles.

There are passages wide enough for three men to walk abreast which cut through the solid rock, connecting the old Temple site with Mount Zion, a half mile away. Some of these remain unexplored.

I have heard of one set of rock-strewn galleries that leads down as much as a hundred feet below the surface.

Another closed and secret tunnel travels almost two miles from the Temple Mount to a spot near the Plaza Hotel in west Jerusalem. Near the Damascus Gate, at the entrance to Solomon's quarries, is a sign which theorizes Hezekiah's escape route around 700 BC.[2] It suggests that one of the caved-in tunnels exiting from the massive chambers of the quarries leads to the Temple Mount. And we are led to believe that the tunnel continues outside the city walls.

An underground passage (Photo: Edith Breeden)

It is possible to get into some of the tunnels. But that is not always easy.

Occasionally a few adventurers, with written government sanction, have been allowed to enter, but even then, those guarding the entrances were very reluctant to let them proceed.

The Ark in Hezekiah's Tunnel?

There was a rumor circulating that the Ark of the Covenant was stored in a shaft of the 1,750 foot Hezekiah's Tunnel to which we have just referred.

Early this century, one Walter Juveliu, with this very idea in mind, gained access into the area. Over three years, he cleared the debris-choked tunnel, but found nothing of value. A side benefit of Juveliu's effort is that visitors to Jerusalem can now wade through Hezekiah's Tunnel.

Under the Temple Mount?

When I began researching, I learned of a further rumor that a secret chamber lay deep within the Temple Mount and that the Ark lay hidden within that chamber. One story began circulating after some excavations were made under the mount. Rabbi Matiyahu Dan Hacohen told a David Lewis in a taped interview that:

> ... they were excavating along the lower level of the Western Wall of the Temple mountain. At one point during the night, they came to a doorway in the Western Wall. Passing through this doorway, the crew entered a fairly long tunnel. At the end of the tunnel, Rabbi Hacohen said, "I saw the golden ark that once stood in the Holy Place of the Temple of the Almighty." It was covered with old, dried animal skins of some kind. However, one gold, gleaming end of the ark was visible. He could see the loops or rounds of gold through which the poles of acacia wood could be thrust so that the ark could be properly carried by four dedicated Levites. Hacohen and his friends rushed out to the home of Chief Rabbi Shlomo Goren. They awakened the rabbi and excitedly told him that they had discovered the holy ark of the covenant. Goren said: "We are ready for this event. We have already prepared the poles of acacia wood and have Levites who can be standing by in the morning to carry out the ark in triumph." [3]

American author Randall Price subsequently asked Rabbi Goren concerning the factual nature of this account, since it was supposedly reported to him. His response was nothing short of emphatic:

> They are all liars! They are just telling you stories! How can anyone say they saw the Ark? The Ark is hundreds of meters down.... If (anyone) would see the Ark he wouldn't remain alive even for one minute![4]

Today Rabbi Hacohen denies that he ever told such a story. He asserts that his statements were misunderstood.

Another Temple Mount story

Another "sighting" claim had been made concerning Rabbi Getz. It was alleged that when the chamber leading to the supposed site of the Ark was discovered, the rabbi used a mirror to look around a corner of the tunnel, and saw the reflected image of the Ark. There was also a story circulating that Rabbi Getz heard the sound of a bellows or breathing, indicating that a Divine immanence still attended the Ark.

A fax from Rabbi Getz to a Mr. T. Green, dated June 13, 1993, stated:

> I can confirm to you that we know the location of the Ark of the Covenant.[5]

In an interview on Australian television, according to *Petah Tikvah* magazine, Rabbi Getz said that he and others had actually seen the Ark of the Covenant.[6]

Randall Price confronted Rabbi Getz, asking for clarification of these claims. The rabbi said he was surprised at such stories. He wanted to set the record straight. His comments were:

> No... no... that is not what I said. These are all stories... I am not responsible for someone else's remarks. It is important to know the truth, since millions of Christians and people who live in Israel read such material.[7]

In both stories, the claim was of the Ark being in a chamber beneath the site of the former Temple – and that the excavators reached this spot.

Rabbi Getz, however, calculated that excavators never got closer than 96 feet from this part of the mount. But according to Rabbi Goren, such a chamber would be located deeper still. He contended that excavators would need to dig not a few meters, but hundreds of meters to reach such a spot – and that would have taken another 2½ years, he estimated.

Price asked Rabbi Getz whether he had actually been in the room where the Ark was speculated to be. His reply was consistent with Goren's statement:

> We know where it is, but we did not discover it. According to the (rabbinic) writings it is called the **Gear He'Etzem** ("Chalk of the Bone") and is located deep within the ground. I wanted to go through the tunnels (and reach this area), since I knew the direction – I might be off only 15 to 18 feet - but it is impossible (to reach) because it is deep under the water (which flooded the tunnels).[8]

If one could take these two rabbis, Goren and Getz, who directed the Temple Mount excavation, at their word, then there is no way they could have even come close to the alleged hiding place of the Ark – much less have seen it.

Other rabbis in Israel, such as Rabbi Nahman Kahane of the Institute of Talmudic Commentaries, have stated that they doubted that Getz and Goren knew the true location of the Ark.

In the 1860s, a young lieutenant, by the name of Charles Warren, who was in Britain's Royal Engineers, excavated in the area of the Temple Mount.

In 1985, four rabbis actually broke through the Western Wall and entered an area that Warren had previously excavated and documented. However, they did not enter to search for archaeological relics. The real reason for their excursion we shall reveal in a later chapter. When they were apprehended, they told the authorities that they were looking for the Ark of the Covenant. But that was their cover story.

In the bowels of the earth?

I came across another ancient document, The *Apocalypse of Baruch*, which says that the Ark and other items were taken from the Temple by four angels, who, only moments before the

Babylonian army broke into the Temple, commanded the earth to swallow them until Jerusalem is "restored for ever".[9]

This purports to be an eyewitness account by a certain "Baruch":

> And I saw him descend into the Holy of Holies, and take from it the veil, and the Holy Ark, and its cover, and the two tablets. And he cried to the earth in a loud voice, "Earth, earth, earth, hear the word of the mighty God, and receive what I commit to you, and guard them until the last times, so that, when you are ordered, you may restore them, and strangers may not get possession of them." And the earth opened its mouth and swallowed them up.[10]

It is now known that this document was not written in the 6th century BC, when Jeremiah lived, but in the late first century *AD*. Despite its eerie and evocative tone, it cannot, therefore, in any way be an eyewitness account. Rather, it is, from beginning to end, a piece of imaginative fiction, possessing no historical merit at all.[11]

Other speculated sites

One archaeologist thought to find the Ark at **Masada,** the cliff-top fortress where Jewish patriots made their last stand against the Romans in the 2nd century AD.

Another felt he was on the verge of locating the prize in the **Qumran** caves area near the Dead Sea, after he found what were believed to be ashes of the ceremonial red heifer.

A cave at **Engedi**, one of the hideouts of David, was also considered to be a possible hiding place for the Ark. But soundings made at the proposed spot, initially thought to be hollow, showed it to be nothing but solid ground.

Still another speculation put the Ark of the Covenant in a secret spot on the **Mount of Olives** just east of the old city of Jerusalem. While another suggested it was in a cave near **Bethlehem.**

Transported to heaven?

A most unusual suggestion was that the Ark was transported to heaven.

In support of this idea, some refer to a New Testament book which mentions a Temple in heaven containing "the ark of his testament".[12]

Yet, according to another part of the Scriptures, the Hebrew tabernacle and its furniture were merely replicas of those in heaven.[13] There is the heavenly original and the earthly copy.

Because the heavenly Ark has always been in heaven, the earthly Ark had no reason to be there.

A restored Temple with the Ark?

I have heard people asking, "If found, would the Ark be used in a Third Temple built by the Jews?"

It is worth mentioning that when the Jews went into captivity in Babylon and the First Temple was destroyed, the prophet Ezekiel wrote that the Lord had issued new instructions regarding the sacrificial system – instructions which no longer included the Ark of the Covenant.[14]

And so it was that, when the Jews returned from exile, they continued the sacrificial system according to those instructions, without the Ark of the Covenant. During the time of Jesus Christ, they were still performing the sacrificial system – but without the Ark.

There is no reason why the Israelis would need the Ark to perform the sacrificial system. They would need only to build a "table of the Lord" as instructed in the book of Ezekiel.[15]

Still hidden

Well, my investigation had led me into numerous localities in a number of countries. I was satisfied that the Ark had not gone to any of these places; that it had not been taken by the Babylonians or the Romans and that it had not been destroyed either.

According to tradition, the Ark and other Temple treasures had remained hidden throughout the time of the Babylonian invasions, the 70 year exile of the Jews and the entire Second Temple period. They remained hidden throughout the centuries while Jerusalem was under foreign domination – and they remained hidden to the present day.

A "fake" shooting that went wrong?

Upon my first visit to Israel in 1967, I sensed the electric mood, the excitement, the energy of a people on the move. It was a young, vibrant land, full of expectation.

It still is. But the political situation continues to heat up.

After the assassination of Mr. Rabin in 1995, Mr. Peres took over for a short time. The state of affairs was deteriorating so badly with Mr. Peres that even Mr. Arafat was predicting a civil war among the Jewish people.

The very existence of the nation hung in jeopardy. By less than one per cent of the popular vote, Binyamin "Bibi" Netanyahu (Hebrew for "gift of God") was elected Prime Minister of Israel.

Meanwhile, there was a great deal of crisis management going on behind the scenes.

Controversy was swirling that the assassination of Rabin may have been a staged fake attempt on his life with blank bullets. However, someone put real bullets in the gun. Stimulating this assertion, a Government Security agent, Yoav Kurial (Rabin's bodyguard) shouted out near Rabin as the shots were fired, **"They're blanks. This is an exercise."**

Reporting on the incident, John Barala of Tulsa, Oklahoma, commented:

> This was done to promote sympathy for Rabin during the election campaign.[16]

The same agent was murdered a few days after Rabin died. He was buried in a closed funeral. Even Leah Rabin, the widow, stated that she was told first that Rabin was only shot with blanks.

Yigal Amir, the alleged assassin, was first asked at the scene, "Did you shoot blanks?" It was GSS agents who asked this question.

Later, Amir called out to reporters at his first court appearance that he had knowledge that would bring down the whole Israeli government and called on reporters to investigate the GSS agent's death.

Yitzhak Rabin

Barala asked:

> Did Yigal shoot Rabin as part of a planned charade (fake
> assassination) to clamp down on peace process protesters,
> or was he part of a double cross that resulted in Rabin's
> death? One thing is for sure, Rabin's death did cause a major
> clamp down and bolstered the peace process tremendously,
> and almost enabled Peres to be elected!... Rabin had been
> leading Netanyahu when Bibi entered the race, by anywhere
> from 14 to 18 points. However, Netanyahu closed the gap to
> the point where they were almost neck-and- neck. Perhaps
> this was the strategy behind the phony assassination at-
> tempt that was supposed to be the one that used blank
> bullets, that back-fired.[17]

It is against such a volatile background that the search for the Ark of the Covenant must be considered. We need to be aware that this much sought relic could be, potentially, the most explosive artifact on earth.

Let's go back in time and look at a little history. I am going to show you a lot of information that is incredibly important.

We shall need to dig into history. And many chapters will be devoted to this. The big picture, once grasped, will help us to understand the significance of the find.

Enough said. Let's go...

CHAPTER 4

DARING RESCUE PLAN

"That'll do, guys. There's enough space now to squeeze through. Let's go."

Five men – two archaeologists, two geneticists and a cameraman – scramble into a tunnel leading under the streets of Jerusalem.

As he slides down behind the stones blocking the entrance, Ron turns to face the others and whispers:

"Even Indiana Jones would never dream of being here."

The last man through trembles excitedly. "Can you believe it? We are now inside the original tunnel. This tunnel has never been opened. And this is the way to the Ark?"

"The Temple priests used it, " Ron whispers. "Further along is another wall. If we get through that, we'll see the chamber."

Jewish sages predicted that the Ark of the Covenant in its secret chamber would be discovered. Did the chamber contain other Temple treasures?

The chamber would be opened tonight.

••••••

One day soon – very soon, we believe – this scenario is to take place.

Before we go any further, let me say it. The significance of the golden Ark goes beyond anything you have imagined. It brings us eyeball to eyeball with issues we may prefer to avoid. I shall raise these issues and ask respectfully that you consider them with me. They will be vital to our understanding of what the Ark is all about.

So you might as well humor me. Because just as fascinating as its discovery, is the Ark's background story - a history that is at times exciting and suspense-packed.

Because the Ark was a religious artifact, we shall find ourselves dealing with some basic facts of life. Archaeology – history – religion: in dealing with the Ark of the Covenant, we shall find these three aspects interwoven.

During twelve years' research for *Dead Men's Secrets*, a book on the lost secrets and technology of the past, I sifted through thousands of artifacts, records and traditions of the ancient world.

If we are to believe these traditions, the original inhabitants of our planet Earth were like gods - that is, they were members of a superior civilization, which ceased to exist after some great disaster.

Egyptian records would contend that the reign of the "gods" before the First Dynasty was one of superior and miraculous powers.

The Popol Vuh (the sacred book of the Quiche Indians of Guatemala) records: "The first race of men before the Flood possessed all knowledge; they studied the four quarters of heaven and the round surface of the earth."[1]

Understood in this light, even Greek mythology begins to make some sense. We see it as the recollection by a degenerate race, of a vast, mighty and highly civilized empire, which in a remote past covered the world.

Pause for reflection. Can we possibly imagine that all of the people of all continents independently invented such a story? Did they all speak of an original Golden Age by chance, without any foundation?

Indeed, I am tempted to ask, if man evolved from beasts, then why is it that there existed a long tradition of a Golden Age instead of that of a savage past? Will anyone explain that?

Even where there was lack of writing in conditions of savagery imposed by catastrophe, the same memory of the Golden Age was passed from mouth to ear.

You may want to ask at this point, can we really place much credence in ancient legends?

Surprisingly, a great deal. Too often, I'm afraid, we have been prone to dismiss folklore and mythology out of hand. But is this not unscientific, especially since traditions have often led us to discover physical remains?

Legends usually based on a core of fact

Pertinently, William Prescott, the great Americanologist, reminds us: "A nation may pass away and leave only the memory of its existence, but the stories of science it has gathered up will endure forever." [2]

You see, folklore is a fossil of history; it preserves history in the guise of colorful tales. Far from being a collection of fables, it is a recital of actual past events, even though from generation to generation some facts have become distorted or forgotten.

Professor I.A. Efremov, of the former Soviet Union, cautions that "historians must pay more respect to ancient traditions and folklore." He accuses Western scientists of snobbishness in rejecting the tales of the "common people." [3]

We must face it: legends are usually based on a core of fact.

Take the legend of Troy. No scholar took *The Iliad* or *The Odyssey* of Homer as history. But Schliemann, putting faith in it, discovered the "mythical" city of Troy. The *Iliad* spoke of a cup decorated with doves which Odysseus used. In a shaft Schliemann found that 3,600-year-old cup.

A griffin

Herodotus told a fabulous story of a distant country where griffins guarded a golden treasure. This land (Altai, or Kin Shan) has now been found, together with ancient gold mines, and decorations from a high culture prominently display the griffin. The vague myth is seen to be a fact.

41

Mexican Indian legends spoke of a sacred well of sacrifice, into which maidens and jewelry were hurled. Historians dismissed this as a mere tale, until the well, at Chichen Itza, was discovered in the 19th century.

More than any document, the Bible was assailed as a collection of fanciful myths. Yet, to the embarrassment of the critics, archaeological discoveries proved time and again that the fabled cities, mythical persons and impossible events were true and reliable reporting in every detail. Indeed, the Bible can now be regarded as the most accurate and trustworthy source of history we possess.

Our ancestral memory of the golden era

If we are to credit the collective testimony of all ancient races, man's early history was truly an incredible one. It was a Golden Age of advanced civilization, of original giants who had superior intelligence and technology. This appears to have been a universal truth, known to everyone in ancient times.

Sacred records affirm that at the very beginning (soon after the fall from Paradise) men possessed extraordinary mental abilities. Beginning with the raw earth, they mastered a high level of civilization in just the first six generations of their existence. In that short time they were able to build cities, play complex musical instruments and smelt metals. Indeed, with their scientific complexes, these earliest men, it seems, were no fools.

Did you know that when Alexander Graham Bell gave us the telephone, he hinted that it had been done before? "The old devices have been re-invented," he observed.[4]

Yes, you read it right. That is exactly what Bell said.

In fact the question was pressed further by the eminent British scientist Frederick Soddy, winner of a Nobel Prize in physics. He wondered whether the ancients might "not only have attained our present knowledge, but a power hitherto unmastered by us?"[5]

Physical remains also

Where did Bell and Soddy get their information? Quite possibly from some musty old records.

Nevertheless, our quest is not based on ancient texts and reports, but on accepted scientific discoveries. There are recently discovered artifacts that cannot be dismissed, namely, objects of metal sitting in museums, unquestionably made in the ancient world, that would have required very advanced technology to produce. A technology not to be repeated until our day.

A "fall" from paradise

And something else. Would it surprise you to learn that nearly all writings of ancient peoples worldwide tell the same story, that of a fall from an original paradise state of peace, love and happiness? A beautiful world. No suffering at all.

The earliest records ever unearthed were written by the ancient Sumerians of Mesopotamia, more than 4,000 years ago. Preserved in their records are their laws, history and culture, as well as stories concerning events that had occurred before their time.

Their writings speak vividly of a time when animals were neither wild nor harmful, when there was no rivalry or enmity among men, when there was plenty, security, harmony, and right living on earth in all directions.[6]

Sacred records affirmed, however, that there had been a departure from harmony with God. Such accounts are not confined to the Bible. They are in the oral and written history of many ancient nations.

The loss of immortality caused by man's disobedience to divine law seems to have been keenly felt by more than one ancient writer.[7]

Many prayers and hymns of the ancients impressively reveal how these people clearly understood the principles of the biblical Ten Commandments and knew quite well what was right and wrong.[8] They were fully conscious of their rebellious condition and were longing for forgiveness. One prayer of an ancient penitent may serve as an example:

O my god, who art angry, accept my prayer;
O my goddess, who art angry, receive my supplication,
Receive my supplication and let thy spirit be at rest.
O my goddess, look with pity on me and accept my supplication.
Let my sins be forgiven, let my transgressions be blotted out.

Let the ban be torn away, let the bonds be loosened.
Let the seven winds carry away my sighs.
I will send away my wickedness,
Let the bird bear it to the heavens.
Let the flowing waters of the river wash me clean.[9]

Although the people had now slipped into polytheism, they realized their true spiritual condition.

In ancient Babylon, man was felt to live under a curse, a spell, from which only a divine act of cleansing could free him.

Egyptian writings reveal a similar understanding that the people were aware of a condition of wrong doing, that they had a longing for eternal life and even felt a need for some kind of rescue.

Alienated and dying

They were aware that their Creator had surrounded them with evidences of His love, yet they had failed Him. Disobedience had marred the original harmony. Human nature had become so weakened through wrong-doing that it was impossible in one's own strength to resist the power of evil.

And it was worse. Now they were separated from the Life-giver, so the consequence had been the entry of death, a process now passed onto all their children.

In the ancient writings, one senses a cry of regret at an event they firmly believed had occurred.

What an intensely painful experience! And how vividly had it become etched into the racial memory!

According to some archaeologists, the oldest piece of art known to the human family is that which is termed the *temptation seal*. This pictures a tree, on the opposite sides of which are seated two persons. Behind one of them is the upright form of a serpent, who is whispering to one of them.

A Sumerian poem laments that "the maiden ate that which was forbidden, the maiden, the mother of sin, committed evil; the mother of sin had a painful experience."[10]

Mankind's entrapment by the "evil serpent" was remembered from Egypt to China to the Americas.[11]

Rescue plan

But there was a hope of future deliverance. This is reflected in the traditions and mythologies of all ancient peoples.

They believed in the one Creator, in beings called angels, and in the fall and depravity of man through the subtlety of Satan (represented by a serpent).

They also believed in the Creator's love for human beings – and in a rescue plan that He had promised them immediately after the Fall - the coming down of a mightier One, who was to assume human nature and die for mankind. They believed in the ultimate triumph of this Rescuer, the eventual restoration of all that was lost, and the vanquishing of the Serpent.

All nations awaited him

Dupuis, in *L'Origine des Cultus,* has collected a vast number of traditions prevalent in all nations concerning a divine person, born of a woman, suffering in conflict with a serpent, but triumphing over him at last.[12]

He came, or was to come, from heaven for the purpose of delivering mankind, sacrificing himself, but rising to life again and returning to heaven.

Notice how two different heathen poets contemplated these prophecies:

> * A golden progeny from heaven descends,
> O chaste Lucinda! speed the mother's pains,
> And haste the glorious birth!...
>
> ...virtue shall restore,
> And crimes shall threat the guilty world no more...
> The warring nations he in peace shall bind,
> And with paternal virtues rule mankind.[13]

> * Hail, great Physician of the world! all hail!
> Hail, mighty Infant, who, in years to come,
> Shall heal the nations and defraud the tomb!...
> Thy daring art shall animate the dead,
> And draw the thunder on Thy guilty head;
> For Thou shalt die, but from the dark abode
> Rise up victorious, and be twice a God! [14]

45

The Babylonians and Persians expected a king-redeemer and hero-sage, who would establish a new age of happiness. The Chinese also believed that a great wise man would appear. The Hindus believed that the supreme God would reveal himself to humans and that ultimately would come a new world. The ancient Germans looked forward to the renewal of the present world. And the Druids of Britain expected the coming of the "Curer of all ills," whose symbol was the mistletoe (or Branch).

Likewise, in the earliest Egyptian texts are found prophecies proclaiming the coming of this Savior of the human race - prophecies that were already ancient. [15]

To cap it all, the ancient Romans were convinced that a master and ruler of the world was to come out of Judea.[16]

A teaching device

To help mankind understand the rescue plan, a teaching device was set up: it became known as the **sacrificial system.**

The requirement was that when a person was sorry for his sins, he would take an innocent lamb and kill it with his own hand.

The message was that just as an innocent victim (the animal) now died at the hand of the repentant wrong-doer, so at some future date, an innocent deliverer would die for guilty man and free mankind from the curse of everlasting death. The sacrificial rite was an act of faith in future deliverance.

Archaeology has shown that this sacrificial system was handed down and became part of the culture of all nations. There was a belief that the rite had been imparted by God Himself to the parents of the human race after they fell, along with the promise of eventual rescue.[17]

46

So it was that the ancient races feared sin and sought forgiveness through blood sacrifice. They spoke of a Deliverer coming to suffer, of resurrection from death through him and the eventual restoration of all that was lost. [18]

This good news is, therefore, as old as the race; and never was there a time when it was not known. The divine promise to mankind was known as the **everlasting covenant.**[19] It was a **Covenant of Blood.**

And in God's foreknowledge, He was able to accept the sacrifices of His people BEFORE the Deliverer came into the world. That future deliverance - and the death of the Messiah - would be the HUB of history. They looked forward. We look back. Each person who would accept the rescue would do so in FAITH.

Eventually, the ARK OF THE COVENANT would be constructed to encapsulate this incredible rescue plan.[20]

But first, gross perversions were about to take place. I shall relate that chilling story now...

Jivaro tribesmen of the Amazon headwaters sacrifice a pig to the fire god of Mount Sangay. Below the pig hangs a chicken sacrifice.

CHAPTER 5

FIRE GOD OF THE AMAZON

I looked up – and shuddered. The war paint, poison darts and blowpipe screamed out that he was a killer. Those wound-scars on his face and body spoke of head-taking raids.

Here, at the eastern edge of the Andes mountains, stretches the headwaters of the mighty Amazon, a vast, unknown region of barely-explored tropical rain forest. Rugged, trackless and isolated, this region is infested with vicious insects, wild beasts and wilder men.

And here was one of them, glaring down at me... a savage who thought that all men in the world were killers like himself!

Better be careful. I felt in my bag and drew out a balloon. He squinted at it, stuffed it into his mouth to chew, pulled it out, fiddled with it – and looked totally puzzled. His young son came to the rescue. And soon this fierce warrior was prancing around the yard, showing his family how smart he was. Giggling with delight, he blew it up and let the air scream out. Oh, now he was friendly enough!

... In this land of never-satisfied hates, the Jivaro Indians believe in two main deities – the Earth Mother (to whom they address songs and prayers) and the Great Serpent (represented by sun and fire). An earthly embodiment of this sun or fire god is the active volcano, Mount Sangay.

To this smoking mountain, the natives sacrifice a pig, by strangling. After this, they kill a fowl and sprinkle its blood over their legs – just in case they have incurred some guilt by killing the pig!

What do we see here? In this fowl's blood that "cleanses" them from sin – what is this but a carry-over from the original knowledge of an atonement, a reconciliation by blood?

•••••••

The sacrificial system, committed to our first parents, was perverted by their descendants. Superstition, idolatry, cruelty and licentiousness corrupted the simple and significant service that their God had appointed.

How this occurred may surprise you.

Monotheism at first

As research penetrates into the most inaccessible portions of the world, it becomes apparent that all men are from one central point. Human culture history is a single connected story.[1]

In his voluminous work on the origins of ancient religion, George Stanley Faber writes:

> The various systems of Pagan Idolatry in different parts of the world correspond so closely, both in their evident purport and in numerous points of arbitrary resemblance, that they cannot have been struck out independently in the several countries where they have been established, but must have all originated from some common source.[2]

The evolutionary theory that the first men worshipped many gods and that the idea of 'one God' evolved later, has been largely demolished by archaeology. It now appears that MONOtheism (one 'high God') lay at the root of all religions, but that after about 2000 BC monotheism degenerated into pantheism, polytheism and animism.

Archaeologists and historians of unimpeachable accuracy (Horn, Faber, Rawlinson, Waddell and Budge, to name a few) insist from their discoveries that the earliest Sumerians, Iranians, Phoenicians, Egyptians and Indians were monotheists. Ancient textual evidence shows that the trend was to **increase** the number of gods as time passed, rather than decrease them.[3]

This harmonizes with biblical claims. It was only the later nations who were POLYtheists (worshipping many gods).

Gradual corruption

The corruption was gradual. It can be shown that the various systems of pagan mythology originated from a common source. That source is Babel, Mesopotamia, in the time of Nimrod, shortly before 2000 BC.

Notice these stages:

Gradually the universal worship of a Creator who was behind the sun, moon and stars, degenerated into veneration of these visible heavenly bodies themselves.

As migrants scattered from Babel, such influence spread worldwide. Everywhere, under different names, the counterfeit took hold, the gods of each nation bearing the same functions and symbols and represented in the same way.

This counterfeit ultimately usurped the true.

Idolatry began with the worship of heroes and heavenly bodies and degraded into the worship of bulls, goats, cats and crocodiles and hawks and beetles.

In the **earliest** Egyptian texts we are brought face to face with prophecies concerning a Messiah **who was to come**. It was held that "the teacher awaited since the creation of the world" had not yet been manifested on earth. His coming was to end in his sacrifice and bring about the regeneration of mankind.

Only in the **late** Egyptian literature (from late in the 18th and early in the 19th Dynasty) did Osiris and other gods usurp the functions and attributes of the Promised One.[4] By then, religious degeneration had set in well and truly.

Prior to that time, the position of Osiris was not messianic.[5] Osiris was no more than an allegorical patron of corn, a personification of the agricultural seasons.[6] Much, much later he became "a god who had been originally a mortal and had risen from the dead."[7] So confirms Sir E.A. Wallis Budge in his *Book of the Dead*, a British Museum publication.

The added attributes of the Promised One were thus given to him.

Professor Budge points out:

The beliefs which were conceived by the Egyptians in their lowest states of civilization were mingled with those which reveal the existence of high spiritual conceptions.[8]

Owing to this perversion of the messianic prophecy having spread worldwide, modern scholars were led to conclude that Christianity had been borrowed from pagan religions. The archaeological evidence now available shows that these scholars were mistaken.

How sun worship began

The prophesied Messiah, in the earliest times, was associated with the bringing of **spiritual LIGHT**. This symbolic meaning was soon displaced by 'actuality', **physical LIGHT**, represented by the **SUN**.

From this desire for physical images, it was a simple matter to begin worshipping the sun.

All over this planet, sun-plates and sun-pillars were erected and the smoke of strange altars ascended. The sun god became the highest god. At dawn services, from Asia to Europe to South America, royal families, nobles and common people stood silent and still, their eyes turned toward the east, awaiting the great moment when the first brilliant red rays should shine forth above the horizon. In some countries, a human image representing the sun was worshipped by casting live children into the fire in its belly.

The burning of incense took place not merely to the sun and moon, but also to the other heavenly bodies. These came to be regarded as gods. Astrology was a form of polytheism. These 'gods' were consulted on behalf of the nation.

The perversion developed further. The predicted **resurrection** of the coming Deliverer was actually deemed to be enacted in the annual decay and regrowth of vegetation. **Regeneration** became less important and was confused with **reproduction**. The solar year and its vegetational 'death and resurrection' therefore became the literal enactment of the death and resurrection of the sun god.

And along with the sun developed the worship of its earthly symbol, the snake, who, it was held, had 'enlightened' mankind.

Snake cults spread worldwide. Evil, represented by the snake, had indeed become the "god of this world".[9]

Human sacrifice and cannibalism

In the sacrificial symbol which spoke of the promised Rescuer, the participant partook of the flesh of the animal. This implied acceptance of the benefits of the promised atonement, as well as digesting the "Word" of the Savior.

In this connection, the Pharaoh Unas (5th Dynasty) is quoted as "eating the gods". Budge comments that "in eating them he also ate their words of power and their spirits."[10]

An idea of lost integrity seems to have pervaded the world, and to have entered into the pagan mysteries.[11]

Among all nations, sacrifice was plainly designed to avert the wrath of the Deity, which would instead fall upon the substitute victim, thus sparing the forfeited life of the guilty worshipper or guilty nation.[12]

Always hand in hand with idol worship (worshipping a physical representation of the god), went immorality, sexual perversions, witchcraft, astrology and a sadistic love of cruelty.

Later, when animal sacrifice was degraded into human sacrifice, the messianic rite gave way to a sacrament of cannibalism.

Instead of **rejecting** the doctrine of deliverance, the world at large **corrupted** it. Such adaptation runs through all their rites, whether the sacrifice was animal or human.

Thomas Johnston, who researched first hand pagan religions in the Pacific, writes that human victims:

> ...were offered in seasons of war, at great national festivals, during the illness of rulers, and on the erection of temples. I have been informed by several of the inhabitants of Maeva (Tahiti) that **the foundations of some of the temples for the abode of the gods were actually laid in human sacrifices.**
> The only motives by which they were influenced in their religious homage or service were, with few exceptions, superstitious fear, revenge toward their enemies, a desire to avert the dreadful consequences of the anger of the gods,

and to secure their sanction and aid in the commission of the grossest crimes.[13]

I can vouch for the truth of one of Johnston's findings. In 1967, on the island of Vanua Levu, Fiji, I personally went into a chief's house which had been erected upon human sacrifice as recently as 1923. Four robust young men who were lowered into holes to embrace the corner posts, had been packed over alive with earth. They still hold up the building!

According to Jeff Houser, resident in India, sacrifice of street children is even today practised in the laying of foundations for buildings in the Orissa region of that country.

Heathenism taught men and women to look upon the Supreme Being as an object of fear rather than of love – a malign Deity to be appeased by sacrifices.

The Hebrew prophets saw this as an important development in the intensifying conflict between the Creator who desired man's best good and the forces of evil out to destroy the human race.

Society was becoming more degraded.

The next stage of the rescue plan was now activated.....

CHAPTER 6

"SACRIFICE YOUR SON"

It was a seering hot afternoon in October that I tripped down the steps from an upper room in the old walled city of Jerusalem.

Pushing along through the bewildering maze of narrow streets with ancient cobble stones, I climbed some steps to a hawker's stand and stood there to order a falafel.

Then I ambled out through the Damascus Gate. Peddlers sat around, spreading out their wares hopefully. Four young Israeli soldiers in uniform - two of them girls – stood, rifles in hand, surveying the passersby.

I continued across the road and around the corner through the Arab bus station. Some buildings abutted the hill. The Calvary escarpment, some called it.

And there it was, in a back yard, the cave.

My eyes roved across the banana crates inside.

Curiously, this hole in the cliff face had acquired the impressive appellation of *Jeremiah's Grotto*. (This was not the real McCoy, however.)

I gulped in the fresher, cooler air.

And the thought struck me that here I was, standing close to a place of sacrifice! This was the very mountain to which the famous patriarch Abraham had come to sacrifice his son Isaac.

In recent years the authenticity of the book of Genesis, which tells of Abraham, had come under attack. Critics had charged that the stories were fables, written hundreds of years after the alleged events.

Then came other ancient texts that confirmed the authenticity of Genesis.

The Bible had dated the patriarchs Abraham, Isaac and Jacob at shortly after 2000 BC. Newly discovered texts, such as those at Nuzi, described for us the customs of that period. G. Ernest Wright of Harvard University noted that:

> (Abraham's) life and times, as reflected in the stories about him, fit perfectly within the early second millennium, but imperfectly within any later period.[1]

The reciting of customs peculiar to that period in both the Nuzi tablets and the book of Genesis bred confidence that the Genesis story was told as only a contemporary could describe them.

All available evidence showed that Abraham certainly was a real character.

Two great races, the Jews and the Arabs, trace their ancestry to Abraham.

Near the river Euphrates, on the fertile plain of Mesopotamia, stood the highly civilized and sophisticated city of Ur.

During the closing years of the 20th century BC, one of its better-educated and wealthier citizens was a man called Abram, or Abraham, a Semite.

Abraham was called to leave Ur and migrate to Canaan, present-day Israel.

A prophecy: "For all nations"

In whatever manner came the divine call, it was direct and specific. "Abraham, I want you to leave Ur, for I plan to make of you a great nation through whom all nations of the earth will be blessed."[2]

It was probably after much family discussion, that Abraham and his close relatives moved south to Haran. In Haran, there was repeated this promise of a nation in which all other nations were to be blessed.

Perhaps it might be wondered why the eternal God would select a special people in the first place. Did He have no concern for other nations? Why the apparent exclusiveness?

Such an idea as this, that one nation should be destined by the Deity to be the vehicle of blessing to all nations, was totally foreign to the thinking of the ancient world. For instance, Rome sought to spread her customs over the nations by means of the sword, but had no conception of being a blessing to the rest of the world. Likewise with Greece, even though she governed more by the arts of peace.

But here is something **unique**. A chosen people is formed for the purpose of blessing all nations through a foretold Deliverer. This was intimately locked into God's plan to save as many of mankind as possible.

Abraham now moved south to Canaan, the land of modern Israel. And here, after a time, he was plunged into the greatest of traumas.

"Sacrifice your son"

The citizens of Canaan regularly sacrificed their sons to their gods. Abraham had often told them that the Creator did not approve of such sacrifice.

Then suddenly the unthinkable happened. Abraham was faced with a divine command to do just that. That he was stunned would be an understatement. It was, after all, this very child of his old age from which the promised nation was to spring. Why then this?

Yet, ever loyal, the patriarch sorrowfully set out with Isaac on a journey to Mount Moriah. His heart was breaking. How could he reveal to his son the purpose of this trek?

Isaac helped him gather wood for a fire. And then came the question: "But dad, where's the lamb for the burnt offering?"

The old man simply stared at him, trembling. Never had Isaac seen such a strange look on his father's face. At length the old man replied, "God will provide Himself a lamb, son."

And eventually came the moment to break the news.

Was Isaac shaken? More likely he was filled with horror. But from infancy there had been instilled into him a total commitment to God's way. And Isaac believed in the integrity of his father. He understood that the direction **must** have come from God.

He was full of sadness at his separation from his father. But he was willing.

Though strong enough to resist his aging parent, the lad cooperated. Soon he lay bound on the altar. His father embraced him and wept. Then, with a trembling hand, he raised the knife.

"Abraham, Abraham!" The urgency of the voice held his arm.

"Do not lay your hand on the lad or do anything to him; for now I know that you reverence God, seeing you have not withheld your son, your only son, from me."[3]

Then it was that Abraham saw a ram caught by its horns in the bushes. He took it and offered it instead of his son.

Was this incident a capricious whim on the part of God? Not at all. It was a graphic object lesson to the father of the selected nation – intended to impress on him and his posterity the reality **that God Himself would some day make an agonizing sacrifice** of a Precious One in order to deliver mankind.

"God will provide himself a sacrifice... in the mount of the Lord it shall be seen."[4]

Could this be a prophecy that, one day in the future, the Messiah, God's Son, would himself be sacrificed as a lamb on this very mountain?

And centuries later, a well-known person would declare, "Abraham rejoiced to see my day, and was glad."[5]

By faith, Abraham looked forward to that future One in whom all nations would be blessed.

Thus began the nurturing of a race, the intended vehicle of this purpose.

●●●●●●

The drama was soon to begin.....

CHAPTER 7

ESCAPE AT MIDNIGHT

Josephine snorkeled along the surface. A large part of her life had been spent with coral reefs, so she found it comparatively easy to identify objects as natural or not.

Suddenly she saw it.

"That's coral. But it' s NOT coral!" she thought.

Descending quickly to inspect the object, she stared at it. Indeed, it was a length of coral, with one end cemented to a stone.

As she tried to raise it, half of the length snapped off.

Her heart skipped. Inside that coral was **iron**!

On-shore examination confirmed the coral to be dead; it was very old. The object inside was the precise length, width and shape to be the dislodged spoke of an ancient Egyptian chariot wheel. We would take it for testing.

"This whole area is a massive graveyard!" exclaimed Dane, after four dives. "But the underwater land bridge is so vast. It's so difficult to find what we're looking for, amid all this coral. The coral is coating over a lot of the evidence."

"I was snorkeling over almost flat seabed," Brett cut in. "And suddenly came this sharp drop of about seventy feet. It was scary. On both sides of the 'bridge' it dropped off quite steeply."

David undid his belt. "I photographed what is apparently a horse's head," he said calmly. "The coral matt held it tight. Also the vertebrae of a horse. And some wheels. They've collapsed outward. Bad condition. Photos would not prove good evidence."

This was the latest of three expeditions I had accompanied or led to the bottom of the Red Sea.

In November, 1993, after the first of these, I was able to report in *Update International,* my quarterly newsletter:

> I have some stunning news for you! We have just returned from diving on the floor of the Red Sea – and checking the immediate land area. With me was a six-member, international team. Ron Wyatt first saw it. We went down to confirm it. The discovery – true, I believe, beyond any doubt: the long-sought Exodus crossing site, complete with parts of the drowned Egyptian army.[1]

I also reported on the chariot parts photographed in 60 feet of water and deeper, in my book, *The Ark Conspiracy.*

As I explained in the very first chapter of this book, my initial reaction upon hearing of Wyatt's discoveries was disbelief. He had to be a liar, an egotist, or at the very least a deluded crank who thought he'd found things when he hadn't.

That was three years ago, now. At that time, I had believed the negative opinions of others.

But I had not met Ron Wyatt personally, nor checked out his claims. My opinion was not valid. I merely believed what I was told. I had been prejudiced against his claims by the ill-informed bigotry of a "scientific" writer.

But it didn't stop there! I had enough curious interest - which others might term foolhardiness - to check out Wyatt's claims personally.

The result was to prove stunning. In each instance in which it was possible to check his claims, I found Wyatt to be telling the truth. The scholarly-sounding arguments against the man's work fell apart, one by one.

Ron Wyatt, with helpers, had several times been diving in the Red Sea. He had found chariot parts, four, six and eight spoked wheels and skeletal remains of horses and men, scattered over the sea floor. One wheel had been retrieved and presented to the Antiquities Director in Cairo, Mr Nassif Mohammed Hussan.

Was this the evidence that had eluded searchers for centuries? Physical proof of the Hebrew Exodus from Egypt, in which the pursuing Egyptian army was lost in the sea?

Who were these Hebrews? And what really happened that day?

It should be understood that a Hebrew is not necessarily a Jew. The term Jew applies to a member of the tribe of Judah, one of the twelve tribes of Israel. The Hebrews were the Israelites, descendants of Abraham through his son Isaac.

The Jewish "miracle"

On one occasion, King Frederick of Prussia demanded of a preacher that he prove in one word that the Bible was true. Without hesitation, the preacher replied:

THE JEW, YOUR MAJESTY, THE JEW!

Nowhere in all the world is there anything so strange, so remarkable, yet so sad, as the Jew.

The Jewish race is about the oldest in the world.

When ancient Rome in her hey-day wielded the scepter of universal power, the Jews formed but a small province of that mighty empire. Today, however, Rome's ruins lie smoldering in the dust. But the Jews, whom she conquered and slaughtered, live on as virile as ever.

It is significant that every nation that persecuted the Jews, in time has waned, crumbled, vanished. Two ancient nations around Judea that remain (Persia and Greece), were nations that befriended the Jews.

These mystery people, the Jews, are descendants of Abraham the Semite.

They migrated to Egypt while yet a family. And while there, they were forced into bitter bondage under the Egyptians. On account of their phenomenal growth, which was considered a menace to Egypt's security, the Pharaoh endeavored to slay all the Jewish male infants. Nevertheless, Egypt's efforts to stem the increase were in vain.

Finally, through Moses, the Lord God miraculously delivered Israel from Egypt, to make of them a great nation settled in the land of Palestine.

The evidence of archaeology increasingly confirms the biblical records concerning these events.

61

A preview of history given

Before Moses died, God gave him a preview of the history of the Hebrew people. This was recorded 3,500 years ago; and its remarkable fulfillment is taking place before our eyes today.

God will set you on high above all the nations of the earth...
The Lord shall make you the head and not the tail.[2]

This was to be fulfilled in the glorious reigns of David and Solomon. Solomon was the greatest monarch of the oriental world. All nations came to Jerusalem to behold his glory and hear his unexcelled wisdom.

Israel became the head in her central geographical position, where all the routes of trade met and crossed. She was the instrument in the divine hand for disseminating the knowledge of the Creator God.

She was "set on high above the nations." She was "the head and not the tail."

While the Jewish nation was destroyed in 70 AD, nevertheless, it is remarkable that in almost every field of endeavor they are at the top. Even their enemies admit this!

For example, in the *Who's Who* of the United States, Britain, France, Germany, Russia, and so many more countries, there is presented an extended list of Jews.

In the musical world, Mendelsohn, Bach, Schubert, Schuman, Rubinstein, and others, were Jews.

Herschel and Einstein, among others, led in the scientific world. Among physicians, Jews stand almost unexcelled.

Insulin, cocaine, salvarsin, the Waserman test, serum for meningitis, vitamins and the beri beri cure, as well as endless other discoveries, were made and developed by Jews.

Of all Germans awarded the Nobel Prize, 30 per cent were Jews.

Again, 3,500 years ago, Moses enunciated this prophecy:

You shall lend and not borrow.[3]

While this referred to the prosperity of the past Jewish nation, yet it also intimates the financial genius of this people.

During the Middle Ages, Christians in many lands were forbidden by Canon Law to lend money on interest. This enabled the Jews to become the bankers and financiers of Europe.

Columbus in his expedition to the New World was financed by Jews. Napoleon's ambitions were blasted by the Jewish gold of the Rothschilds. George Washington, in his struggle of the Revolutionary War, was saved by the finance of the Salomons, Sevys, and others, of New York and Philadelphia. Germany claims her defeat in World War I was due to the Jewish gold, talents, and influence.

In the United States, the Jews control the dry goods and clothing business of that great nation. Theater ownership and management, the motion picture industry and numerous other enterprises are likewise under their control.

"You shall be the head and not the tail." Similar facts could be repeated for almost every country.

But back to our story...

The exodus

Four centuries after Abraham, his descendants in Egypt were groaning under the slave-master's whip. The future seemed not to exist, let alone the promise that through them all other nations would be blessed.

It was April, 1446 BC. Sudden and dramatic came the rescue. Even most Bible critics now acknowledge the Exodus as historical fact.

Archaeologists have noted that every one of the ten plagues that at that time fell on Egypt seemed aimed at some aspect of the corrupt Egyptian religion. Each of their gods (those of the frog, the fly, cattle, medicine, the elements, the sun, the fertility of fields, and the goddess of birth) suffered tremendous loss of prestige in the minds of the Egyptians.

If one is tempted to think that these ten plagues were a little harsh, it should be remembered that the Lord had warned Pharaoh what was coming if he did not let Israel go. So the king knew what was involved. First of all came the frogs and flies and lice – annoyances that did not threaten life. Pharaoh received chance

The Hebrew exodus from Egypt

after chance – each time being warned of what was coming next, so that he could escape it if he would.

But he let love and compassion harden his heart instead of melt it. He eventually destroyed himself by his own choice.

And the people of Egypt were given every opportunity to accept the message. Many did just that – and left Egypt with the Hebrews.

This was the Hebrew month Abib (later called Nisan). It was the 14th. On this day, the Hebrews were asked to demonstrate their faith, being protected from the final plague, if they first sacrificed a lamb (a symbol of the promised Deliverer) and placed its blood on their door post. All the way through, the message was that they could not save themselves.

Probably in their oppression as slaves, they had lost sight of the real significance of the blood, but obedience to the command was nevertheless rewarded.

As for the plagues, some recent researchers contend, with considerable evidence in support (though this has not yet been accepted by most Egyptologists) that an error in Egyptian chronology, once corrected to the extent of 600-800 years, will yield an Egyptian account of the plagues parallel to that of the Bible.

Immanuel Velikovsky has presented a detailed analysis of two records, the *Papyrus lpuwer* and the *el-Arish shrine inscription*, which appear to be Egyptian versions not merely of a great catastrophe, but of the ten plagues.[4]

According to the book of Exodus, the last night the Israelites were in Egypt, death struck instantly and took victims from every Egyptian home. The **Pass-over** of the "angel of death" was at midnight. And "there was a great cry in Egypt."[5] The select and the flower of Egypt lay dead.

The Egyptians looked upon the ten rapid sequence calamities as acts of God and the slaves. "And the Egyptians were urgent upon the people, that they might send them out of the land in haste; for they said, We be all dead men."[6]

And now the Hebrews, whom Pharaoh had refused to let go, were **driven out**. The Lord had delivered His people – but at what a cost, what needless cost!

Drowning of the Egyptian army

The *Papyrus Ipuwer* clearly describes three consequences of the catastrophe: the population revolted; the wretched and poor men fled; and the pharaoh perished under unusual circumstances.

The Bible records that after the Hebrew escape, the Egyptians tried to restore order. They pursued the slaves. The Hebrews found themselves trapped by the sea.

The drowning

However, "a cloud of darkness" kept the Egyptian army at bay "all the night". Yet the **same** cloud became a **great light** to the Hebrews, flooding the entire camp with the radiance of day.

Under instruction, Moses, the humble Hebrew leader, stretched out his rod over the sea. Then, the Lord did, as He will now, surprising things through chosen, humble instruments.

"And the Lord caused the sea to go back by a **strong** east wind."[7] A channeled wind exceeding the force of the mightiest hurricane drove back the waters. The waters became "congealed," [8] or frozen, as a wall on the right hand and the left.

All night they advanced across the sea bottom, the last rows climbing up the opposite shore to safety as the morning light broke.

The Egyptian soldiers poured onto the sea bed after them. The mysterious cloud changed to a pillar of fire before their astonished eyes. The thunders pealed and the lightning flashed. The clouds poured out water.

Soon the wheels of the chariots began to sink deep into the soft sand and the charioteers struggled to free the wheels.

Again was Moses instructed to lift his rod toward the sea. Here was a humble human servant being used to deliver his people. You could call it divine-human cooperation. That, apparently, is how the Lord likes to work.

Suddenly, the piled up mass of waters, hissing and roaring, thundered back over the Egyptian army, swallowing them into its black depths.

The monarch and the nation's army and priests were in that place of fearful danger by their own choice. They had destroyed themselves!

This was a **dramatic deliverance** for the people the Lord was leading, and a **dramatic and traumatic death** for the Egyptian pursuers.

In both the Bible and the Egyptian records, the Pharaoh perished in a whirlpool during or after the days of the great darkness and violent hurricane.

Mouth of the canyon

The *el-Arish inscription* states that the event occurred "on this place called *Pi-Kharoti*".[9]

The Bible says that Pharaoh overtook the Hebrews "by the sea, beside *Pi-ha-hiroth*(Khiroth)." [10]

It is the same place, the same pursuit.

The name *Pihahiroth* means "Mouth of Gorges" [11] – a most accurate description of the locality opposite which our archaeological team has been finding the chariot parts and skeletal remains of horses and men.

A prophecy

The disaster to the flower of the Egyptian army and nobility was so overwhelming that Egypt succumbed to looting, disorganization and anarchy for several years.

There was no longer any royal power. Egypt was largely depopulated. And she was defenseless.

Thus were the words of a prophecy fulfilled:

> For this cause I have raised you (Pharaoh) up, to show in you my power, AND SO THAT MY NAME MAY BE DE-CLARED THROUGHOUT ALL THE EARTH.[12]

One wonders if any event in history, except those connected with Jesus Christ, has been so extensively "declared throughout all the earth", and for so long, as this description of the deliverance of a people who at that time were minor and insignificant.

It cannot be denied that the news of their Exodus from Egypt and the name of their God has been "declared throughout all the earth" – **a precise fulfillment of prophecy**. Epic films have been made of it; the story has been translated into over a thousand languages.

But the prophecy meant more than this. Pharaoh had been "raised up" for the purpose of showing, by the extent of his fall, the puny and insecure nature of the greatest kingly power when measured against the power of the world's Creator.

Moses, motivated by the grand mission for which God had called him, refused the throne, the wealth and splendor of the world's most pompous nation. Today his name is honored. And the once majestic pharaohs? Just listen.

Early this century, when some of their mummies were being transported down the Nile to Cairo, the shippers were in a quandary. There was no cargo classification for "royal mummies", so do you know what they did? The pompous pharaohs had to travel under the designation, "dried fish"!

Israel's planned role

It had seemed that freedom would never come. Yet the Lord had promised. And suddenly it happened – a series of judgments upon Egypt in rapid succession – and they were free!

Sketch by Darren Hunter

Now the plan was activated to bond Israel together as a nation in a common trust in the Creator God. Organized by Moses at Sinai in a public covenant relationship with God (a unique event in any nation's history), the Hebrews became the recipients of the plan for the coming Deliverer of the human race. They were entrusted with written revelations of the divine purpose.

The Ten Commandments

At Mount Sinai, the people stood trembling, as the earth shook violently, lightning flashed and thunder rolled. Clothed with majesty of fire, the Lord descended upon the mountain – and once only in history He spoke audibly before a whole nation of people.

He formally restated the Ten Commandments. Ten laws, brief, comprehensive and authoritative – laws which cover the duty of man to God and to his fellow man – and all based upon the great basic principle of love. You could call them God's ten-point character reference.

These commandments are an expression of the eternal moral law of God. They embody the basic principles of life, and state what would be true even if the commandments had not been formally announced by our Maker.

Love to God and man was enshrined in the Ten Commandments.

The Lord God wrote them as with a finger of light, incising them onto tablets of imperishable stone.[13]

Then He delivered them to Moses, to be placed in a tent of worship, known as the **tabernacle**.

The Hebrews were given specific guidance in family relationships, in diet, in dress, in business, in public health, and in civil government – guidelines that are still beneficial today.

For all nations

The Hebrew prophets clearly enunciated God's plan:

My house shall be called a house of prayer for all peoples.[14]

The instructions were not for Israel alone, but for all nations. Israel was merely the vehicle through which the world was to be blessed. Thus an entire nation was raised up to function as a spiritual beacon in a world losing its knowledge of God and degenerating fast.

Their chief responsibility was to reveal to other peoples of the world the Lord's generous kindness. For that reason, the Hebrews were soon to be planted on the land bridge of Palestine, a focal point between three continents – Africa, Asia and Europe. According to the prophets, the Lord was saying:

I have set her in the center of the nations, with countries round about her.[15]

The divine schedule for the Hebrew nation was clearly set out in advance.[16]

Through His servant, the prophet Moses, God outlined the future history of Israel if they remained faithful to His commission.[17] And their alternate destiny should they turn aside from the plan.[18] The choice would be theirs.

◆◆◆◆◆◆

And right there at Mount Sinai in the Arabian desert,[19] the Ark of the Covenant was constructed.   But, why was it built?

A wonderful play was about to be enacted......

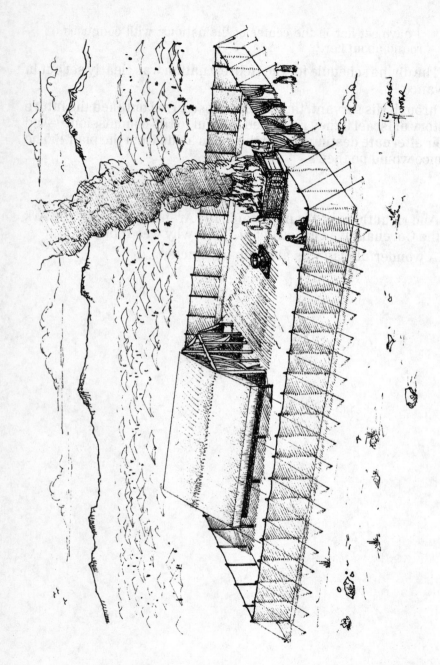

The Hebrew tabernacle erected at Sinai (Sketch: Darren Hunter)

CHAPTER 8

COVENANT OF BLOOD

He entered cautiously. The chamber was windowless. And empty, except for the golden chest. A light of dazzling brilliance hovered over it.

He came in waving incense.

The people outside breathlessly awaited his return. So long as they could hear the bells on his robe, they were assured he was still alive.

•••••••••

To teach the people His rescue plan for mankind, the Lord instructed the Hebrew leader to build a sanctuary in the camp.[1]

God's way – God's plan – for mankind, His **modus operandi**, if you like, was to be enacted before their eyes, by means of the sanctuary rituals. As the psalmist later put it, "Your way, oh Lord, is in the sanctuary."[2]

The sanctuary outlined God's perfect plan for dealing with the sin problem.

If we want to know **how** God intends to save us, we will investigate the Hebrew sanctuary. You see, the age-old sacrificial ritual (which taught the principles of the divine rescue plan) was incorporated into the sanctuary, or Temple, worship.

In simple terms, God wanted to impress upon them: **(1)** His holiness in contrast to their unholiness; **(2)** His eagerness to forgive their sins in response to their turning from them; and **(3)** His desire to cleanse their lives and win each person's heart.

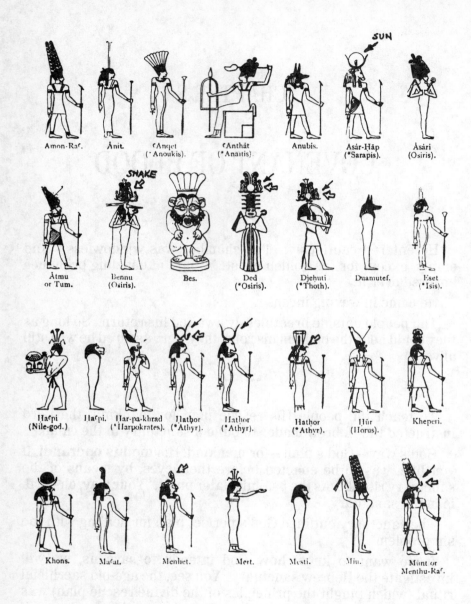

Amon-Raʿ.	Ánit.	ʿAnqet (*Anoukis).	ʿAnthât (*Anaitis).	Anubis.	Asár-Háp (*Sarapis).	Ásári (Osiris).
Átmu or Tum.	Bennu (Osiris).	Bes.	Ded (*Osiris).	Djehuti (*Thoth).	Duamutef.	Eset (*Isis).
Haʿpi (Nile-god.)	Haʿpi.	Har-pa-khrad (*Harpokrates).	Hathor (*Athyr).	Hathor (*Athyr).	Hathor (*Athyr).	Hūr (Horus). Kheperi.
Khons.	Maʿat.	Menhet.	Mert.	Mesti.	Miu.	Mūnt or Menthu-Raʿ.

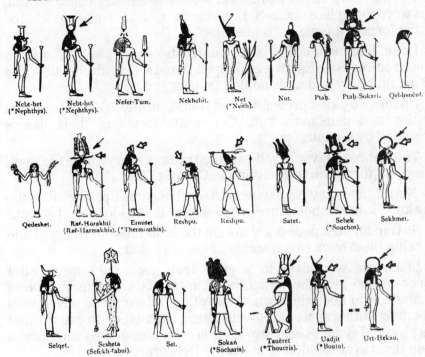

Nebt-ḥet (*Nephthys). Nebt-ḥet (*Nephthys). Nefer-Tum. Nekhebit. Net (*Neith). Nut. Ptaḥ. Ptaḥ-Sokari. Qebḥsnêuf.

Qedeshet. Raf-Horakhti (Raf-Harmakhis). Ernutet (*Thermouthis). Reshpu. Reshpu. Satet. Sebek (*Souchos). Sekhmet.

Selqet. Sesheta (Sefekh-ʿabui). Set. Sokaň (*Socharis). Tauēret (*Thoueris). Uadjit (*Bouto). Urt-Ḥekau.

So long as the Hebrews had not yet reached their promised land, but were living like nomads, this sanctuary was to be constructed in the form of a tent, or "tabernacle".

Israel had been in Egypt for hundreds of years. Egypt was an idolatrous nation. Egypt worshipped the sun, the Nile, beetles, and so on, and they had idols depicting each god.

On the two pages preceding, are representations of the principal deities and demigods, with the Greek forms of their names preceded by an asterisk (*).

The Hebrew slaves saw these illustrations everywhere in Egypt. They had forgotten to worship the Creator God.

Notice the many places the **sun** symbol came up, as well as the **snake.** Both symbols were predominant in the idolatry of Egypt.[3]

So God found it necessary to lead the Israelites out of Egypt and to bring them back to a worship of the true God.

Since they were used to "seeing" their gods, the Lord found it necessary to give the Israelites a "bite, taste and feel" type of symbolism to keep the plan of salvation before them. Even with this their faith was weak. It would have been much worse without the physical symbols and prophetic ceremonies of the sanctuary to keep them ever mindful of a coming Deliverer.

Accustomed as they had been in Egypt to material representations of the Deity, and these of the most degrading nature, it was difficult for them to conceive of the existence or the character of the Unseen One. In pity for their weakness, God gave them a symbol of His presence. "Let them make me a sanctuary," He said, "that I may dwell among them."[4]

The courtyard – place of sacrifice

Enclosing it was a "courtyard", in which stood an altar for sacrifices, as well as a "laver", a basin containing water for ceremonial washing.

Twice a day, a lamb was offered on the altar. This, as we have already seen, was symbolic of the Coming One, who would at some time in the future – in real life – be "led as a lamb to the slaughter".[5] Whenever a person who had done wrong brought an animal for sacrifice to the courtyard, he would lay his hands on the animal and personally take a knife and kill it. He himself killed it. By laying his hands upon the animal, the wrong-doer now symbolically transferred his own guilt to the innocent victim – and the animal became, as it were, a substitute for him.

The *Jewish Encyclopedia* thus comments:

> The laying of hands upon the victim's head is an ordinary rite by which the substitution and the transfer of sins are effected.
> In every sacrifice there is the idea of substitution: the victim takes the place of the human sinner.[6]

However, to confess the wrong, as well as to restore whatever had been taken, was necessary in all cases, before the atonement could be made for the individual.[7] Some blood from every sacrifice was sprinkled on the altar, to teach the people that "it is the blood that makes reconciliation."[8]

Of course, the Lord God took no delight in the shedding of blood. But there were two reasons for the sacrificial system.

Firstly, man needed to feel a **HORROR** for wrong-doing, a desire to turn away from it.

Can you visualize a man shuddering as he gazed upon the lifeless form of that animal, realizing that his own act had just caused the death of an innocent creature?

You see, the sacrifice was a constant and vivid reminder of the terrible cost of sin. The death of the sacrifice drove home the painful truth that the result of sin is death. Sin causes death so irrevocably and inevitably that God cannot merely overlook it. It would cost God dearly to save us.

A second reason for the sacrifices was that mankind also needed **HOPE**. He must be reminded that his wrong-doing would one day cost the life of the innocent Lamb of God.

This teaching device had to do with the restoring of broken relationships.

No man could feel good about himself as he raised the knife to kill an innocent lamb - and knew that his guilt would one day take the life of the Rescuer. But, by faith in the Coming One, he knew he could be freed from guilt.

Of course, a sacrificial animal could not take away a man's or woman's guilt, but the sacrificial rite was an act of **faith** and **acceptance** of future deliverance.

77

The priest

The slaughtered animal represented the DEATH of the Coming One.

But there was more that needed to be done.

After the animal was sacrificed – and was dead – it could no longer play a role in the symbolism. This is where a priest took over.

This priest represented the same Coming One, who would, after his death, be raised to life again (resurrected) – and would subsequently enter God's presence on behalf of each of us. Sanctuary priests were thus appointed, who cooked a portion of each sacrifice and ate it.[9] In this way, the priest – like the promised Coming One – symbolically bore the sins of the people in his own body.[10] Thus, when the priest entered the tent after offering a sacrifice for his own sins, he carried therein blood that now symbolized forgiveness for the people's sins as well as his own. He went into the holy place to represent the people before God.

Two rooms

The tent itself was divided into two chambers.

The **first room** was known as **the holy place**. Here there were three items of furniture.

1 – A solid gold 7 branched Lampstand burned, representing the divine Light of the world – the coming Messiah, who would bring light into our darkened lives.

2 – The "table of the bread of the Presence" (the Table of Shewbread) was gold-plated and about the size of a coffee table. On it were placed twelve flat loaves, symbolic of the Coming One, who would spiritually nourish us and bring eternal life to all who would accept him.

3 – A golden Altar of Incense, before which the priest stood on behalf of the people, and applied the blood of a sacrifice. The incense smoke symbolized the perfection of the Coming One, which would render the people's ascending prayers acceptable to God.

The second room

The second chamber, termed the **Most Holy Place,** contained one object – THE ARK OF THE COVENANT. The Ark constituted the very heart of the sanctuary.

Ark of the Covenant

Expertly fashioned from acacia wood, this gold-plated chest enshrined the tablets of stone upon which God engraved the Ten Commandments. The lid of the Ark, known as the **Mercy Seat**, was of pure gold. Attached to it and beaten out of the same piece of gold, were two angel-like carvings called **cherubim**. These faced each other, looking down toward the law and the Mercy Seat. The Ark had its own light. A brilliant, supernatural light – later known as the **Shekinah** – shone above the Mercy Seat as a symbol of the Divine Presence.

The Ark was considered to be the holiest object on earth.

One might ask, Why was such importance attached to it? I can think of three reasons.

Symbol of God's throne

1 – The Ark was the special place for the manifesting of God's presence on earth.

The book of Numbers depicts Moses coming to the Ark and hearing the voice of God speaking from between the cherubim upon the Ark.[11]

God said, "There will I meet with you; and from above the mercy seat, from between the two cherubim which are upon the ark of the testimony, I will speak to you about all that I will give you in commandment for the sons of Israel."[12]

The Ark was merely a means of **manifesting** God's presence on earth, since we are told God is able in His omnipresence to fill both heaven and earth,[13] yet remains in His heavenly Temple.[14]

The Ark was symbolic of the Great Throne in heaven, the center of rulership for the universe.

Thus two cherubim (representations of angelic beings) were attached to the cover of the Ark. Cherubim always appear in Scripture as immensely powerful beings who attend the visible

Illustration: Tom Dunbebin

presence of God. The cherubim had a "covering" function, preventing God's glory from breaking forth upon men. These "covering cherubim" symbolically protected Israel while God's presence was manifested at the Ark in the sanctuary.

The position of the cherubim with their faces turned toward each other, and looking reverently downwards toward the Ark,[15] represented the reverence with which the heavenly beings regard the law of God and their interest in the plan of salvation. Various Scripture passages picture the Lord as sitting enthroned between the cherubim[16] with the Ark as His footstool.[17]

Enshrines the Ten Commandments

2 – The Ark's main purpose was as a repository for the holy law of God.

It was for this reason that this golden chest was named the ARK OF THE COVENANT (or ARK OF THE TESTIMONY). It enshrined **"the words of the covenant, the ten commandments", also known as "the testimony"**.[18]

That law was a transcript of the character and will of God. As such, it was inscribed by God's own hand. And it was honored as the most sacred object in the sanctuary. The Ten Commandments on earth are the humanization of the heavenly original. The tables of the law within the Ark testified to the fact that God's kingdom is founded on an unchangeable standard of right living.[19]

A teaching model of God's plan to save mankind

3 – The Ark was a teaching model of God's great plan to save fallen man.

The message was that God will be gracious to those who come to Him in His appointed way.

Firstly, man has sinned. He has broken that **law** which is the foundation of God's government. Says John, "Whosoever commits sin transgresses also the law: for sin is the transgression of the law."[20]

But, **secondly**, over this law is the Mercy Seat. The Lord's **mercy** is over His **law**. It is the prerogative of the law-giver to provide mercy.

The location of the TEN COMMANDMENTS below the MERCY SEAT of the Ark taught that God's government and law isn't arbitrary, but is based on LOVE.

From the divine Throne emanates not merely "justice and judgment" but also "mercy".[21]

While the tablets of the law within the Ark testified against the wrong-doer, the Mercy Seat pointed to a way in which the claims of the law (for obedience) could be met by the Coming One - and the wrong-doer saved from death, the penalty of the law.

On the basis of the law alone there could be no reunion between God and man, since sin separates each person from his Maker.[22]

The Mercy Seat must intervene.

Blood on the Mercy Seat

So it was that, in addition to the regular sanctuary features, once a year, on the Day of Atonement, the blood of an animal

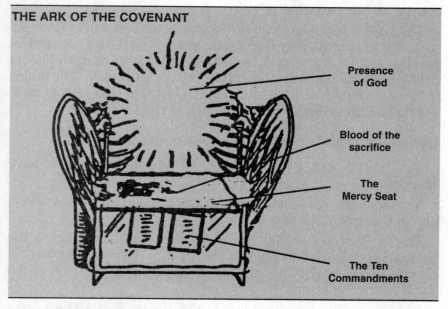

THE ARK OF THE COVENANT

Presence of God

Blood of the sacrifice

The Mercy Seat

The Ten Commandments

sacrifice was sprinkled onto this Mercy seat.[23] The Lord appeared over it in a cloud at that time.

The sacrificial blood placed upon the Mercy Seat over the Ten Commandments was an impressive symbol of the price that our sins have cost and which the Deliverer would be willing to pay.

So in a nutshell, it meant simply this:

The blood of the Coming One shall be shed as a sacrifice and God will grant mercy to all who accept that sacrifice on their behalf and turn from their wrong-doings.

Before we leave this point, something I found interesting was that on the annual Day of Atonement the blood was sprinkled **on the Mercy Seat once**, and **before it 7 times**. Just so, the coming Lamb of God, the Messiah, would be offered once for all. Seven is the number of perfection and completeness.

"Patterns of things in the heavens"

All of the objects in this tabernacle built by Moses were "patterns of things in the heavens".[25] "They serve a copy and shadow of the heavenly sanctuary." [26]

Many references in the Scriptures indicate the existence of a heavenly Temple, which is the center of God's government.

It is recorded that the Lord showed Moses – and later David – some sort of model or pattern by which they could construct the tabernacle (and later the Temple), including the Ark.

Notice the two following accounts:

> Let them construct a sanctuary for Me, that I may dwell among them. According to all that I am going to show you, as the **pattern** of the Tabernacle and the **pattern** of all its furniture, just so shall you construct it...you shall make a mercy seat of pure gold...you shall make two cherubim of gold.. . the cherubim shall have their wings spread upward, covering the mercy seat...And see that you make them after the **pattern** for them, which was shown to you on the mountain.[28]

David said:

> All this the Lord made me understand in writing by His hand upon me, all the details of this **pattern**.[29]

Evidently, the earthly Ark of the Covenant was patterned after the Great Throne in heaven. And the divine law enshrined within

83

the Ark was modeled on the great original, which is the foundation of God's Throne.

Other objects with the Ark

At the **side** of the earthly Ark was placed the **Torat Moshe** (autograph of the Pentateuch, the five books of Moses), to be removed and read at the festival of **Sukkot**.[30]

At one time Aaron's rod and a pot of manna were placed in front of the Ark as a memorial of God's provision and the Israelites' rebellion.[31] But when the Ark was later placed in Solomon's Temple, we find that those were no longer there.

Says the record, "There was nothing in the Ark save the two tables of stone."[32] Only the tablets of the Ten Commandments remained permanent fixtures inside the Ark.

The Old Testament, Josephus and Philo are unanimous in their verdict that the only items in the Ark were the tablets of the Ten Commandments.[33]

✦✦✦✦✦✦✦

Soon the Ark was to begin its march into the promised land. And what incredible events were to attend it - and the people who bore it!

CHAPTER 9

WHY WERE THE CANAANITES EVICTED?

The Philistines [the then inhabitants of today's Gaza Strip] took the captured Ark of God from the battleground at Ebenezer to the temple of their idol Dagon in the city of Ashdod. But when the local citizens went to see it the next morning, Dagon had fallen with his face to the ground before the Ark of Jehovah. They set him up again, but the next morning the same thing had happened – the idol had fallen face down before the Ark of the Lord again. This time his head and hands had been cut off and were lying in the doorway; only the trunk of his body was left intact. (That is why to this day neither the priests of Dagon nor his worshippers will walk on the threshold of the temple of Dagon in Ashdod.)

Then the Lord began to destroy the people of Ashdod and the nearby villages with a plague of boils. When the people realized what was happening, they exclaimed, "We can't keep the Ark of the God of Israel here any longer. We will all perish along with our god Dagon."

So they called a conference of the mayors of the five cities of the Philistines to decide how to dispose of the Ark. The decision was to take it to Gath. But when the Ark arrived at Gath, the Lord began destroying its people, young and old, with the plague, and there was a great panic. So they sent the Ark to Ekron, but when the people of Ekron saw it coming they cried out, "They are bringing the Ark of the God of Israel here to kill us too!"

So they summoned the mayors again and begged them to send the Ark back to its own country, lest the entire city die. For the plague had already begun and great fear was sweeping across the city. Those who didn't die were deathly ill; and there was weeping everywhere.

The Ark remained in the Philistine country for seven months in all. Then the Philistines called for their priests and diviners and asked them, "What shall we do about the Ark of God? What sort of gift shall we send with it when we return it to its own land?"

"Yes, send it back with a gift," they were told. "Send a guilt offering so that the plague will stop. Then, if it doesn't, you will know God didn't send the plague upon you after all."

"What guilt offering shall we send?", they asked. And they were told, "Send five gold models of the tumor caused by the plague, and five gold models of the rats that have ravaged the whole land – the capital cities and villages alike. If you send these gifts and then praise the God of Israel, perhaps he will stop persecuting you and your god. Don't be stubborn and rebellious as Pharaoh and the Egyptians were. They wouldn't let Israel go until God had destroyed them with dreadful plagues. Now build a new cart and hitch it to two cows that have just had calves – cows that never before have been yoked – and shut their calves away from them in the barn. Place the Ark of God on the cart beside a chest containing the gold models of the rats and tumors, and let the cows go wherever they want to. If they cross the border of our land and go into Beth-shemesh, then you will know that it was God who brought this great evil upon us; if they don't, (but return to their calves) then we will know that the plague was simply a coincidence and was not sent by God at all."

So these instructions were carried out. Two fresh cows were hitched to the cart and their calves were shut up in the barn. Then the Ark of the Lord and the chest containing the gold rats and tumors were placed upon the cart. And sure enough, the cows went straight along the road toward Beth-shemesh, lowing as they went; and the Philistine mayors followed them as far as the border of Beth-shemesh.

86

So reads the ancient biblical account.[1]

Dangerous plunder

Of all the plunder the Philistines seized from the Israelites, the Ark, foolishly taken into battle on this occasion, was the most valuable. Not only was it overlaid with gold. These superstitious people thought it was the secret of Israel's strength. But they found to their horror that it was a most dangerous piece of booty.

This episode must have made them think how wonderful was the power of the God of heaven.

The Israelites had mistakenly regarded the Ark as some sort of magic charm that would bring them victory no matter what sort of lives they were living or how much evil was in their hearts. But the Lord intended to teach them that the power was inherent not in the Ark, but in their faithfulness to their God and a living connection to Him. That is why He permitted the Ark to be captured when they took it out of the tabernacle and brought it into battle with them.

It became dangerous plunder for the Philistines... and a lesson for the Hebrews.

The Hebrews were settling into the promised land of Canaan. And they still had much to learn concerning loyalty to the Lord who had brought them there.

It might be asked, Why did other people have to be evicted so that the Hebrew invaders could come in? Wasn't that unfair to the existing population of Canaan?

This is my answer:

According to many traditions of the ancient world, sometime after the great World Flood, the earth was divided by lot among the three sons of Noah, the leader of the Flood survivors. Eusebius tells us that this solemn division by Noah took place about twenty years before his death.[2]

Each of the three groups had its own portion assigned to it for the future. Japheth and his descendants were to occupy initially Europe and northern Asia; Shem southern Asia intermingled with Ham's offspring; while Ham was to settle Africa and southern Asia.

Moses refers to this event in his writings.[3] Among the nations, the remembrance of this triple division remained. Out of it, a certain territory, well-known to all the rest of mankind, was reserved as the lot of the future race through whom the Deliverer would come.

Why were the Canaanites dispossessed?

A prominent post-Flood leader, Nimrod, slighted this ordinance, however. He and his clan conceived the project of a universal empire over which they themselves should preside. The Lord interposed, according to ancient writings, and scattered them over the earth.

The district reserved as a holy land was necessarily **crossed** by the descendants of Mizraim and Phut en route to settle Africa, but it appears that everyone religiously abstained from **occupying** it – until the descendants of Canaan (another family related to Nimrod's tribe) had the temerity to seize it.

Then we find the Lord God reclaiming this usurped territory and solemnly promising it to Abraham, for the yet future chosen nation through whom the world's Messiah will come.

Archaeology has uncovered evidence of the Canaanites' unspeakably vile culture. They had degenerated into savagery, involving sexual perversions and the burning of little children alive – practised under the guise of religion.

The Canaanite religious texts discovered in ancient Ugarit in northern Syria between 1929 and 1937, fully corroborate the estimate of such older scholars as Lenormant, who said of Canaanite religion:

> No other people ever rivaled them in the mixture of blood-shed and debauchery with which they thought to honor the Deity.[4]

Even so, the Lord God patiently tolerated this situation for 400 years more. The reason was: "for the iniquity of the Amorites [of Canaan] is not yet full."[5]

Now the time had arrived. Such depravity and cruelty must be stopped.

The judgment on the Canaanites was also an act of mercy, designed to spare generations yet unborn the terrible contamination and deadly influence of the Canaanite culture.[6]

Unless they were removed, their influence on the incoming nation of Israel was bound to be corrupting in the extreme. In fact, history demonstrated this to be so. Surviving Canaanites so

88

contaminated later generations with their beliefs and practices, that the Lord had to remove Israel from the land as well. As they entered Canaan, the people of Israel were a theocracy, a nation ruled directly by God. God made the decisions. He communicated with them, whenever His glory cloud descended upon the Ark of the Covenant.

When God the Creator, the One who imparted life to all, ordained the destruction of a nation, it was only after He had done everything possible to save it from such an end.

But it was the people, not God, who thought they had to have weapons to expel the usurpers occupying the promised land.

By contrast, the expressed divine plan was to drive out the Canaanites with hornets![7] A most effective method if you ask me!

Why such miracles for the Hebrews?

In the Old Testament narrative, one reads at times of such astonishing miraculous happenings on behalf of the Hebrews. Admittedly, such accounts almost strain credibility. We are tempted to ask, Could the writers have been exaggerating a bit?

It is true that we do not often witness such spectacular displays on behalf of any one nation today.

Events that we might call miracles are constantly occurring, however.

Whether one accepts them as such depends upon one's attitude concerning the existence of God. If one accepts the reality of a Superior Being who was establishing a particular group of people for a unique role in history, it may make sense.

What we might call "supernatural" could be perfectly natural to a Superior Being, quite natural to His power. If He created laws of nature, might He not override such laws? Using even natural phenomena in a "supernatural" way?

Could I suggest that even when supernatural events find explanation in the framework of understood natural phenomena, does that lessen the divine, miraculous wisdom behind them?

THERE WAS A REASON FOR THE SPECTACULAR DEMONSTRATIONS witnessed during Israel's establishment.

Long had they been oppressed by slavery. God cared for them tenderly, supplied their every need, protected them from enemies and illness. And He worked spectacular miracles, time after time, **to show that they could trust Him**.

Time and again they were led into situations from which there appeared no way out.

As when death took all the flower of Egypt, including the son of Pharaoh, in one night – and Israel, spared, was suddenly freed from slavery.

As when the Red Sea was parted for their escape, and then the angry waters rolled back upon the Egyptian army.

Israel, after this, was not a nation unacquainted with God. Move by move, she was acquiring an incomparable heritage.

The Lord God gave these spectacular demonstrations **TO PROVE that He was APPOINTING that nation to a UNIQUE ROLE in history**. And other nations saw it too! Through these displays for Israel, God created a **"field of influence"** in the history of mankind.

"Peculiar" strategy

The ways of the Deity seemed peculiar, even bizarre. No general alive would approve of His strategy for fighting a war.

Imagine it, if you can! He told them to just march around Jericho City and blow trumpets. But it worked! The walls, with their massive towers, teetered and heaved, and crashed outward to the earth. "The wall fell down flat",[8] permitting the taking of the city. The walls were caused to fall outward! Now walls of cities do not fall outward; they fall inward.

When Jericho was excavated this century (1930-1936), Middle Eastern archaeologist Professor Garstang found something so startling that he and two members of the team signed a statement concerning it:

> As to the main fact, there remains no doubt: the walls fell outwards so completely that the attackers would be able to clamber up and over their ruins into the city.[9]

It was discovered that the city at that time had been burned, not looted – again corresponding to the Bible account.[10]

Another strange strategy occurred in the days of King Jehoshaphat, when the country was invaded by an army that would make anyone tremble. But the king, with God's encouragement, sent out a choir at the head of the army to praise God for victory – before the battle even started! What a seemingly ridiculous act! But it worked. When the enemy heard the singers claiming victory, they were so alarmed and confused that they simply turned on each other, destroying themselves.[11]

Then there was Gideon's army of 32,000 men. The Lord told him that was too many. So Gideon (although fearful and perplexed at the instructions) kept sending men home, until he had only 300 left.

In the dead of night, these men approached the Midianite camp from three directions. On a signal, every trumpet sounded. Then, breaking their jugs so that 300 blazing torches were displayed, they rushed in shouting, "The sword of the Lord, and of Gideon."[12]

Awakened by the noise and the lights on every side, the enemy thought an overwhelming force was upon them. Fleeing in panic, they mistook their own men for enemies and destroyed one another!

What strange methods! Again and again it happened. Time after time, by doing that which appeared not very sound, by violating all the rules of war, God made it plain that there was no way man could have done it. He Himself was at work.

Joshua's long day

Consider the account of Joshua's "long day", described in the book of Joshua.[13]

This amazing account states that in the battle between the Hebrews and the Amorite confederation, "the Lord fought for Israel" by providing two related miracles:

Firstly, the sun stood still in the sky, so that it "hasted not to go down about a whole day." (This was to give Joshua time to defeat the enemy completely before they could escape and regroup under cover of darkness.)

Secondly, a devastating hailstorm. (This must have given Israel's army relief from the heat; but it also helped to decimate the Amorites, a Canaanite group.)

A miracle is, of course, by scientific definition, impossible. A miracle is an interruption to natural law. But if there is a God who **made** the atom He would surely know how to **control** it.

Clearly, the earth's rotation must have slowed to a crawl, or even stopped. The Scripture does not say that the stoppage was sudden. A sudden stop in a fast moving automobile produces chaos, but if it gradually slows to a halt, no disturbance is felt.

Of course, during a slow down of the earth, atmospheric conditions would be drastically affected. This fact may have been the cause of the tremendous hailstorm that ensued.

Such an event was also recorded in the ancient non-biblical book of Jasher.[14]

Is there any independent historical evidence of this strange occurrence? Although written records of that period (1406 BC) are scarce and fragmentary, it is significant that the fact of a long day (or, on the other side of the world, a long night) is noted in the racial memory of numerous peoples. To name a few: the Hindus, Buddhists, Chinese, Mexicans, many American Indian tribes ("the theft of the sun for a day"), the Polynesians, Greeks and Egyptians. These are found in oral history, inscriptions and other written records.

Such an event was an important intervention in natural law, because the success of Joshua's entire campaign to take Canaan depended on the outcome of this battle, and hence the fulfillment of the Lord's promises to the world through the nation of Israel.

Perhaps it was also a demonstration for the benefit of the sun worshippers that it was the Creator who had ultimate control, and not the sun god.

I doubt if there was a child in Israel who didn't know these events all by heart.

A harsh God?

As I was reading the biblical history of Israel, I used to think the God of the Old Testament appeared to come through as harsh, even cruel.

Eventually, it struck me that the Lord would have to do things the way He did. He was forced to condition the revealing of Himself to the spiritual state of the people in their circumstances.

The lash of the whip and the slavemaster's curse had effectively choked out the language of love. Sometimes the Lord had to reach them with the language they understood – thunder, smoke and sword.

"I will apply to you the same rules you apply to others,"[15] was His approach. "If in your spiritual state of being you demand an eye for an eye, then so be it, I shall demand the same of you. I will be to you a God of justice and rectitude."

The Creator has had to communicate with people where He found them – and, from there, lead them as far as He can toward the ideal.

But the love is still there. As when a mother has to shout at a child about to grasp a razor blade. The shouting, the sternness, are as much a part of love as the gentle voice.

Meanwhile, in the sacrificial system, the Lord gave them a preview, repeated daily, of forgiveness through the Coming One.

And all the time, with tears in His heart, He waited patiently for the day when that Deliverer would demonstrate this incredible love in a way that even slaves would understand.

Planted on the crossroads

Israel's history in the land of Palestine was to last about 1,500 years.

Under the great King David, and then under Solomon, the nation began to be the spiritual agent God intended and Israel became one of the strongest powers in the Middle East.

Solomon publicly voiced the prayer that "all the peoples of the earth may know thy name and fear (reverence) thee, as do thy people Israel."[16]

And during Solomon's reign many did come to learn the secret of Israel's prosperity. We shall catch a glimpse of the geographical extent of Solomon's influence in the next two chapters.

Had she continued faithful, Israel would have become so well known for the justice of her laws, for the honesty of her merchants, for the fertility of her farms, for the good health of her citizens, and, above all, for the purity of her faith, that she would have been the wonder of the world.[17]

All over the globe, communities would have sprung up copying the Israelite pattern, and the God of love would have been loved everywhere. And now something wonderful happened that could have brought this about and changed history...

Come with me now, far back into the center of the Great Unknown. Our destination: the remotest corners of the earth, 3,000 years in the past.

This is where our research must lead us.

You see, the Ark of the Covenant was so important to a king of Israel, that he spent billions of dollars (in today's terms) simply to house it. The most opulent golden structure in the world was erected in Jerusalem specifically to enshrine this golden chest.

The builder – King Solomon – sent huge ships to the ends of the earth in his quest for gold and silver.

And the question arises, Where did the ships go?

Why did each voyage take three years?

And where was that land of gold, the fabled land of Ophir?

Scholars have driven themselves wild on the matter for years, but no one seems to have a satisfactory answer. In my search for the truth, I determined, if possible, to find out...

CHAPTER 10

SOLOMON'S FLEET MYSTERY

I stumbled into it. And hating secrets, I just had to find out.

Mount Moehau, on New Zealand's Coromandel Peninsula, plunges steeply into the sea. Draped in subtropical rain forest, downcut by waterfalls and precipitous gorges, the region oozes mystery and enchantment.

Here, says Maori legend, the Turehu people, light-skinned, with reddish hair, made their last stand.[1] The Maoris say they found them in parts of New Zealand. As the Maoris encroached, the Turehu retreated further into the hills, particularly of the Coromandel Peninsula. Here the mountains of Moehau, steep and remote, became their final refuge. Since they sought concealment near the misty summit of Moehau, the Turehu were sometimes spoken of as the "Mist People". Their voices and the ghostly piping of their flutes could often be heard in the dense forest. Huge gourds they grew. They built forts from interlaced supplejack, a long thick woody vine that trailed across the tall forest trees.

According to other Pacific islanders, people answering the same physical description had come from the east – from the direction of South America – long, long ago.

And would you believe, in South America I ran into similar traditions of a light-skinned, red-haired, blue-eyed race. According to legends, these people had settled and built cyclopean stone cities (whose ruins survive), but following a war had fled **westward** across the Pacific.

Was there some link, here? Could they have been the same people?

And pushing the question a little further, could these people of historical tradition have been the descendants of some ancient traders whose story we shall now relate?

◆◆◆◆◆◆

... Even as Israel took possession of the promised land, another power was being established on the sea coast adjacent to the north, a people whose career was definitely marked out for them.

It was the destiny of Phoenicia that she should become to the ancient world in material things, what the Hebrew was called to be in spiritual things.

Phoenicia was the great manufacturing nation of the ancient world. Her dyed textiles, glass technology, superb stonework, ceramics and gem engraving were unsurpassed.

Indeed, L. A. Waddell (citing Sir Flinders Petrie) asserts that the Phoenicians "had a civilization equal or superior to that of Egypt, in taste and skill... luxury far beyond that of the Egyptians, and technical work which could teach them rather than be taught."[2]

The city of Tyre was the London of antiquity, the centre of a vast global trading network.

Mistress of the seas

Phoenicia, mistress of the seas, sent ships to all ports and traversed all oceans. From the thirteenth century BC she was the dominant naval and commercial power. Her mercantile operations were enormous. This great naval power had the trade of the planet in her hands. She was a great distributing nation; her people were the carriers of the world.

The famous Indian epic, the *Mahabharata*, states that:

> The able Panch (Phoenicians) setting out to invade the Earth, brought the whole world under their sway.[3]

They were termed "leaders of the Earth".[4]

And Phoenicia was, in the tenth to eleventh centuries BC as great as Babylon or Egypt.

The coasts and islands of the Mediterranean were rapidly covered with colonies. Today's "Venice" preserves the ethnic title of "Phoenicia".

The Straits of Gibraltar were passed and cities built on the shores of the Atlantic. They founded Gades (Cadiz) on Spain's west coast, 2,500 miles from Tyre, as the starting point for the Atlantic trade.

In the expanding range of their voyages, Phoenician ships out of Spain were battling the wild Atlantic en route to the tin of Cornwall and even to Norway (2,000 miles beyond Gades).

Eastward, there is evidence that Phoenicia built factories on the Persian Gulf and traded as far as Ceylon.

London founded

An interesting sideline concerns the founding of London.

It has been adduced from substantial evidence that some 89 years after the fall of Troy (a Phoenician colony), Brutus, a descendant of the Trojan royalty, sailed up the River Thames in Britain and founded Tri-Novantum ("New Troy"). This ultimately became London.[5]

Thus, contrary to popular misconception, there existed a highly civilized dynasty, which survived in Britain even until the Roman invasion. It left behind gold coins, at least one surviving stone inscription and a detailed chronology. Indeed, Julius Caesar and other contemporaries testified to its cultured, well-dressed city-dwelling subjects, though untamed tribes did flank the western and northern borders.[6]

Researcher L.A.Waddell gives an authenticated unbroken chronology of highly civilized independent British kings reigning in London from Brutus (c. 1103 BC) to the Roman conquerors.[7] There is evidence that a large proportion of the people of Britain are descendants of the sea-going Phoenicians.

Sophisticated instruments

Phoenician ships probed ever further. Navigation across open ocean was no problem to these explorers.

Due to the insufficient attention paid to this aspect of the subject, we have tended to belittle the size and sophistication of Phoenician shipping.

If we conceive of it as represented by types of marine craft as outlined on Phoenician coins and tombs, we shall not be able to suppose that the nation was ever employed on such voyages as those that shall shortly engage our attention.

There is evidence that they had the benefit of sophisticated instruments and large, fast, modern vessels carrying over 500 people.[8] This will be a surprise to many readers.

"Ships of Tarshish"

The type of vessel built especially for ocean travel was designated "ship of Tarshish" to distinguish it from the smaller craft which merely plied the eastern Mediterranean.

The name of the original Tarshish (in Spain) became displaced as the horizon of the Phoenician navigators moved westward.

Herodotus records a Phoenician clockwise circumnavigation of Africa about 600 BC, on behalf of Pharaoh Necho – a distance of 13,000 miles. Herodotus sniffed at their report that the sun was on their right, that is, to their north.[9]

This establishes the fact that Phoenician nautical prowess and daring was at a level not to be seen in modern times until the century of Columbus.

It is only due to the proud announcement of the Pharaoh who sponsored the trip that we know of this voyage. The Phoenicians were not publicists.

So what other trips were being made – from perhaps as early as 1200 BC?

At La Venta, Mexico, was found a sculpture with distinctly Phoenician characteristics: bearded faces, upturned shoes, twisted rope borders and other details. It has been dated to around 850 BC. From Nicaragua to Mexico, on jade figurines, the backs of slate mirrors, funeral urns and other objects, appear bearded men who bear little resemblance to American Indians.

A well-known colony of Phoenicia was Carthage. An ancient historical work records the voyage of a convoy of as many as 60 ships, each carrying 550 people. This was around 500 BC.[10]

Strabo writes that Phoenician colonies (300 colonies, he estimates) were planted prolifically well down the Atlantic coast of Africa.[11]

From West Africa, it would be a simple matter to follow the trade winds to - you guessed it - South America.

To some, the idea that ancient mariners would have known the Americas may appear too ridiculous to consider, and it will be cast aside. But before such actions are taken, surely the evidence for this position should be carefully considered.

As Michael G. Bradley aptly put it, "The truth is just now being glimpsed by a handful of specialists - it is still almost completely unsuspected by the average civilized citizen."[12]

Voyages to the New World at around the time of King Solomon of Israel now seem more likely than not.

Some twelve years' research for the book *Dead Men's Secrets* finally convinced me that these colonists of a forgotten age were indeed part of a great network of ancient civilizations that once maintained a flourishing trade between Europe, Asia, and the Americas, some 3,000 years ago.

I was surprised to discover that Harvard professor Dr. Barry Fell, from his own research, had reached the same conclusion. He considered the ancient visitors to North America were probably not explorers, but rather merchants, trading with well-established fur trappers and very likely also mining **precious metals** on those sites where ancient workings have been discovered.

Fell states:

> Because of the depth of ignorance into which Europe fell during the Dark Ages, at times we are apt to forget how advanced were the ideas of the ancients, and how much they knew about the earth and about astronomy and navigation.[13]

Fell is also convinced that "America shares a history with the Old World, and ancient Americans must have been well acquainted with much of that history as it took place."

Dr. Fell is now recognised as one of the world's foremost epigraphers.

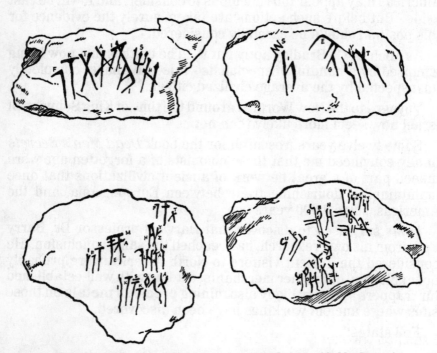

Stone inscriptions from the Amazon regions (letters added by Ramos)

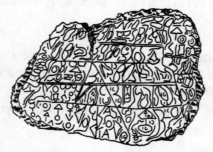

Rock inscriptions from Pedras, Rio Utama, Amazonas (from Ramos)

Phoenicians in America?

In 1780, on a rock on the shores of Mount Hope Bay in Bristol, Rhode Island, there was discovered an inscription, which Fell deciphered in 1975 to read:

> VOYAGERS FROM TARSHISH
> THIS STONE PROCLAIMS

This suggests strongly that here on the eastern seaboard of North America there was once a port for "ships of Tarshish".

On the island of Hispaniola, Columbus discovered immense ancient mines. In Haiti, he thought he could trace furnaces in which gold had been refined.[14]

Between 1850 and 1910, travelers in the Amazon region and other parts of Brazil were reporting the finding of old inscriptions on rock faces.

Former rubber tapper Bernardo da Silva Ramos, in a now rare book in Portuguese, has published 1,500 reproductions from such rock carvings. They are all covered over with the letters of the Phoenician alphabet.

Investigator Pierre Honoré, discussing the finds of other Brazilian travelers and explorers of last century, states:

> Today there is a whole library full of their reports; and they too were firmly convinced that the inscriptions were Phoenician texts. They were sure that King Solomon (975-935 BC) had once come to the Amazon with his ships; that the gold countries of Ophir, Tarshish and Parvaim were not to be looked for in the Old World at all, but here in the Amazon region on the Rio Solimoes, Solomon's River.[15]

It is reported that in Havea near Rio de Janeiro are letters several feet high inscribed upon a sheer cliff face in cuneiform. The inscription reads:

> BADEZIR OF THE PHOENICIAN TYRE.
> THE FIRST SON OF JETHBAAL..[16]

(Jethbaal ruled Tyre from 887 to 856 BC.)

In 1872, on the coast of Brazil near Paraiba, Joaquim Alves da Costa found on his property a stone that bore numerous characters which no one understood. He copied them and sent them to the President of the Instituto Historico. A translation is as follows:

We are Sidonian Canaanites from the city of the Merchant King. We were cast

(2) up on this distant island, a land of mountains. We sacrificed a youth to the celestial gods

(3) and goddesses in the nineteenth year of our mighty King Hiram

(4) and embarked from Ezion-geber into the Red Sea. We voyaged with ten ships

(5) and were at sea together for two years around Africa. Then we were separated

(6) by the hand of Baal and were no longer with our companions. So we have come here, twelve

(7) men and three women, into "Island of Iron". Am I, the Admiral, a man who would flee?

(8) Nay! May the celestial gods and goddesses favor us well.

This eight-line inscription proved to be in Phoenician characters. There are reasons to believe that the king referred to was Hiram III (553-533 BC). Brazil was known, anciently, as Hy Brasil. The incorporation of 'I' or 'Hy' is typically Phoenician.

According to Cyrus Gordon, Head of the Department of Mediterranean studies at Brandeis University, Massachusetts, the Phoenicians certainly knew Brazil, which they called "Island of Iron". Hy Brasil means "Island of Iron". Iron is still the country's main resource.

When I first learned of this inscription, I was skeptical. Mention of it was omitted from my book *Dead Men's Secrets*, since I preferred to publish only discoveries which could be confirmed beyond doubt as genuine. Others also considered it to be a fraud.

As we noted, at the time the alleged inscription was found, the script was not known. No one other than the original translator could read it. That has now changed.

Significantly, it contains Phoenician idiosyncrasies that were unknown in 1872 but which are now authenticated by other inscriptions found since.

Concerning many such initially rejected finds, Barry Fell says:

One by one competent scholars who hold responsible positions in universities and museums are now coming forward with confirmations of the decipherments.[17]

Facsimile of a Phoenician text carved on stone near Paraiba, in Brazil. It describes a transatlantic sea voyage in the 6th century BC.

Shipping routes westward at first

The trend of Phoenician colonial development prior to 1000 BC was mainly in a westerly direction.

However, it is quite certain that they did not long rest satisfied with that.

With their overland routes to the east at risk from unrest in Babylonia, the Phoenicians gave careful attention to an alternative eastern route.

We know that Hiram I, king of Tyre, shared a friendship with Israel's King David, and with his son Solomon.

There was also a religious sympathy. These early Phoenicians – contrary to the now current notions of popular writers – were **monotheists**.

As a result of a commercial treaty, Hiram assisted in the erection of Solomon's Temple and Israel granted Phoenicia the two ports of Eilat and Ezion-geber on the Gulf of Aqaba.

Like Gades in the west, the Persian Gulf colonies must now be viewed not as an end of Phoenician navigation in the east, but as the starting point for more distant navigation.

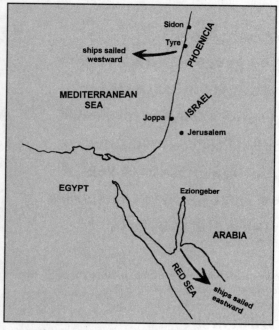

Phoenician-Hebrew sea voyages began from Tyre (for the west) and Eziongeber (for the east and west)

Fortunately, a mass of undigested historic data leaves no doubt concerning this fact.

King Solomon's silver

We find that the ships employed in the prosecution of the silver trade in both easterly and westerly directions were now "ships of Tarshish".

Suddenly we find gold and silver in such abundance in Jerusalem that Solomon "made silver to be in Jerusalem as stones... for abundance."[19]

And why? "... for the king had at sea a navy of Tarshish with the navy of Hiram: once in three years came the navy of Tarshish, bringing gold and silver, ivory, and apes, and peacocks."[20]

There can be no question that the peacocks came from south-East Asia. But whence the abundance of silver?

Says Heeren:

> Silver is also found in Siberia and in China or South Asia,
> but the large annual importation of the metal from Europe
> in consequence of the high price it bore in the East suffi-
> ciently prove that it was found there in small quantities. We
> may therefore conclude with certainty that the greater por-
> tion of the silver possessed of old by the Asiatic nations was
> imported, and there can be no question that the Phoenicians
> were the channel of importation.[21]

Ultimate destination: Ophir

The ultimate destination of the ships of Hiram and Solomon was
a place or region called Ophir.

"And they came to Ophir," says the Scripture, "and fetched from
thence gold." "And the navy also of Hiram, that brought gold from
Ophir, brought in from Ophir great plenty of almug trees, and
precious stones."[22]

From the books of Genesis[23] and Josephus,[24] it can be found
that Ophir was the general name for the rich southern countries
lying on the African, Arabian and Indian coasts.

But when we ask, Where was that Ophir which could be reached
from Ezion-geber that provided silver in such abundance, we are
faced with a problem.

It can be shown that the source was not Asia, the greater portion
of whose silver was imported.

Silver was so scarce in Arabia, that it was assessed at ten times
the value of gold.[25]

Yet in Solomon's Jerusalem it became **as common as stones**.

I am aware of the nineteenth century explorers' tales that
supposedly identified the mines of Ophir with central Africa.
There are people who refuse to accept that the massive stone
fortress known as the ruins of Zimbabwe (and situated in that
country) could have been built by native Africans.

Such identification with King Solomon must be regarded as
romantic fiction.

Zimbabwe is AD not BC and almost certainly it is the work of a powerful indigenous African empire.

"Three year" voyages

That the expeditions pushed into regions much more distant than the Indian Ocean is apparent from the "three years" required for the double voyage, only nine months being required for a return journey to the extremities of Arabia.[26]

Thomas Johnston suggests that Ophir "must be looked for in the farther East, and in a territory that was not only capable of supplying silver in practically unlimited quantities, but of affording conclusive evidence of occupancy by the Jews and Phoenicians."[27]

Johnston argues persuasively that the route of the expeditions can be traced beyond the peacock lands, through Indonesia, the Torres Strait (at the north of Australia), and via Samoa and Tahiti to Mexico and Peru. It appears that they founded colonies along the route.

An American destination accords well with the fact that the world's largest silver deposits are in the Americas – in the United States, Mexico, Canada and Peru.

Reached from two directions

The Bible says that the distant land of Tarshish was rich in silver, iron, tin and lead.[28] It could be reached from the Mediterranean port of Joppa (Jaffa),[29] or the Red Sea port of Ezion-geber.[30]

A glance at the map tells us that the only part of the world that one would reach by ship from either the Mediterranean or Red Sea ports is the Atlantic seaboard.

Cyrus Gordon of Brandeis University, Massachusetts, says that a text mentioning "gold of Ophir" found at Tell Qasile on the Mediterranean coast of Israel, suggests that Ophir could be reached via Gibraltar. I am aware that many places have been suggested as the location of Solomon's fabled mines. New respect for the seagoing capabilities of early navigators makes the Americas a strong possibility.

"Ofir"

The Ugha Mongulala tribe of north-west Brazil preserve written records of an ancient city called *Ofir* (Ophir) which once stood at the mouth of the Amazon River.

This is the ONLY independent mention of a specific locality called Ophir, outside of the Bible. Could this be significant?

Their tradition states that:

> Lhasa, the prince of Akakor... commanded the construction of *Ofir*, a powerful harbor city at the mouth of the Great River (the Amazon). Ships from Samon's (Solomon's?) empire docked there with their valuable cargoes. In exchange for gold and silver...[31]

Perhaps, like that of Tarshish, the name *Ophir* became displaced, and as the trade of the Phoenicians moved further eastward and westward, it moved with the trade, until in course of time it came to be applied to a more distant region controlled by the Phoenicians.

Corroborating this, the Phoenician *Ophir* or *Ofor* means, in their ancient language, **the Western Country**.[32]

And what land lay to the west? The Americas, no less.

Mixed crews

While the expeditions were under Jewish and Phoenician direction, they undoubtedly carried crews and marine force of composite nationality. In the next chapter we shall touch on evidence suggesting that considerable numbers of Scythians and Thracians were employed on the Phoenician fleets. At this time in history Hebrew, Phoenician, Scythian and Thracian were the dominant factors in the national life of the eastern Mediterranean. The Thracians and Scythians were then the two great nations of south-eastern Europe.[33]

Eastward

There must have been, from Ezion-geber, a general push of the giant "ships of Tarshish" toward the east.

If we continue the line to Java and Sumatra, we will have reached the native home of the peacock, which was collected on the return journey of Solomon's and Hiram's expeditions.

The servant of Hiram of Tyre bringing presents to King Solomon

Penetrating beyond Indonesia, we shall discover some facts of a rather startling nature.

CHAPTER 11

INTO THE UNKNOWN

Already one ship had gone down in the vortex of the whirlpool.

The others had watched, helpless, while that huge vessel just vanished, sucked down into the gigantic sink hole.

Experienced mariners, these were, seasoned to danger. But this had been pure terror.

Now, just hours later, the survivors were caught in a hurricane. The winds and rain ripped and pounded the vessel in a frightening display.

The deck would heave itself up, then suddenly drop down, leaving one's stomach hanging in the air.

Mountainous waves crashed against the deck, swelling and rushing over it.

The young Jewish deckhand riveted himself to the mast and twisted another rope around his wrist. The current swirled over him with a powerful motion, tumbling into the sea.

He knew a moment of fear.

This was his first voyage. He felt squeamish. And he was thousands of miles from home.

He would not see his beloved wife again for three years. He reflected on the tales he would share with her. And those unbelievable trinkets of gold and silver and gemstones, crafted exquisitely in the land of Ophir...

The "ships of Tarshish" encountered unknown perils as they ventured into new regions. One particularly dangerous passage was along the north-western coast of Australia.

••••••

To control the South Arabian markets could not have been the sole purpose of Solomon building his great ships. If these ships had been merely constructed to trade with Yemen, and back, and if, as the Scripture says, the journey had taken three years, then Solomon and Hiram were inept investors. The cost of the ships, the expense of working them, the interest on capital for such a long interval, as well as the deterioration of cargo in such a climate, would have outweighed any advantage of using sea transport, as against an overland route.

Furthermore, it seems most unlikely that expeditions to a place as close as Yemen could have wakened such enthusiasm, as to have brought Solomon and his court from their safe capital into the heart of a discontented country to witness the departure of the ships and their crews, as 2 Chronicles 8:17 records.

••••••

Any mariner approaching the north-west coast of Australia could find the West Kimberley area near Derby one of the most dangerous on the coast. A violent rip runs up to ten knots and creates whirlpools. To come in at the entrance to King Sound, ships must run through this riptide. There are many reefs and shoals. Navigation is hazardous.

Around the entrance to King Sound lie the islands of the Buccaneer Archipelago. King Sound itself is about 90 miles long and at its widest about 35 miles across.

A feature of this area is the extreme rise and fall of tides: up to 35 feet, which leaves ships high and dry.

Here salvage diver Allan Robinson found what he believed to be the wreck of an ancient Phoenician ship.

He noticed that in the mud of the swamp off the mainland, there was a strange shape. Small pips of mud seemed to project above the surroundings to form a shape more like a banana than a ship.

110

The contour was quite plain. A bronze plate was retrieved and declared by a university official to be of Phoenician origin.

The Phoenician wreck was near an overgrown mine of galena. And galena is an ore of silver, lead and zinc.

It is not surprising that, if the ships of Solomon and Hiram came as far as Java and Sumatra (which, as we said, was the native home of the peacock – one item of Solomon's cargo), that they would have found the nearby coast of Australia.

Their route would have taken them through Torres Strait. And, conceivably, they could have sailed down the eastern coast of Australia.

Should it surprise us, then, that Phoenician-style engravings have been found on a marble slab in North Queensland? Or that further south along the coast, in New South Wales, many strange symbols, ships, and figures of Egyptian, Phoenician and Syrian style have been discovered carved on rocks along the Hawkesbury River?

Ancient Aboriginal legends tell how people in large ships like birds (the bird-headed prows of the old Phoenician triremes?) sailed into Gympie (now 34 miles inland), dug holes in the hills, erected the "sacred mountain" found nearby and interbred with local inhabitants. Interestingly, evidence of ancient mining and smelting was recently found here, as well as traces of a causeway or stone quay.

Near Toowoomba in Queensland, recently, a group of seventeen granite stones was discovered, bearing ancient inscriptions. These were identified as Phoenician. One of them has been translated to read **"guard the shrine of Yahweh's message"**. Another says, **"God of gods"**.

Some years ago, a farmer in the Rockhampton area plowed up a large ironstone slab. Today the slab sits in the museum of Rex Gilroy near Tamworth, New South Wales. It bears another Phoenician inscription that reads, **"Ships sail from this land under the protection of Yahweh to Dan"**.

Dan was an ancient trade center in north-west Israel just south of Tyre, a Phoenician port. These discoveries were reported in an issue of the Ravenshoe *Northern Star* dated July-August-September, 1996.

*The small rock inscription found near Toowoomba, Queensland, bearing
the ancient Phoenician script, "Guard the Shrine of Yahweh's Message"*

As I commented in the book, *Dead Men's Secrets*, fiction
couldn't challenge your imagination more. And yet here it all is,
fact after fact, story after story, about the lives and discoveries of
a people thousands of years ago.

Now naturally these exhibits will **not** be popular with some
people. The majority of the scientific community has greeted them
with deathly silence because of early indoctrination in the theory
of evolution. It tries to ignore them for the sole reason that it
cannot explain them.

I ask, was it simply to control the nearby Arabian trade that
Solomon and Hiram created the costly fleet of large armed ships of
Tarshish? Or were these large, sophisticated vessels fitted out to
travel the earth's surface?

The biblical account suggests the latter. And the implications
are dynamite.

Into the Pacific

As an eastern port on the Red Sea became a reality, the Phoenicians, with Solomon of Israel, now pursued with eagerness a further expansion eastward, to parallel that in the west.

And beyond Australia, they left a trail right across the Pacific.

Samoa rises up dramatically from the sea. But its native population has traditionally not pronounced it as Samoa, but as *Samo*. And this was also the name of a Phoenician colony (pronounced the same way) on the coasts of Asia Minor – *Samos*.[1]

The name *Samo* means, according to Pliny, "a mountain height by the sea". Both locations have a similar appearance, rising up from the sea. In fact, modern navigators term the Pacific Samoa "high islands", in contrast to the low coral atolls that surround it for hundreds of miles in all directions.

The principal island of Samoa is named *Upola* – the equivalent of the Scythian deity *Apollo*. And the main town of Western Samoa is *Apia* – which is the name of the Scythian deity, the Earth,[2] as well as the name of the Peloponnesus[3] – a Phoenician locality.

Next, traveling east, the ships of Solomon and Hiram would have reached the Society Islands. Here is *Tahiti,* with a silent "h". This is identical to *Tabiti* (probably also with a silent "b"). Tabiti was the Scythian Vista. Both names would be pronounced *Ta-iti*.

The name of Tahiti's chief settlement, *Papeete*, is only a slightly modified form of the name of the Scythian Jupiter, or father, *Papeus*.

Morea, the name of an island separated from Papeete by a narrow strait, is the same as *Morea,* a principal district of the Hellenic Peninsula in the Mediterranean, colonized by the Scythians shortly before the period of Solomon's expeditions. Morea was given that name because the contour of the shoreline resembled a mulberry leaf. This explanation is also applicable to Morea of the Pacific.

It would seem that in the Pacific the Phoenicians followed the same policy as in the Mediterranean. They established stations for the ships to call at on these long voyages. It appears that these colonies were placed under the care of responsible governors, drawn from the Scythians of the marine corps, since most of the names we have referred to were clearly drawn from this source.

Phoenician ships sailed into the Pacific Ocean. (*Scene: Tahiti*)

There is no other explanation for the presence of Scythians in the heart of the Pacific.

Enormous stone remains in many of the Pacific Islands can be linked with local traditions.

Strong's Island is one example. An ancient tradition says that "an ancient city once stood round this harbor which was occupied by a powerful people called Anut, who had large vessels in which they made long voyages, many moons being required in their prosecution."[4]

Early European missionaries to the Pacific found in these islands evidence of numeric skill, cosmogony, astronomical knowledge and religious system which was plainly Phoenician.

For example, the Phoenician skill in the use of numbers and astronomy is reflected in the same extraordinary skill of the Society Islanders. And their names of stars and constellations and the use to which they applied their knowledge of the heavenly bodies was the same as that of the Phoenicians.

Their sacred groves, open-air temples or marais, their human sacrifices, and their methods of initiation and practice, were identical to those of the priests of Astarte on the eastern Mediterranean.

It should be noted that, throughout the period of the Solomon-Hiram voyages, both Israel and Phoenicia were monotheistic, worshipping the one true God, the Creator. But later, both nations descended into the worship of Baal the sun-god and Astarte (Ashteroth) the "queen of heaven". The expeditions were, however, continuing during this period. Thus, although true worship had been planted first throughout the world wherever the expeditions went, this was eventually corrupted as new generations of sailors brought their practices with them.

The Phoenician alphabet of 16 letters was the same as the Samoan. The natives of Samos (Samo) in the Mediterranean were famous as seamen; likewise the Pacific Samoans were famed for their nautical skill.

The gymnastic systems used in the Mediterranean, as a means of training for war, as well as the implements used (including spear, javelin, bow and arrow, dart, sword, falchion, and sling and boomerang) are found over the entire route of the ships across the Pacific to the Americas.

115

The historical traditions, practices, circumcision and some other customs such as test of virginity were clearly Jewish.

Further customs (tattooing, spear and javelin throwing) were clearly Thracian.

Their worship of the skulls of ancestors, cannibalism, and use of bow and arrow as a test of strength were peculiarly Scythian.

Research has established that the implements of war and the festivals and games among these Polynesians were the same as those found in the ancient Mediterranean. And the foregoing is just a small sampling of the many parallels.

Here are startling facts, pointing to the presence together of four races – Hebrew, Phoenician, Scythian and Thracian – in the mid-Pacific in the remote past.

How can this be explained, if not through the instrumentality of the historic expeditions of Hiram and Solomon?

The *Encyclopaedia Brittanica* notes concerning the Polynesians that, while their facial features sometimes suggest Mongoloid affinities, their light skin, wavy hair and full beards, as well as their blood types, suggest European ties.[5]

This is certainly consistent with the planting of outposts in the Pacific by European members of Solomon's and Hiram's crews, such as Scythians and Thracians.

And on to the Americas

The Maya population already inhabited central portions of the American continent.

Votan, the first historian of the Maya (c.1000 BC), actually reported the arrival around that time, on the Pacific coasts of Central America, of seven large ships.

In his book on the origin of the race, Votan declares himself a descendant of Imos, of the land of Chan, of the race of Chivim.

Research shows that present-day Tripoli in Syria was, in the time of Solomon, a town in the kingdom of Tyre, and was anciently known as Chivim.

Votan is said to have led some of his people to Yucatan in Central America, where he found inhabitants already there. Here he established the kingdom of Xibalba and built the city of Nachan (probably Palenque).

A copy of Votan's book, written in the Quiché language, existed until 1691, when it was very likely burned, along with other native relics, by the Spaniards at Huehuetan, but not before extracts had been copied from it.[6]

Fray Lizana set down in his *Historia de Yucatan* the tradition that from the west (that is, from the direction of the Pacific) "many" people had come.[7]

Indeed, there is abundant physical evidence in Central America which appears to indicate Phoenician and Hebrew penetration of these remote regions. Evidence of occupancy, linguistic features, physical characteristics, intricacies of customs, as well as traditions and place names.

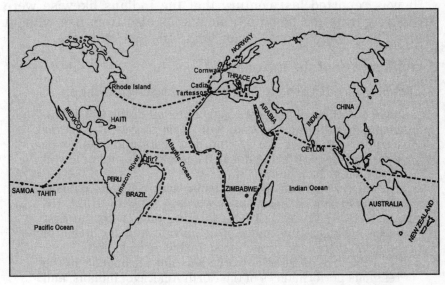

Phoenician global trade routes, according to latest information

Some resemblances

It will be of interest to note a few similarities to be found between the indigenous peoples of America and the Hebrews.

The religion of the Mexicans strongly resembled that of the Hebrews in numerous minor details. De Bourbourg noted the perfectly Jewish dress of the women at Palin and on the shores of

117

Lake Amatitlan.[8] Like the Hebrews, the Mexicans tore their clothing on receipt of bad news. Another similarity was giving a kiss on the cheek as a token of peace.[9]

The Hebrew nation were ordered to worship Yahweh the true and living God. James Adair, a trader with the "wild" Indians of the south-east of North America, discovered that the North American Indians styled the living God as *Yahewah*.[10]

Like the Hebrews, the North American Indians offer their **first fruits**, they keep their **new moons**, as well as the **feast of Atonement** at the **same time** as the Jews. The brother of a deceased husband marries his widow. In some places, circumcision is practised. There is much analogy in rites and customs, such as the ceremonies of purification and the manner of prayer.

It was reported last century that the Indians likewise were abstaining from the blood of animals, as also from fish without scales. They had various "clean" and "unclean" animals.

A replica "Ark of the Covenant"?

Researchers Rivero and Tschudi indicated that they:

> have a species of ark, seemingly like that of the Old Testament; this the Indians take with them to war; it is never permitted to touch the ground, but rests upon stones or pieces of wood, it being deemed sacreligious and unlawful to open it or look into it.
> ......(they) celebrate the first fruits with religious dances, singing in chorus these mystic words: – YO MESCHICA, HE MESCHICA, VA MESCHICA, forming thus, with the first three syllables, the name of Je-ho-vah, and the name of Messiah thrice and pronounced, following each initial.
> ...... The use of Hebrew words was not uncommon in the religious performances of the North American Indians, and Adair assures us that they called an accused or guilty person **haksit canaha**, "a sinner of Canaan"; and to him who was inattentive to religious worship, they said, **Tschi haksit canaha**, "you resemble a sinner of Canaan". Les Carbot also tells us that he had heard the Indians of South America say "Alleluia".[11]

Adair, who wrote these facts in his *History of the American Nations* (pp.15-212), lived 40 years among the Indians.

The evidence suggests that a significant portion of the early American civilization came from the eastern shores of the Mediterranean. Its intermediaries were Phoenicians and Hebrews, who were accompanied by Thracians and Scythians, who were accustomed to hire themselves out as mercenaries.

They sailed from Ezion-geber on the Red Sea to a destination called Ophir, whose actual location has been traditionally difficult to determine.

This should, however, occasion no surprise, since the Phoenicians adopted a policy of secrecy as to their routes and destinations after the Greeks displaced them on the eastern Mediterranean some 150 years before the expeditions that sailed from Ezion-geber.

Their route may be tracked across the Pacific by observing such traces as still exist of the presence of nations which formed the personnel of these expeditions. This is possible because the Phoenicians, on their longer routes, were accustomed to establishing stations for repairing and revictualling their ships and ports of call.

For how long?

How long did these voyages continue? We have no means of determining accurately. However, it is likely that they continued for some 300 years, until the Assyrians and Babylonians occupied strategic land and closed areas of Middle East territory that were crucial to the continuance of the voyages.

Lighter skinned peoples

At the time of the conquest of Peru, the Spaniards noticed that many of the Inca ruling caste were paler of skin and had reddish tints in their hair, as distinct from the native mountain peasants of the Andes, who were generally of distinctly Mongoloid ancestry.

Inca legends spoke of certain white and bearded men who advanced from the shores of Lake Titicaca, established an ascendancy over the natives, and brought civilization.

Ancient representations in stone, as well as portrait jars from the ruins of the city of Chan, in coastal Peru, show white, bearded men. And mummified corpses of chiefs from the oldest layers of graves in this region bear hair that is auburn or blond, wavy and fine.

119

Maori retreat, Coromandel Peninsula, New Zealand (Alexander Turnbull Library)

Reports frequently surface concerning ancient "white" tribes still surviving in isolated pockets of the Americas.

South American legend records that some of the bearded white men who built the enormous stone cities found in ruins there eventually left to sail westward... into the Pacific Ocean.

Polynesian legends still current are living proof that the bearded white men arrived safely in Polynesia.

But there is evidence more substantial than legend on some of these islands: pyramids, helmets and panpipes. As well as proof that irrigation , trepanning and head-deformation were practised. These same Pacific Islanders knew that the earth was round – and they had a vast astronomical knowledge, as well as a calendar curiously similar to that in the Americas.

On some of the islands, early missionaries found people of a lighter skin, who sported reddish hair and blue eyes. Which made me prick up my ears when I learned of a discovery on the other side of the world.

Some sarcophagi had been found at the old Phoenician city of Sidon. On these were some lavishly colored representations which suggest that some of the deceased were blue-eyed and had dark red hair.

Now I prefer not to speculate. It's just a thought. In the introduction to Chapter 10, I was musing on a New Zealand Maori tradition of light-skinned people with red hair and blue eyes, having long ago been driven by the Maori people into a last refuge on the Coromandel Peninsula.

And the thought just crossed my mind. Could some descendants of the crews of the Hiram-Solomon maritime expeditions have reached even the remote land of New Zealand?

In distributing their products to the ends of the earth, the Phoenicians brought within the range of their influence practically every center of population, civilized and uncivilized, known to the ancient world.

A divine plan?

Johnston perceives something significant in this. He says:

> The time, however, was appointed for the coordination of what was already in existence of the divine plan.[12]

121

Solomon's Temple

Two nations superimposed in location and time. What a power for good, they could have been! Phoenicia to open up the lines of communication globally, and Israel to plant its blessings among all nations. The opportunity that could have changed history!

That could well have been the divine plan. The Lord gave the Hebrews their world mission. Then He placed the Phoenicians alongside them, to make it possible.

Johnston notes:

> It is true that neither Jew nor Phoenician achieved their manifest destiny, but will we, in the face of what we now know of the history of these two peoples, believe that the plan of their career was any the less divinely appointed?

For a time, this softening influence left its stamp upon the beliefs and practices of many remote peoples – and is identifiable even today.

But now we shall return to Israel, where King Solomon was constructing his famous Temple...

Solomon's magnificent temple

The tremendous wealth that poured into Israel from these global expeditions can be appreciated to some extent when we reflect on the magnificence of Solomon's Temple.

It has been calculated that this famous building contained 86 tons of gold and 126 tons of silver.

And the technological expertise involved was ingenious.

The first book of Kings reports that it "was built of stone made ready before it was brought thither: so that there was neither hammer nor axe nor any tool of iron heard in the house, while it was in building."[13]

Can you imagine it? Some of those massive stones were as long as a bus... from 10 to 40 feet long by 6 feet wide. One of them at least weighed approximately 445 tons. They were pre-cut, then transported from the quarry and slid into place so accurately that it would be difficult to find the seams.

The splendor of Solomon's Temple would defy comprehension. Nowhere on the face of this planet did a structure of such size and beauty command the awe of man. Travelers from many lands would travel great distances just to set eyes on this Temple, never to be disappointed. Its array of shining metals and precious stones was dazzling beyond belief.

This enormous Temple featured planks of cedar and cypress – fir trees hand-crafted to expose their elegant grains. The entire structure was overlaid on the inside with gold.[14] Precious stones of onyx and marble were seen in abundance.

Silver, brass and iron were used in the Temple. Outer courtyards and inner chambers were adorned with high-reaching palm trees and colorful flowers.

Using modern equipment capable of determining very precisely the isotopic content of different metals, it has been shown that the lead used in drainpipes in the area of Solomon's Temple came from the Mendip Hills in Somerset, Britain. This type of analysis is made possible because lead samples from different locations contain varying amounts of the isotopes of lead, resulting from the decay of radioactive materials.

Similarly with tin. The Temple was adorned with plenty of bronze, and this alloy was made by adding tin to copper in the smelting. The presence of tin caused the copper to become much harder and less easily tarnished. It was British tin that was used by Solomon. The date was about 1000 BC.

Technology used

Two cast pillars of brass stood boldly at the entrance.

According to an old tradition, the two great pillars were hollow. Stored inside them, according to the same tradition, were "ancient records" and "valuable writings" pertaining to the past of the Hebrew people.[15] And included among these records had been information on something known as the *shamir*.[16]

What was this mysterious shamir?

Moses had instructed his people not to use "any iron tool" in the construction of the holy places.[17] And Solomon likewise directed that no hammers, axes or chisels should be used to cut and dress the stone blocks with which the Temple would be built.

Instead, according to Jewish sources, he provided the workmen with an ancient device called the shamir, that had been used in the time of Moses to engrave writing on the precious stones of the high priest's breastplate.[18]

Known as "the stone that splits rocks,"[19] the shamir was capable of cutting the toughest materials without friction or heat.[20] This included "the remarkable property of cutting the hardest of diamonds".[21]

There must have been something special about the shamir, for it was said:

> The shamir may not be put in an iron vessel for safekeeping, nor in any metal vessel: it would burst such a receptacle asunder. It is kept wrapped up in a woolen cloth, and this in turn is placed in a lead basket filled with barley bran... With the destruction of the Temple the shamir vanished.[22]

Islamic traditions concerning the shamir paralleled those of the Jews, with the additional statement that it had been quite noiseless while it was at work.[23]

Built specifically for the Ark

The Temple was first planned by David as a "house of rest for the ark",[24] but constructed by his son Solomon.[25]

That magnificent Temple of fabulous wealth and world renown was specifically conceived and built, for what purpose, but to enshrine the Ark of the Covenant! That was its reason to be!

The actual room known as the Holy of Holies, in which the Ark stood, was a perfect cube - and immensely strong. It measured just over 34 feet long, by 34 feet wide, by 34 feet high.[26] Its floor, walls and ceiling were lined with fine gold, weighing an estimated 45,000 pounds, that is, more than 20 tons![27] And it was all riveted with golden nails.[28]

We observed that the Temple was built with the stated purpose of housing the Ark of the Covenant.

And we recall that the Ark itself was constructed to enshrine the two tablets of the law, the Ten Commandments written with the finger of God. That's why the Ark of "the Covenant" was thus named.

One stands in awe at the sacredness, the considered importance, of this Ten Commandment law – that billions of dollars (by today's estimate) was spent merely to house it!

Queen of Sheba visits Solomon

I took time to ponder on this – and realized that it is our modern disregard for these very laws that lies at the root of society's greatest problems.

Murder, adultery, robbery, violence, war, hatred, loneliness... not to mention disease, pain and death. It affects us all. If we could be rid of these problems, what price would we be willing to pay?

Votan's trip to the Mediterranean

You remember we spoke of Votan, the first historian of the Maya, in Central America, who lived around 1000 BC. Votan had come originally from the Phoenician city of Chivim.

He records that he later made four or more visits to his former home. On one of these trips he visited a great city wherein a magnificent Temple was in the course of erection (thought by the researcher Ordonez to have been Jerusalem). En route, he had visited a place where men had erected a tower which had been intended to reach heaven, an object defeated by a confusion of tongues. Upon returning to Palenque, he found that several more of his nation had arrived. Legend and pictorial evidence suggests that they may have been Carthaginians.[29]

Was it Solomon's Temple that visitors from as far away as the Americas came to see? Possibly. We are informed that "all the kings of the earth sought the presence of Solomon, to hear his wisdom that God had put in his heart." [30]

The plan sabotaged

What enormous potential Israel now had within her grasp. She had been placed at the crossroads of the world, in order to prepare the whole planet for the coming of the Deliverer.

What a responsibility! What a privilege!

But the prince of evil was hostile to this plan... and was preparing a trap for Israel. Heathen rites would soon be mixed in with their pure worship.

Israel was about to go down...

The sad fate of Queen Jezebel

128

CHAPTER 12

JEZEBEL, SEDUCTRESS

In the drain lay her left foot. Her skull and the palms of her hands turned up on the sidewalk. A dog finishing off her right foot, they chased away.

That very afternoon, large as life, she had been bathing herself in luxury. She highlighted her sexy blue eyes, carefully rouged her sensuous lips, teased her soft, auburn hair. Now a few caresses of perfume, and he would not resist her. She glowed with anticipation, a wicked smile curling her lips. She would have him eating out of her hand.

An hour later, the servants hurled her down from the window. And "some of her blood was sprinkled on the wall, and on the horses: and he trod her under foot."[1] Dogs ate her shattered corpse, dug holes and buried every bone. Minus certain parts.

The Bible tells it like it is. Queen Jezebel herself, the stunning beauty who had seduced a nation into witchcraft, was no more.

••••••

And so it was. After that glorious period of David and Solomon, the history of Israel reverted to one long mournful sequence repeated over and over again: apostasy, invasion, repentance and deliverance; apostasy, invasion, repentance and deliverance; and repeat...

Their subsequent recorded history is one of stubborn rebellion against their God.

History shows that when spiritual decline got particularly bad, some of the surrounding nations were permitted to invade. This was perhaps a hard way to bring them to their senses, but it often worked.

The Lord sent messages through prophets to assure the people that He still loved them, even though they were too half-hearted about their agreement with Him.

After Solomon's death in 931 BC, his son Rehoboam had rebellion on his hands. Ten of the tribes seceded forever. They retained the name Israel. The remaining two **southern** tribes continued as the kingdom of Judah, with Jerusalem as the capital.

Born in rebellion, the **northern kingdom** degenerated rapidly. Idolatry and bloodshed became rampant.

Less than a lifetime after the death of King Hiram of Tyre, the high priest Eth-baal assassinated the then Tyrian king and seized the throne of Tyre. Eth-baal was a high priest of the goddess Astarte (Ashtoreth), and under his rule idolatry took rapid root.

His daughter Jezebel wedded Israel's King Ahab, and brought to Samaria, Israel's capital, an entourage of 400 priests of Baal, the sun god, as well as 400 priests of Astarte, the "queen of heaven". This persuasive young woman soon had her husband build a sanctuary in which the Babylonian deities adopted by Phoenicia were installed.

Dollinger describes the practice of this religion:

> ....the principal sacrifice was children. This horrible custom was grounded in part on the notion that children were the dearest possession of their parents, and, in part, that as pure and innocent beings, they were the offerings of atonement most certain to pacify the anger of the deity.... The sacrifices were consumed by fire.... and the sound of complaint was drowned in the din of flutes and kettledrums.[2]

At the spring festival, children...

> were put into a leathern bag and thrown the whole height of the temple to the bottom, with the shocking assertion that they were calves and not children.[3]

Whipped up into a tumult of excitement by this act and music accompanying it, temple eunuchs and spectators were seized by a desire to lacerate themselves and run bleeding through the city.

The second book of Kings records that Israel "left all the commandments of the Lord their God... and served Baal. And they caused their sons and daughters to pass through the fire."[4]

Children were sacrificed to the god Molech

This sun and fire cult, this dark religion, dragged Israel to its doom.

Finally, the kingdom that didn't want God went down in utter defeat and extinction. The Assyrians overwhelmed them and carried the population into exile. From that moment they were lost to history.

Prophets sawn apart

The southern kingdom of Judah failed to profit by Israel's experience. The spiritual revivals encouraged by such kings as Hezekiah and Josiah did extend Judah's history a little longer.

131

The trouble was, they didn't want to be different from the other nations. They mixed heathen rites with their worship of the true God. They ate what the heathen ate; and they suffered the same diseases. They were complacent.

Yet if the promised Deliverer, the Messiah, was ever to come, he must come **through them**.

Can you imagine how the Lord of the Universe must have felt? This world He had created was in revolt. And now here was the nation He had chosen, tramping, even running, after fake gods!

Constantly, He raised up men, prophets, to call the people back to their purpose. The forces of evil did everything possible to keep God's messages from getting through.

Enemies were stirred up to silence the messengers, to mock, scourge and imprison them. Others were stoned, thrust through with the sword, or sawn in pieces.[5]

The powers of evil were determined to divert the people's minds, to make God's character look black. The enemy worked through priests and rulers to make religion so complicated; to push God so far away; to make Him so exacting and tyrannical, in the people's eyes.

When Jezebel's daughter, Athaliah, married one of Judah's kings, she introduced the same orgies, the same revolting practices. A cemetery, containing many graves of sacrificed children, has been unearthed outside the gates of Jerusalem.

For 150 years after Israel's destruction, the people of Judah generally followed the religious views of the reigning king. If he restored the true way, they followed him. If the king served idols, they gave up God and served idols. Few worshipped from personal conviction.

We reap what we sow. When men deliberately choose evil, it runs its course to destroy them.

The remedy

Long before it happened, the prophets of God warned the nation that evil would fall upon them "which they shall not be able to escape" and they would cry to their idols "but they shall not save them at all in the time of their trouble";[6] "for now shalt thou go forth out of the city... **even to Babylon**."[7]

132

How ironic! They were going to be dragged to the very headquarters of the counterfeit religious system that had corrupted them. The Lord intended that they would become so sickened by it, that they would be cured of idolatry. (And so they were!)

Moses himself had given a prophecy that they would be taken away **with their king**! The prediction that they would have a king is significant – and was not fulfilled for over 400 years.[8]

These prophecies were accurately fulfilled.

In 606 BC, Nebuchadnezzar, crown prince of Babylon, entered Jerusalem, looted its Temple and took away some of its young men, including Daniel.

During the next few years, Babylonian armies returned several times, until the city and Temple were virtually destroyed. Thousands of higher class citizens were dragged in chains to Babylon. This included successive kings, Jehoiakim, Jehoiachin and Zedekiah.[9]

Ark not taken to Babylon

When Nebuchadnezzar sacked Jerusalem and destroyed the Temple in 586 BC, the Ark of the Covenant was not among the items seized. The Bible gives a list of things taken to Babylon, but the Ark is not included! The books of 2 Kings and Jeremiah[10] give parallel inventories, which do not contradict each other in any way. And they make no mention of the Ark.

The gold and silver items taken consisted only of relatively minor utensils. At the first Temple robbery, the Babylonians "took the bowls, the censers, the sprinkling bowls, the ash containers, the lamp-stands, the goblets and the saucers: everything that was made of gold and everything of silver."[11]

The objects **not** taken at this time are also named. Jeremiah prophesied that they would be taken after the next conquest of the city:

> But if they be prophets, and if the word of the Lord be with them, let them now make intercession to the Lord of Hosts, that the vessels which are left in the house of the Lord, and in the house of the king of Judah, and at Jerusalem, go not to Babylon. For thus saith the Lord of Hosts concerning the pillars, and concerning the Sea, and concerning the bases,

133

and concerning the residue of vessels that remain in the city, which Nebuchadnezzar king of Babylon took not when he carried away captive Jeconiah... king of Judah from Jerusalem to Babylon... Yea, thus saith the Lord of Hosts, the God of Israel, concerning the vessels that remain in the house of the Lord, and in the house of the king of Judah and of Jerusalem; They shall be carried to Babylon, and there shall they be until the day that I visit them, saith the Lord; then will I bring them up, and restore them to this place.[12]

Because Jeremiah foretold – and even welcomed – the destruction of Jerusalem by the Babylonian king, whom he saw as God's chosen instrument for chastising the nation of Judah, he faced the hostility of the official religious leaders. Frequently was he in personal danger. He was physically assaulted and even had to go into hiding for several years.

In the above lists of items snatched from the Temple, the most precious objects of all – the Table of Shewbread, the 7-branched golden lampstand, the Altar of Incense and the Ark of the Covenant are omitted.

Temple priests had evidently hidden them from the Babylonians.

And at the restoration of the Temple some 70 years later, they would not be listed among the items brought back from Babylon to be reinstated in the Temple.[13]

Ark of the Covenant hidden

In Jerusalem at the time, were some faithful men who determined to place beyond the reach of ruthless hands the sacred Ark containing the tablets of the Ten Commandments. With mourning and sadness, they secreted the Ark in a cave.[14]

From that moment, the Ark was lost to history.

Most Jewish legends agree that it was not destroyed or stolen, but hidden by God to await the end times. Several legends claim that the prophet Jeremiah was involved in hiding the Ark and other Temple treasures. It is not unreasonable to conclude that Jewish priests secretly hid it at the instigation of Jeremiah the prophet.

The apocryphal book of 2 Maccabees (c.163 BC) asserts that Jeremiah took the Ark to Mount Nebo, far away from Jerusalem, and there hid it.

Another legend states that Jeremiah took the Ark to a secret place between Mount Nebo and Mount Hor and sealed it within a rock. The Ark will be brought out **when Israel is regathered and the glory-cloud appears.**[15]

Still another work says that Jeremiah, accompanied by Baruch, was commanded by God to take "holy vessels of the worship-service" and bury them. They will reappear only **at the time of Israel's regathering.**[16]

There is also the claim that Jeremiah was told by God to bury the Temple vessels **"until the coming of the Beloved One"** – an allusion to the end times.[17]

It was commonly held by the ancient rabbis that the Ark would be found at the coming of the Messiah.

Some other prophecies

Those dragged off to Babylon included some faithful Jews who knew the divine purpose.

God also loved Babylon and He loved its proud king. He wanted Babylon to know what He was like. Later, Daniel, a Jewish prince, was promoted to high office in the court of Babylon. Nebuchadnezzar was fond of Daniel and trusted him. Ultimately this arrogant monarch became a humble and devoted adherent of the One God.

God also loved the Jews. Through His prophet He promised that, after a captivity lasting 70 years, they would return to Palestine. This prophecy was given through Jeremiah.[18]

Deportation to Babylonia took place in three stages, commencing in 606/605 BC. The exile continued for 70 years inclusive, until the time of the Persian king Cyrus, in 537/536 BC.

More than a hundred years before he was born, Cyrus was named by the prophet Isaiah as the man who would be the instigator of the return of the Jews and the rebuilding of the Temple.[19] Now that says something about the accuracy of Bible prophecy!

The promised return to Palestine was fulfilled exactly as predicted. Completely fulfilled.[20]

The Babylonian captivity was the result of their departure from God. He promised to bring them back to their own land after they had learned their lesson. This occurred.

And this brings me to what must be the most amazing prophecy of all. Stay tuned!

CHAPTER 13

THE PROPHECY AND THE RABBIS' CURSE

POLAND. 1656. Behind closed doors a group of intense, determined Rabbis forge a curse:

> May his bones and his memory rot who shall attempt to number the seventy weeks.

That curse is EVENT NUMBER 3.

◆◆◆◆◆◆◆◆

JUDEA. 27 AD. A young Jewish man strides into the villages of Galilee. He electrifies the people with his dramatic proclamation:

> The time is fulfilled, and the kingdom of God is at hand. The Lord has anointed me.

Messiah; anointed – they're the same word! Who is this audacious person? And what does he mean by the words, "**The time is fulfilled**"?

That announcement is EVENT NUMBER 2.

◆◆◆◆◆◆◆◆

BABYLON. 536 BC. The Jews are still exiles in Babylon. Jerusalem lies in ruins. But a heavenly being, identified as the angel Gabriel, comes to the Jewish prophet Daniel to instruct him that the prophetic clock will begin again for Israel – with a decree

Babylon captured by the Medo-Persian armies

to rebuild and restore Jerusalem. And "seventy weeks" will be allotted during which the eternal God plans to accomplish certain things.

That prophecy is EVENT NUMBER 1.

•••••••••

This prophecy is recorded in the book of Daniel, Chapter 9. And we shall not worry too much about the rabbinic curse upon those who try to decipher it. The prophecy may be summarized thus:

"Seventy weeks are determined upon your [Daniel's] people [the Jews] and upon your holy city [Jerusalem],

- to finish the transgression,
- and to make an end of sins,
- and to make reconciliation for iniquity,
- and to bring in everlasting righteousness,
- and to seal up the vision and prophecy,
- and to anoint the most Holy."[1]

This is followed with more detail:

> Know therefore and understand, that from the going forth of the commandment to restore and build Jerusalem UNTO MESSIAH THE PRINCE shall be seven weeks, and sixty-two weeks: the street shall be built again, and the wall, even in troublous times.
>
> And after the sixty-two weeks shall Messiah be cut off, but not for himself: and the people of the prince that shall come shall destroy the city and the sanctuary; and the end thereof shall be with a flood, and unto the end of the war desolations are determined.
>
> And he shall confirm the covenant with many for one week: and in the midst of the week he shall cause the sacrifice and the oblation (grain offering) to cease, and for the overspreading of abominations he shall make it desolate, even until the consummation, and that determined is poured upon the desolator.[2]

Here is an outline of a prophecy that was to be fulfilled over "seventy weeks", along with other events which are not confined to the "seventy weeks" but are related to them.

This prophecy unveiled the future history of Israel and the precise time of Messiah's appearance. It's a prophecy of "seventy weeks".

So tell me, how many days are there in a week? Seven, of course, you reply. How many days in 70 weeks? 490, that's easy.

According to this prophecy, how many things are going to happen during "seventy weeks"? For one thing, a whole city built.

Now just do a little figuring here. Think it through and you will see that we are dealing with a period of time that is longer than a mere 490 days.

Scholars recognize that these seventy weeks (490 days) are symbolic of 490 years, each day representing a year. The year-for-a-day principle appears in Numbers 14:34 as a divinely established identity in prophetic symbolism; as also in Ezekiel 4:4-6 – "I have appointed thee each day for a year."

- On "seventy weeks" (70 x 7 years), Jewish commentator J.J. Slotki states: "The cryptic phraseology may have been suggested by the seven-year cycle of Lev. xxv. The expression 'week of years' occurs in the Mishnah (Sanh. v.i)."[3]

One could compare the expression "weeks of years" with "seven sabbaths of years..., seven times seven years;... forty and nine years" in the book of Leviticus.[4]

Other Jewish scholars concur:

- On "he shall confirm the covenant with many for one week" (Daniel 9:27), *Midrash Rabbah* reads: 'Week' represents a period of seven years."[5]

- On this same reference (v.27), the *Talmud* says: " 'One week' in Dan. ix means a week of years."[6]

- On seventy weeks are determined" (v.24), the *Talmud* states it to be "490, i.e. seventy weeks of years".[7]

- Isaac Lesser refers to "Ancient Jewish writers", Rashi and other commentators as recognizing "year-weeks".[8]

Here, then, we have a period of 490 years allotted to the Jewish nation, during which certain events will occur. You'll notice that the prophecy deals with the coming Messiah, as well as the history of Jerusalem.

	A	B
	THE MESSIAH	**JERUSALEM**
v25	**At the end of 7 + 62 wks** Messiah will arrive	Will be rebuilt, but under conditions of distress
v26	**After the 7 + 62 weeks** Messiah will be killed	A desolater prince will destroy it again
v27	**During the 70th week** Messiah will keep covenant with many people	
	In midst of the 70th week Messiah will cause sacrifices to cease	The desolater himself will be destroyed as predetermined

There is a clear structure to this prophecy, in which each verse deals firstly with Messiah, then with Jerusalem.

The events of Column A are unmistakably and closely dated to the seventy weeks. However, the events of Column B are not explicitly dated. Nor do they directly fulfill the spiritual purposes of the seventy weeks as specified in verse 24.

When was this "seventy week" period – which we now know to be 490 years – when was it to commence? If we can find the starting point, the rest of the prophecy will be easy to understand.

Jerusalem to be restored

> Know therefore and understand, that **from the going forth of the word to restore and to build Jerusalem** unto Messiah the Prince shall be seven weeks, and threescore and two weeks: the street shall be built again, and the wall, even in troublous times.[9]

It begins, you notice, from **the decree to restore and build Jerusalem.**

When did this take place? The Bible itself tells us: it was in the seventh year of the reign of the Persian king Artaxerxes,[10] when he issued his first "decree" [11] to rebuild the city.

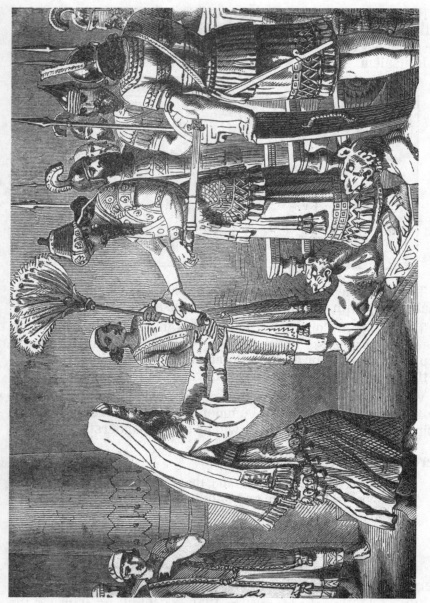

Artaxerxes presents his letter to Ezra

Leading up to this decree were two others - those of Cyrus and Darius - which related only to the building of the ruined Temple.

In 536 BC, Cyrus allowed the Jews to return and rebuild the Temple.

In 520 BC, Darius reaffirmed and expedited Cyrus' decree concerning the Temple. And in March, 515 BC, the Temple was dedicated. [12,13,14]

But the construction of Jerusalem itself was accomplished "according to the decree of Cyrus, Darius, and Artaxerxes king of Persia".[15] Ezra the biblical scribe considered the third decree to be the culmination of the three.

His use of the singular word "decree" to cover the three documents indicates the unity of the decrees. It also directs attention to the third one, without which the first two were incomplete.

It was this third decree, in the seventh year of Artaxerxes in 457 BC, which gave Jerusalem its legal rebirth, restoring full autonomy in legal judgments, including the death penalty.[16]

It made possible the restoration of Jerusalem to capital city status - necessitating its rebuilding as a visible administrative center.

It was this third decree which the prophecy had in mind when it spoke of a decree to "restore and rebuild Jerusalem".

It took the three decrees - of Cyrus, Darius and of Artaxerxes I - to implement the "commandment" of God, as Ezra terms it.[17] But when 457 BC arrived, the "commandment" of God was complete.

It is from this date, therefore, that Daniel's 490 years begin.

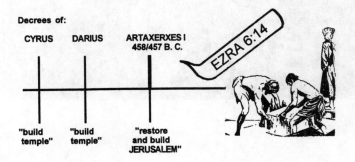

Decrees of:

CYRUS   DARIUS   ARTAXERXES I
                   458/457 B. C.

EZRA 6:14

"build   "build   "restore
temple"   temple"   and build
                      JERUSALEM"

Building Jerusalem's walls

Can this date - 457 BC - be confirmed?

The date is now firmly established as 457 BC by four independent sources:

- Greek Olympiad dates
- Ptolemy's Canon
- Elephantine Papyri
- Babylonian Cuneiform tablets

For example, one of the Jewish Elephantine papyri written between Tishri, 465 BC, and Nisan, 464 BC, is dated "accession year of Artaxerxes".

All four lines of chronological evidence point unanimously and harmoniously to the fact that the seventh regional year of Artaxerxes I extended from Nisan (month 1) in the spring of 458 BC to Adar (month 12) in the spring of 457 BC. From the extensive amount of evidence available, these dates can be considered as firmly and irrevocably fixed.[18]

To be built in troubled times

"The **street** shall be built again, and the **wall**, even in **troublous times**." So says Daniel's prophecy.

Ezra notes that both the "street",[19] that is, the broad empty space where the houses were formerly built, and the "wall" enclosing the city,[20] were rebuilt.

Nevertheless, the builders were hindered and their plans thwarted by the opposition of the Samaritans, who hired counselors to frustrate them. At the Persian capital, Shushan (Susa), Nehemiah received a report that his fellow Jews were in "great affliction and reproach" and that the newly-built "wall of Jerusalem" had been broken down and the gates "burned with fire".[21]

Distressed, Nehemiah sought permission from Artaxerxes to visit Jerusalem and "build it",[22] that is, repair the damage. The Persian king issued letters,[23] giving him permission to go to Judah and to receive lumber for gates.[24]

In Chapter 3 of his account, Nehemiah used the word "**repaired**" 33 times! "Now it came to pass, when...our enemies heard... that there was no breach left (in the wall)... they thought to do me mischief."[25] Nevertheless (in spite of troubles) "the wall was finished... IN FIFTY TWO DAYS".[26] A 52 day repair job.

This wall construction in 444 BC was **not** the predicted building of a **new** wall, **but** the **repair** of that damaged by opponents. Indeed, as Daniel predicted, these turned out to be "**troublous times**".

The prophecy of Daniel allows for the building of the city and the wall, a total period of "seven weeks" (49 years).

Here, then, are our first seven "weeks" in Daniel's prophecy.

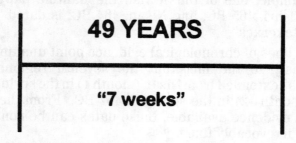

49 YEARS

"7 weeks"

Since historical records from Palestine are so scant, we cannot find independent evidence that Jerusalem was precisely 49 years in rebuilding.

However, the wording of the prophecy that "from the going forth of the commandment to restore and to build Jerusalem, UNTO MESSIAH THE PRINCE, **SHALL BE 7 WEEKS + 62 WEEKS**", provides us with a specific time for the more important event – the appearance of the Messiah.

- 7 plus 62 equals 69 "weeks of years"
- 69 times 7 equals 483

If we calculate 483 years from the "commandment to restore and to build Jerusalem", we should get the very year when Messiah would appear.

Now I suggest you follow this closely and check it yourself. There is no date in Bible history of which we can be more sure.

◆◆◆◆◆◆◆◆◆

146

Daniel wrote the prophecy. Ezra recorded the commencement date.

(There is no doubt that this prophecy existed. It was translated into a Greek version by seventy Jewish scholars in Alexandria between 285 and 180 BC, and circulated throughout the Greek-speaking world.)

Then for 400 years there was silence – while Israel and some others waited. The countdown began...

EVIDENCE NO SKEPTIC CAN ANSWER

AN OUTRAGEOUS CLAIM

The Bible claims that God selected holy men and revealed messages to them. As they wrote, they were under some mysterious control.

Expressions such as "God said," "the Lord commanded," and "the word of the Lord" occur in the Bible more than 3,800 times.

THIS PROBLEM OF VERIFICATION IS IMPORTANT

And for this reason there is a type of information which might be compared to a seal on a document that attests the document's genuineness.

PREDICTIVE PROPHECY SUPPLIES VERIFICATION

We humans can be sure of nothing even seconds ahead - just ask any horse punter! Remember the oracle of Delphi

and Croesus? The prophecy was so vague, that whatever happened, it would come true.

However, someone behind the Bible makes an audacious claim:

"So that you will know I am God," He says, "I am giving you the 'GAME PLAN' of history before it happens. Test it. Prove all things. I have told you before it happens, so that when it does happen you will believe." 1

And then? He proceeds to give us A THOUSAND or more predictive prophecies - dealing not merely with broad, general outlines, but often with minute details.

He names men, cities and nations, and even specific dates far into the future. He says, "I will cause these most unlikely events to take place."

Centuries pass... Suddenly events start happening - and a great variety of predictions, highly improbable when given, are progressively fulfilled.

THERE IS NOTHING VAGUE ABOUT THESE PREDICTIONS.

Bible prophecy is as far from Delphic style as midday is from midnight.

A PROOF OF GOD

Since man can't predict world history, it should be self-evident that if we find a series of predictions and they take place precisely as foretold, then we have proof of a source that comes from beyond mankind.

The united wisdom of man can only guess. God alone knows WITH IN-FALLIBLE CERTAINTY what is to come.

Predictive prophecy establishes that there is a Divine Intellect behind the Bible. It establishes the fact of God.

1 Isaiah 46:9,10; 41:21-23
1 Thessalonians 5:20,21
2 Peter 1:19-21
2 Timothy 3:16

CHAPTER 14

MESSIAH'S APPEARANCE FORETOLD

The wealthy King Croesus went to visit the oracle at Delphi. He wanted to know whether he should fight the Persians. According to the historian Herodotus, the "wise" oracle told him that "by crossing Halys, Croesus will destroy a mighty power."

Croesus took this as a prophecy that he would destroy the great Persian army. So he went into battle. But he was defeated.

He **did** destroy a mighty power: his own!

Whichever way the battle went, the augury would be true.

Human prophecy, I have found, is much like that.

However, an investigation of Bible prophecy proves it to be as far from human prediction as midday is from midnight. Bible predictions burn all bridges. They are specific.

And Daniel's prophecy, into which we shall now continue, is a notable example of this. And later, we may well ask, How did the prophet know?

483 years "to Messiah the Prince"

"Until Messiah the Prince there will be seven weeks and sixty-two weeks." [1]

That is, seven "weeks of years" (49 years) to rebuild the city, followed by 62 "weeks of years" (62 x 7 = 434 years) duration of the restored city – till the Messiah!

149

The Jewish writer, J. J. Slotki, says: "Jerusalem will be a fully restored city during a period of 434 years." [2]

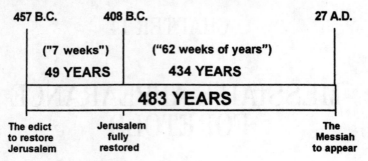

If the rebuilding of Jerusalem was to occupy 49 years, this would bring us to the year 408 BC. When we calculate another 434 years, we should get the very year when Messiah would appear.

It must be remembered that there was no 0 BC (zero BC) year. Thus, when we count from BC dates to AD, one year must be deducted from the total.

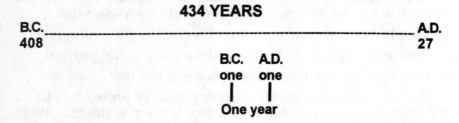

You will see that 434 years after 408 BC reaches to the year 27 AD.

These 434 years would reach to the *Messiah*, a name meaning the "**Anointed**" one. So the Messiah must appear in that year. And if that year passed and he didn't come, then we might well say that any future claimant to the role is NOT the promised Messiah!!

Do you see how clear that is? The eternal God in His revealed Word has given us a tremendously solid platform on which to base our faith. Did something significant occur during that year? Let's see.

The expectation

At the time, the land of Judea (Israel) was in the hands of the powerful Roman Empire. Many a Jewish heart longed to throw off the imperial yoke. Soon news filtered up to Jerusalem that a powerful speaker had appeared in the Jordan Valley east of the city and was calling on everybody to repent and be baptized. John the Baptist, as everyone called him, understood the chronology of Daniel's prophecy, and had caused quite a stir by announcing, "the kingdom of heaven **IS AT HAND**", [3] that the promised Messiah was about to appear.

As the time drew near, those who knew Daniel's time prophecy were **expecting** the appearance of the Messiah. Luke records that "the people were **IN EXPECTATION**".[4]

For centuries, almost every Jewish mother prayed with longing that her firstborn son would be the Messiah. Thus there developed a custom that if a boy was born there was great joy. If a girl was born... they wept.

Early Jewish documents, such as the *Septuagint* translation of the Scriptures (285-180 BC)[5] and the *Testament of the Twelve Patriarchs* (c. 100 BC),[6] interpret Daniel's time prophecy as referring to the Messiah.

Indeed, whether Essene, Hellenistic, Pharisaic or Zealot, the most usual interpretations of Daniel 9:24-27 within Judaism, until after 70 AD, were of the messianic kind.[7]

The Herodian group knew that the time for the appearance of Messiah was at hand. In their worldly perception of the event, they regarded King Herod himself as the Messiah.[8] From Daniel's prophecy, they correctly found that the term of 490 years was approaching its completion in the time of Herod.

The Essenes of the Qumran community likewise interpreted Daniel's prophecy messianically. That understanding was worked out prior to 146 BC.[9]

Clearly, the general expectation of the Jews was that the time for Messiah's appearance had arrived.

This is why the Jews sent priests and Levites to John the Baptist, to ask him, "Who are you?"

Although he confessed, "I am not the Messiah",[10] there were still many who speculated that John was "that prophet that should come into the world".[11]

Certainly John the Baptist understood the chronology of Daniel's prophecy and made it one of the bases of his appeal, "Repent ye, for the kingdom of heaven IS AT HAND."[12]

"The time is fulfilled"

In the crowd pressing around John was a young man approaching thirty. He came to John to be baptized by immersion in the River Jordan.

From this time onward, there followed a series of statements which, had they been accepted at face value, would have prepared their hearers for what was to occur three and a half years later.

The first was John's announcement upon seeing Yeshua: "**Here is the Lamb of God**, who takes away the sin of the world."[13] As symbolized by the ancient sacrificial system, this young man would ultimately go "as a lamb to the slaughter",[14] for claiming to be "the Son of God".[15]

Yeshua began his public ministry by declaring, "THE TIME IS FULFILLED."[16] With his own lips, he announced the termination of the prophetic time period.

"I'm here," he declared, "ON TIME."

Emperor Tiberius

Thus, one of the crowd who had been to the Jordan reported back to his brother, the fisherman Peter, "We have found the MESSIAS... the Christ."[17] The term "Christ" is the English equivalent of the Greek "Christos", meaning "ANOINTED ONE", and the Hebrew "MASHIACH" (MESSIAH).

Soon after this, Yeshua entered the synagogue of Nazareth, his home town, and announced, "The Spirit of the Lord is upon me, because he hath ANOINTED me."[18]

152

The year

And what year was this? You're not left to speculate. The first century writer Luke informs us that it was **"in the fifteenth year of the reign of Tiberius Caesar,** Pontius Pilate being governor of Judaea, and Herod being tetrarch of Ituraea and of the region of Trachonitis, and Lysanius the tetrarch of Abilene, Annas and Caiaphas being the high priests,"[19] that John the Baptist commenced his ministry.

Notice how careful a historian is Luke. He takes pains to confirm the date by seven independent lines of evidence.

F. F. Bruce, of the University of Manchester, offers this tribute to the historical accuracy of Luke:

> A man whose accuracy can be demonstrated in matters where we are able to test it is likely to be accurate even where the means for testing him are not available. Accuracy is a habit of mind, and we know from happy (or unhappy) experience that some people are habitually accurate just as others can be depended upon to be inaccurate. Luke's record entitles him to be regarded as a **writer of habitual accuracy.** [20]

Clark Pinnock, Professor of Interpretations at McMasters University, Toronto, concurs:

> There exists no document from the ancient world witnessed by so excellent a set of textual and historical testimonies, and offering so superb an array of historical data on which the intelligent decision may be made. **An honest (person) cannot dismiss a source of this kind.**[21]

Luke gives you seven historical facts, in order to pinpoint a date. You can check and re-check.

Tiberius' 15th year

We have an abundance of facts on the Caesars of Rome. And we can identify the fifteenth year of Tiberius' reign. It is 27 AD.

Tiberius commenced reigning on August 19, 14 AD.

The Jewish New Year began in September-October (on the date known in Jewish terminology as Tishri 1).

153

It was Jewish practice to reckon the years of foreign kings from Tishri 1 (New Year's day by the civil calendar).

Thus Tiberius' short first year (commencing August 19) ended - and the second year of his reign began – on Tishri 1 (in September-October, according to Jewish reckoning.)

The accompanying chart shows the first fifteen years of Tiberius' reign.

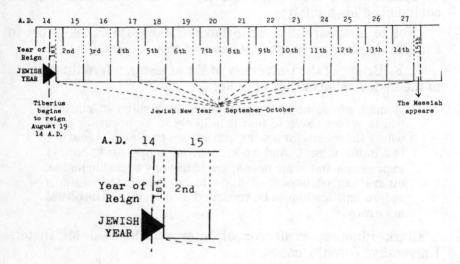

Tiberius' fifteenth year began in September or October, 27 AD.[22]

According to Daniel's prophecy, the Messiah should appear 483 years from the decree to restore and rebuild Jerusalem. That is, in 27 AD.

And right in that very year, Yeshua of Nazareth appeared, stepped into the Jordan to be baptized, and began his appointed work as the "Anointed One". [23]

May one conclude by this public announcement of Yeshua, that the prophecy given 600 years earlier was fulfilled ON TIME?

Paul, a former skeptic, seems to have believed this when he wrote, "**When the time had fully come,** God sent forth his Son, made of a woman."[24]

154

The covenant to prevail 7 years

Daniel wrote, "He shall confirm the COVENANT with many for one week."[25]

This "week" is the final one of the seventy weeks allotted in a special sense to the Jews.

An equally valid translation of this passage is: "One week shall **establish** the covenant" or "For one week the covenant shall **prevail**." Of course, "one week" denotes seven years.

The prophet Malachi called the coming Messiah "the messenger of **THE COVENANT**".[26]

This is the everlasting covenant of mercy that God had made with the human family, the promise that He had given to Adam.

By the events of this seven year period, the covenant would be forever confirmed and strengthened. It would prevail "with many" of Daniel's people, the Jews.

This divine covenant was to triumph in the ministry of the Messiah to Israel – a ministry which was to be a unique demonstration of patient, forgiving love.

(False interpretations of this passage have had it that some evil character will "make" a covenant with the Jews, then break it. However the original Hebrew word here is never translated "make". It is usually translated "prevail". **Nobody** was to "make" a covenant.)[27]

For 3½ years Yeshua came publicly to Israel.[28] He confirmed the covenant in person by his life and teachings.

Then, just before his death, he lifted a cup of wine and said to his disciples, "This is my blood of **THE COVENANT**, which is poured out for **many** for the forgiveness of sins."[29] Evidently, he was thinking that night of Daniel's prophecy, "He shall confirm **THE COVENANT** with **many**."[30]

To become effective, the covenant would require his death.

This period of 3½ years – and a second period of 3½ years that would follow his death – were definitely directed at the Jews ("thy people" of Daniel's prophecy). And as a consequence **many** Jews did recognize Yeshua as the Messiah.

The New Testament writers bear witness that after Yeshua's death on the cross, the same covenant message was **confirmed** to the Jewish nation for a further 3½ years.

Seven weeks after the crucifixion, on the day of Pentecost, the Jew Peter called his countrymen to repentance and forgiveness. "For the **promise** is to **you** and to your **children**," he said. [31]

On that occasion, 3,000 Jews accepted the offer. Soon after, 5,000 men, as well as women and children, accepted the offer, when Peter told them, "**You** are the sons of the prophets and of the **COVENANT** which God gave to your fathers.... God, having raised up his servant (Yeshua), **sent him to you first, to bless you** in turning every one of you from your wickedness." [32]

70 WEEKS OF YEARS (490 Years)

69 Weeks (483 YEARS)		1 Week (7 YEARS)
Jerusalem rebuilt 7 weeks (49 years)	62 weeks (434 years)	70th week
Artaxerxes' Decree	Messiah to Appear	End of the Jewish Period

So persuasive was this superlative sort of love, so attractive was the appeal of a God who continued to share His promise in spite of rejection and crucifixion, that (as Luke records) "the word of God increased: and the number of disciples multiplied greatly in Jerusalem, and a great many of the priests were obedient to the faith."[33]

Mark, another writer, states that when the disciples went publicly to Israel, that their Lord was "**confirming** the word with signs following."[34]

Again, Paul wrote to his Jewish kinsmen, "How shall we escape, if we neglect so great salvation; which at the first began to be spoken by the Lord, and was **confirmed** to us by them that heard Him."[35]

156

Can you see? In a very real sense, the ministry of the disciples was a **continuation** of the ministry of Yeshua himself.

This is how the Messiah would "**confirm the covenant**" with many (that is, the Jews) for one week (seven years).

Yeshua's use of "Messiah" and "Son of man"

In the popular mind, messiahship was tied to the idea of kingship, of one who would violently overthrow the Romans and bring on a Golden Age. Messianic ideas were nationalistic, destructive and vengeful.

To play that part was the last thing Yeshua desired. Any suggestion that he might do so was a hindrance to his cause. So he told his followers not to say that he was the Messiah, not in public.

Then, abruptly, he "began to teach them that the Son of man had to undergo great sufferings and to be rejected," that his role was to be essentially that of the innocent sufferer. "Your Messiah is a conqueror," he told the disciples; "God's Messiah is a servant."

Yeshua accepted the messianic faith of the Jews but interpreted it by means of the suffering servant passage of Isaiah chapter 53. He knew what lay ahead and was doing his best to prepare the disciples for it.

Rather, he preferred to call himself "the Son of man". It was his favorite title; it identified him with mankind.

However, at the end of his ministry, when he had to confront the high priest preparatory to his arraignment, he was asked point-blank, "Are you the Messiah?" And he replied, "I am."

It is clear that Yeshua allowed himself to be condemned to death for claiming the messianic role. Even if contemporary ideas of the title "Messiah" were mistaken, Yeshua still could not simply repudiate the title to save his life. He was voluntarily taking a course that would lead to his death.

After 3½ years: a violent death

"And after **the** 62 weeks," says the literal Hebrew language of Daniel's prophecy, "shall Messiah be cut off."[36] That is, AFTER the full 62 week period of the sequence of events in the prophecy, shall Messiah die. During the 70th week, in other words.

It does not tell us how soon "after". We need a specific phrase to place the timing of the event. We shall see, shortly, that the prophecy gives that timing in the next verse.

The expression "CUT OFF" implies that Messiah would not die a natural death; he would be murdered!

7 weeks	62 weeks	1 week
69 weeks		70th week
		"Messiah... cut off"
---------------- 483 years ----------------		------------ 7 years ------------

The prophet Isaiah spoke in similar terms regarding the coming Messiah. He will be "despised and rejected", "stricken", "wounded", "bruised", "brought as a lamb to the slaughter", "taken from prison and from judgment" and "CUT OFF out of the land of the living".[37]

Daniel prophesied that Messiah was to die "not for himself".[38] True, he would not die for his own sins, but for those of others; it was to be a substitutionary death.

"... and shall have nothing.[39] – no people, no place, no recognition, no kingdom, no adherents. He shall be deprived of everything.

Yeshua was crucified virtually alone and without even his clothes.

Bring sacrifice to an end

"In the midst of the week he shall cause the sacrifice and the oblation to cease." [40]

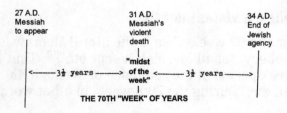

158

This is the final "week" of Daniel's prophecy. From Messiah's appearance to the time of his death would be half of the week, or 3½ years. And the disciple John, by recording the annual Passovers that Yeshua attended, provides evidence that three and a half years did indeed elapse between Yeshua's baptism and his crucifixion.[41]

The fourth Passover came in the spring of 31 AD – just 3½ years after his first public appearance – just as Gabriel had indicated to the prophet Daniel.

I would have to agree with writer Mervyn Maxwell that "If Gabriel were an athlete instead of an angel, we would stand on our feet and cheer!"[42]

"... he shall cause the sacrifice and the oblation to cease."

" How would Messiah bring the sacrificial system to an end? And why should he? Are you wondering?

A few chapters earlier we noted that for millennia men and women of the nations of earth anxiously awaited a coming Deliverer, and meanwhile they confessed their sins upon the heads of innocent animals which were sacrificed on their behalf.

Now Daniel is informed that the Messiah will be "cut off" – will die violently – "but not for himself."

Did this mean that the Messiah would die as the substitute sacrifice for the sins of mankind?

Would the Messiah, by his death, abolish the necessity for further sacrifice? Could it be that in the sight of heaven, Yeshua's death was the Sacrifice to end all sacrifices?

One ex-member of the Jewish ruling body, the Sanhedrin, certainly believed so! Paul wrote that Yeshua's crucifixion "in the flesh" had abolished the sanctuary "ordinances" for the sacrifice of animals in the flesh.[43]

His sacrifice had terminated the significance of the Jewish sacrifices forever.

••••••

Is that why Daniel wrote that the "70 weeks" were set aside to accomplish these things:

- "to finish the transgression"
- "to make an end of sin"
- "to make reconciliation for iniquity"
- "to bring in everlasting righteousness"
- "to seal up the vision"
- "and to anoint the most Holy"?

Is this what the Messiah was to achieve?

I believe so. But we shall leave these aspects of the prophecy to a later chapter. And we may discover a prophetic link with the Ark of the Covenant.

Questions arise, however.

This controversial person – was he for real?

Did he actually claim to be God's Son?

Did he really heal the sick?

If he was the Messiah, then why did the learned men of Israel, the doctors of religion, the leaders of the nation, reject him?

Vital questions indeed.

And we shall discover this man as his enemies saw him...

CHAPTER 15

BORN INTO DANGER

In the northern heavens... beyond the glories of the Orion Nebula... at the center of the universe.

Just ponder this...

Bethlehem

On the Throne of majesty, the Prince hears the cries of his suffering people. He is stirred with pity. All this splendor cannot be enjoyed while a tiny world on the edge of the universe suffers without hope.

So, from the place where he is adored by all, the Prince steps down, disguises himself, and goes out to suffer with his subjects in a cold and thankless world.

It is by his own act and by his own consent.

This is the scenario painted by the biblical prophets.

••••••

Place: Bethlehem in Judea, in the Middle East. Time: 5 to 4 BC. What a distance between the mighty God and a helpless child! One of the greatest of all-time miracles was when the co-Creator[1]

161

himself came down and became a helpless human baby, clinging to the breast of a sinner.

What humility was this! It stunned the universe.

He came down to the level of those he wished to save. Only thus could he rescue man from the lowest depths of degradation.

What humiliation! Who can comprehend it? Yet, in stooping so low, he lost not one atom of dignity and glory.

Into enemy territory, where the devil claimed dominion,[2] the great God permitted His Son to come, a helpless babe, subject to the risk of failure and eternal loss.

The rescue plan was made with the Father's full consent and deepest involvement. It was His act, His love and sacrifice also.[3]

On earth, the powers of evil had painted a false picture of God as harsh and cruel, just waiting for an excuse to dump calamities on people's heads. The people were tense and fearful.

So the Son of God assumed a human body in order that he might, without forcing man's will, woo him to himself. Perhaps if we knew him better, we would love him too. He would give people evidence of his love, and win from them their answering love. Without force. In the end, nobody would be able to say, We would have loved you, God, if only you had given us more evidence.

To appear as man, with all of the problems that men and women and children face, is the ultimate in communication. It is, in effect, to say, "This is an example of how I want you to live."

His coming to our planet Earth would add a great deal to our confidence that he understands our problems.

According to the biblical records, this person would be known as Yeshua, or Jesus. He would grow up in the northern town of Nazareth and, around the age of 30, commence a 3½ year public ministry.

Religious leaders call it a non-event

The priests and elders of Jerusalem were not as ignorant concerning the birth of Yeshua as they pretended. The report of the heavenly beings' visit to the shepherds with news of the birth had been brought to the capital. But the rabbis treated it as unworthy of notice. They themselves might have found Yeshua, and might have been ready to lead the Maji who came seeking him, to his birthplace. But the opposite occurred: those wise men from the east came to the rabbis to call their attention to the birth of the Messiah.

" Where is he that is born king of the Jews?" they asked. "For we have seen his star in the east, and have come to worship him."

Now pride and envy closed the door against the knowledge. If the reports brought by the shepherds and the wise men were credited, they would place the priests and rabbis in a most unenviable position, disproving their claim to be the exponents of the truth of God. These learned teachers would not stoop to be instructed by those whom they termed heathen. It could not be, they said, that God had passed them by, to communicate with ignorant shepherds or uncircumcised Gentiles.

They determined to show their contempt for the reports that were exciting King Herod and all Jerusalem. They would not even go to Bethlehem five miles away to see whether these things were so. And they led the people to regard the interest in Yeshua as a fanatical excitement. It was just a "sensational report".

Here began the rejection of Yeshua by the priests and rabbis. From this point their pride and stubbornness grew into a settled hatred of the Messiah. While the Lord God was opening the door to the Gentiles, the Jewish leaders were closing the door to themselves.

He knew suffering

Suffering was more keenly felt by this man, since his spiritual nature was free from the taint of sin. (We shall see testimony to this effect, shortly.) Therefore his desire for the removal of suffering was stronger than you and I experience. He went about healing people. He could not bear to see people hurting and not do anything about it.

He walked among the thoughtless, the rude, the discourteous. When he healed the sick, he was accused of being a Sabbath-breaker. When he cast out demons, they accused him of being Satan himself. He could not win!

The capacity to suffer, far from limiting his perfection, fulfilled him in the greatest possible perfection. Never was there another whose sympathies were so broad and tender.

What opposites meet in Yeshua! The co-Creator of all, yet in a world of his creating, often hungry, thirsty and weary, without a place to lay his head! Possessing eternal riches, yet living the life of a poor man!

Yes, after a long day of teaching, healing, climbing the mountainside, giving of himself days on end, he knew what it was to be tired – dead tired!

Has your love for another person been rejected? Yeshua suffered **more** than we. Because he was capable of deeper love – and he was to be harshly rejected. Yeshua would know what it was to suffer.

And he would be able to help mankind. He would care deeply.

He healed the sick

To anyone who would insist that such miracles were impossible, against natural law, I shall say: miracles must be observed as God coming in and interrupting the ordinary course of things. They are an inherent part of God's communication to us. The whole question depends ultimately on the existence of God.

True miracles are above nature, not against nature. They are manifestations of a higher law, which the lower laws must obey.

Let's face it. A Messiah who, being the Son of God and seeking to be mankind's Deliverer, who wrought no miracle, would be less credible than the Yeshua whom the New Testament records.

Evidence of hostile witnesses

Far from denying these miracles, Yeshua's enemies attributed them to the power of evil. It is of historical value that his enemies actually wrote of his miracles. They attributed them to sorcery.

The Jewish Babylonian *Sanhedrin* states :

> On the eve of the Passover they hanged Yeshu (of Nazareth).... he hath practiced sorcery and beguiled and led astray Israel.[4]

Julian the Apostate, Roman emperor from 361 to 363, who strongly opposed Christianity, wrote:

> Jesus did nothing in his lifetime worthy of fame, unless anyone thinks it a very great work to heal lame and blind people and exorcise demoniacs.[5]

Justin Martyr, around 150 AD, refers to official Roman records:

> That he performed these miracles you may easily be satisfied from the 'Acts' of Pontius Pilate.[6]

Yeshua's miracles demonstrated power over nature, power over disease, demons and death, as well as powers of creation. This power over natural forces seemed so ordinary to this man. It was a natural and necessary outcome of his life.

Yeshua's miracles occupied, however, a comparatively insignificant place in his ministry; they were worked with restraint, and only in love and mercy, for the benefit of men and women.

Often they were performed before the public for open scrutiny and investigation by skeptics.

When he raised Lazarus from the dead, it is significant that his enemies did not deny the miracle, but, rather, tried to kill him before all men believed in him.[7]

He loved everybody

Never would there be a man so kind as he, so generous, so helpful, so lovely – or so loving.

While abhorring sin, he wept with compassion over the sinner. He was able to be on the side of the sinner without ever once condoning the sin.

Though he was not soft on sin, Yeshua had come, as he said, "to heal the broken hearted", not to create new hurts. He was always sensitive to the feelings of others. He never needlessly embarrassed anyone or exposed a guilty one publicly. He associated with the rejected and approached the frustrated with compassion. He went down to the seamy places of the cities where prostitutes were kept and told them that God loved them, that He would forgive their sins and make them into dignified women again. How they appreciated that! They had never been shown love before. Exploited, lusted after, yes, often. But never loved.

There never was another like him, so tender and compassionate, so wise and strong. Yeshua gave abundant evidence that God is love.

What gracious, lovely things Yeshua said! He always made religion easy to understand. He proved that God was all-powerful and inexorably just, but kind and loving and merciful too. Just being near Yeshua made a person want to be good.

Becoming one of us, here with us for a time, was the best way God could communicate with us what He was like and how He wanted us to live.

His perfect life was a miracle

It is evident that Yeshua believed himself to be sinless. We never read of him confessing or asking forgiveness of his wrongs,

166

although he told his followers to do so. It appears he had no sense of guilt.

In their close contact with Yeshua, the disciples never saw in him the sins they saw in themselves.

They got on one another's nerves, they grumbled and argued, but never did they see this in Yeshua. Peter declared that he "did no sin, neither was guile found in his mouth."[8]

John went so far as to state that if anyone declared himself to be without sin he would be making God a liar and was a liar to himself. Yet of Yeshua he said, "And you know that he was manifested to take away our sins, and in him is no sin."[9]

And Yeshua allowed his dearest friends to believe this.

His enemies bear witness

But perhaps more important was the witness of his enemies. When Yeshua asked, "Which of you convicts me of sin?"[10] he received no answer.

Eventually Governor Pilate would testify, "What evil has this man done?" A criminal crucified with him would cry, "This man has done nothing wrong." And a Roman centurion would bear witness, "Certainly this man was innocent."[11]

However hard his enemies tried to bring forth an accusation of wrong, they could not.[12]

Yeshua seems to have lived in an unbroken relationship with God. His character was too far above that of every man, a moral miracle of history.

It had been claimed that the divine law was unreasonable and could not be obeyed by men and women. But Yeshua kept it.

Taking human nature and standing as man's representative, Yeshua said he was out to show that man, connected to God, could obey every divine requirement.

Quite obviously, Yeshua demonstrated that God's commandments were given to men and women in love. He showed us what it is like to have heaven in the heart.

Say others:

In the very perfection of his human nature his life stands forth as miraculous in a degree no other of the miracles of Scripture can attain (Morton).[13]

His sinless perfection is a miracle, in the sense that history is ransacked in vain for another fact like it (Whale).[14]

There never has been a more real or genuine man than Jesus of Nazareth (Thomas).[15]

When one reads his name in a list beginning with Confucius and ending with Goethe we feel it is an offense... against decency. Jesus is not one of the group of the world's great... Jesus is apart. He is not the Great; he is the Only (Stott).[16]

Sinless perfection and perfect sinlessness is what we would expect of God incarnate, and this we do find in Jesus Christ. The hypothesis and the facts concur (Ramm).[17]

What his antagonists say

Goethe wrote:

If ever the Divine appeared on earth, it was in the Person of Christ.[18]

Said H. G. Wells:

He was too great for his disciples.... Is it any wonder that men were dazzled and blinded and cried out against him?.... Is it any wonder that to this day this Galilean is too much for our small hearts?[19]

Even Rousseau admitted:

Yes, the life and death of Socrates are those of a philosopher, the life and death of Jesus Christ are those of a God.[20]

And in the *Koran*, the book of Islam, Yeshua is referred to as "the greatest above all in this world and in the world to come."[21]

His Words – a puzzling paradox

How simple was everything he said, how easy to remember, yet how profound!

168

Yeshua was not a political activist. He knew that the problem was in the hearts of men. And he worked on the heart!

To estimate his influence on history, consider the difference between Yeshua and all philosophers and moralists. To gather all their wise and good precepts, you must first sift out all the error, immorality and absurd superstition, which would be an enormous job.

The fact is that a single person, unlearned in men's wisdom, not only opposed the practices and maxims of his own country, but formulated a system so admittedly superior to others.

Joseph Parker declares:

> After reading the doctrines of Plato, Socrates or Aristotle, we feel the specific difference between their words and Christ's is the difference between an inquiry and a revelation.[22]

Socrates taught for 40 years, Aristotle for 40, Plato for 50 – and Yeshua for only three; yet those three years surpass in influence the combined 130 of these three greatest men.

Former Yale historian Kenneth Scott Latourette says:

> As the centuries pass the evidence is accumulating that, measured by His effect on history, Jesus is the most influential life ever lived on this planet.[23]

Latourette speaks also of:

> ...the baffling mystery... that no other life ever lived on this planet has evoked such a huge volume of literature among so many peoples and languages, and that, far from ebbing, the flood continues to mount.[24]

Let's face it. The life, the words, the character of this strange Man are the enigma of history. Any naturalistic explanation makes him a more puzzling paradox, a fathomless mystery.

His words are "the greatest ever spoken" (Ramm). "He shed more light on things human and divine than all the philosophers and scholars combined" (Schaff). One cannot fail "to see... that since the days of Christ, in spite of all the progress of thought, not a single new ethical idea has been given to the world" (Thomas).

Erstwhile skeptic Josh McDowell said it all:

If God became man, then certainly his words would be the greatest ever spoken.[25]

I wondered. **Could this explain the paradox and solve the mystery?**

His preposterous claims

Who was Yeshua? A superman? A fake?

He made seemingly impossible assertions and promises – strange statements that would normally brand a man either a preposterous liar or a mad fanatic.

Take these, for example:

- I am the light of the world.[26]
- Heaven and earth shall pass away, but my words shall not pass away. [27]
- I am able to give life to whom I wish.[28]
- I have moral authority over all men.[29]
- Only I can save men.[30]

Who is this person who places his own authority side by side with the authority of God?

You see? Yeshua claimed to be no mere holy man – he claimed uniqueness.

According to those who personally heard him teach, he said:

- I am one with God. [31]
- I am God's only Son.[32]
- I was with the Father before the world was made. [33]
- Before Abraham was, I AM.[34]

(And that was the name, according to Scripture, that God gave Himself when He communicated to Moses that He was the self-existent One: "I AM who I AM... Say to the people of Israel, I AM has sent me to you."[35] The name of God in Hebrew is YHWH or I AM.)

And Yeshua made still other audacious claims:

- You will see me sitting at the right hand of God the Father.[36]
- I am equal with God.[37]
- Worship is due to me as it is to the Father.[38]

(Hence Yeshua commanded and accepted worship as God.)[39]

And, as if that were not enough, he predicted:
- I will judge the world, and arouse the dead.[40]

These were all claims to divinity – and were recognized as such at the time, by those who heard him.

Yeshua is the only religious leader who has ever claimed to be God.

He made the incredible claim that he, a simple carpenter's son among the shavings and sawdust of his father's workshop, was in reality God in the flesh!

He never "guessed" or "supposed". His teachings were ultimate, final.

Yeshua was crucified not for his actions; **the issue was his identity.** This is unique among criminal trials.

He was crucified for blasphemy – saying that he was God. And indeed, unless he were equal with God his words **were** blasphemy.

Was he a great moral teacher?

C.S. Lewis, who was a professor at Cambridge University, and once an agnostic, wrote:

> A man who was merely a man and said the sort of things Jesus said would not be a great moral teacher. He would either be a lunatic – on the level with the man who says he is a poached egg – or else he would be the Devil of Hell. You must make your choice. Either this man was, and is, the Son of God; or else a madman or something worse.[41]

He adds:

171

Let us not come up with any patronising nonsense about his being a great human teacher. He has not left that open to us. He did not intend to.[42]

Was he a liar?

If this man's claims were false, there were two alternatives:

1 – **He knew his claims were false.** If this is so, then he made a deliberate misrepresentation. He was a liar, a hypocrite, a demon – and he was a fool, because he died for it.

If he made such claims and none were true, then he was the most unprincipled deceiver in all history.

He told others to trust him for their eternal destiny, even to die for his claims. If he could not back up his claims and knew it, then he was unspeakably evil. He was a liar and a hypocrite, because he told others to be honest, whatever the cost, while himself teaching and living a colossal lie.

Yet there is not a skeptic who will admit he was a deceiver. They concede he was honest and earnest.

A bad man could not have taught such great truths as he taught – truths which perform miracles of character-change on people. And a good man could not have deceived the people for whom he gave his life.

Indeed, how in the name of common sense could an impostor have continued to demonstrate from beginning to end "the purest and noblest character in history, with the most perfect air of truth and reality"? (Schaff).[43]

So I say, he could not possibly have been a fraud.

Was he a deluded madman?

That leaves us with the second option:

2 - **He did NOT know his claims were false**. If this is true, he was sincerely deluded; he was a lunatic.

Yet the facts show his mind was so keen that it was more than a match for the sharpest intellects of his day.

Tell me. How could he be a deluded madman, who never lost the even balance of his mind, who sailed serenely over all the troubles and persecutions, as the sun above the clouds, who always returned the wisest answer to tempting questions, who calmly and deliberately "made predictions which have been literally fulfilled"? (Schaff)[44]

The noted British historian William Lecky, a dedicated opponent of organized Christianity, said:

> The simple record of these three short years of active life has done more to regenerate and soften mankind than all the disquisition of philosophers and all the exhortations of moralists.[45]

We will have to face it: if his claims were FALSE, whether he be a deceiver or self-deceived, in either case, if he was NOT God he was not good.

Or were his claims true?

In my search for the truth of the matter, it came back to this.

This person is either EVERYTHING for mankind or NOTHING – either the highest certainty or the greatest fake.

If his claims are true, then I must either accept or reject his Lordship.

There needs to be a moral honesty in this, I told myself.

Yeshua prophesied that he would be the great spiritual magnet that would draw men and women of all nations to himself.

That prophecy has proved true. Something to think about?

Why did they reject him?

From my research into the prophecies concerning the Coming One, I was struck by prophecies that seemed to indicate the Messiah would be rejected by the very people who foretold his coming, but would be accepted by others.[46]

And I began to ask myself, **Why did the nation's leaders reject this Person?** Didn't they have enough evidence to know?

I uncovered ten reasons:

173

1 – **They were biased against him.** The human heart, according to the Scripture, is self-deceived and corrupted by sin. We are naturally rebellious toward spiritual matters.

2 – **It hurt their national pride.** They were expecting a Messiah who would deliver them from the Roman occupation. Because Yeshua did not come in the power and glory of a physical deliverer, they rejected him. Even to think that their expectations might be disappointed, enraged them. (He told them he had come to conquer sin in the life.)

3 – **His humble way of life offended their snobbery.**

4 – **He had not been taught by them.** They were unhappy with this brilliant young teacher because he had not attended one of their schools. He was in no way a product of their teaching. And his ministry was independent.

5 – **His character showed them up.** Yeshua's compassion stood out in bold contrast to their own rigid, uncaring attitudes. His large-hearted love made their littleness look exceedingly small. Frustrated and angry, they began to hate him.

6 – **In argument he outclassed them.** These learned men asked him one difficult question after another, determined to trap him into saying something for which they could condemn him. His mind was so keen that it was more than a match for them. Yeshua silenced one attack after another until his enemies gnashed their teeth in frustration and retreated. He had a way of telling little stories and asking them to comment. And often in their response they condemned themselves before they realized that they were the culprit in the story. Clearly outclassed, they became furious.

7 – **His growing popularity endangered their influence.** Yeshua's healing was making him ever more popular with the people. His personality was so warm and loving that huge crowds flocked around him. The religious leaders were thoroughly alarmed. More and more people were coming under his influence. Their own influence was endangered. They were losing their control of the people.

8 – **They feared incurring the wrath of Rome.** Since 63 BC a dozen rebellions in Palestine had been subdued – most of them by Roman force. Another uprising under Yeshua of Nazareth might bleed Rome's patience dry and lead to tighter occupation. For political reasons, Yeshua was perceived as a menace.

Yet, although men in their wickedness would demand the death penalty, it would be Yeshua himself who would voluntarily take a course that he knew would lead to his death. That was the reason he had come. His death was a key part of the divine plan to rescue mankind... as many as would accept it.

The Sanhedrin meets

We might note that those who sought to violently kill him, chose that role for themselves. It didn't have to be that way, unless they chose it.

Did I say **ten** reasons why he was rejected? There are two more – and they applied to most people in his day.

9 – They were asked by Yeshua to leave the majority and follow an insignificant little group. Yeshua told them: "Broad is

175

the way that leads to destruction, and many... go in thereat: Narrow is the way that leads to life eternal, and few there be that find it."[47]

It was a sad fact of life then. As today. Truth is rejected because of peer pressure. Yet history shows that the majority is usually proved wrong.

10 – **They were asked by Yeshua to "forsake all and follow me."** In those days, it meant to lose your job and even to be despised.

♦♦♦♦♦♦

To accept the claims of Yeshua was not easy. It meant there was **much rethinking** to do.

This was no superficial, surface change. It was a total transformation of a person's life.

The solution...

Eliminate him.

A climax was fast building between Yeshua and the religious leaders. Something must be done... SOON.

CHAPTER 16

"HIS BLOOD BE ON US"

"DEATH... DEATH... DEATH!" chants the mob. "Crucify him, crucify him."

The accused is calm. He surveys them with tender pity. How he longs to protect them from the events that lie ahead! But they have chosen not.

It is the eve of the Jewish Passover feast. The setting: Jerusalem.

Spitting upon this man, they drag him toward Skull Hill, for execution on a Roman cross.

......Fast forward, thirty-nine years. The Roman general Titus is besieging Jerusalem, currently packed with visitors for another Passover. The surrounding hills swarm with crosses, thick like a forest. And those who once asked the Romans to put that young man on a cross, now see thousands of their nation also sacrificed upon Roman crosses.

When the Jews returned to their homeland as a functioning state subject to Persian control, the nation was given a final opportunity as well as ample time in which to accomplish God's intentions through them. During those five centuries they could have enlightened and prepared the world for the coming Deliverer.

But 90 years after their resettlement, the prophet Malachi found them in a lapsed, and self-justifying condition. What more could God do for His people? The prophetic voice ceased.

The final appeal would come in the visible person of the Messiah himself.

But, although great crowds followed him, few in the nation were to accept him as Messiah. The simple record throbs with anguish: "He came unto his own, and his own received him not."[1]

Pilate washes his hands

All but a few hated this "Son of God"... rejected and despised him. Some spat in his face. Others in mockery placed upon his brow a crown of thorns.

They were among the crowd that demanded the Roman governor to give him the death penalty on a Roman cross.

Finally, at the governor's judgment hall, to Pilate's question, "Shall I crucify your king?" the chief priests replied, "We have no king but Caesar."[2] And the rabble added, **"His blood be on us, and on our children!"**[3]

Afraid of the mob, the governor called for a bowl of water and publicly washed his hands. "This innocent man is yours. See you to it."

Years later, it is told,[4] a forlorn Pilate was exiled to Gaul (France). He was seen down by the river. He was washing his hands... and washing... and washing... and washing... and washing his hands...

A friend stood at a distance, watching him... and then pressed closer to ask, "Why are you washing your hands like that? Can't you get them clean?"

Pilate looked up in desperation. "No," he replied, "I can't wash off the blood of Jesus Christ." Pilate eventually committed suicide.

A vast crowd followed Yeshua from the courthouse to Skull Hill. The news of his conviction had spread through Jerusalem and people of all classes and ranks flocked toward the execution spot.

"And they bring him unto the place Golgotha, which is, being interpreted, The place of a skull."[5]

It is 9 o'clock in the morning.[6] The execution is about to commence...

CHAPTER 17

A PLANNED TIME TO DIE

"He never existed!" shouted the communist official.

"What newspaper have you in your pocket?" asked the other man. "Is it *Pravda* of today or yesterday? Let me have a look."

The official pulled it out. Was this man for real?

"Aha!" exclaimed the other, looking it over. "August 8,1990. 1990 counted from when? From the One who did not exist or played no role? You say he never existed, but you count the years from his birth. Time existed before him. But when he came, it seemed to mankind that everything which had been before had been in vain and that the real time began only now."

If you say he was only a man, then a Jew did it! He split time in two!

History is replete with ambitious men who tried to hinge history upon themselves – and failed.

You can mention any name in history and nobody will turn a head. But mention "Jesus" (Yeshua} and they get uneasy.

He wrote his name on time itself. Every newspaper, cheque and letter, every legal transaction we enter, is dated from that event... dated from the wonder man of the ages, who cut time in two.

Who was this person? He claimed to be God, visiting man in the flesh.

•••••••

181

He died on time

Detailing a succession of events to occur in the future Roman empire, that prince of prophets Daniel pinpointed the time in Roman history when the Messiah would appear.

Daniel wrote concerning a ruler who would be characterized as **"a raiser of taxes"**.[1] The emperor who fulfilled this specification is clearly Augustus Caesar. We now know that there was in the Roman empire a system of census-taking regularly every fourteen years. The idea was associated with taxation. We also know that the system was inaugurated by the emperor Augustus.

His successor was also accurately described.[2] History gives the name of this successor as Tiberius. Daniel predicted that during this man's reign **"the prince of the covenant"** would be **"broken"**.[3] This accords with Daniel's earlier prophecy concerning **"Messiah the prince"** who shall **"confirm the covenant"** and be **"cut off."**[4]

We would expect the Messiah to suffer a violent death, therefore, **during the reign of TIBERIUS.**

Well, did he?

Cornelius Tacitus, a Roman historian (born 52-54 AD, who wrote in 112 AD) bears witness as follows:

> Nero, in order to stifle the rumor (as if he had himself set Rome on fire) ascribed it to those people who were hated for their wicked practices, and called by the vulgar Christians; these he punished exquisitely. The author of this name was Christ, who, in the reign of Tiberius, was brought to punishment by Pontius Pilate the procurator.[5]

The New Testament writer Luke, of course, indicates the same.[6]

Indisputably, Yeshua was crucified under Pontius Pilate, who was administrator ("procurator") of Judea between the years 26 and 36.

There were at least eleven attempts on Yeshua's life, during his 3½ year ministry, but all of these failed until the time was due. His enemies attempted to take him, "but no man laid hands on him, because **his hour was not yet come.**"[7]

On various occasions, Yeshua said, **"Mine hour is not yet come"**,[8] **"My time is not yet come."**[9]

However, just prior to his betrayal and death, Yeshua announced, **"My time is at hand."**[10] And finally, **"The hour is come."**[11]

There was a definite time in the divine plan for Yeshua to die. **"In due time,"** says Paul, "Christ died for the ungodly."[12]

In 536 BC, Daniel had defined the time of the Messiah's death by the exact date, 31 AD.

Yeshua of Nazareth died in the prime of life in the prophesied year.

And what is more, he died at the RIGHT TIME OF THE YEAR.

When one examines carefully the system of sacrifices that pointed forward to the Messiah and his self-sacrifice, one is forced to conclude that Yeshua Messiah died ON THE VERY MONTH AND DAY predicted in that symbol.

A male lamb without blemish was to be slain each year on the Passover day in the **month of Abib** (later called Nisan).[13] It was to be slain on the **14th day** of the month.[14]

And did you know, this age-old custom was linked prophetically to the Messiah!

The noted Jewish commentator Abrabanel states that

> ... **during the month Nisan in which the messianic re-demption is to occur**, the cup of Elijah **at the Passover meal** preserves in symbolism the idea that the new redemption will come during the same season as the exodus from Egypt.[15]

Did that click? Here is a Jewish commentator suggesting that the redemption that will come through the Messiah will occur at the time of Passover!

Traditional Jewish observance of Passover is called **Seder shel pesahh.** This joyous annual feast is inextricably linked with the messianic idea.

Zman-heruteinu, the name by which Passover is known among Jews, means that this is the season of freedom. How significant, when one considers that this event prefigured the Messiah who was to free the sinner from his chains.

Should we be surprised – or not – that rabbinical writings suggest that during Nisan a much greater redemption will someday be accomplished by the God of heaven?[16]

And that rabbinical tradition holds that Elijah will appear at Passover time and announce the coming of the Redeemer?[17]

Significant, also, is the practice which follows the Passover supper. As the participants sing the so-called Hallel, they repeat in song the messianic words of Psalm 118:22, which says: "The stone which the builders refused is become the head stone of the corner."

A most significant and intriguing allusion to the Son of God in the Passover observance is the centuries-old ritual which involves three cakes of unleavened bread (**matzos**) – always and invariably three – neatly wrapped in snow-white linen and placed on the Passover table before the host.

Early in the meal, the presiding person (usually husband and father) reverently takes the **middle** cake from between the other two, and after pronouncing a blessing upon it, breaks it into two equal parts. One half is broken into small fragments and distributed among the participants, who eat it with solemnity and reverence. The remaining half of the middle cake, called the **Afikomen**, is neatly wrapped in a linen cloth and hidden somewhere in the supper chamber, usually under the pillowed seat of the host.

At the end of the supper, when the third cup of wine has been emptied, the Afikomen, or hidden manna, is recovered, and then broken and distributed among those sitting around the table.

Thus ends the Passover celebration.

What is the meaning of this ceremony of three cakes of unleavened bread? Why **three** cakes? What do these symbolize?

There is a wide divergence of opinion among the rabbis. Does the ceremony of the three cakes represent the triune God – with the upper matzo denoting the Father, the middle matzo the Son, and the third cake the Holy Spirit? Between the *Talmud* (which denies the trinity) and the *Zohar* (which affirms the trinity), there has raged a battle for ages. The *Zohar* became dangerous to Judaism, since many found in it a confirmation of Christianity.

But I am curious. What is the significance of the **breaking** of the middle Matzo? And the **hiding** of it? And then the finding of the other half, called the Afikomen?

Could the middle cake actually represent the Messiah, the Son of God – whose body was to be broken for the sins of the world?

Could the hiding and the recovering of the Afikomen, which was wrapped in a linen cloth for burial, represent him who would die, his body then being wrapped in linen [18] – and who would later be resurrected to become the Messiah triumphant?

This ceremony of three unleavened cakes was doubtless practiced in Yeshua's day, since we read in the writings of Paul that the night Yeshua instituted the "Lord's Supper" to replace the prophetic Passover, he broke Afikomen and said to his disciples, "Take, eat: this is my body, which is **broken** for you."[19] John, in the Revelation, speaks of him also, as the "hidden manna."[20]

The meaning that this was intended to convey was that the resurrected Savior, now at the Throne of the universe with his Father, offers us, children of dust, the hidden manna – himself – in the infinite abundance of his resurrection power! By drawing upon this dynamic spiritual force, one can live above the foul swamp of sin and finally be counted among the overcomers to receive the overcomer's reward.

You see, the annual Passover, celebrated on the fourteenth day of Nisan, not only commemorated the deliverance from Egyptian slavery back in 1446 BC, but something more. The Passover lamb was a prophecy of the death of the long-promised Messiah, God's Lamb.

"Pass-over" predicted the Crucifixion, that is, the Passing-over of death from mankind, by Someone dying in his place.

Just prior to his betrayal and death, Yeshua announced to his disciples, "You know that after two days the Passover is coming, and the Son of man will be delivered up and crucified." [21]

There was one day on which the Jewish leaders did not want to kill Yeshua, and that day was Passover.[22]

But this date had been divinely appointed, and Yeshua's murderers had no choice but to meet this exact appointment.

But, we ask, did Yeshua the Messiah's crucifixion really occur on that precise day of the year? No doubt at all. The Jewish Talmuds confirm it:

> On the eve of Passover they hanged Yeshu (of Nazareth)...
> But they found naught in his defense and hanged him on the
> eve of Passover.[23]

Incredible! And this discovery has turned rabbis into Christians.

But there's more....

Not only was the year predicted. Not only the month. And not only the day...

The very hour of the Messiah's death was foretold in the Passover practice!

Divine appointment had long ago decreed: "In the fourteenth day of the first month at even (literally, in Hebrew, 'between the two evenings') is the Lord's Passover."[24]

The first "evening" began when the sun began to visibly decline from the zenith, around midday. The second "evening" was at sunset. Mid way between these was 3 pm.

Passover lamb was always killed in the **first month** (Nisan), on the **14th** day, "**between the two evenings**", which was the **9th hour** of daylight.

According to the first century Jewish historian Josephus, it was the custom in his day to offer the sacrifice at "about the ninth hour" (3 pm).[25]

Yeshua was lifted up onto the cross at Skull Hill around the third hour of daylight, at 9 am. He died six hours later, at 3 pm. [26]

The time it happened, and the fact itself, are recorded in a curious and valuable passage of a respectable Roman Consul, Aurelius Cassiodorius Senator, about 514 AD:

> In the consulate of Tiberius Caesar Aug.V. and Aelius
> Sejanus (U.C. 784, 31 AD), our Lord Jesus Christ suffered,
> on the 8th of the calends of April, when there happened such
> an eclipse of the sun as was never before or since.[27]

As to the year and day, agree also:

– The Council of Cesarea, 196 or 198 AD

- Maximus Monachus
- Nicephorus Constantinus
- Cedrenus

As to the year, but differing in days:
- Eusebius
- Epiphanius
- Kepler
- Bucher
- Patinus
- Petavius

Some of these reckon it the 10th of the calends of April, others the 13th.

Thus a host of credible authorities locate it in the Spring of 31 AD.

There is no question but that Jesus' death occurred at 3 pm, on the 14th day of the Jewish month Nisan, in our year 31 AD.

He fulfilled the prophecy not only to the **YEAR, MONTH**, and **DAY** of death, but to the **VERY HOUR!**

At that hour, the Temple priest would be raising his knife to kill the Passover lamb. Suddenly, as if by unseen hands, the massive Temple veil is ripped noisily from top to bottom.

In great fright, the priest drops the knife... and the lamb escapes.

The priest stands in stark amazement!

A man rushes in, his face white. The words spill out:

"HE'S DEAD. HE'S DEAD!"

The priest, with trembling lips, asks, "Who's dead?"

The man replies, "YESHUA OF NAZARETH."

••••••

The "cutting off" of Yeshua at the precise moment at which it was foretold, has become the pivot of the world's history, just as his birth has become the central epoch of the world's chronology.

The prophecy of Daniel 9 is irrefutable proof, mathematical proof, that Yeshua was who he said he was. Yeshua constantly appealed to the prophets as proof of his identity. Yet the most startling evidence, as we shall later see, is the discovery of the Ark of the Covenant, to which this information relates.

As Adam Clarke states: "The **whole** of this prophecy from the times and corresponding events has been **fulfilled to the very letter.**"[28]

As I investigate it more thoroughly, I am discovering Bible prophecy to be so accurate.

Why was it given? The disciple John replies, "That you might believe."[29]

••••••

Weird things began to happen in Jerusalem, following the crucifixion.

Some people would call them omens...

188

CHAPTER 18

THE WOMAN WHO ATE HER SON

At 3 o'clock there was an earthquake. The massive curtain which shielded the Holy of Holies in the Temple ripped downward from the top, as though by invisible hands.

That moment, north of the city wall, Yeshua died.

The Jewish temple sacrifices had lost their reason to be.

Daniel's prophecy had suggested that the Messiah would bring an end to sin offerings. At this time the sacrificial system of the Temple would cease to have meaning. In the divine plan, it would be ended. No longer must lambs be slain to point to the Lamb of God who should come.

It is true that for some forty years more, the outward shell would remain. That shell was to be removed in the physical destruction of Jerusalem in 70 AD. The Jewish ritual then ended. It has never been restored. Since then there has been no priesthood to make atonement, since every "son of Aaron" (the priesthood succession) was at that time slain.

Strange events begin

After they crucified Yeshua, some weird events began to transpire.

Take, for example, the **Yom Kippur** lots. On the annual Day of Atonement (Yom Kippur), according to custom, the Temple priest would cast lots to select a sacrificial goat to be the "sin offering".

189

It was considered a good omen if the lot came up in the high priest's **right** hand, for right is symbolic of good, and left is the symbol of evil.

The ancient Jewish rabbis related that during the forty years prior to the destruction of the Temple in 70 AD, this lot always came

The Second Temple, Jerusalem

up in the high priest's **left** hand. They wrote that it was one of the signs of the impending doom placed by God upon the Temple.

The Talmud also records that during the second Temple period it was customary on the Day of Atonement to tie some red wool to the Temple gate which would turn white as a sign that the people had been forgiven.

However, the Talmud bears witness to an astonishing event that occurred forty years before the destruction of the Temple in 70 AD. (Note that 40 years before the destruction of Jerusalem is about the time Yeshua was crucified – although the Talmud does not refer to this.) It reads:

> Forty years before the Holy Temple was destroyed the following things happened: The lot for the Yom Kippur goat ceased to be supernatural; the red cord of wool that used to

190

change to white (as a symbol of God's forgiveness) now remained red and did not change and the western candle in the sanctuary refused to burn continually while the doors of the Holy Temple would open of themselves.[1]

This Temple gate, I might add, was secured by immense bars of iron fastened deep in the pavement of solid stone. It was so heavy that it could hardly be shut by twenty men – yet it swung open, unaided.

The turning of the red cord of wool to white was considered to be in accordance with the words of the Lord through the prophet Isaiah: "Though your sins are like scarlet, they shall be white as snow...as wool."[2] From the cessation of this phenomenon in 30 AD the rabbis concluded that God was saying, "I will not forgive; I will not forgive."

Calamities predicted

Daniel prophesied that **after Messiah's rejection**, a succession of **calamities would sweep over Jerusalem** like a flood of desolation.[3]

Six centuries later, and only five days before his death, Yeshua was riding on an ass into Jerusalem. Thronged by adoring crowds, he paused. From the top of the Mount of Olives, the Temple looked resplendent, gleaming in the setting sun. Unknown to the crowd, the sun was setting on their nation too.

The front walls of that magnificent Temple were plated with gold, dazzling to behold when the sun shone upon them. Elsewhere, the Temple stones were of such pure whiteness that at a distance it appeared to the stranger like a mountain covered with snow. Its marble buildings, terraced courts, with the golden spikes atop the holy place, not to mention its massive proportions, must have stirred every Jewish heart.

This was not an old, crumbling building, since its renovation had been initiated by Herod as late as 20 BC. Work on the entire complex of courts and buildings had already been in progress for fifty years and would not be completed until about 63 AD. – a mere seven years before it would be totally destroyed.

Yeshua burst into tears. His voice breaking with compassion for Jerusalem, he predicted its terrible suffering.

The apostle Paul speaking on Mars Hill, Athens

Three days later, making his final visit to the Temple, he announced, "Your house is forsaken and desolate."[4]

On the way out, he pointed to the huge Temple stones and confided to his disciples, "Truly I say to you, there shall not be left here one stone upon another, that shall not be thrown down."[5]

Puzzled, four of them seized a private moment, to ask the question, **"WHEN will this be, and** what shall be the sign of your coming and of the close of the age?"

Linking in their minds those two events, they reasoned that such a substantial building would not be destroyed until the end of the age. "But when will that be?"

Then Yeshua dropped a bombshell. "All these things shall come upon **this generation.**[6] YOU yourselves shall see it happen."[7]

He confirmed that Daniel, also, had predicted it.[8]

Seven omens

Seven omens that would precede that dreadful event were listed - signs that were to find a remarkable fulfillment.[9]

1 **Many deceivers or false Christs:** Josephus confirms that during the time of governor Felix, preceding 70 AD, the land of the Jews was filled with impostors whom Felix had put to death EVERY DAY!

2 **Wars and rumors of wars:** When Yeshua spoke this prophecy, the Roman empire was experiencing a general **peace** within its borders. But this changed. The *Annals* of Tacitus, giving a Roman history of the period prior to 70 AD, refer to "Disturbances in Germany", "commotions in Africa", "commotions in Thrace", "insurrections in Gaul", "intrigue among the Parthians", "the war in Britain" and "war in Armenia". Before the fall of Jerusalem, four emperors died violently in eighteen months.

3 **Famines:** Historians such as Suetonius, Tacitus, Eusebius and Luke record famine during those years in Rome, India, Greece and throughout the world.

4 **Pestilences:** Plagues and epidemics in Italy and Babylonia wiped out tens of thousands of people.

5 **Earthquakes in divers places:** Seneca, writing in 58 AD, referred to earthquakes in Asia, Achaea, Syria, Macedonia, Cyprus, Paphos and Campania. "News has often been brought to

us of the demolition of whole cities at once," he wrote. Hierapous, Colosse and Laodicea were overthrown. In 63 AD, Pompeii was greatly damaged, and earthquakes rocked Apamea, Crete, Smyrna, Miletus, Chios, Samos, Rome and Judea. Earthquakes in divers places!

6 **Persecutions against the disciples of Jesus Christ:** It is a matter of history that wherever the message of Yeshua was taken, persecutions broke out.

7 **Before Jerusalem falls, the gospel will be preached to all nations:** Daniel had predicted that the covenant (God's promise to save mankind) would first be confirmed with the Jews for "one week" (seven years).

Moses and Isaiah had foretold that the Jewish nation would slip away from God; that He in turn would set the nation aside, as His special agents, and would use another people, thereby provoking Israel to jealousy.[10]

For 3½ years Yeshua walked in Israel's midst to fully disclose the will of God to them and to the world.

Then for a further 3½ years, his followers continued their appeal to Israel – until the good news was formally rejected by the Jewish Sanhedrin. General persecution broke out upon the Christians, as Daniel's prophesied 7 years came to an end. The time for Israel to officially accept their role as God's agents to the world had run out.[11]

From then on, those who in faith truly followed Yeshua as the Messiah, whether Jew or Gentile (foreigner), were now "God's own people" to perform the task that once belonged to the nation of Israel.

This time of transition was marked by a number of supernatural events. The Gentile centurion Cornelius received a heavenly visitation telling him to contact Peter the Jew. Peter, prejudiced against Gentiles, was shown in a vision that he must share the message of salvation with them. Paul (Saul), a fanatical persecutor of Christians, was suddenly confronted by the risen Yeshua; his life and career were reversed overnight. All of these events were timed perfectly.

Taking up the responsibility, the early Christians carried the good news everywhere. Even their enemies conceded that they "turned the world upside down".[12] The apostle Paul could later write that the word had been taken "to every creature which is under heaven."[13]

In recent years, reports have come in from explorers, anthropologists and archaeologists that suggest Paul was not exaggerating.

Some puzzling findings raise questions, such as, who was it that around the first century of our era went to the peoples of India, China, Japan, Tahiti, Peru, Brazil and North America? Who went there and healed the sick, raised the dead, even walked across water, calmed storms with an uplifted hand, gathered around him little children, and taught the message of salvation – as so many independent traditions of isolated tribes insist?

One such historical tradition was reported by Dr. Buck of the Bishop Museum in Honolulu. Dr. Buck wrote *Vikings of the Sunrise*. He was a full-blooded Polynesian and a scholar of the past of his people.

He wrote of a man coming in a flotilla of three Roman-type ships from the direction of the Red Sea and anchoring off Tahiti. He indicated that the event could definitely be assigned to the first century of the Christian era, plus or minus some fifty years.

The account goes as follows:

> To an island where men were fighting for the possession of the good land came three ships with giant sails like enormous birds with wings up-lifted, glowing goldenly in the dawn-light. Suddenly frozen to immobility were the warriors as the ships moved around a jutting headland.
>
> "What manner of monsters are these with the great wings?" "Perhaps they have come to devour the people!" Forgotten was the heat of the battle. Friend and foe stood facing seaward, weapons clutched in paralyzed fingers, staring in wide-eyed wonder.
>
> The ships' oarsmen, whose paddles looked like a hundred centipede legs touching the water, rested now from their task of moving the giant monsters forward.[14]

They saw the form of a man walking over the water, toward the shore. He was unlike their people, fair, with long, curly, light-brown hair and a beard. As he came up onto the wet sand, the warriors stared first at his garments, then into his eyes. They were grey-green.

They saw him going among the injured and dying, who arose from their pain to find themselves well of body as he touched them.

Small boats now left the Great Birds and brought other strangers to shore. After a short stay, these others departed, leaving this one man to remain with the natives.

Wakea, as they called him, learned Polynesian quickly. He visited the islands throughout the group, teaching them of the One God who ruled the heavens and whose law was based on love. They gave up war and the sacrifice of children. Finally, he departed in one of the Polynesian migration canoes in the direction of the Dawning (that is, eastward).

Similar racial memories have been found throughout the Americas, as well as in Asia.

There is good reason to believe that indeed, by the year 70, when Jerusalem fell, the good news had been taken to the remotest corners of the earth.

This was the seventh sign Yeshua foretold. "Then shall the end come," he said. The end of the Jewish Temple, that is.

(In his prophecy, he also looked ahead to the end of the age – and gave these same seven signs, to be repeated down in the end times.)

The Sanhedrin could sentence Yeshua to death, BUT THEY COULD NOT OVERTHROW HIS PROPHECIES!

Wait for THE sign, then flee

Now Yeshua gives **THE** sign – a **specific** sign that would let them know Jerusalem was about to be destroyed. "WHEN you shall see the abomination that makes desolate, spoken of by Daniel the prophet, stand in the holy place; WHEN you see Jerusalem **SURROUNDED BY ARMIES,** you will know that its desolation is near. WHEN this happens, then get out of the city quickly."[16]

Among the Jews an idol or other heathen symbol, such as a banner, was often termed an "abomination", or something offensive from a religious point of view. This would apply to the banners of a Roman army appearing outside the city.

A most unlikely prophecy

But, I hear someone say, why ever would the Romans want to attack Jerusalem? Since it was part of the Roman empire, they already had jurisdiction over it.

And another question. How on earth could anyone leave the city when it was already surrounded by armies?

It does seem a senseless type of prediction - as well as advice - to give.

So it would seem. You see since the days of Julius Caesar, Rome had treated the Jews leniently. They lived by their own religious law, were exempt from military service, and even retained puppet kings, the Herods.

Something happens

However, the Roman officials became more grasping. Crushed by taxation, the Jews turned to the Zealots – the fanatical leaders to whom Rome was a foe to be rooted out with the sword.

In 65 AD, the Roman agent Floris did something that really upset the Jews. And they revolted. Led by John of Giscala, a rich merchant of Galilee, and Simon bar Gioras, the Jews rose in mass revolt. Roman garrisons were surprised and cut to pieces. Jerusalem itself was seized by these Jewish fighters and fortified.

Cestius Gallus, Roman legate of Syria, took command of Judea and in the autumn of 66 marched against Jerusalem, **surrounding** it with his troops.

If it had not been for the Jewish rebellion that year, the Romans would have had no reason to besiege Jerusalem. And Yeshua foretold it. "When armies surround Jerusalem," he said, "then flee."

Pagan banners betokening the presence of Gentile arms not only appeared near and around the city, but were eventually in the holy place. They fought about the holy Temple – attempting in vain to enter.

"When you see the abomination stand in the holy place," said Yeshua.

IT WAS THE SIGNAL FOR THE CHRISTIANS. BUT HOW COULD THEY FLEE? The attackers encircled the city! And the furious war party in the city, the Zealots, would have prevented any attempted flight.

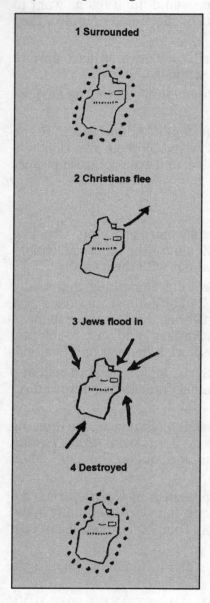

1 Surrounded

2 Christians flee

3 Jews flood in

4 Destroyed

Cestius' Roman troops were so successful that the Jews were ABOUT TO SURRENDER. Encouraged by a promise of the loyalist party in Jerusalem to open the gates for him, Cestius gathered his troops to a strong assault. He penetrated as far as the northern wall of the Temple.

THEN AN ASTOUNDING THING HAPPENED.

Suddenly he withdrew from the city, "without any reason in the world."[17]

THE CHRISTIANS KNEW THE REASON.

As the Zealots **opened the gates** and set out in pursuit of the retiring Romans, the watchful believers knew THEIR MOMENT HAD COME.

Latching on to Yeshua's warning of 35 years earlier, **every Christian fled out through the open gates at the proper time**.

They fled to Pella, in the foothills of a mountain range across the Jordan River, a place completely separated from Judea by the Jordan Valley.

"Prior to Jerusalem's siege by Titus (in 70 CE)," *Encyclopedia Judaica* states, "its Christian community moved to Pella."

"It is hard to account for this escape if (Yeshua's) prophecy was written after the event," states G. A. Williamson in his introduction to *Josephus - The Jewish War*.

Not one Christian perished in the subsequent destruction of Jerusalem. They had been watching for the sign – and they obeyed Yeshua's instructions.

THE PROPHECY WAS SPOT ON!

A prayer answered

The Christian believers had been praying, in harmony with Yeshua's instruction, that this event would not occur during winter, nor on the Sabbath day.[18]

Graetz, the Jewish historian, has computed the days involved, showing that Cestius must have withdrawn from the city on WEDNESDAY, October 7. The Christians did not have to travel on the Sabbath.

Haste necessary

Yeshua had predicted that the flight out of the city would require such haste that the man on the housetop or in his garden should not try to gather any extra clothing.[19]

History shows that such haste was necessary. Time was of the essence. To postpone flight would entail great danger. As events proved, this advice was appropriate, because the ROMAN ARMIES SOON RETURNED. The temporary respite was the last opportunity the Christians would have to escape.

As the Romans devastated one town of Judea after another, people fled when possible to Jerusalem, swelling the numbers there to be fed and kept in order. This continued, since united action from Jerusalem appeared to be the safeguard. During a comparative lull in the storm, thousands more people poured in.

The moment the Zealots returned, the gates were closed and desperate preparations were begun for the next encounter. No Christian would have escaped then.

Before long, the invading Romans returned to the siege. Fearful scenes of famine and bloodshed were to follow, until Jerusalem would be laid waste.

But – and note this point – history records that NOT ONE CHRISTIAN PERISHED IN THE SIEGE OF JERUSALEM.

The great tribulation

"For then shall be great tribulation"; "the days of venge-ance... great distress in the land... wrath upon this people."[20]

The horrendous flood of destruction that followed the Jewish revolt was a dramatic fulfillment of Yeshua's prophecy!

As the Roman pressure intensified, inexpressible horrors took place within the cities of Judea and especially in Jerusalem.

Factions began to slaughter each other, torturing and killing as many as thousands a day. Josephus says that the people inside the city "never suffered from the Romans anything worse than they made each other suffer." Some of them, "taking up a mad rage from those dead bodies under their feet, became the fiercer... and omitted no method of torment or of barbarity!"

Some who tried to escape the besieged city, swallowed pieces of gold to take with them. Word got around – and many were cut open, 2,000 in one night.

The fighting was incessant, day and night. As the miseries grew worse and worse, the terror of the people increased. The multitude of carcasses that lay everywhere in heaps produced a pestilential stench.

Famine

Long centuries earlier, when Moses had been given a vision of the future of Israel, the Lord had said,

"I will bring a sword upon you that shall avenge THE QUARREL OF MY COVENANT: and when ye are gath-ered together within your cities, I will send the pesti-lence among you." [21]

Titus the Roman general occupied the Mount of Olives in the spring of 70 AD and laid siege to Jerusalem in earnest. By May 25, Titus had captured the outer wall, and a week later he held the second one.

Within the city, where thousands had crowded together at the time of Passover, misery became extreme. Their stores of provisions, which, if carefully preserved, would have supplied the citizens for years, had previously been destroyed through the jealousy and revenge of contending factions. And now all the horrors of starvation were experienced.

When provisions ran short, a measure of wheat was sold for a talent. In simple terms, a dry quart sold for over $600.

Disease erupted. Between May 1 and July 20, in just 80 days, 100,000 corpses were carried outside the city for burial.

Many, wasted to shadows, died of starvation as they tried to bury others. Many went and lay in their coffins before their hour of death had come.

Says Josephus:

> There was no wailing or lamentation heard. The famine stifled all natural emotions. Those who were about to die looked upon their dead with dry eyes and smiling mouths. A deep silence and kind of deadly night had seized upon the city.
>
> At first, orders were given to bury the corpses out of the treasury (the stench being unbearable). Later, when they could no longer do that, they had them cast down from the walls into the ravines outside.
>
> When they were no longer able to carry out the dead bodies of the poor, they laid their corpses on heaps in very large houses, and shut them up therein.
>
> Later, when it was not possible to obtain food, some persons were driven to such terrible distress that they searched the common sewers and old dung-hills of cattle, and ate the dung there.
>
> At last they were reduced to chewing girdles and shoes, and pulled off and gnawed the very leather which belonged to their shields. Wisps of old hay became food to some; and some gathered up fibers.[22]

Oh, if only they had heeded the words of their Messiah and his messengers!

Moses, writing concerning the siege, had predicted that in the famine, a man's **"eye shall be evil toward his brother"**.[23] This refs to a man watching and begrudging every morsel he may see in the possession of other members of his house, and to evil designs against his own kin.

Josephus records the fulfillment of the prophecy:

> If so much as the shadow of any kind of food anywhere appeared in any house, a fight ensued, and the dearest friends fell to contending with one another for it, snatching from each other the wretched supports of life. Nor would men believe that those who were dying had no food, but the robbers would search them even when they were expiring, lest anyone should have concealed food in his bosom and counterfeited death. And the robbers themselves gaped for want, and ran about staggering like mad dogs, and reeling against the doors of houses like drunken men, and would also in their dire distress rush into the same houses two or three times in the same hour.

> When they saw any house shut up, this was to them a signal that the people within had got food, whereupon they broke open the doors and ran in, and took pieces of what they were eating almost up out of their very throats, by force.

> Children pulled the very morsels their fathers were eating out of their very mouths. So did the mothers as to their infants.[24]

Cannibalism

Looking ahead to this siege, Moses had prophesied: **"And thou shalt eat the fruit of thine own body, the flesh of thy sons and of thy daughters."**[25]

It happened exactly as Moses wrote. Flavius Josephus, eyewitness to the tragedy, recorded the facts 1500 years after the prophecy.

> Here is a fact such as no history records either among Greeks or Barbarians, horrible to speak of it, and incredible when heard:

> There was a certain woman that dwelt beyond the Jordan, whose name was Mary. She was eminent for her family and wealth, and had fled to Jerusalem with the rest of the community, and was besieged with them at this time. All her

202

personal effects that she had brought for safe keeping to Jerusalem, had been seized by plunderers within Jerusalem who were taking advantage of the siege; and any scraps that she had treasured up besides, and any food she had contrived to save, had also been carried off by the rapacious guards who came every day running to her house. They grew to hate her for her strong protests. If she found any food, she sorrowfully realized that her labors were for others. And as it was now almost hopeless for her to find any food, and the famine pierced through her very bowels and marrow, her passion was fired to a degree beyond the famine itself. So she proceeded to a most unnatural thing, and, snatching up her son, who was a child sucking at her breast, she exclaimed, "O thou miserable infant! for whom shall I preserve thee in war, famine and sedition? As to the Romans, even if they preserve our lives, we must be slaves; but the famine will get us before slavery does; yet these robbers are worse than both Romans and famine. So be thou my food, and be thou a fury to these seditious persons, and a by-word to the world, which is all that is now wanting to complete the calamities of us Jews." When she had said this, she slew her son, and then roasted him, and ate half of him, and kept the rest by her concealed. And straightway the seditious came in, and smelling the scent of this uncanny food, threatened to cut her throat immediately, if she did not show them the food she had dressed. She replied that she had saved a very fine portion of it for them, and uncovered what was left of her son. Thereupon they were seized with horror and amazement of mind, and their blood ran cold at the sight. And she said to them, "This is my own son, and this is my doing. Come, eat of this food, for I have eaten of it myself, and be not more tender than a woman, or more compassionate than a mother. But if you are too scrupulous, and abhor my sacrifice, as I have eaten half, let the rest be reserved for me also."

At this they went out trembling, and with some difficulty prevailed upon themselves to leave the remainder of it with the mother.[26]

"All is well"

The distress was worsening. Many people were calling on their priests, urging them to help end the siege.

To the very last, the leaders continued to assure the people: "Hang in there. Is not the Lord among us? No harm can come upon us."

The blind obstinacy of the Jewish leaders and the detestable crimes perpetrated within the besieged city, excited the horror and indignation of the Romans.

The fury of the Romans

According to both Moses and Daniel, in their prophecies, the attackers besieging Jerusalem **would be of a fierce countenance.**[27]

It is true that the Roman leaders endeavored to strike terror into the Jews, and thus cause them to surrender.

Those who ventured out into the valleys in search of food were caught by the Romans and crucified, as many as 500 a day, until the number of crosses within view of the city walls became so great that there was not room enough for the crosses. Nor were there enough crosses, so that several people were often crucified on the same cross.

Sallies by the Jews delayed the Romans, and the tricks they played in fighting, infuriated the besiegers, and prepared their minds for the unmitigated cruelties they were soon to commit.

When the Romans finally broke into the city, their desire for revenge would know no bounds.

CHAPTER 19

THE END APPROACHES

Within the city itself, some weird occurrences were being noted.

- According to documents dating from that time, a great
  light shone around the Temple altar for half an hour
  during the ninth hour of the night – making it like day
  time.
- An astronomical phenomenon shaped like a sword
  hung menacingly over Jerusalem.
- Toward sunset, chariots and troops of soldiers in their
  armor were seen running about among the clouds
  preparing for battle. Josephus realized that such a
  fabulous tale stretched one's credulity, so he wrote, "It
  would seem to be a fable, were it not related by those
  that saw it."
- When the day of Pentecost arrived that year, the
  officiating priests felt the Temple precincts tremble as
  many voices were heard crying, "Let us depart hence."[1]

●●●●●●

Another incredible prophecy

It was one of the world's great buildings, the Jerusalem Temple.
Individual stones reached up to 36½ feet long by 11½ feet high by
17½ feet thick, and weighing hundreds of tons each.

The excellent construction of the building gave assurance that
it would withstand the elements indefinitely. The city of Jerusalem

was held to be, for all practical purposes, impregnable, but Yeshua predicted that it would be destroyed by force.

And concerning the Temple, he said, **"THERE SHALL NOT BE LEFT ONE STONE UPON ANOTHER, THAT SHALL NOT BE THROWN DOWN."[2]**

Think about it! How many ancient buildings still stand, wholly or partly, with their building stones still standing atop other stones? Tourists to old sites find them all over the place.

But not so, said Yeshua, with this massive Temple. It would totally vanish. Now that is really sticking one's neck out.

During the five months of the siege, fighting continued to be bitter. In July, the Castle of Antonia was taken – and the sacrifices in the Temple ceased.

In August the Temple was conquered.

Titus tries to save the Temple

The blind obstinacy of the Jewish leaders, and the detestable crimes perpetrated within the besieged city, excited the horror and indignation of the Romans.

The siege dragged on.

The fall of Jerusalem (Sketch: Darren Hunter)

The Roman general Titus decided to take the Temple by storm. However, he gave **strict orders** that when his army should enter the city, the magnificent Temple **should be spared**. He held a council with his generals and instructed that the Temple be saved as a priceless ornament of the Roman empire.

HAD HIS ORDERS BEEN OBEYED, THE PROPHECY WOULD HAVE FAILED.

But because a Roman soldier **disobeyed** a command (an unlikely event), this prophecy came true.

Command disobeyed

It was August 30. Titus had retired to his tent for the night. Suddenly the Jews, sallying from the Temple, attacked the soldiers without.

Reports Josephus, who was present at the siege:

> ...in spite of Titus' decision, during the excitement of the attack one of the soldiers, awaiting no orders and with no horror of so dread a deed.... snatched a brand... and, hoisted up by one of his comrades, flung the fiery missile through a low golden door.[3]

The silver-embroidered curtaining was set on fire. Immediately, the cedar-lined chambers about the holy house were ablaze.

Titus rushed to the place, followed by his generals and legionaries, and commanded the soldiers to quench the flames.

His words were unheeded. In their fury the soldiers hurled more blazing brands into the side chambers, and then with their swords they slaughtered in great numbers those who had found shelter there.

Blood flowed down the Temple steps like water, forming large pools.

> As the flame shot up, a cry, as poignant as the tragedy, arose from the Jews, who flocked to the rescue, lost to all thought of self-preservation.... now that the object of all their past vigilance was vanishing.[4]

Above the sound of the battle, voices were heard shouting, "Ichobod! The glory has departed."

The golden plates, melted by the fury of the fire, ran down the cracks between the stones. After the fire died, the gold-hungry soldiers prized the massive blocks of the foundations apart stone by stone in search of the precious metal, LEAVING NOT ONE STONE UPON ANOTHER.

Lange's Commentary on Matthew 24:2 says of Yeshua's remarkable prophecy:

> A prophecy literally fulfilled forty years after its utterance, fulfilled by Jewish fanatics and Roman soldiers in express violation of the orders of Titus, one of the most humane of the Roman emperors.

"This generation"

"This generation will certainly not pass away until all these things have occurred," said Yeshua. "Daughters of Jerusalem, weep not for me, but for yourselves and for your children." "ALL THESE THINGS shall come upon THIS GENERATION."[5]

"When shall the Temple be destroyed?" his disciples asked.

He replied: "In this generation."

The precise year foretold?

Yeshua predicted the **generation** of Jerusalem's destruction, but what about the **year**?

Could it be that Yeshua gave the precise date in Luke, when he said, "And they (the Jews) shall fall by the edge of' the sword, and shall be led away captive into all nations: and Jerusalem shall be trodden down of the Gentiles, until the times of the Gentiles be fulfilled."[6]

Listen to this observation by Colin Deal:

> The Hebrew alphabet, as is well known, attaches certain numerical values to each of its twenty-four letters. By adding the value of certain letters in a word or phrase you can find a total numerical value which can denote a given year or number. The terminology in the Hebrew language of the phrase, **trodden down of the Gentiles** is **Yerushalam Tel** – Jerusalem will become a heap. Tel denotes a man-made mound, usually formed as a result of an attack upon a city which is destroyed or abandoned. When Yeshua said the Gentiles will make a heap of Jerusalem, a **Tel of Jerusalem,**

the equivalent of these letters in figures come to 3,830, reduced to the Hebrew calendar, then to the Gregorian calendar, the figure becomes exactly the year 70 AD! Thus the precise year of Jerusalem's destruction and the Jewish dispersion was foretold by Yeshua. "And now I have told you before it come to pass, that, when it is come to pass, ye might believe" – John 14:29.[7]

Just in case you missed that, I should repeat that the Jewish people have their own calendar. The date Jerusalem was destroyed, according to the Jewish calendar, was the year 3830. That is equivalent on our Gregorian calendar to the year 70.

Coincidence?

And it gets more amazing.

The very date the Temple was burned by Titus' armies was the SAME DATE that the armies of Babylon had burned it centuries before – the tenth day of the month Ab.[8]

How could there be anything less than a divine message in this uncanny repetition?

The end approaches

Josephus narrates:

The flame was also carried a long way, together with the groans of those that were slain...nor can one imagine anything greater or more terrible than this noise... the ground did nowhere appear visible, for the dead bodies that lay on it.[9]

After the destruction of the Temple, the whole city soon fell into the hands of the Romans. The south-west hill of Jerusalem (the Upper City) fell in September. The leaders of the Jews forsook their impregnable towers, and Titus found them solitary. He gazed upon them with amazement.

According to Josephus, the Roman commander confessed that neither his armies nor his siege engines could have been successful in breaching the walls of Jerusalem UNLESS GOD HIMSELF HAD SO WILLED IT.

As a last place of refuge, thousands crammed into the city sewers. Two thousand were found dead there; the survivors were dragged out and slain.

During that fierce tribulation, 1,100,000 people perished. Never have so many citizens perished in the fall of any city. Only about one-tenth as many people were killed in Hiroshima as in the fall of Jerusalem.

Josephus sums it up:

> I shall therefore speak my mind here at once briefly:– that neither did any other city suffer such miseries, nor did any age ever breed a generation more fruitful in wickedness than this was, from the beginning of the world.[10]

The city and Temple were razed in order to show the world that even the strongest fortifications were no match for the Roman army.

Only the three towers of Herod's palace and part of the western wall were left standing as monuments of Jerusalem's former glory, and to furnish a military post for the Roman garrison. Both the lower and upper city were set on fire, and the walls were broken down. As far as topography permitted, the site was leveled.

The anguish of a disillusioned people

It is probably safe to say that suffering never reached a greater degree of awfulness and intensity.

Nevertheless, even the bestiality of Jew to Jew, and Roman to Jew, was nothing compared to the ANGUISH OF A PEOPLE who knew they were forsaken by God.

And this is the saddest part of the whole story. During the siege, many Jews expected divine intervention.

To the very LAST they had held out, assured of eventual deliverance, for did not the prophecies all say that **THE CITY AND THE TEMPLE WILL NOT FALL UNTIL MESSIAH HAS COME?**

Jacob... Micah... Haggai... and Daniel... all agreed on that![11]

And in a thousand years of Hebrew history, no biblical prophecy had been known to fail. Of that, they were certain.

But now, the Temple was falling. Here was destruction – of everything! EVERYTHING! And the Messiah hadn't come. What had gone wrong?

Can you grasp it? – the utter anguish, the unspeakable despair, the black hopelessness, that now fell upon "God's chosen ones"?

The desolator of Daniel's prophecy had come. The holy city and Temple were in ruins, the desolation accomplished.

Aftermath of the rejection

They were familiar with the prophecy in Scripture that the scepter would not depart from Judah until first the Messiah had come.

And now the scepter was gone. The Talmud records this dismay:

> Woe unto us, for the scepter has been taken from Judah, and the Messiah has not appeared![12]

Did he come, and had they somehow missed him?

It was no mere accident that things happened the way they did. This was the fearful aftermath of Israel's official rejection of God's Son.

By putting Jesus to death the Jews virtually destroyed their Temple.

The name of YESHUA (JESUS) in the Old Testament

Think back, for a moment. Just a few years earlier there was **a general expectation** among the Jews that the time for Messiah's appearance had arrived (see chapter 14).

This expectation was gained from some very clear prophecies.

Did you know that even the name of the coming Messiah was woven into the Hebrew Scriptures?

In Hebrew the name of *Jesus* is *Yeshua*, or some say *Yashua*.

In translating the Holy Scriptures, his name was rendered in Greek *Iesous* and in the English it became *Jesus*.

211

However, his name in the land of Israel with his earthly parents was **Yeshua**.

Every time the Old Testament uses the word **SALVATION** (especially with the Hebrew suffix meaning "my", "thy" or "his"), with very few exceptions (when the word is impersonal), it is the very same word, **YESHUA** (Jesus) used in the New Testament.

In ancient times, the meaning of a person's name was considered very important. For example, Lamech called his son *Noah* (meaning Comfort), saying "This same shall comfort us..."[13] Eber called his firstborn son *Peleg* (meaning Division), "for in his days was the earth divided".[14]

The same is true of the names Abraham, Sarah, Isaac and Jacob (changed to *Israel,* meaning "God's Prince"), as well as the names of all of Jacob's sons.

Thus when the heavenly messenger spoke to Joseph, husband of Mary, who was to conceive Jesus, here is what Joseph actually understood:

> And she shall bring forth a son, and thou shalt call his name SALVATION [YESHUA – same word]: for he shall save his people from their sins.[15]

The message would have been spoken in the Hebrew language.

Thus the baby was named YESHUA (Jesus).

Arthur Glass was a Jew who had accepted that Yeshua was the promised Messiah. Glass lived in the United States.

One spring in St. Louis, he met a fellow Jew in the home of a mutual friend. The conversation gravitated to the subject of Yeshua (Jesus).

And the other Jewish man flung at Arthur Glass the challenge: **"If Yeshua is our Messiah, and the whole Tenach [Old Testament] is about him, how come his name is never mentioned in it even once ?"**

"But it is," responded Arthur.

"Rubbish. I'm a Hebrew Scholar. And I tell you, you **can't** find the name of **Yeshua** in the Old Testament."

Arthur paused for an instant. Then he bent down, opened his briefcase and took out his Hebrew Bible.

212

"My friend," he said, "would you translate into English the passage of Isaiah 62:11, for me?"

The Jewish scholar did so with the utmost ease. He translated rapidly and correctly. And this was his translation of the text, verbatim:

> Behold, Jehovah has proclaimed unto the end of the world, Say ye to the daughter of Zion, Behold thy YESHUA [Jesus] cometh; behold, his reward is with him, and his work before him.

Immediately he crimsoned. It dawned on him what he had done. He fairly screamed out, "No! No! You made me read it 'thy YESHUA', Mr Glass! You tricked me!"

"No, I did not trick you," was the reply. "I just had you read the Word of God for yourself. Can't you see that here SALVATION is a Person and not a thing or an event? HE comes, **HIS** reward is with **HIM**, and **HIS** work before **HIM**."

The other man rushed to open his own Old Testament. He was talking frantically as he did so. "I'm sure mine is different from yours."

He found the passage, looked it over, and dropped like a deflated balloon. His Hebrew Bible was, of course, identical.

You see, the name YESHUA (Jesus) is found in the Old Testament about 100 times all the way from Genesis to Habakkuk! Yes, the very word – the very NAME – that the angel Gabriel used when he told Mary about the Son she was to have.[16]

Yes, in the Hebrew Bible the Messiah is referred to as Yeshua. [17]

In Habakkuk, we read literally from the original Hebrew:

> "Thou wentest forth with the YESHA [a variant of YESHUA – Jesus] of [or for] thy people; with YESHUA thy MESSIAH [thine Anointed One] thou woundest the head of the house of the wicked one [Satan]."[18]

Here you have it! The very NAME given in the New Testament –Jesus Christ! (Christ is the equivalent of the word for Messiah, or Anointed) And there it is in the Old Testament – the Hebrew Bible.

As a matter of fact, even in the Jewish Prayer Book it is written:

May it be Thy will that the sounds of the Shofar [ram's horn] which we have sounded today be woven into Thy tapestry **Yeshua**, the Prince of Thy presence and Prince of might. So mayest Thou receive our pleas and extend to us Thy compassion.[19]

One may ask how the sages who wrote the Prayer Book knew that the name of the MESSIAH was **Yeshua** (the Hebrew equivalent of **Jesus**), as quoted in the Mahsor for the New Year? The answer is that they understood what the Bible teaches concerning the Messiah.

Moreover, on the same page of the Prayer Book is this prayer to God:

May He appear the second time.

Why did the Hebrew sages write that? Evidently, because he came once, which most of the Jewish people do not believe. Let us remember that among the Hebrew sages were many honest men who knew and wrote truth. And there were others who were not so honest. "May he appear the second time." That some did know the prophecies is evident. Though they wrote honestly knowing that the MESSIAH had to come during the time of the Second Temple, because of prevalent prejudice, they may not have known the true identity of the MESSIAH.

Well, there it is. Yeshua came – and at the precise time foretold by Daniel. And he fulfilled the predicted messianic role.

But he was rejected – a fact which had also been foretold by the prophets. The rejection of the true Messiah was prophesied in Isaiah, Daniel and the Psalms – in prophecies which were acknowledged by the early Jews to be messianic.[20]

The Jewish leaders rejected Yeshua because he did not fit their mistaken assumptions; because he did not come in the power and glory of a king, to bring immediate, national deliverance from the Roman rule. If only they had read the prophecies more carefully – and understood his real purpose! Their prejudices got in the way.

Evidence might be conclusive and even overwhelming, but it does not necessarily produce conviction. The will and the affections must necessarily enter into it.

Once men have committed themselves to a certain position, it is very difficult to look at evidence impartially – and more so when private interests are involved. David Cooper expresses it well:

> The subtleties of the human mind are indeed deceptive and will lead to dangerous errors unless one is a truth-seeker and examines every matter microscopically with an eye focused upon undisputed facts.[21]

They had their calculations right. But they rejected the Coming One when he arrived. So it was that "when the true Messiah was rejected, and the time for His coming had gone by," states Anstey, the Jews "corrupted their Chronology and shortened the duration of the kingdom of Persia, so as to be able to apply the prophecy to Theudas and Judas of Galilee... and at length to Bar Cochab..."[22]

This shortening of the chronology can be adequately traced. Authorities such as Sir Isaac Newton[23] and D. Davidson[24] have addressed this deliberate corruption of history which occurred in the first century of the Christian era.

It is partly as a result of this shortening of world history, that the Jewish year count (in 1999 AD it would be counted as the year 5759), falls short of the year count as arrived at from the Hebrew Scriptures – a curious anomaly.

A greater rejection, a greater desolation

The Jewish Temple was destroyed, along with Jerusalem city, on two occasions. Each time, the nation was exiled.

The first time was for their rejection of the prophets and their failure to heed the word of God.

Could it be that the second time was for their rejection of a greater Prophet, even the Messiah himself – and a refusal to accept the word of God through him?

If the first captivity of 70 years was an adequate punishment for the rejection of their ancient prophets, what can be the enormity of the national sin which brought these people of God to exile, grief and woe for nearly 2,000 years?

According to the Scriptures, it could be nothing less, and nothing more, THAN THE REJECTION OF THEIR MESSIAH... nationally.

Moses, in looking ahead to the siege of Jerusalem by the Romans, said God would bring the sword upon them, "that shall **avenge the quarrel of my COVENANT**."[25]

Daniel wrote that the Messiah was to come in order to "**confirm the COVENANT**." [26]

You see, it was all about the COVENANT. The same covenant for which an Ark was prepared.

While the leaders of the people were rejecting the covenant and the Prince of the covenant, the sacred Ark – **the Ark of that COVENANT** – lay out of their reach. And probably out of their thoughts. Through all of this, the Ark of the Covenant remained safely hidden.

Yes, the Messiah came to CONFIRM THE COVENANT. And he sealed it with his Blood.

Then followed DESOLATION upon Israel. And he told them why. "Because you did not recognize the TIME of God's coming to you."[27]

He told them they were now left **DESOLATE**.[28] Soon the **DESOLATOR** predicted by Daniel would be knocking on the gates of Jerusalem. [29]

I must say this. It is always wrong when people try to lay the blame on individual Jews for the crucifixion of Jesus Christ.

The crucifixion was the clash between the love of God and the sinfulness and selfishness of the whole human race. Those who crucified Yeshua are representatives of the whole human race.

It is for no one to point the finger of accusation at anyone else.

Rabbinical curses on Daniel 9

Daniel the prophet! "Read him," said Yeshua. "No," said the rabbis. "We'll place a curse on you."

Let me tell you what happened.

In 1656, a dispute occurred in Poland between some distinguished Jewish rabbis and the Christians. The dispute concerned Daniel's "70 weeks" prophecy.

"Look," said the Christians, "this prophecy proves Yeshua to be the Messiah. It tells exactly when the MESSIAH was to suffer."

The rabbis were so hard pressed by this argument, it was embarrassing. So they broke up the discussion.

The rabbis then held a meeting. As a result, they pronounced a curse upon any Jew who should attempt to work out the chronology found in this prophecy.

This was their curse:

MAY HIS BONES AND HIS MEMORY ROT WHO SHALL ATTEMPT TO NUMBER THE SEVENTY WEEKS.

And in the Talmud this curse is recorded:

Rabbi Samuel B. Nahmani said: "Blasted be the bones of those who calculate the end.[6] (Note 6: i.e. Messiah's advent) For they would say, since the predetermined time has arrived, and yet he has not come, he will never come." [30]

Now ask an eyewitness who was at the destruction of Jerusalem. "Josephus, what do you think about the prophecy of Daniel?"

Listen to his reply:

Daniel also wrote concerning the Roman government, and that our country should be made desolate by them. All these things did this man leave in writing, as God had showed them to him, insomuch, that such as read his prophecies, and see how they have been fulfilled, would wonder at the honor wherewith God honored Daniel. [31]

217

CHAPTER 20

HOLOCAUST

Although he was innocent, Josiah Scamp did not hesitate to confess to a crime which carried the penalty of DEATH.

And he knew the law would accept his confession and HANG him.

The crime was horse-stealing. And the real culprit was Scamp's son-in-law.

But to save his daughter the sorrow – and disgrace – of losing her husband on the gallows, Scamp, a gypsy, of Odstock, in Wiltshire, England, decided to take the blame.

To divert suspicion from his son-in-law, Scamp hurried to the stable of a farmer who had reported to police the theft of his horse, and under some straw Scamp placed his coat.

The coat was soon found and Josiah was arrested and charged with stealing the horse. At the turn of the 18th century horse-stealing was punishable by death.

Josiah Scamp pleaded guilty to the charge and was hanged at Salisbury.

But Scamp's noble sacrifice was in VAIN. For the son-in-law stole ANOTHER HORSE shortly after his death.

Police caught the thoughtless man and he was found guilty of the theft.

He also was HANGED.

The MESSIAH did everything he could to save Israel. He even died for them. They had the world's best opportunity to turn from their wrongs and avert the disaster that followed. As do we, individually.

With uncanny accuracy, Old Testament prophets had foreseen what would follow if they rejected his rescue offer. They foresaw Jerusalem's fate and the events of the centuries that would follow.

"Therefore shall Zion... be plowed as a field," said the prophet.[1]

After the final destruction of the Temple and Jerusalem, Rufus Turnus, the Roman general left in charge, had a plow furrow run right across the Temple grounds and the city.

As recently as 1865, Josias Porter wrote:

> I have seen the plow at work on it, and with the hand that writes these lines I have plucked ears of corn in the fields of Zion.[2]

Amazing prophecies

The prophecies do not stop at the destruction of Jerusalem. They reach ever onward, through history, describing the situation to this present day!

For the remainder of this chapter I shall briefly overview a sample of these.

Prophecy: THE INHABITANTS WILL BE LEFT FEW IN NUMBER[3]

> **Fulfillment:** Those who died from the siege, both during and after, reached the almost unbelievable figure of 1,100,000. The large majority of those who perished, though Jews, were visitors to the city rather than dwellers there.

> In 70 AD, the Jews were crushed, but not really dispersed. However, in 135 AD, all the land was confiscated and sold to Gentiles by Hadrian. The Hebrew civilization and culture was all but demolished.

Prophecy: THE JEWS WILL BE SOLD INTO SLAVERY IN EGYPT

"And the Lord God will bring you into Egypt again with ships... and there ye shall be sold unto your enemies for bondmen and bondwomen, and no man shall buy you."[4]

Fulfillment: Some 97,000 were sold as slaves, some being taken to Egypt, "into bonds, and sent... to the Egyptian mines... and (they) sold the rest... at a low price, and that because such were sold were very many, and the buyers few." The slave markets of the world were so glutted with Jewish captives that they could not be sold.[5]

Prophecy: THEY WILL BE SCATTERED AMONG THE NATIONS FROM ONE END OF THE WORLD TO THE OTHER

"I will scatter you among the heathen"; "thou shalt be removed into all the kingdoms of the earth."[6]

Fulfillment: Today, wherever mankind is found, whether it be barbaric or highly civilized, there you will find the Jew. He is in every land and every race.

Prophecy: WILL BE OPPRESSED AND SLAUGHTERED

"Thy life shall hang in doubt before thee and thou shalt fear day and night"; "and ye shall have no power to stand before your enemies." "And they that are left of you shall pine away in your enemies' lands."[7]

Fulfillment: In many countries, the Jews could find no fair protection under the law. Wherever the Jews have set foot, they have felt the cruel stroke of persecution. Almost every nation has persecuted them. On several occasions, atrocious massacres have aimed at, and almost secured, their complete extermination.

Their history has been one long, bloody commentary on the uncanny accuracy of this prophecy.

Of all events in the Nazi assault on Europe, the Jewish holocaust still makes one's flesh creep.

There sits on the table before me a report in the London *Daily Mail* of July 30 1996.

The writer, Tom Bower, reveals that Swiss bankers received from the Nazis gold bars shipped by train to the Swiss capital Berne. Some of this gold had been extracted from the teeth of Jews gassed in the extermination camps. Bags of small fillings which had arrived in Berlin's Reichsbank, were melted, stamped and dispatched as German bullion to Berne.

221

The saddest feature of the Jewish torments is that they have often been engineered by so-called Christians. No genuine, enlightened Christian will persecute a Jew or anyone else. On the contrary, he will do his best to assist another, since God loves each one.

And although the nation as a whole certainly erred, many godly men and women adorn the pages of Jewish history from antiquity to now.

Prophecy: "SHALL BE WANDERERS AMONG THE NATIONS"[8]

Fulfillment: This prophecy hardly needs comment. We have all heard the expression "wandering Jew". There is even a vine with that name!

Prophecy: WILL EXPERIENCE "FAILING OF EYES" DUE TO WEARINESS FROM LOOKING FOR DELIVERANCE THAT FAILED TO COME [9]

Fulfillment: Many Jewish people are still wistfully longing, looking in vain for the Messiah. Arthur Michelson comments: "In an Orthodox Jewish home we hear so much about the coming of the Messiah. My father and my rabbi told me repeatedly that when the Messiah would come he would deliver the Jews from all their trouble and would bring peace to the world. Very often, especially at Passover night, I saw my father standing in the backyard of our house, where he looked so anxiously to the heavens and to the stars for the coming of the Messiah while tears were running down his cheeks, and he prayed: 'Oh, God, have mercy upon us, and send us the Messiah.' Oh, what a tragedy! I am convinced that every Christian man and woman would be stirred up at such a sad sight, which I had the opportunity to witness on several occasions."[10]

Prophecy: WILL BECOME A PROVERB AND A BYWORD

"And thou shalt become an astonishment, a proverb, and a byword, among all nations whither the Lord shall lead thee"; "a reproach and.. a taunt."[11]

Fulfillment: Wherever he has wandered, the Jew has been taunted and reproached. Through history, when one wished to express contempt for a person, he would call him a Jew. Who has not heard such derogatory expressions as "wandering Jew", "as mean as a Jew", and so on. All too frequently, I'm afraid - and often undeserved. But the inspired biblical prophets foresaw it. And their enemies fulfill the prophecy even as you read this.

Prophecy: DESPITE ALL PERSECUTIONS THEY WILL NOT BE TOTALLY DESTROYED

"I will make a full end of all the nations whither I have driven thee, but I will not make a full end of thee." [12]

> **Fulfillment:** The Jewish nation has survived more dispersions, persecutions, and martyrdoms, than any other people on the face of the earth. The amazing preservation and longevity of the Hebrew race is a standing enigma, a curious paradox, to the world. It is significant to notice that every nation that has persecuted the Jews has, in time, crumbled and vanished. Two nations around Judea that remain today, Persia and Greece, were those who befriended the Jews.

Prophecy: JERUSALEM WILL BE CAPTURED AND DESTROYED, BUT IT WILL REMAIN

"Jerusalem shall be trodden down of the nations until the times of the nations be fulfilled."[13]

> **Fulfillment:** Present-day Jerusalem is the 17th edition of the original city! There is no spot on earth so blood-soaked as Palestine. The armies of the world from time immemorial have marched and clashed there in battle. Jerusalem City has suffered 40 major sieges, been partly destroyed 35 times and totally destroyed 4 times. Her valleys have been filled and her hills leveled, her streets and buildings destroyed, and her people slain and exiled.
>
> Babylon, a monstrous capital – built on a plain, with beautiful soil and plenty of water – has vanished (as biblical prophecy said it would!).
>
> Jerusalem was so INSIGNIFICANT by comparison, and built on barren rock.
>
> Bible prophecy said Jerusalem will remain, even though the great city of Babylon would never rise again. Jerusalem has been trodden down by the nations - the Romans, the Persians, the Romans again, the Saracens, the Crusaders, the

223

Saracens again, the Khwarazm Turks, the Egyptians, then the Ottoman Turks, and finally the British.

Now, for the first time in almost 2,000 years, it has returned to Israeli hands.

Why has the Jew survived?

Isn't there a tremendous lesson in all this? Could it be that God has preserved the Jew for several important reasons?

I can think of three. Firstly, to preserve His word – the Holy Scripture. Don't you think this amazing?: the records telling of their shame have been faithfully handed down to us by the very people who should want them destroyed. Such fidelity to truth is

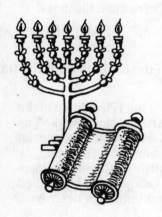

unknown anywhere else in history.

Secondly, to prove that His word is true. "I tell you before it happens," said Yeshua, "so that when it happens you may believe."

Thirdly, to show that the man who rejects the love of God as revealed through Yeshua will be far worse off.

In the ancient books of Leviticus (Chapter 26) and Deuteronomy (Chapter 28), there was clearly outlined the history of the Jews for the next 3,500 years, that is, from 1500 BC to this present day.

The Lord gave them glowing promises and plans which were conditional. "If" they were faithful, He would do certain things for them.

Yet, despite their unfaithfulness as a nation, the Lord has, in His magnanimity, kept certain promises that had been conditional on their obedience. For example,

You shall lend to many nations, and you shall not borrow.[14]

And five of you shall chase an hundred, and an hundred of you shall put ten thousand to flight, and your enemies shall fall before you... [15]

It might be remembered that in recent wars, the Arabs have outnumbered the Jews twenty to one.

••••••

During World War II, in Nazi Germany, hatred for Jews knew no bounds.

Carl Benz simply loathed the sight of a Jew. He declared, "I never want any of my children to ever have to look upon a Jew."

His pregnant wife was eventually driven to hospital, where, in the maternity ward, she was placed in a one-bed room.

Carl Benz went to visit his wife, as she lay, waiting for the event. Casting his eyes around the room, he noticed a picture on the wall. It was a picture of Jesus Christ. The blood flushed to his face. He began to shake. In a rage, he rushed to the sister-in-charge. "What is that picture of that Jew doing in my wife's room?" he demanded.

"I cannot remove it, sir."

"Do you hear me?" he roared. "I never want any of my children to look upon that Jew!" They did not remove it. A few hours later, the child was born. It was a boy. But it did **not ever** have to look upon that picture of a Jew. That baby was born blind.

Damascus Gate, Jerusalem (Photo: Jonathan Gray)

The rubbish dump to which Ron Wyatt pointed (Photo: Ron Wyatt)

CHAPTER 21

THE SEARCH

She lost her false teeth. And the United Nations was needed to get them back for her.

••••••

1948. After almost two thousand years of prophetic wandering, persecution and despair, the Jewish people once more had a homeland. Some saw this as a fulfillment of biblical prophecy. To others, it was a sign that the end of the age was imminent.

Yeshua had foretold: "Jerusalem shall be trodden down of the Gentiles (nations), until the times of the Gentiles be fulfilled."[1]

Yet, in spite of this return of the Jews to Palestine, Old Jerusalem city remained in the hands of Gentiles. By an odd twist, the territory of the new Israel almost encircled, but did not include, the most sought after prize of all, the Old City. That remained firmly Arab. Obviously the "times of the nations" was not yet "fulfilled"!

A strange reality was the bulldozed no man's land that twisted and turned through the built-up area, separating Jordanian-held territory from that of the Israelis.

One morning in 1956, at a hospice which sat precariously on the edge of the city's dividing line, an elderly woman leaned from an upstairs window and her false teeth dropped into no man's land.

It took the combined talents of the Israeli and Jordanian liaison officers and a staff of United Nations observers to get them back for her.

This incident highlighted the unnatural state of affairs that persisted until the Six Day War of 1967.

In June that year I found myself roaming the cobblestone alleys of the Old City.

Two tiny Arab boys off loaded from their perspiring little arms, tasty bagel rings, which they sold four for a shekel. A veiled woman flitted elegantly through the crowd, a basket atop her head. And I saw two caged sparrows "sold for a farthing", as in Jesus' time.

Just days before, in a lightning war, Israel had retaken Old Jerusalem.

Now the stage was being set. A series of events would soon start coming together. The ancient saga of the Ark of the Covenant was about to spring to life.

Go Back!

If you started reading this book only five minutes ago and you are already here, I want you to go straight back to Chapter 1. If you do not first read carefully the preceding chapters, you may neither understand nor accept the truth of what follows. And in that case you will not be qualified to make a rational judgment concerning this discovery.

The pointing arm

It was late 1978. Biblical archaeologist Ronald Wyatt was in Jerusalem.

With his two sons Danny and Ronny, Wyatt had been diving in the Red Sea. Wyatt was badly sunburnt, so they returned to Jerusalem to await their return APEX flight home to the United States.

A few days later, after the swelling had eased a little, Ron decided to go sightseeing in the immediate area around the hotel in which he was staying, near the Damascus Gate.

He was accompanied by a local official, who invited him to inspect a property which he managed.

As they passed close to the base of an ancient stone quarry, known to some as "the Calvary escarpment", the two men were discussing Roman antiquities. For a moment they stopped walking.

Suddenly, to his total shock and dismay, Ron's left arm went out and pointed to a site being used as a trash dump, with a dead cat lying on it. And his mouth said:

"THAT'S JEREMIAH'S GROTTO AND THE ARK OF THE COVENANT IS IN THERE."

Immediately he thought, "Why did I say that?" His action had not been consciously done. In fact, that was the first time he had ever thought about excavating for the Ark.

I like the way Ron recalls it: "I was speaking to this archaeological gentleman when my mouth said something my brain didn't go along with, or had no idea about."

While Ron stood in stunned silence, the other man, quite out of character, also reacted strangely.

"That's wonderful!" he exclaimed. "I want you to excavate. We'll furnish you with a permit, fix you up with a place to stay, do your laundry. Yes, we'll even supply your meals."

Was Ron hearing right?

The man looked at him. "And we'll furnish you with all the diggers you need."

Ron Wyatt didn't know what to think. He had done archaeological work in several places, but never had he experienced anything like this. Somehow he sensed this had to be a "supernatural" experience. In his mind, he knew it could be of God... or of "someone" else.

Ron Wyatt

It was like a thunderbolt out of the blue.

"Look, thanks. But I'll have to decline your offer for now," mumbled Ron. "I'm ready to fly home."

But he also needed time to think. He had to figure out if there was any reason to believe the Ark could be in that location.

Jeremiah's Grotto. Perhaps I should remind you at this point that we've already spoken of an open cave often referred to as Jeremiah's Cave.

229

It is in the escarpment a little to the south of Skull Hill. We mentioned it in Chapter 6.

But don't go rushing off there, please. It's only a banana merchant's cave. He stores crates in there. And better not ask him about the Ark of the Covenant. He'll know nothing.

An Australian archaeology writer who didn't like Ron Wyatt – or Jonathan Gray, for that matter – did just that. He went and spoke to the humble Arab banana seller. Then he rushed into print quite seriously with the hot news that the banana man knew nothing about the Ark of the Covenant being in there!

We had a chuckle over that one.

You see, that's just a shallow cave open to the street. And it was **not** in the direction Ron had pointed. His arm had thrust out in the opposite direction.

An official permit

In Tel Aviv, just before catching his plane, Ron went for a drive with a head of the Department of Antiquities. He told him of his experience and showed him the permit from the land owner. Immediately the Israeli official granted him an exploratory permit.

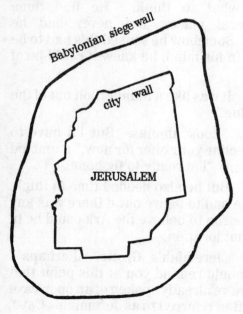

Let me explain here that it is the practice to grant an official excavation permit only to a full-time archaeologist, who should be connected with an acceptable sponsoring institution, such as a university.

I saw a report from the *Jerusalem Post*, in which Avi Eyton, a recent head of the Antiquities Department, confirmed this procedure.

In the above respects, Wyatt did not qualify. But the permit was not only granted – it was **offered** to him!

Evidently, the offer must have been built on confidence and trust from the earlier work Ron had done.

Here was a miraculous situation. First Ron's strange outburst about the Ark of the Covenant. Then the authority's enthusiastic response to a foreigner, especially as it related to the **most holy** artifact that Israel possessed.

Was a divine hand involved?

Clues to the location

So Ron Wyatt and his sons Danny and Ronny returned home. And then began some serious research.

I would eventually go down the same trail of investigation. And the following facts would emerge:

1 – The Ark vanished from recorded history between the 18th year of King Josiah (when it was moved back into Solomon's Temple) [2] and 35 years later, at the siege of Jerusalem, when the Temple was destroyed by the Babylonians.

2 – It was **not** seized and taken to Babylon, according to the list of items taken, which the Scripture gives us.[3]

3 – It was most likely hidden just prior to the destruction of the Temple.

4 – The city had been surrounded by Babylonian "forts... round about", a siege wall at a distance from the main city wall.[4] It would have been humanly impossible to take the Ark outside the siege wall. But it may have been possible for someone to have hidden the Ark near the city within the siege wall – in that no man's land – and not be detected. It could have escaped only by **not** being anywhere in the city.

Well, how far out from the city wall would the siege wall have been?

Siege walls were built by invading armies around cities at a distance beyond the range of weapons used by the defenders. We do know the type of weapons used some 100 years **before** the time of the Babylonian destruction of Jerusalem. The Second Book of Chronicles says that the defenders of Jerusalem had "engines" on the "towers" and "bulwarks" which shot "arrows" and "great stones".[5] "ENGINES INVENTED BY CUNNING MEN," it says.

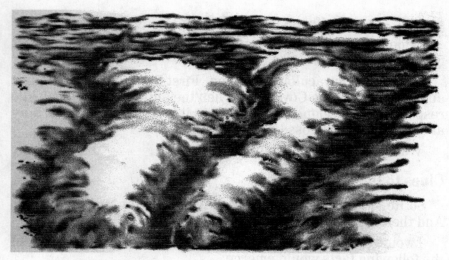

The hills Jerusalem was built upon: "Mt. Zion" is on the left; "Mt. Moriah" centre; the beginning of the Mt. of Olives can be seen far right

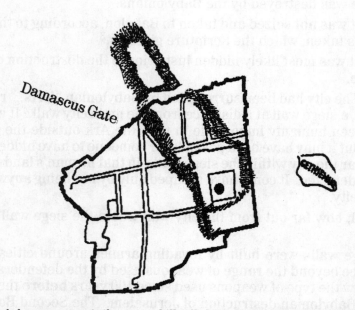

The shaded area represents the eastern hill called "Mt. Moriah". Outside of the northern city wall is a "dry moat" or "trench", cutting the hill into two sections. A portion of the northern section was once used as a quarry.

232

Labels on image:
- Dome of the Rock
- temple mount
- Mount Moriah
- North Wall
- "dry moat" or trench
- "the Calvary escarpment"
- The Moslem cemetery
- Mount Moriah

Aerial view of Jerusalem from the north-west. The white outline represents the approximate line of "Mt. Moriah".

Since catapults were capable of reaching over 1,000 feet, the siege wall would have been located beyond the range of these devices. This would position it further from the city wall than the site to which Ron had pointed.

So the site to which Ron had pointed would be outside of the ancient city wall, yet within the siege wall. That made sense.

And although it was a supposition, it was based upon study. It was enough upon which to base a decision. So Ron decided to go ahead and excavate.

Part of Mount Moriah

Old Jerusalem spreads over two hills, Mount Moriah and Mount Zion. Moriah was the place to which Abraham had been told to take his son for a sacrifice – and where later the Temple was built.[6]

On the western, southern and eastern sides of Jerusalem, there were valleys, but on the northern side the city was more vulnerable to attack.

So to protect the city on this northern side from foreign invasion, a "dry moat" or trench had been quarried out of Mount Moriah. This was to prevent an enemy from being able to break through the wall along this ridge. Then, at some unknown point in time, the northern portion of Mount Moriah outside the city was used as a stone quarry. Stone was cut out of the mountain, lowering the ground level to that of the trench which extended just outside of the north wall. In this way, the north part of Moriah became separated.

As we noted, the site to which Ron Wyatt pointed was along this quarried face of Mount Moriah. This cliff face is sometimes called "the Calvary escarpment", since it contains the "skull face" that many believe was *Golgotha* or *Calvary* where Yeshua was crucified.

Skull Hill execution site

We are informed in the New Testament writings that Jesus was crucified "**outside the city**"[7] at a place called "the Skull". [8] That word "**skull**" translates to "Calvary" in Latin, or "Golgotha" in Hebrew.

234

There is only one place around Jerusalem which has borne, and still bears, the name **Skull Hill**. It is just outside the North Wall, about 250 yards north-east of the Damascus Gate. A portion of this hill bears a striking resemblance to a human skull.

It is also the traditional site of burials for Moslems, Jews and Christians. And it was here, according to local tradition, that criminals were stoned to death. In the *Mishna,* this place is called **Beth ha-Sekelah**, literally, "House of Stoning".

Nearby is St. Stephen's Church, built over an old basilica that was erected to commemorate the stoning of Stephen, who became the first Christian martyr here, in 34 AD.

This was the recognized place of public execution for Jewish criminals. As late as the beginning of the 20th century, Jews would spit at the hill, throw stones and curse the "destroyer of their nation". It is such a site that the Roman authorities would have selected for executions.

We noted that the crucifixion of Yeshua occurred **outside** the city.

Skull Hill is just outside the Damascus Gate, the only direct exit from the Castle of Antonine (alleged place of trial).

Recent archaeological opinion also holds that the Damascus Gate, which today marks the northern boundary of the Old City, likewise marks the northern boundary of Jerusalem in the 30s, the time of Yeshua's crucifixion.

All this tends to add weight to the feasibility of Skull Hill, outside the wall, advocated by Otto Thenius (1842), Colonel Couder (1875) and General Gordon (1883), being the actual site.

One might note, in passing, that this rocky outcrop contains also what is known as a large complex of Jewish tombs dating from the First and Second Temple periods - and in particular, what is known as the "Garden Tomb", in which many believe Yeshua was buried.

The quarried face is hundreds of feet long.

Excavation begins

In January, 1979, Ron returned to Jerusalem with his two sons. They were to come back time and again, having little idea where they were even supposed to work.

Golgotha (Skull Hill) (Photo: Jonathan Gray)

Over the next few years the team was to spend hundreds of hours digging at that location.

A condition of the team's being permitted to excavate was that they must completely restore the above ground area before they departed.

An early member to the team was Bob Murrell. Bob, a dear friend, and an ex-Pan Am airline pilot, recalled to me that there was so much rubbish in front of the hill, that it filled several truckloads, before they could even start digging. Wheelbarrow loads of earth and rock were thrown onto the truck to be taken away.

To the human eye, the trash dump to which Ron had pointed appeared to hold very little promise.

In the area adjacent to the cliff, the ground had been raised to a much higher level today. That is, the original rock floor was many, many feet below the present ground level.

Over the centuries Jerusalem had been destroyed numerous times. The procedure with ancient cities was to rebuild on top of the destruction level. Today we do it differently: the debris is removed before rebuilding. But in the Middle East archaeologists are able to find evidences of many cities which have existed on the same site. In excavating down through each successive level to the next until they touch bedrock, they reach the first city to be established on that particular site.

An old photo of the "skull face" (known as Golgotha) in the "Calvary escarpment". Notice how the ground level rises to the left of the photo.

The spot the team was to excavate had a ground level many feet higher than the quarry floor to the south near the city wall. So they realized that, for starters, they would have to dig straight down.

At the location to which Ron had pointed, there was an extremely large boulder just barely exposed. So it was decided to dig several yards to the right.

Ron Wyatt in the excavation trench in front of the Calvary escarpment

One of the first photographs of the chiseled out "niches" in the cliff-face that the team discovered as they began to remove the earth along the escarpment (Photo: Ron Wyatt)

Many tons of rock and debris would eventually need to be removed And the men would have to sift through all of it for artifacts. This was a requirement of the Department of Antiquities. The teams always comply with such orders.

The job proved to be of mammoth proportions.

Niches in the cliff face

The "niches" after they had excavated down several more feet (Ron Wyatt)

The men dug straight down along the cliff face, forming a steep wall with the earth they removed. As the face of the cliff was exposed, almost immediately they noticed a large niche, like a shelf, cut into the cliff.

Further digging was to expose two more niches, each cut into the cliff, with another smaller niche to the right of these.

It appeared that these had been cut out to hold plaques or signs.

These were close to the "skull face", the place of executions. Three of them.

Ron concluded they were probably for placement of notices stating the crime of the execution victim in three languages.

Crucifixion as a deterrent

Available information on Roman crucifixions indicates that this form of punishment was used as a deterrent. The Roman writer Quintillian stated:

> Whenever we crucify criminals, very crowded highways are chosen, so that many shall see it and may be moved by fear

239

The author (right) and Bob Murrell, with one of the "niches" on the left (Photo: Jonathan Gray)

of it, because all punishment does not pertain so much to revenge as to example.[9]

The three basic elements of Roman crucifixion were:

1 - the scourging

2 - the carrying of the crossbeam by the condemned, to the site

3 - the nailing or binding of the condemned to the crossbeam, followed by attaching the beam onto the upright post and setting it up.

These three are perfectly described in the account of the crucifixion of Yeshua Messiah.

But for crucifixion to be a DETERRENT the CRIME of the condemned must be posted in clear sight of those passing by. A board covered in gypsum and inscribed with black letters (known as a "titilus") was posted above the cross.

Signs were large

In the report of Yeshua's crucifixion, John relates:

> And he bearing his cross went forth into a place called the place of a skull, which is called in the Hebrew Golgotha: Where they crucified him, and two other with him, on either side one, and Jesus in the midst. And Pilate wrote a title, and **put it on the cross**. And the writing was JESUS OF NAZARETH THE KING OF THE JEWS. This title then read many of the Jews: for the place there Jesus was crucified was nigh to the city: and it was written in Hebrew, and Greek, and Latin.[10]

We commonly assume that when Jesus was crucified a single sign was nailed to his cross above his head. This may be correct.

However, in order for passers-by to read signs written in THREE languages, such signs would have needed to be quite large, much larger than a hand-written notice on a paper. Such a sign nailed to a cross would have been almost impossible to read even by persons standing directly at the foot of the cross.

You can experiment yourself. Go down to a shopping center. You will find that shop signs even with letters 8 inches (20 centimeters) high are very difficult to read from across the street, or even closer.

Ron had signs made up in Greek, Latin and Hebrew — "Jesus of Nazareth, King of the Jews" — and set them up in the "niches". These signs, it was found, were quite visible from a distance and could have been seen easily by passers-by. (Ron Wyatt)

242

Three different languages were common in Jerusalem - Hebrew, Greek and Latin. The signs in three languages above Jesus' head were probably much larger than has been commonly assumed.

"Above the cross"

In reading and re-reading the accounts of these signs at Yeshua's crucifixion, one discovers that although John's account has been translated to read "ON the cross", the original Greek could just as accurately be translated "ABOVE the cross" or "OVER the cross".

In the above passage from John, we read that the "title" was put "on" the cross. The Greek word translated **on** is *epi*.

But in the following quote from Luke, the same word *epi* is translated to read **OVER**:

> And a superscription also was written **over him** in letters of Greek, and Latin, and Hebrew, THIS IS THE KING OF THE JEWS.

The word *epi* could not be translated to read **on** here! ("And a superscription also was written *epi* **(on)** him."? Obviously not.)

This same word *epi* is translated in other passages to read **above**.

Also notice Matthew's account:

> And they crucified him.... And sitting down they watched him there; And set up **over his head** his accusation written THIS IS JESUS THE KING OF THE JEWS.[12]

This much is clear. The comparative evidence from Scripture does not specify that the "title" was nailed onto the physical cross. All it states for sure is that the "title(s)" were placed **over**, **above** or **about**, the cross.[13]

So, with this understanding, and the information on Roman crucifixions and the "titulus" covered in gypsum and written in black ink, that the Romans were known to use, we consider that this conclusion - that large titles were placed in niches above the cross - should not be ruled out.

So the next morning, Ron said, "I'm going shopping."

"Food?" Danny queried. "We still have plenty."

"No," said Ron, "I'm going to buy some boards and paint."

An hour later, he was back, grinning. He had what he wanted. "OK, guys, a paint brush for each of you. I want you to splash these letters on."

They penciled on the Greek, Latin and Hebrew characters, shaped them in strong black paint and spread them over the earth to dry off.

An hour or so later, the plaques were set up in the niches in the cliff face, and photographed.

This demonstration proved to be useful. Subsequent digging showed that there were no more niches below these. Ron believed the much smaller niche was for the ever-present Roman eagle.

Digging continues

The team members continued to excavate straight down the cliff face, but the earth wall on the outer side began to show signs of instability and was so high they feared it could collapse upon them.

It was decided to move back along the cliff face to the original site to which Ron had pointed. That huge boulder just under the surface had deterred them, and they dreaded going back there to work, but now felt there was no choice.

Ron had felt justified in beginning the dig several yards from the original site, since it was in the same general area.

Now they began to dig around the large boulder and discovered there was enough space behind it to resume their dig.

But they were not prepared for what awaited them...

CHAPTER 22

GRUESOME FIND

The cliff face was different here. While at the first dig site it was fairly vertical like a wall, here the cliff face slanted inward, forming a "roof" over the place they were digging.

They started to dig downward behind the big rock, looking for an entrance to a cave or tunnel in the now buried lower cliff face.

Soon they came upon a hole carved into the cliff face. It was similar to the eye of a needle. A rope or something similar could be inserted through it.

"What can that be?" asked Danny.

"It's probably not important," replied his brother.

"Let's wait and see," suggested Ron. "It could be for anything. One thing's sure. It was chiseled out of the rock very carefully."

As we noted, the cliff slanted out overhead here.

During the course of digging, many pottery shards began to be uncovered. Some pieces were still intact.

Circular shaft

This turned out to be a long, long dig. They kept going straight down, looking for a buried opening in the cliff. Bedrock was reached at about 38½ feet down.

Now they began to clear sideways, gradually removing debris from all around. They found that they were standing at the bottom of a round chamber. It was approximately 15 feet across and carved out of the solid rock.

"Rope hole" chiseled into the cliff face (Photo: Ron Wyatt)

The grain bin that Ron and the boys discovered was a circular shaft with steps descending into it very similar to this water-shaft discovered in El-Jib which is believed to be the "pool of Gibeon".

246

Chiseled into the side were steps descending in a spiral from the top to the bottom.

There were signs that this had been a grain storage bin, but that over time it had been remodeled and plastered for reuse as a water cistern.

This could explain the "rope hole" higher up in the cliff. A rope which held a jug or a bucket could be lowered into the shaft, to retrieve either grain or water.

Chiseling through the plaster, Ron and the boys found much pottery among the debris that had been used as fill to form the cistern.

How old could this be? The men retrieved some of the pottery pieces and went off to the Antiquities Department to report the find.

The officials examined the pieces. "Some of these date back to the Jebusite period," said one of the men, an authority on ancient pottery of Palestine.

"That's before David took Jerusalem!" exclaimed Ron. "That's 3,000 years or more ago."

"Well, there are some later pieces here, as well," reported the Antiquities officer. "These would be from the Roman period."

This fact would indicate that the grain bin had been filled in partly with this pottery, then plastered over for a cistern, during Roman times.

This was indeed an exciting find. But it was not the purpose of the dig.

Back to work.

As the digging descended, it was possible to distinguish the Roman level from pottery pieces and some coins found inside the circular shaft. But, again, this was not why the men were here.

They covered over the shaft, taking care to preserve everything, then began to tunnel sideways below the present ground level, back toward the site they had originally dug – in the direction of the plaque holes. These were about 28 feet away.

Somewhere, it was felt, there had to be a hole in the cliff face – the entrance into a cave or tunnel.

So they tunneled underground against the cliff face. They were not prepared for the next find. It was gruesome.

The "place of stoning"

As the tunnel proceeded, it was discovered that the rock floor surrounding the cistern abruptly ended about three or four feet beyond it.

The men paused.

"I say we dig straight down here," said Ron.

They began to dig. But only three feet down they came upon something quite unusual. There was an enormous quantity of fist-sized stones, as well as larger ones.

Sorting through these rocks, they came upon a number of human bones, and in particular, some finger bones.

Now, to find rocks in an excavation is quite common. But it is not normal to find so many rocks of this particular size all together in such a large pile.

This was certainly not a tomb. The bones among the rocks – disarticulated bones – led to one conclusion: this had been a "stoning ground".

The book of Acts, describing the stoning of the apostle Stephen, says:

> Then they cried out with a loud voice, and stopped their ears, and ran upon him with one accord, and **cast him out of the city, and stoned him**.[1]

When it dawned on Ron what he had found, he quickly climbed out of the shaft. He was shaking. "Let's get on with the tunnel, boys."

Forever afterwards, that gruesome find would reflect on his face whenever he talked about it.

The tunnel continued to move in the direction of the original dig – toward the site of the plaque holes in the cliff face. The digging was slow, hard and tiring.

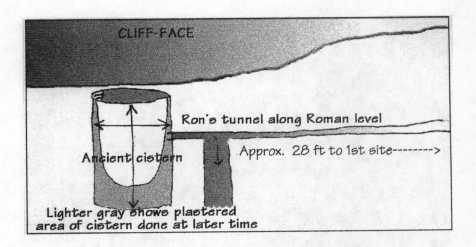

This simple diagram shows the buried Jebusite grain silo plastered and used by the Romans as a cistern, and the tunnel Ron dug along the Roman level. He found the massive pile of very large stones mingled with human bones in the narrow shaft to the right of the cistern. He did not excavate to discover how wide this area was. (Diagram: Ron Wyatt)

An ancient building

Soon the team members uncovered the remains of a buried structure. This building was adjacent to the cliff. Part of the rear wall actually ran along against the cliff face.

The foundations of this building were still in place. The structure was later determined to be 22 feet wide and 40 feet long.

From the rear wall there extended out horizontally a hewn stone. Ron's first impression was that this was an altar. Its top displayed smooth wear.

The plug

In front of this "altar stone", and below it, lay a large, squarish rock. It had become coated in travertine. (Travertine, for those who don't know, is deposited limestone, such as occurs when stalactites and stalagmites are formed.)

This squarish rock appeared too symmetrical to have been shaped naturally. Ron decided to pick it up and examine it more closely. In doing so, he found that there were actually finger handles on the two sides where you could put your fingers under it and lift it up.

Part of the building's foundation (Photo: Ron Wyatt)

More of the building (Photo: Ron Wyatt)

250

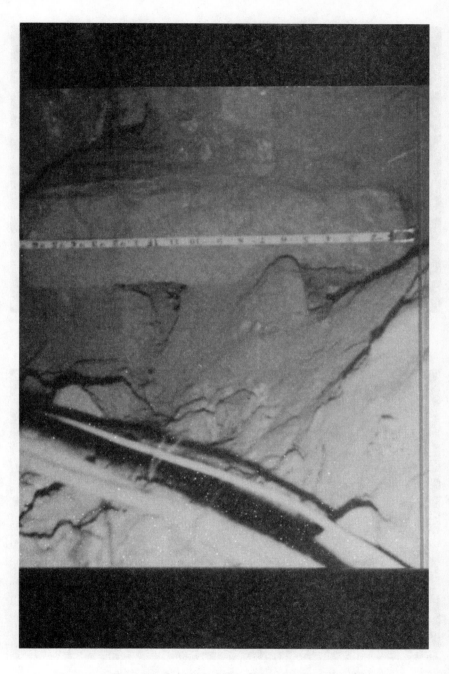

The "altar" extending out from the interior wall (Photo: Ron Wyatt)

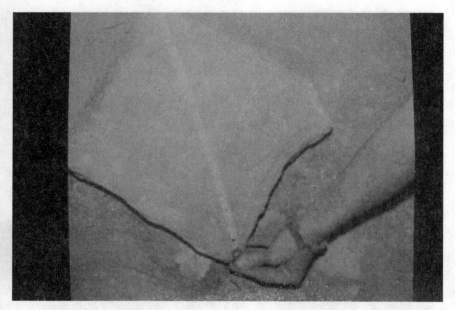

Measuring the squarish stone covered in travertine. It is approximately 13 inches square. (Photo: Ron Wyatt)

Jonathan Gray with the stone (Photo: Josephine Gray)

252

Photo: Jonathan Gray

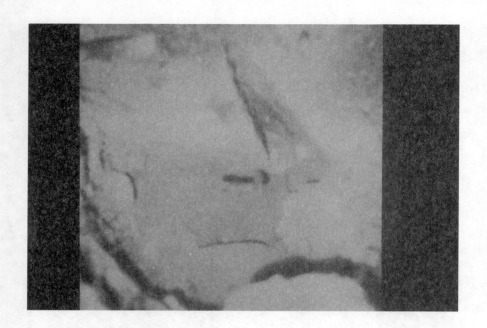

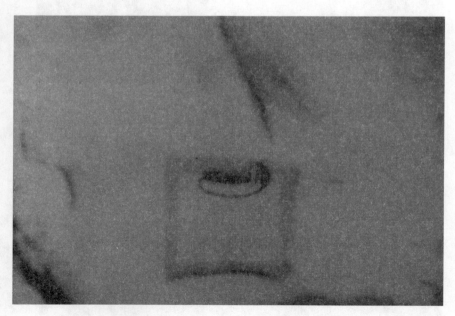

The squarish hole chiseled into the elevated 'bedrock "shelf" with a large crack extending out from it. There is a crow bar standing up within the hole to show the depth. (Photo: Ron Wyatt)

Raising this stone, the men found that it was covering a squarish hole chiseled into the bedrock.

The rock around the hole was recessed so that this "plug" would not fall all the way into the hole. The hole was similar to a post-hole, 13 inches by 14 inches in width, cut out of solid rock and going down about two feet. It was empty.

The squarish stone "plug" in the top of it was approximately 4 inches thick.

A tremendous volume of debris and dirt covered the whole site. As the boys cleared away the surrounding dirt, they discovered that the hole had a large crack extending out from it.

Crucifixion platform

As more rubble was cleared away, a shelf of limestone became visible. It extended out from the cliff face for about eight feet. A platform, if you like. And it was into this platform, or shelf, that the squarish hole had been chiseled.

They started digging out in front of the platform, into an area of packed earth.

Below this pack of earth, four feet lower down, was another, lower level of bedrock. Clearing this, they uncovered **three more** squarish holes, chiseled into this lower rock in front of the platform.

The excitement was mounting.

"Bring me the tape measure," Ron shouted.

They climbed up onto the higher platform which contained the first square hole with the crack. The tape measure was thrust up the cliff face, toward the three cut-out niches.

It was determined that the platform was 14 feet directly below the niches in the cliff face.

It had already been suspected that these niches on Skull Hill could be for signs stating the crucifixion victim's crime in the three languages of Jerusalem. Now the team had found more squarish holes, each 12 to 13 inches wide, cut into the bedrock – holes which, apparently, had once held crosses.

Danny looked back up at the hole elevated above the rest, on the shelf-like platform. It appeared that this was the place where the

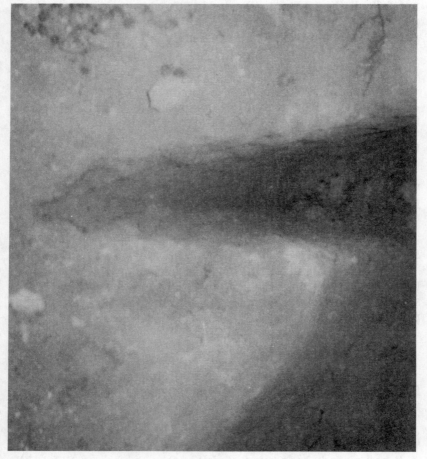

Closer-up of the crack in the cross-hole on the elevated bedrock shelf (Photo: Ron Wyatt)

"featured" criminal-victim was crucified, being elevated several feet above those crucified around him.

Had this hole held that of Jesus Christ?

The "plugs" in the cross-holes had the obvious use of preventing the holes from filling up when not in use, as well as preventing people and horses from breaking their legs.

Building encloses the site

Attention again focused on the building structure. From the intact remains, it was evident that a building had covered the entire site.

The stone wall extended along the base of the cliff directly behind the cross-hole on the platform-like shelf of bedrock.

A point of interest was that the "altar stone" (set in the stone wall) extended out horizontally almost directly above the elevated cross-hole.

The "crack"

As we have noted, there was a split in the rock running from the left side of the higher cross-hole. It was large. There was also another crack, this one vertical directly behind the cross-hole. The crack displayed no evidence of having been chiseled. Rather, it appeared to have been caused by an earthquake.

After the removal of debris, the cross-hole was measured and found to extend 23½ inches into the solid bedrock. The crack, however, appeared to extend much deeper.

But for now, no attempt was made to clear it out, or to measure it. It would be more than a year later before the team would find that the crack extended about 20 feet into the bedrock.

Not on a hilltop

We noted that these cross-holes were **not** on top of a hill, but on a **ledge** in the front of the hill.

Popular assumption has it that Jesus was crucified on TOP of a hill.

I suppose we got that idea from our artists. And so we assumed it to have been that way.

But did you know that the Scripture implies otherwise?

Matthew and Mark both record that "they that **PASSED BY** railed on him (reviled him), wagging their heads."[2]

From this we learn that the crucifixion site was at a place where people were PASSING BY – that is, **beside a public road.**

We have already noted that the Romans liked to crucify victims as an **example**, or a **warning**, to the populace. And to erect the crosses beside a crowded thoroughfare fulfilled this purpose well.

And now the team had uncovered the crucifixion site – and found it to be up against the Calvary escarpment close to the place of the Skull. It was near the Damascus Gate, on a ledge facing toward a public road, the old highway that led to Samaria.

Dating the building

Coins found during the course of the excavation helped to narrow the date of the building.

Ron Wyatt found a Roman coin bearing the impression of Tiberius Caesar, who reigned from 14 to 37 AD. This was the earliest dated coin the team found.

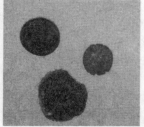 

Coins of the reign of Tiberius and the First Century AD *Penny of Emperor Tiberius*

The latest coins were from about 135 AD, but no later. This was consistent with the known history of Jerusalem and placed the date of the building between the time of the crucifixion of Yeshua and 135 AD.

After Jerusalem was destroyed in 70 AD, the area was only a Roman camp with the occasional non-Jew living there. Apparently, there was a measure of toleration of Christians by the local Roman authority. In 130, when the emperor Hadrian came to rebuild Jerusalem as a Roman city, calling it Aelia Capitolina, he showed favor to Christians, while forbidding any Jew to ever set foot in the city again. This and other acts helped to trigger a Jewish revolt in 132, which was disastrous for the Jews.

Since the coins found in the ancient building cease at about 135, it appears that whoever built and used this structure abandoned it shortly afterward.

Gradually, over time, it was covered in debris. The evidence showed that the structure had not been disturbed since Roman times.

"A very great stone"

Continued clearing of the area out from the cliff face revealed the building to be very simple in shape. The rear wall abutted the cliff face and ran along the top of the elevated platform section of bedrock. Two walls ran out, one from each end of it, at right-angles.

As the men dug within the building, they uncovered a portion of a large, flat rock, which was a little less than **two feet thick**. I would like you to remember that measurement. We shall meet it again.

The edge now exposed was curved, somewhat like that of a large, thick, rounded table-top.

As the men cleared away more dirt and debris, it became apparent that the stone was enormous.

They stopped digging. The dirt and debris piled over it was ten feet deep. It would be several years later before its true dimensions were to be determined by sub-surface radar from above the ground. The diameter was found to be **13 feet 2 inches!** Thirteen feet two inches. Remember that measurement also, as we shall return to it again.

If the building had been constructed to enclose BOTH the crucifixion site AND this great, round stone, then **WHAT COULD BE ITS SIGNIFICANCE?**

Why had this great stone been placed inside the building?

One found it hard to sleep. The questions began flooding in...

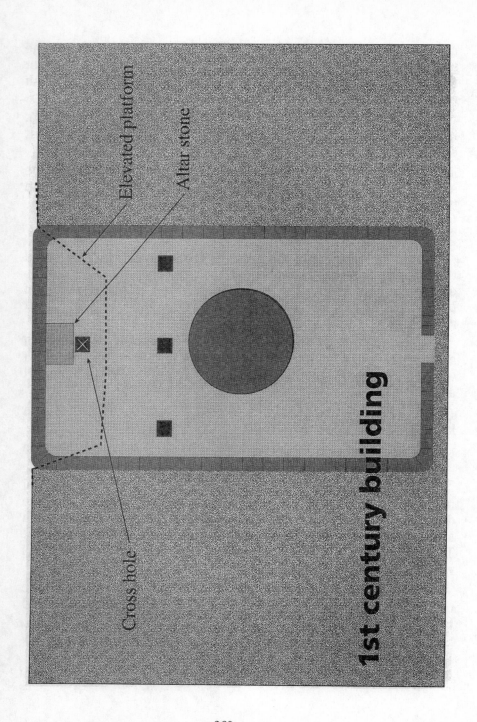

Elevated platform

Altar stone

Cross hole

1st century building

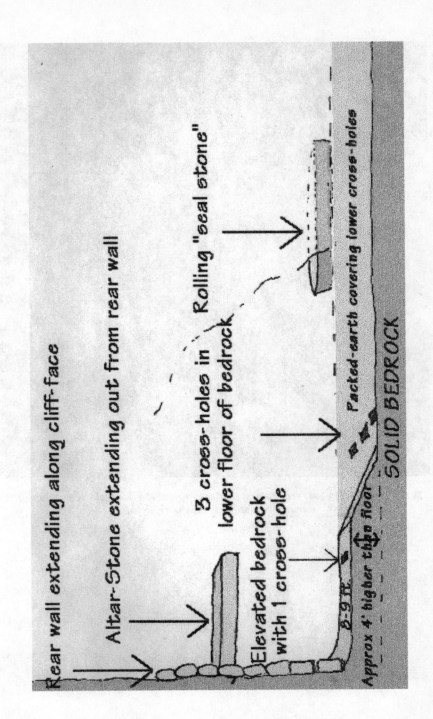

Rear wall extending along cliff-face

Altar-Stone extending out from rear wall

3 cross-holes in
lower floor of bedrock

Rolling "seal stone"

Elevated bedrock
with 1 cross-hole

Packed-earth covering lower cross-holes

8-9 ft.

Approx 4' higher than floor

SOLID BEDROCK

The Garden Tomb in 1867 soon after it was discovered. The door, which was damaged during excavation, was later repaired.

CHAPTER 23

THE LINK

"Now **in the place where he was crucified** there was a garden; and in the garden a new sepulchre, wherein was never man yet laid. There they laid Jesus... for **the sepulchre was near at hand**."[1]

John, a first century witness, furnishes us with a THREE-STRAND LINK:

1 – the Skull Hill crucifixion site

2 – a surrounding garden, and

3 – a nearby tomb.

Nearby... a tomb

In 1867, in the same cliff face not far from where our team would later work, a landowner was digging a cistern on his property, when he discovered a tomb cut into the cliff face. As with Ron's excavation site, this tomb was beneath the current ground level, covered in the debris of many centuries. It was at about the same depth as the sites our team was excavating.

Several cisterns were also unearthed at this spot. These suggested that in the first century an olive grove could have existed here.

One of the cisterns was very large – and it dated back to the first century or earlier. Lying some twelve feet below the pavement against the east wall, it could hold about 200,000 gallons of water, sufficient to keep a large plantation green throughout the eight dry months of the year.

The Garden Tomb (Photo: Jonathan Gray)

In 1924, a very fine wine press was excavated near the present main entrance to the garden. This indicated that there was also a vineyard nearby.

Of course the discovery of a tomb in this vicinity could hardly be described as sensational. Many tombs had been found in this large, ancient burial area of Jerusalem.

But this tomb was of special interest.

When a tomb is seen to be unusual (and we shall address that shortly), and is seen to be adjacent to an ancient execution site, as well as in the setting of a garden, such a combination of factors is not to be taken lightly.

In 1883, General Gordon, the notable British soldier, came to the area – and became convinced that the "skull face" was the true Golgotha.

This prompted him to go looking for a tomb that was "near at hand", as indicated in the Bible.

And just a few hundred feet away was this tomb, today known as the Garden Tomb.

Although first discovered in 1867, it was not excavated until 1891. At that time, Dr. Conrad Schick prepared a report with diagrams, which was published in the *Palestine Exploration Fund Quarterly* of April, 1892.

This tomb became the prime suspect for being the tomb of Jesus Christ. However, strenuous opposition arose from adherents of the traditional "Holy Sepulcher" tourist site inside the Old City.

The Church of the Holy Sepulcher had been built by the Roman emperor Constantine in 333 AD, on a site selected by his mother, Helena. Helena, by the way, bequeathed to future tourists something else – the "fake" Mount Sinai in Egypt.[2]

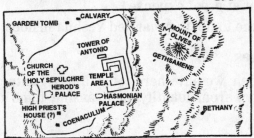

265

Many scholars have asserted that this site of the Holy Sepulcher church could have been outside the city wall in Jesus' time. It is INSIDE the wall today.

However, prevailing archaeological opinion is that the wall is now just where it was in Jesus' day. And also that the actual place of Yeshua's crucifixion was the "Skull Hill" outside the city wall.

Soon this new tomb site, the "Garden Tomb", gained some supporters.

"First century"

Once excavation of the tomb was completed, characteristics were noted which did prove it to be dated to the first century of the Christian era, the time of Yeshua the Messiah.

Dame Kathleen Kenyon, the famous British archaeologist, said in 1970, "It is a typical tomb of about the first century AD." [3]

Joseph of Arimathea

It was the Jewish Sanhedrin, a council of leading men, who had plotted Yeshua's death. One of their number, who had previously defended Jesus, now came forward and asked the Roman governor for the condemned man's body.

This council man was Joseph, of a town called Arimathea. Joseph was one of the wealthiest men in Israel.

Joseph and a colleague named Nicodemus lowered the body from the cross, covered it with myrrh and aloes they had brought, and wrapped it in a white linen shroud.

Joseph and his helpers did not go far with their precious burden, since there was a garden nearby, and in that garden was Joseph's own sepulcher, which Joseph had built for himself and his family, no doubt at great expense.

Arriving at the tomb, they carried Yeshua inside.

Eight vital clues

Very well, then, we have here today a first century tomb. But that is a far cry from identifying it as the tomb of Joseph of Arimathea.

We need evidence. Is there any way the biblical accounts might assist us? Indeed, in those ancient writings I was able to find eight clues.

According to John, Matthew and Luke, the tomb of Joseph had special characteristics:

1 – It was near the place of crucifixion.[4]

2 – It was in a garden.[5]

3 – It was carved out of the rock.[6]

4 – It was a rich man's tomb.[7]

5 – The disciples could look into the tomb from outside.[8]

6 – There was standing room for a number of persons.[9]

7 – It was a new tomb and not an old tomb renewed.[10]

8 – The tomb was closed by rolling a GREAT stone over the entrance.[11]

In every one of these particulars, the tomb discovered in 1867 matched the biblical description. It fitted like a glove.

A rich man's tomb

Entering the tomb, one is impressed with the size. Certainly, only a rich man could have afforded a tomb such as this. Inside the tomb, to the right, was a spot for the owner of the tomb to be laid – and close to that, another spot, possibly for his wife. To the left, a large room was cut out for mourners to stand.

Used by a different person

But this tomb was **not** used by the person or persons for whom it had been cut out. Inside the tomb, one section carved out of the rock to fit one man, has clearly been enlarged for somebody else – someone who was taller than the man for whom the tomb had been measured. This enlarged section indicates that not the owner, but **some other person**, was laid in this rich man's tomb.

The ancient record states that Joseph, a member of the Sanhedrin, took the body of Yeshua and "laid it in his own new tomb", "wherein was never man yet laid."[12] Is this spot in the tomb that was enlarged for someone's feet, another link in the evidence?

A most remarkable feature of Jesus' entombment is that, although he was executed as a criminal and so should **not** have

267

Inside the tomb: the place where the body was laid

received the dignity of normal burial, yet his body was rescued from 'disgrace' and laid in a grave of highest rank!

Yet this very event was prophesied concerning the Messiah, many centuries earlier:

> He made his grave with the wicked but with the rich in his death.[13]

The mathematical odds against such an event are enormous.

A new or uncompleted tomb

The existence of the cavity in the receptacle at the tomb's north-east corner, and the absence of this cavity in the south-east receptacle, as well as the unfinished groove toward the north end of the west wall, show clearly that the tomb was never completed.

A "great" stone

Something else. Matthew records that Joseph, after placing the body in his own new tomb, "rolled a great stone to the door of the sepulchre, and departed."[14]

The text goes out of its way to say **"great"** stone. This clue, that it was a GREAT stone, is another evidence that the owner of the tomb was a rich man.

Someone else was also interested in this tomb. The Jewish chief priests and Pharisees went to Pilate, the Roman governor, saying:

> Sir, we remember that that deceiver said, while he was yet alive, After three days I will rise again. Command therefore that the sepulchre be made sure until the third day, lest his disciples come by night, and steal him away, and say unto the people, He is risen from the dead, so the last error shall be worse than the first. Pilate said unto them, Ye have a watch: go your way, make it as sure as ye can. So they went, and made the sepulchre sure, sealing the stone, and setting a watch.[15]

The missing seal stone

Immediately in front of the tomb is a stone trench, or trough. This was for the rolling of a stone to seal the doorway.

At the left end is an incline. The stone was rolled onto the trough at this end.

Josephine Gray in the trough that runs in front of the tomb for rolling the seal-stone

(Photo: Jonathan Gray)

Late in 1995, I took another archaeological team to Jerusalem. We measured this trough which was built to channel the rolling stone. We found this trough to be – wait for it – about **two feet** wide!

At the right hand end of the trough is a large stone block, positioned to prevent further movement of the seal-stone toward the right. Above that, on the right hand face of the tomb itself, a ridge was cut in the rock, which would block the stone from rolling further in that direction.

In the face of the tomb were two evidences which showed that a very, very large seal-stone was once used to seal this tomb.

In the right side of the tomb face, team member Dr. Nathan Meyer had on an earlier visit pointed out a hole which was pierced into the cliff face. The hole held the oxidized remains of an iron shaft. This has since been removed, but the hole remains.

On the left hand side of the tomb face, another hole had been pierced into the rock for the insertion of a metal shaft, to prevent the seal-stone from being rolled to the left and the tomb being opened.

On Friday, October 20, at 4 pm, team members Dr. David Wagner and Peter Mutton measured across the tomb face from the shaft hole on the left to the ridge at the right. The distance was discovered to be – you guessed it – precisely **13 feet 2 inches!**

This shows that the seal-stone was "a very great stone" - over twice the diameter of any other seal-stone found! To our knowledge, the largest seal-stone previously found was 5 feet 6 inches.

This and the size of the buried stone were a PERFECT MATCH.

The link

Now for the LINK.

We have noted that close to Golgotha, the place of the Skull, is the crucifixion site, now enclosed by the remains of a first century building.

A short distance away is a rich man's tomb, not used by him, but by someone else.

The "great stone" from this tomb is missing.

The block which prevented the seal-stone from rolling any further to the right (Jonathan Gray)

The author examining the "catch flange" at the right hand side of the tomb, which stopped the rolling-stone (Photo: Jonathan Gray)

But nearby – right inside that first century building – we find a seal-stone which matches perfectly.

Excitement was hard to suppress as we saw absolute proof of something we had until now only suspected – the link between this burial site and the nearby crucifixion site.

Who did it? Who considered it **so important** as to place a building around both the crucifixion site **AND** that seal-stone, enclosing them **together?**

Who, in the first century, during the reign of Tiberius, considered this LINK to be significant?

My mind was racing. Did Joseph of Arimathea acquire that whole garden area surrounding his tomb and the nearby crucifixion site? Was it he? Did the early Christians make this connection?

Of this much I was certain. By placing a building to enclose both the crosshole AND the seal-stone from the tomb, someone had linked the two.

Oh, I should tell you. In front of the tomb there was cut out of the bedrock what appeared to have been a font for baptisms by immersion (now mostly filled in), as well as a squarish trough for foot-washing – both early Christian practices.

Such evidence suggests that the early Christians revered this particular tomb site as special.

There is evidence that in later times Christians continued to have a special regard for this spot.

On an inside wall of the tomb is a cross. On the front of the tomb, outside, is the sign of an anchor, an early Christian symbol. And there are indications that a building, possibly a church, was erected in front of the tomb itself.

To date, the custodians of the Garden Tomb have shown a responsible attitude in stating only that this **could** be a candidate for the tomb of Jesus Christ.

Is this Garden Tomb the tomb of Joseph of Arimathea and the one in which Yeshua rested over the Sabbath, and from which he arose, gaining the victory over the grave for each of us? I believe the new evidence deserves serious consideration. I consider it to be overwhelming.

273

Our crew members noted chisel marks radiating inward across the face of the tomb where the great slab of stone was removed to be shaped into a giant seal-stone.

Mystery of the iron shaft

Now let me comment on something wonderful.

We photographed and video-taped the spot where the Romans drove the iron shaft into the stone face of the tomb at the left edge of where the thirteen foot seal-stone would have been. They had done this in an attempt to prevent the stone from being rolled to the side and the tomb being opened. The record states that the stone was "sealed".[16]

The metal shaft on the left which held the stone in place was about two fingers in thickness. It would be impossible to bend this shaft, much less snap it off, simply by pushing the seal-stone against it. To move the great stone even one inch, the shaft must first be taken out.

However, when we examined the hole that held the metal shaft, we found that the shaft was still in there! What was left of it, that is. It was sheared off, level with the wall. The appearance of the metal was consistent with its having been sheared off when struck with a tremendous force from the right-hand side.

According to an engineer, the shear strength of this peg was approximately 60 to 80 tons. To put it another way, a metal peg of such thickness would withstand 60 to 80 tons' pressure before it actually snapped off.

Imagine, if you can, ten tip trucks all compressed together -or all the materials for two brick houses squeezed together - and suddenly dropped onto the iron peg. That is the pressure involved.

However, being soft and malleable, the peg might have taken **more than** 60 to 80 tons' pressure, bending first before it sheared right off.

The engineer confirmed my conclusion. "I could see that the end had been torn slightly sideways - perhaps a quarter inch - to the left, even though it was now rusted some. It was an incredible sight, to witness what had happened," he said. "Accomplished by moving the stone in one simple move." He calculated that the stone itself weighed around 13.8 tons.

It would be impossible, humanly speaking, to snap off that metal shaft **from a dead stop.** There was no leverage.

The seal-stone has gone.

Someone pushed the stone aside without taking out the metal peg... Who was it?

The disciple Matthew informs us that the power involved was angelic – super human: "... the angel of the Lord descended from heaven, and came and rolled back the stone from the door."[17]

The evidence shows that the stone was moved **with great speed**, by some colossal force WITHOUT TAKING OUT THE METAL ROD.

Could that sheared off metal shaft still visible in the wall be proof of a supernatural opening of the tomb? Is this a physical witness to the miraculous resurrection of Yeshua the Messiah?

A wonderful find... but where was the Ark of the Covenant cave? Ron's search must continue.

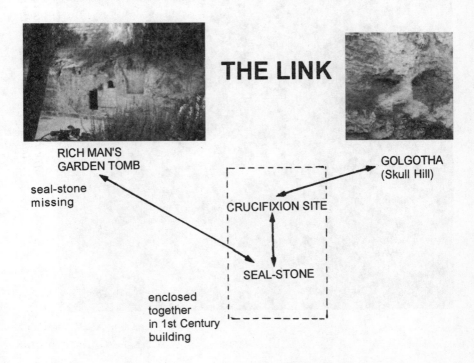

THE LINK

RICH MAN'S
GARDEN TOMB

seal-stone
missing

GOLGOTHA
(Skull Hill)

CRUCIFIXION SITE

SEAL-STONE

enclosed
together
in 1st Century
building

The distance was measured from the hole for the iron shaft on the left to the "catch flange" on the right (Photo: Jonathan Gray)

Dr. Nathan Myer points to a hole in the right hand side of the tomb face which held the oxidized remains of an iron shaft that was used to help secure the seal-stone.

How the seal-stone would have appeared in place

The hole on the left, with the iron shaft still in it (Photo: Jonathan Gray)

CHAPTER 24

"THE DEAD MAN'S ALIVE!"

The following could have been an "on the spot" news account by a reporter in Jerusalem on Nisan 16, in 31 AD:

NAZARENE REPORTED ALIVE

Executed Victim Reported Alive by Roman Guards

City in Uproar

JERUSALEM, NISAN 16, 3rd Hour.

Early this morning, not long before daybreak, several Roman soldiers were seen running toward the city from Skull Hill north of Jerusalem. According to witnesses they were very frightened. As they ran by in frantic haste they cried, "HE'S ALIVE! The dead man's ALIVE!" They sped past the tower of Antonia, on by the Temple area, and were just passing the Council Chamber when several priests stepped out and hurried them inside.

Those soldiers were a special detail that was assigned to guard the tomb of the man who was crucified the day before yesterday. He was a teacher from Galilee, called Yeshua.

Quite a crowd had gathered by the time the Romans left the building. The soldiers passed the word through the crowd that the disciples of Yeshua had stolen the body out of the sepulcher while they were asleep. Gradually the people dispersed, but there are some unanswered questions in the minds of many in Jerusalem this morning.

Why did the soldiers go into the Council Chambers telling one story and come out telling quite another? Why were they so self-assured in confessing to sleeping on duty? The death penalty is mandatory for this offense. It very much appears that this tale about sleeping on duty is concocted to keep the truth from the people. But what is the truth? Where are the facts?

This whole affair has been conducted with unusual secrecy as if there were something to hide. The accused was taken prisoner sometime after midnight the day before yesterday in an olive garden east of the city on the west slope of the Mount of Olives. He reportedly put up no resistance and would not permit any of his followers to resist.

The authorities and the mob were led to Gethsemane Garden by a disaffected disciple, Judas Iscariot. He was aware of this private retreat used by Yeshua and his followers.

The trial was conducted before daybreak, which is highly irregular – in fact, illegal. Before the city was awake to what was happening, or before the followers of Yeshua could organize an opposition to the proceedings, they were faced with a "fait accompli". The trial had been held and the Roman Procurator had reluctantly given his consent to the execution.

Yeshua was crucified about three hours after sunrise. Six hours later he was dead. It is very unusual for death to take place so soon after crucifixion. If Yeshua had been sick or old it would not be so surprising, but he was only a little over thirty-three years of age, and was in perfect physical condition. He was buried in a tomb near Skull Hill, the place of the execution.

It seems highly probable that an innocent man has been accused, condemned, and put to death. If this proves to be so, the responsibility for this act will rest on the Sanhedrin, and especially the chief priests Annas, and Caiaphas, his nephew. Their hatred and jealousy of Yeshua of Nazareth have been obvious for quite some time.

The story is circulating that the trial was conducted under these secret conditions because the authorities were afraid of the people. As a matter of fact, Yeshua had a tremendous following, especially among the common people. He is said to have healed their sick, and some say that he raised a man from death in Bethany a few weeks ago.

He has on several occasions made astounding predictions which have happened just as he said they would. For several weeks he has been predicting his own death. He also predicted that on the third day after his death, he would miraculously rise from the dead. Today is the third day!- *Simon Abrahams.*

◆◆◆◆◆◆

If it was a hoax that established worldwide Christianity, if its central character Jesus Christ never rose from the dead, then what became of his body within three days after burial must be THE WORLD'S MOST INTRIGUING UNSOLVED MYSTERY.

We all love mysteries. And I remember the day I sat in a backpacker's hostel discussing this very matter with a tourist from Sweden. His name was Leif.

Yeshua's "resurrection": a later invention?

"For starters," said Leif, "I do not believe that Jesus Christ rose from the dead. That story is history's biggest fraud."

"Oh yes?"

"That tale was inserted into the writings years later, to glorify a dead hero." Leif was serious.

"I see. Tell me, Leif, the people involved in this fraud, as you call it... that sect known as Christians. When did it actually come into being? Would you agree it was during the reign of the Roman emperor Tiberius?"

"I suppose."

"Leif, that is firmly established, historical fact, is it not?"

"No contest on that, Jonathan. But the resurrection tale, that evolved later."

I leaned forward. "Let me ask you, Leif, what was it that brought these Christians into existence IN THE REIGN OF TIBERIUS? I suggest to you, it was nothing less than the **belief** that Jesus had recently **risen from the dead**! Even pagan writers and scholars attest this.

"Since this is so, Leif, then how could the resurrection of the dead be a **later** invention of Christians? Rather, it was the **very beginning** of their belief, the very **strength and impetus** of their faith. It was the very **reason** for their religion and their fervent hope!

"What I am saying, Leif, is that the CAUSE and BEGINNING of Christian faith was the bodily resurrection of Jesus."

"Oh, come off it, Jonathan, the story of Jesus was not written down until the second, third or fourth century. Quite a long time after the alleged event!"

It just happened that in my bag was some information on this question. I bent down, opened my briefcase and pulled it out. "Have you heard of Professor William Albright?" I asked.

"Who's he?"

"One of the world's foremost biblical archaeologists, no less. Listen to his summary of the findings:

> Regardless of whatever else the Dead Sea Scrolls tell us, one thing is certain. We know now that none of the New Testament could have been written after AD 80."[1]

Leif stared at the statement.

"This means, Leif, that the complete account was already written before the death of the first disciples, and much of it a long time before."

"You mean," he said, "it did **not** come to be accepted, or inserted, into the Bible later."

"Right," I responded. "These people at first had no written records of Yeshua's resurrection. Rather, they had PERSONAL attestation, LIVING eye-witnesses, PERSONAL EXPERIENCES OF THEIR OWN upon which to base their faith. They rested their sound and fervent faith, NOT on some 'records' but on what they had seen WITH THEIR OWN EYES! Any subsequent records of a LATER date were the **RESULT OF THEIR FAITH**. What I am trying to say is, it was **not** written records that brought their faith into existence.

"Paul, himself a one-time skeptic, could later say before King Agrippa, 'For the king KNOWS of these things (of the resurrection of the dead), before whom also I speak freely, for I am persuaded that NONE of these things are HIDDEN from him, for **THIS THING WAS NOT DONE IN A CORNER.**'[2]

"The resurrection of Jesus was a TALKED-OF, DISCUSSED, WELL-KNOWN EVENT that swept the entirety of the Roman empire in a short time."

Leif flushed a little. "It had to be a face-saving device, I tell you, on the part of a small bunch of fanatics."

"OK, Leif. Suppose you're right. Tell me this. Do invented stories of that kind have the power to transform character and inspire men and women, and even boys and girls, to suffer indescribable horrors of persecution and die martyrs' deaths? If it was just deception, then how do you explain the radiant joy on the faces of the sufferers and the prayers upon their lips as they asked for the forgiveness of those who inflicted the pain? Nothing, absolutely nothing, could withstand their testimony. WHAT THEY SAID 'TURNED THE WORLD UPSIDE DOWN.' When challenged, they replied simply, 'We cannot but speak the things which we have seen and heard.'[3]

"How do you account for this?"

Leif looked thoughtful.

"Peter, on Pentecost day fifty days later, did not speak to the crowd as a man who knew he was proclaiming a lie, but as one conscious of the undeniable fact that Yeshua Messiah had risen from the dead. That was the main theme of his gripping message. Nobody could contradict him. No one attempted to deny it. The evidence of Jesus' resurrection swept on, to close pagan temples, to cast down idols, to lift men into nobility, and bring hope to a society in despair. Yeshua had said, 'I am the resurrection and the life.' Let me ask you, my friend, Could YOU say that?"

"Yes, I could say that!"

"But could you make anyone believe it?"

There was silence.

This greatest of all miracles was **universally believed** throughout the entire confines of the early church. A powerful impact was felt because the immediate followers of Yeshua who had seen him PUBLICLY EXECUTED and PUBLICLY BURIED, had even WALKED AND TALKED WITH HIM AFTER HIS RESURRECTION.

A forceful, firm belief in all that he was, and in all that he claimed to be, has gripped men, delivered them from the power of enslaving habits and accomplished miracles of transformation in human lives, for multitudes in each generation ever since.

If Yeshua had not risen from the dead, there would never have been Christianity – nor the New Testament writings.

But let me tell you about the strange experience of Gilbert West and Lord Lyttleton...

CHAPTER 25

WHO STOLE THE BODY?

Two bright young men – avowed skeptics – went up to Oxford. One was the eminent Gilbert West, and the other was Lord Lyttleton, the famous English journalist.

These two men agreed that Christianity must be destroyed. They also agreed that to destroy it, two things were necessary:

1 – They must prove that Jesus never rose from the tomb.

2 – They must prove that Saul of Tarsus was never converted to Christianity.

Now they divided the task between them, West assuming the responsibility for the RESURRECTION, and Lyttleton and his great mind, caring for the EXPERIENCE OF SAUL on the Damascus road.

They were to give themselves plenty of time - twelve months or more, if necessary.

••••••

West entered the driveway of the Porteur mansion. It had been the second snowfall this winter. Smoke spiraled up from the living room chimney. West's neighbor was a "religious nut", a good "victim" upon which to sharpen his wits.

He was ushered into a large office. Porteur looked up.

"Gilbert, my dear man. Such a rare thing... To what do I owe this pleasure?"

The men sat for a time, exchanging gossip. Then West moved in.

"Porteur, I am going to demolish the resurrection myth. Do you dare give me an hour of your time?"

"Why not?" grinned the other man. "So what's on your mind?"

Did not die?

"Well, to be frank with you, Jesus didn't die on the cross."

"Interesting," responded Porteur. "Then what happened?"

"He took a narcotic drug that fooled the Romans. Or else he was in a swoon when they took him off the cross and put him in the tomb. Somehow he escaped it, and journeyed off to a far place to live out his natural life and die of old age. That's what happened."

Porteur smiled. Was West serious? Yes, he looked like he meant it.

Porteur spoke. "What you say about him taking a drug to induce unconsciousness on the cross, let me tell you something. That is incompatible with the very nature of crucifixion."

"What do you mean?" asked West.

"In crucifixion, the arms being spread out and the hanging body, raises the rib cage and drops the diaphragm to the maximum. This means the victim can breathe only by raising the body - and this requires the use of the large muscles of the legs, if it is to be maintained for any length of time. This is why the legs of those crucified were broken to hasten death: death by suffocation would follow within minutes.

"I tell you, Gilbert, if Jesus had taken a drug in sufficient quantity to induce unconsciousness while hanging on the cross, it would not have taken a spear thrust to hasten his death. He would have been dead before his friends could have taken him down. Your idea falls apart with this one elementary fact."

"Just a minute," retorted West. "The Bible says that after Jesus was laid in the tomb that 'they prepared spices and ointment' and brought these to the tomb. If Jesus was dead, what were the ointments for? A dead body needs no medical treatment."[1]

"Spices and ointment? My dear friend, they were simply to treat the body of the dead, according to custom," smiled Porteur. "A practice related to embalming. Surely you must know that. And ponder carefully: his own mother and others with her had actually seen him die. They weren't coming to treat a sick man.

286

"And something else. Just think! When a person has been BEATEN and WHIPPED until he is so EXHAUSTED he literally COLLAPSES on the public streets, when he has been UP all one day and all one night, and part of another, being BUFFETED ABOUT, KICKED and SPIT UPON, when he has been WITHOUT FOOD OR WATER, and LASHED WITHIN AN INCH OF HIS LIFE, finally to have SPIKES driven through his hands and feet, to HANG IN THE BLAZING SUN for hours, then to have a huge spear PLUNGED INTO HIS SIDE, with great spurts of gushing blood and fluids pouring out of his body; when his lifeless, limp body has been TAKEN DOWN from the stake, carefully wrapped in grave clothes and laid away in a tomb - COULD THERE BE ANY QUESTION THAT HE WAS **DEAD**?

"But... suppose there could be the **remote** chance that Jesus wasn't dead? Tell me, how could he ever, in such a horribly wounded condition, weak and exhausted, remove a huge stone to escape the tomb, a stone that required several Roman soldiers, in all their youth and strength to move?

"Remember, the Jews were carefully **guarding** against this possibility. They had said to the governor, Pilate, 'Sir, we remember that deceiver said, while he was yet alive (showing they FIRMLY believed him now to be DEAD), After three days I will rise again. Command therefore that the sepulcher be MADE SURE until the third day, lest his disciples come by night, and steal him away, and say unto the people, He is risen from the dead, so the last error shall be worse than the first.' Pilate co-operated. He replied, 'Ye have a watch, go your way, MAKE IT AS SURE AS YE CAN.'

"To suggest that Jesus had only 'swooned', as you say, is to deny logic, reason, historical fact, and sanity itself!

"You see, West, they made sure the stone could never even be opened FROM THE OUTSIDE - let alone from the INSIDE, by a mortally wounded man. The record says, 'they went, and made the sepulcher **sure**, SEALING THE STONE, and setting a WATCH.'[2]

"When the stone WAS rolled back, it was NOT done by secretive men at night, but by a powerful heavenly being. The watchers who had been set to guard the tomb FAINTED DEAD AWAY AT THE SIGHT OF HIM. This was **not** some **secretive** thing, but a TREMENDOUS, AWESOME, GLORIOUS EVENT.[3]

"Yet there is even stronger proof that it was more than just a swoon from which he recovered."

"What do you mean?" asked West.

"I mean," replied Porteur, "that it is impossible that a man who had stolen half-dead out of the grave, who crept about weak and ill, wanting medical treatment, who required bandaging, strengthening, and care, could have given to the disciples the impression that he was a conqueror over death, the Prince of Life - an impression that lay at the bottom of their future work. It could hardly have changed their sadness into enthusiasm, or lifted their reverence into worship of him."

"I suppose you've made a fair point," conceded West. "So he died. We all die. But it's really this resurrection nonsense I refuse to swallow."

West excused himself. He would begin his investigation in the town library. Then he'd tear the biblical account to shreds.

Historian, concerning Jesus

However, he was soon a little perturbed to discover what Josephus - who was not a Christian - had written concerning Jesus:

> Now there was about this time Jesus... And when Pilate, at the suggestion of the principal men among us, had condemned him to the Cross, those that loved him at the first did not forsake him; for he appeared to them alive again the third day... And the tribe of Christians, so named from him, are not extinct to this day.[4]

Joseph Scaliger, a man highly familiar with Josephus' work, concludes:

> Josephus is the most diligent and the greatest lover of truth of all writers: nor are we afraid to affirm of him, that it is more safe to believe him, not only as to the affairs of the Jews, but also as to those that are foreign to them, than all the Greek and Latin writers, and this, because his fidelity and his compass of learning are everywhere conspicuous.[5]

Josephus was not to be dismissed out of hand.

West was not unduly worried. He knew the New Testament writers would trip themselves up and be easy to discredit.

The empty tomb

This was a fact no one disputed: three days after the crucifixion, **the tomb was empty**. Romans, Jews and followers of Yeshua all checked it - and all admitted that.

Unless they went to the wrong tomb!

Yes, that was it. Those women who came on Sunday morning and reported the tomb was empty must have gone to the wrong tomb.

But as West thought about it a little more, he saw some difficulty there.

How could three or more people so soon forget the place where they had laid a loved one? After all, they had seen exactly which tomb the body was laid in, because they themselves had put it there![6]

In any case, would not Yeshua's enemies soon have found the right tomb, and exposed those deluded women and other followers of Yeshua who said he had risen?

West the skeptic was determined to be thorough. He noted that this was the private tomb of Joseph of Arimathea. Would this man forget the location of his own donated tomb?

But more problematic for the "wrong tomb" idea was that the Jewish chief priests and elders never questioned that the tomb was empty.

That was it! Somebody must have moved the body to another location. Joseph of Arimathea probably changed his mind and removed the body of Jesus - so emptying this tomb.

But, if that were true, then WHY DID THE GUARDS NOT SAY SO? Why guard the tomb if they knew the body had been moved to another spot? It would have had to be shifted before the stone was rolled over. And if it was empty, it would obviously be seen to be empty by those who sealed the door. Moreover, it would have been a simple story for the soldiers to tell, if Joseph had simply moved the body earlier - **a much safer story**, as far as the soldiers were concerned!

For several days, West turned it over in his mind.

It kept nagging at him. WHY WOULD JOSEPH HAVE DONE SUCH A THING so quickly after he had, at a great risk to himself and to his future popularity, begged to have the body that it might be placed in his own tomb? He made no such explanation to the disciples, who now fully believed that Yeshua had risen from the dead.

Joseph was an honorable counselor, who "also waited for the kingdom of God", "a good man and a just."[7]

Would a man of this caliber and character perpetrate a FRAUD?

West thought not. If there had been any trickery, sooner or later it would have been exposed.

On the other hand, the Roman soldiers had a possible chance to hide his body, secretly, and to bury it elsewhere at a later time.

Not likely. Military law could demand the death penalty upon soldiers[8] asleep on duty. The fear of punishments produced faultless attention to duty, especially in the night watches. Why should the guards want to risk death? And what would be THEIR motive for removing the body?

No motive.

Did the Jews steal the body?

Perhaps, thought West, the Jewish leaders hated Yeshua so much that they stole the body and secretly buried it in another location. Perhaps that's why it was never found.

West held on, like a bulldog. He continued to study and weigh all the inter-playing factors.

The Jewish leaders steal the body? No, it didn't make sense. On many different occasions they had tried to have Yeshua killed. The religious leaders, that was.

They were jealous of his influence and character. They would have done **anything** to discredit Yeshua as the Messiah. Yet, even when he was in the tomb there was something about his prophecies that bothered them.

Firstly, in their own Scriptures were predictions about the anticipated Messiah.

Secondly, in Jesus' life, those prophecies, one by one, were claimed to be coming true. One of those prophecies hinted that the Messiah was to come alive again after a violent death.[9] Yeshua had claimed that he would die and rise again after three days.

So to make sure that Jesus' body could not be snatched from the tomb, the Jewish leaders had themselves called upon Roman help to keep that body in the tomb. At their own suggestion and under their supervision, the tomb was sealed.[10]

So well was it sealed, that no one could break it open - and Roman guards were ordered to watch it.

West continued his investigation of the four New Testament gospel accounts.

That third day after the crucifixion - what a morning it was! Several Roman soldiers were seen running toward the city. According to witnesses, they were very frightened. As they ran by in frantic haste, they cried, "HE'S ALIVE! THE DEAD MAN'S ALIVE!"

As they passed the Council Chambers, several priests stepped out and hustled them inside.

WHY DID THE SOLDIERS GO INTO THE COUNCIL CHAMBER TELLING ONE STORY - AND COME OUT TELLING QUITE ANOTHER?

The record said that the Jewish leaders themselves "gave large money unto the soldiers, saying, 'Say ye HIS DISCIPLES came by night, and stole him away while we slept.' And if this comes to the governor's ears we will persuade him, and secure you. So they took the money, and did as they were taught, and this saying is commonly reported among the Jews until this day."[11]

West asked himself, WHY WERE THE SOLDIERS SO SELF-ASSURED IN CONFESSING TO SLEEPING ON DUTY - when the death penalty was mandatory for such an offense?

AND WHY WERE THE JEWISH LEADERS SO ANXIOUS TO MAKE THE SOLDIERS CHANGE THEIR STORY? The **Jews themselves** paid a large sum of money to the soldiers to spread the story that Jesus' disciples had stolen his body away. If the Jews had stolen the body, why would they bribe the soldiers to say the disciples had done it?

It hit West like a thunderbolt: WHAT WOULD HAVE BEEN ONE OF THE GREATEST PROOFS TO THE PEOPLE THAT JESUS WAS **NOT** THE MESSIAH and that he was still dead?

SURELY THE FINDING AND EXHIBITION OF HIS BODY!

Yes, indeed. Had the Jewish leaders, or any of the Jews of Jesus' day, been able to find Jesus' body, they would have PRODUCED that body!

I shall throw my own bit in here: just as the fickle Italian public dragged the body of Mussolini through the streets of Milan, to hang it ignominiously in a public square, upside down beside the body of his mistress, so would the Jews of Jesus' day have paraded Jesus' broken body through the streets of Jerusalem and all the other towns and villages around, and displayed it publicly as PROOF for all the world to see. You can count on it.

So it dawned on West that all the Jewish leaders had to do to **destroy Christianity** was to DISCOVER AND PRODUCE THE BODY OF JESUS.

Such an event would have been the most important talking point for Jews from that day to this.

If the Jewish religious leaders had stolen his body - and KNEW where that body was, and could produce the dead body, THEN WHY DID THESE SAME JEWS FINALLY PERSECUTE AND EVEN MURDER AT THE JEOPARDY OF THEIR OWN LIVES, IN ORDER TO STOP THOSE WHO WENT ABOUT TEACHING THAT YESHUA HAD RISEN FROM THE DEAD?

Would it make any sense to take vows, as they did, to eat no food or drink no water until they had killed the Christian apostle Paul? Would it make any sense to kill James the brother of John? or to martyr and butcher numerous other disciples and Christians for teaching Yeshua had RISEN from the dead - if the Jews absolutely **knew** he had not risen from the dead - and could prove it by producing his body?

A man would have to be a literal fool in the face of such compelling evidence, to believe that the Jews stole and had Jesus' body.

ALL THEY HAD TO DO TO DISPROVE THE RESURRECTION STORY, WAS TO PRODUCE THE DEAD BODY OF JESUS.

Gilbert West knew it! There was no way that the Jewish leaders stole Jesus body.

The investigation must continue...

CHAPTER 26

DID HIS FRIENDS
STEAL THE BODY?

Somebody must have stolen the body. West was sure of it.

Who else, then, but the disciples of Jesus? They must have come while the guards were asleep, rolled away the stone, stolen the body, reburied it, and covered up the affair, so as to trick people into thinking he had risen from the dead.

He would have to investigate this critically. But Gilbert West felt sure this would turn out to be the answer and he would prove it.

His research indicated that the chief priests never questioned that the tomb was empty. They knew that the guards' report was true.

However... if the disciples had stolen the body, WHY DID THE JEWISH PRIESTS FIND IT NECESSARY TO **BRIBE** THE GUARDS TO SAY SO?[1]

If the guards had slept at the tomb, would not those angry Jewish priests have been foremost in accusing them to the governor? But instead they secured the safety of the soldiers, for telling that story.

Again, if those soldiers **slept on guard**, if while sleeping, their prisoner was taken away, then by military law they merited the death penalty for failing to prevent it. SO WHY WERE THEY NOT PLACED UNDER ARREST BY PILATE'S ORDERS IF THE STORY WAS TRUE?

West was getting more uneasy the more he thought about it.

Was it that Pilate knew the guards had **not** been sleeping when the body came out - but that something else had happened?

THE SOLDIERS' EXEMPTION FROM ARREST WOULD SUGGEST THAT THE BODY OF JESUS WAS NOT STOLEN AWAY WHILE THEY SLEPT!

For that matter, if the body was taken while the soldiers ALL slept on duty, then how could they be sure it was the disciples who had done it?

Perhaps one of the soldiers saw the disciples, West reasoned.

OK, suppose he did. Would he not instantly have alerted the other guards, rather than them all face the death penalty?

Anyway, even if **all** those guards had been asleep, surely they would have been awakened by **the heavy noise** of the rolling of that massive stone door along the hollow pavement outside the tomb?

But something else nagged at Gilbert West. WAS IT LIKELY THAT ALL THE SOLDIERS WOULD BE ASLEEP - ALL AT THE SAME TIME? Especially since provision was made to avoid weariness by changing the guard through the night watches.

Could the disciples really have stolen the body? Frankly, West was now beginning to wonder.

Breaking the seal meant death

And how about the stone? That massive seal-stone had been rolled into place against the door - and then sealed with the official Roman seal, a seal no human power dared break, the strongest seal of authority in all the world.

To break the Roman seal was punishable. So if the disciples had broken it, THEN WHY WERE **THEY** LET GO FREE?

On this point, I would like to share with you an interesting discovery.

From Nazareth, Yeshua's home town, there came to light in 1878 a most interesting slab of marble, inscribed in a Greek text.

For many years it lay in the Froehner collection, its value unrecognized until 1930. It is now in the Louvre, Paris.

The text contains a decree issued by an unnamed Roman emperor prohibiting under penalty of death, any kind of tomb robbery, including tombs of relatives, or the moving of a body to another place. It is believed to be from the early days of the Imperial period.

> Ordinance of Caesar. It is my pleasure that graves and tombs remain undisturbed in perpetuity for those who have made them for the cult of their ancestors, or children or members of their house. If, however, any man lay information that another has either demolished them, or has in any other way extracted the buried, or maliciously transferred them to other places in order to wrong them, or has displaced the sealing or other stones, against such a one I order that a trial be instituted as in respect of the gods, as in regard to the cult of mortals. For it shall be much more obligatory to honor the buried. Let it be absolutely forbidden for anyone to disturb them. In the case of contravention I desire that the offender be sentenced to capital punishment on charge of violation of sepulture.

The dating of this inscription has been placed somewhere between 44 and 50 AD, which was during the reign of Claudius Caesar, who was noted for his persecution of the Jews.[2] This was not many years after the death of Jesus. It is believed that the preaching of the resurrection had already begun in Rome by this time. Perhaps this decree reflected the fact that the enemies of Christianity had faced up to the empty tomb story.

The placing of the decree on a rock in the little, unimportant town of Nazareth where Yeshua was reared, indicates a possible relationship between the decree of Caesar and the empty tomb of Yeshua.

If it came at a time preceding the crucifixion, it would prove that there was evidently no ground for the accusation that the disciples stole the body of Yeshua. Otherwise the authorities would certainly have brought the disciples of Yeshua to trial. And the fact that this was not done would show that the rulers of Judea had no hope of making such an accusation stick.

Gilbert West did not know of the Nazareth inscription, but he was a man of clear perception.

If the disciples had been proven guilty, he reasoned, of stealing Jesus' body, would not their enemies, the priests, have been the first to demand their execution? Was it not strange that, instead, the priests tried to hush up the whole matter?

This was puzzling. West would spend weeks on this question. He was no longer sleeping well.

He recalled how the disciples had deserted Yeshua and fled in fear from the scene of the trial and crucifixion. Eleven timid, terrified men. How would they dare face a guard of armed soldiers?

And the size of the stone... how could eleven of them even move a stone which, according to a fourth century manuscript, the *Codex Bezae*, required twenty men to move ?[3]

West knew he was in trouble.

Unexplainable behavior... unless

The thing that threw West most, was the conduct of the disciples themselves.

The faith of the disciples had collapsed after Jesus' death on the cross.[4]

Each was in abject fear for his own personal safety. At the trial, Peter cringed under the taunt of a maid.

They began their defection by denying Jesus, deserting him, flying in all directions, studiously concealing the fact of their former connection with him. They were not only moved by **fear** to conceal themselves, but by **shame**. They were sorely mortified at having been led astray by him. Because they were **honest**, plain, sensible men. They had originally followed him because they saw in him that moral purity and truth, which formed the elements of their own characters.

To them, the whole thing was now over. They thought it had been 'nice' while it lasted, but now their leader had been martyred. And **they were about to go their own way**, back to their respective jobs and positions of earlier days, and give up the whole thing.

Those disciples were very reluctant to believe he had risen again, according to the records. So they scattered to different areas to forget it, to fishing or some other humble way of life. [5]

BUT... WHAT DO WE BEHOLD!!!

WITHIN JUST A WEEK AFTER THIS, THE RESURRECTION OF YESHUA IS MADE KNOWN **BY THEM**, THROUGH THE LENGTH AND BREADTH OF THE LAND! Those men who had cowered and hidden in dismay, now came **boldly forth**, full of confidence in Jesus... to follow him everywhere. Even back to Jerusalem they came - of all places! To the very place from which they had fled! Now they walked everywhere with ANIMATED STEPS AND HEADS HIGH, like men no longer serving a defeated convict, but like men whose Master was Lord of heaven and earth.

What had re-established their faith? What caused this virtually miraculous change?

These men - all cowards, timid and afraid of the Jews who had killed Jesus - how come they were **suddenly** so filled with power and conviction, that they went out enthusiastically announcing against all opposition, **even at the risk of their lives,** that Yeshua had risen?

West was really troubled now. He asked himself, Would numerous men be torn limb from limb, thrown to wild beasts, drawn and quartered, sawn in two, hung upside down, burnt at the stake - FOR SOMETHING THEY KNEW TO BE A DELIBERATE HOAX?

No one ever could have believed (or would have believed) upon the dead Yeshua as the Son of God, had he not had the evidence for the resurrection.

Gilbert West hated to admit it. But the idea that the disciples stole the body, so defied all logic, reason, and known facts, as to appear ludicrous. They could NOT have done it.

I shall add something that was **not** a part of West's investigation. That is, that the Jews are the most resourceful and untiring race on earth! They searched the whole world untiringly, unceasingly, until they discovered the whereabouts of Nazi war criminal Adolph Eichmann. They investigated, searched, scanned, scoured, until they **found him**.

They were able to find Eichmann, even though he was in South America... yet they were unable to produce the dead body of Yeshua - in tiny Judea!!!

Because there **was** no dead body.

That much was now clear to West. But he also knew that if there was no dead body - that if the resurrection had occurred - there would have to be people who saw him alive.

West's investigation now took this unexpected turn.

CHAPTER 27

THE WITNESSES

Only 50 days after the tomb of Yeshua was burst open, the erstwhile cowardly disciple Peter suddenly stood up before a huge crowd and addressed them.

Thousands of visitors were in Jerusalem for the Pentecost festivities.

In his speech, Peter explained why the ancient prophecies had said that the coming Messiah's body, when he died, would not suffer decay.[1]

Peter's logic convinced 3,000 Jews in that audience that the only solution to the empty tomb was that Yeshua was bodily raised from the dead.

"We all are WITNESSES," said Peter.[2]

It was significant that Peter's first public speech was in that **very same city** where the resurrection was claimed to have happened.

If it was all a hoax, how ever could he have hoped to gain believers among those who were there - among those who were in a position to know whether he spoke truly? Only weeks after the death of Jesus, their testimony right there in Jerusalem was received as true, and multitudes became disciples.

Peter told them, THE EVIDENCE WAS RIGHT UNDER THEIR NOSES!

◆◆◆◆◆◆

Gilbert West went over the evidence that he had been accumulating. He had not expected this to happen. Like Lord Lyttleton, he had been sure it would be easy to discredit the whole thing.

He had started out believing there was no evidence. That the resurrection was a total fake.

Now he went over the facts again, looking for a flaw. And he kept coming back to this: THERE WERE TOO MANY WITNESSES TO THE EVENT FOR IT TO BE DENIED!

These witnesses were **not** resting their faith on an empty tomb, but upon **appearances** of Yeshua after the event - **on many** different occasions!

West had already begun to list them.

Firstly, the soldiers

Because the Jewish authorities made special effort to prevent any resurrection, placing armed guards around the tomb, securing the entrance with a Roman seal over a mighty stone barrier - this very act had resulted in more positive and conclusive proof of what happened.

The greater the number of soldiers placed around the tomb, the stronger it made the testimony that the dead man had risen. A whole guard of pagan soldiers became eyewitnesses.

Knowing that to let a prisoner escape attracted the death penalty, the Roman soldiers were compelled to admit to their own peril that this very thing had taken place, even though the tomb was securely sealed as though for eternity.

Secondly, the Jewish religious leaders

The proof that forces exceeding the power of a group of armed soldiers, had opened the tomb, stunned them.

The fact that [1] they bribed the soldiers to hush up the facts, and that [2] they bribed the Roman governor not to punish the soldiers for their story, demonstrated that what they were trying to hide was AN ADMISSION OF THE FACT.

Efforts to prevent the resurrection and to circulate a false report concerning it, served only to provide additional confirmation of it as an historical fact.

Thirdly, the witnesses to Jesus' actual appearances

Jesus had been seen alive after the "event", not once or twice, but at least ten times, according to records. He was seen, not by just one individual, whose word could be doubted, but by GROUPS of two, seven, ten, eleven, and even 500. More than half a thousand people had seen him after his resurrection and under many different circumstances.

Yeshua TALKED, WALKED, ATE, OPENED THE SCRIPTURES, PREPARED A FIRE FOR BREAKFAST, AND SHOWED THE NAIL SCARS. He permitted them to touch his real body. Thomas skeptically examined the wounds and scars.

During all those occasions, the favored ones **spoke with him**, **touched him** and **dined with him**. And he gave the order to spread the news to the world.[3]

The verdict of a doctor named Luke was that these were "infallible proofs".[4]

Mass hypnotism?

But West was not to give in easily.

These alleged appearances of Jesus after his death could, he considered, have been mass hypnotism, or perhaps an hallucination, resulting from a fervent desire in the hearts of the disciples. Or even an apparition.

But there was a problem with that. The disciples **did not believe he would rise.** They **doubted** that he had risen. They called it an "idle tale".[5]

They did not even WANT to believe he had risen![6]

All the way through the gospel accounts, the writers themselves attest to a very great **reluctance** on the part of his closest disciples to **believe** in his resurrection.

Could the "appearances", then, have been an hallucination?

Do men "conjure up" a vague or nebulous dream in something they are "hoping for", if they really ARE NOT EVEN HOPING FOR IT? Would they have an ecstatic "vision" of something they DIDN'T BELIEVE WOULD OCCUR in the first place?

West had to admit, that would not be logical.

What was more, DIFFERENT GROUPS of people kept on seeing Jesus in DIFFERENT PLACES at DIFFERENT TIMES. It could be neither mass hypnotism nor a dream.

The same dream does not repeatedly keep occurring to totally different people in widely separated areas at totally different times.

West actually found twelve different occasions recorded when Yeshua appeared after his resurrection. It was unlikely that men of such diversity of character would all be deceived and deluded. One could hardly imagine Peter becoming delirious, or Thomas hysterical, or the group of 500 all simultaneously suffering from an hallucination.

It was crystal clear that the disciples of Yeshua DID NOT BELIEVE the resurrection of Yeshua until they simply **had** to believe it.

An ardent unbeliever convinced

As he researched, West came upon the account concerning a man named Saul. A Pharisee, Saul was well educated. His logical mind would not be readily deceived. Yet he gave testimony of his meeting the resurrected Yeshua on the way to Damascus - while he was an ardent unbeliever. That meeting turned his life around.

Only one explanation made sense. All these people saw Jesus, the same Jesus. Alive again. They were all skeptical. They DID NOT BELIEVE his resurrection - until they simply HAD to believe it.

While unlikely for us...

West saw himself in this. His problem was, he was asked to believe something that was really unbelievable. He was asked to believe that a dead man rose from the dead. And he had NEVER SEEN A MAN WHO DID THAT.

West was confronted with testimony that a "miracle" occurred. He could not produce witnesses that it did not occur. All he might do is introduce witnesses who would say they had never seen anything like this happen.

Was he to say that no fact was to be taken as testimony unless he, Gilbert West, had experienced it? Anyone who took his own experience solely as his criteria would cut himself off from the greater part of human knowledge.

In West's mind, there was a tremendous presumption against an ordinary man rising from the dead. However, coming to know Jesus as he was portrayed in the gospels, West saw that, whereas it was unlikely that any ordinary man should rise from the dead, in his case the presumption was exactly reversed. It was unlikely that THIS man should not rise. It could be said that it was impossible that he should be bound by death.

Yes, the evidence for the resurrection was GOOD EVIDENCE.

Other scientists speak

For a moment I shall interrupt this story of Gilbert West.

As I write this chapter, I have before me some interesting comments by a chemical scientist and an historian. Let me share them with you.

Dr. A.C. Ivy, of the Department of Chemical Science, University of Illinois, states his faith in the bodily resurrection of Jesus Christ. He says:

> On the basis of historical evidence of existing biological knowledge, the scientist who is true to the philosophy of science can doubt the bodily resurrection of Jesus Christ, but he cannot deny it. Because to do so means that he can prove that it **did not** occur. I can only say that present-day biological science cannot resurrect a body that has been dead and entombed for three days. To deny the resurrection of Jesus Christ on the basis of what biology now knows is to manifest an unscientific attitude according to my philosophy of the true scientific attitude.[7]

Professor E.M. Blaiklock, former Professor of Classics at the University of Auckland, New Zealand, says:

> I am a classical historian, and as an historian I look upon the empty tomb and the only available explanation of it, as a better authenticated fact than almost anything else I have taught about that century in all my university years.[8]

••••••

303

The two skeptics, West and Lyttleton, met again as planned. Each was a little sheepish, as he approached the other. Each was apprehensive of what the other's reaction would be.

For when they compared notes, it was realized that they had both come independently to disturbing conclusions. West had found the evidence pointed unmistakably to the fact that Jesus did rise from the dead. Lyttleton had found, on examination, that Saul of Tarsus **did** become a radically new man, through his conversion to Christianity.

Both men had become, in the process, strong and devoted followers of Yeshua. Each had experienced a remarkable change in his life, which had occurred through contact with the risen Messiah.

CHAPTER 28

LEGAL OPINION

If you went into court with such evidence, how would you come out? I wanted to be sure. Not being a lawyer myself, I went in search of the best I could find.

And here is what happened. But first let me say this:

When an event takes place in history and there are enough people alive who were eyewitnesses of it or had participated in the event, and when the information is published, one is able to verify the validity of an historical event.

Sir Edward Clarke, K.C., wrote:

> As a lawyer, I have made a prolonged study of the evidences for the events of the first Easter Day. To me the evidence is conclusive, and over and over again in the High Court, I have secured the verdict on evidence not nearly so compelling.[1]

Professor Thomas Arnold, author of a famous three-volume *History of Rome*, who was appointed to the chair of Modern History at Oxford, stated concerning the evidence for the resurrection of Jesus:

> Thousands and tens of thousands of persons have gone through it piece by piece, as carefully as every judge summing up on a most important cause. I have myself done it many times over... I know of no one fact in the history of mankind which is proved by better and fuller evidence of every sort.[2]

Lord Lyndhurst, one of the greatest legal minds in British history, who in one lifetime held the highest offices which a judge in Great Britain could ever have conferred upon him

305

(Solicitor-General of the British government; Attorney-General of Great Britain; three times High Chancellor of Cambridge), wrote:

> I know pretty well what evidence is; and I tell you, such evidence as that for the Resurrection has never broken down yet.[3]

While still Professor of Law at Harvard, Simon Greenleaf wrote a volume entitled *An Examination of the Testimony of the Four Evangelists by the Rules of Evidence Administered in the Courts of Justice.* In it he says:

> The laws of every country were against the teachings of His disciples... Propagating this new faith, even in the most inoffensive and peaceful manner, they could expect nothing but contempt, opposition, reviling, bitter persecutions, stripes, imprisonment, torments, and cruel deaths.... They had every possible motive to review carefully the grounds of their faith....
>
> If then their testimony was not true, there was no possible motive for its fabrication.[4]

A former Chief Justice of England, Lord Darling, said concerning Jesus' resurrection:

> On that greatest point we are not merely asked to have faith. In its favor as living truth there exists such overwhelming evidence, positive and negative, factual and circumstantial, that no intelligent jury in the world could fail to bring in a verdict that the resurrection story is true.[5]

What does the resurrection prove?

Throughout this investigation I had been jotting down some common sense facts.

It dawned on me that if Yeshua's resurrection really happened, then this would affect my life.

Like it or not, no person on earth could remain unaffected.

Here's why:

Firstly, Yeshua's resurrection placed a seal on the genuineness of certain Old Testament prophecies.[6]

Secondly, it placed a seal on Yeshua as being who and what he claimed to be.[7]

Thirdly, the resurrection proved Yeshua's inherent power.[8]

Fourthly, it marked him as the conqueror of death.

Fifthly, unless it happened, we are still without hope beyond the grave.[9]

But more than that, such a resurrection would place a seal on his full authority as King and universal Judge. It would make the Judgment of all men certain. If so, then one should take seriously the Scriptural claim that our Creator has "appointed a day, in which he will judge the world in righteousness by that Man whom he hath ordained; whereof he hath GIVEN ASSURANCE unto all men, in that he hath raised him from the dead."[10]

So, **sixthly**, Yeshua's historical resurrection makes certain our own future resurrection at that day.[11] Each person will be raised - to eternal life or judgment.

And it struck me. By accepting his claims, I had nothing to lose - but the possibility of everything to gain.

The resurrection of Jesus (Sketch: Darren Hunter)

On the other hand, if it was true and I did not accept, I had everything to lose. [11]

Just try to imagine that resurrection morning. Picture yourself there. The night of the first day of the week has slowly worn away. The darkest hour, just before daybreak, has come. Jesus is still a prisoner in his narrow tomb. The great stone is in its place; the Roman seal is unbroken; the Roman guards are keeping their watch.

And there are unseen watchers. Hosts of evil angelic beings are gathered about the place. If it were possible, the prince of darkness with his antagonistic army would keep forever sealed the tomb that holds the Son of God.

But a heavenly host surrounds the sepulcher. Angels that excel in strength are guarding the tomb, and waiting to welcome the Prince of Life. And behold, there is a great earthquake; for the angel of the Lord descends from heaven. Clothed with radiance from God, this messenger leaves the heavenly courts.

The bright beams of God's glory go before him, illuminating his pathway. His countenance is like lightning, and his clothing white as snow. And for fear of him the keepers shake, and become as dead men.

Now, priests and rulers, where is your guard? Brave soldiers that have never been afraid of human power, are now as captives taken without sword or spear. The face they look upon is not the face of mortal warrior; it is the face of the mightiest of the messengers of God. This messenger is he who fills the position from which Lucifer fell. It is he who on the hills of Bethlehem announced Jesus' birth.

The earth trembles at his approach, the hosts of darkness flee and as he rolls away the stone, heaven seems to come down to earth.

The soldiers see him removing the stone as he would a pebble, and hear him cry, "Son of God, come forth. Your Father calls you."

As he exits the tomb in majesty and glory, the angel host bow in adoration before him and welcome him with praise.

The decree of heaven has loosed the captive. Mountains piled upon mountains over his tomb could not have prevented him from coming forth.[12]

What happened to Joseph?

My first visit to the site was a powerful experience. To stand alone inside that tomb, staring at the empty space.

And the truth crashed over me like an avalanche: Yeshua, the One who had lain here, had actually died for me. Personally.

That was overwhelming. It shook me.

Soon I got to thinking about the man who stuck his neck out in donating that tomb for the burial of Jesus.

Joseph must have known that he would be in the firing line, after that.

So what really happened to that man - Joseph of Arimathea?

Did he survive the rage of Yeshua's enemies? Was there any information concerning him?

It was a tantalizing question. And one that deserved an answer. I began to probe... not totally prepared for the surprise.

CHAPTER 29

JOSEPH - A MARKED MAN

"Get in!" shrieked the uniformed officer. "There's room for one more."

He nudged the woman off the quay. She stumbled, almost crashing, into the boat. Stabs of pain shot up her leg as she struck something.

Marcella sighed... and looked around her. There was Joseph... Lazarus... and twelve others crammed in with her. She knew every one. All dear friends. One of them smiled at her.

Another boat came in close, to tow them out to sea. Four strong men gave their craft a push.

From now on, they were castaways. Without oars or sails. At the mercy of the Mediterranean.

Yet... not afraid. That was the wonderful part. Each was very calm and at peace with God.

Adjusting to a more comfortable position, they individually reflected on the events that had led to this moment...

••••••

Joseph, the rich merchant... After Joseph of Arimathea had buried Jesus in his own tomb, he was a marked man. The religious leaders were infuriated.

The 4th century *Evangelium Nicodemi* says that Joseph was imprisoned by those leaders, but was miraculously delivered.

This and other events simply enraged them.

To say that Yeshua's disciples were causing a stir, would be an understatement. Since the resurrection, the disciples – now called apostles – had become courageous. "Filled with the Holy Spirit" and strengthened with a courage they had not known before, they hurried into the streets and began speaking about Yeshua.

In the days that followed, thousands of people were convicted in their hearts and made a personal commitment to Yeshua and were baptized. The news just kept going.

Such success brought opposition from the Establishment. They arrested the speakers, threatened them, whipped and even imprisoned them.

The response of the apostles was to become even more courageous. When ordered not to speak, they answered the authorities, "Is it right in God's eyes for us to obey you rather than God? Judge for yourselves. We cannot possibly give up speaking of things we have seen and heard." [1]

No wonder they were so astonishingly successful!

You see, they were not discussing philosophical ideas which might, or on the other hand might not, have some merit.

Since the resurrection, they had actually seen Yeshua, talked with him, eaten with him, walked dusty roads with him. They knew that what they were saying was true. They knew well that peoples' eternal lives depended on him. Without the Messiah, all mankind was doomed.

When again arrested, they told the authorities, "There is no salvation in anyone else at all, for there is no other name under heaven granted to men, by which we may receive salvation." [2]

The opposition grew steadily worse.

Finally, after 3½ years of such speaking in Jerusalem, one of the young deacons was dragged from his pulpit and publicly stoned to death for speaking about Yeshua.

A great rash of persecution had since broken out in Jerusalem and the new Christians were being scattered everywhere.

As for Joseph and his party, they were being put out to sea. Joseph had made his choice. All his wealth was no longer important to him. He had something that was more precious.

We should not know about this, except for several historical writings that agree concerning Joseph having been cast adrift.

Our inquiry now turns to Joseph in particular. We ask, Who was this man? Why was he so rich?

The "Tin Islands"

In order to appreciate fully the available material which can help us in our inquiry, we must first investigate something about a land that was sometimes known as "The Tin Islands". We refer to ancient Britain.

Herodotus, aptly described as the "Father of History", was a Greek historian who lived in the 5th century BC. During his life he traveled over most of the then-known world, and within his writings we find him referring to Britain as the *Cassiterides* or *Tin Islands*.[3]

The reason for Herodotus' assertion was simply that Cornwall had almost the world monopoly of tin production. Archaeological evidences show clearly that the Tin Islands were exporting tin as early as 1500 BC. Biblical "ships of Tarshish" (a name given to ocean-going vessels, and used in the same way that Victorians spoke of "East-India-Men"), which operated mainly from the Phoenician port of Tyre, were the main agents in transporting this valuable metal to different parts of the world.

Herodotus was not the only writer of antiquity to refer to the mining of tin in Cornwall, Britain. It should be mentioned in passing that the Greek navigator and geographer, Pytheas, who lived at Massilia (now the French port of Marseilles) in the late 5th century BC explored the coasts of Spain, France and the British Isles. He mentions the Cassiterides.

So does Aristotle the Greek philosopher (384 – 322 BC); Polybius, author of *Histories* (205 – 125 BC); Diodorus Siculus, Greek historian of the late first century BC ; and Posidonius, the Greek Stoic philosopher, also of the first century BC. All of these deal at length with the British tin industry in the centuries before Christ.

Sir Edward Creasy, the English barrister, professor and historian (1812 – 1878), said in one of his books, as a result of his research, that:

The British mines mainly supplied the glorious adornment of Solomon's Temple.[4]

Now hear what Diodorus Siculus had to say about the British tin mining industry:

> They that inhabit the British promontory of Belerium, by reason of their converse with the merchants, are more civilised and courteous to strangers than the rest. These are the people that make the tin, which, with a great deal of care and labor, they dig out of the ground, and that being rocky, the metal is mixed with some veins of earth, out of which they melt the metal and then refine it. Then they beat it into four-square pieces like a Die, and cart it to a British island, near at hand, called Ictis. For at low tide, all being dry between them and the island, they convey over in carts abundance of tin.[5]

The island he called Ictis is none other than St.Michael's Mount, just offshore from Marazion in Cornwall, and exactly fits Diodorus' description. In 1969, in the little harbor on the island, skin divers found a stone bowl with a handle, which was subsequently identified by the British Museum as Phoenician, and dating back as far as 1500 BC.

Who were the people who worked the mines? Undoubtedly ancient British men. But records show that others were also involved. The eminent English antiquarian and historian, William Camden (1551 – 1623), wrote a book called *Britannia*, which was published in Latin in 1586 and in English translation in 1610. It was a landmark in the topographical study of Britain. In this work he said:

> The merchants of Asher worked the tin mines of Cornwall, not as slaves, but as masters and exporters.[6]

How did this come about?

In earlier chapters we gave evidence of Hebrew-Phoenician cooperation in trading. The Greek geographer Strabo (63 BC – 24 AD) wrote concerning the traders:

> Anciently the Phoenicians alone, from Cadiz, engrossed this market, hiding the navigation from all others. When the Romans followed the course of a vessel that they might discover the situation, the jealous pilot willfully stranded the

314

ship, misleading those who were tracking him, to the same destruction. Escaping from the shipwreck, he was indemnified for his losses out of the public treasury.[7]

And in fact this ploy worked satisfactorily until 450 BC, when the Carthaginian general Hamilcar sailed through the straits of Gibraltar and northward, thereby discovering Cornwall.

Many of those who used the Phoenician port of Tyre were Israelites, who sailed to various destinations, and even set up distant colonies and settlements.

Hebrews in the tin business

In many of the places where Israelites set up their colonies, we find inscriptions and tombstones bearing witness to the fact. The south of Spain is not wanting in this respect. Neither is Cornwall.

Our particular concern is Cornwall. And this is where the story of Joseph of Arimathea begins to unfold.

In times long ago, Cornwall was literally riddled with mines. The remains of their shafts are still in evidence, and care must be taken in certain areas not to fall into these when hiking. But of all the mines, there remains but one that is still in operation.

However, traditions still linger with considerable strength concerning Joseph's involvement. The miners have always sung songs during their work underground, and the refrain has always been:

> Joseph was a tin miner.
> Joseph was in the tin trade.

Is this an empty 'boast'? Hardly. Throughout the world there are very persistent traditions that just will not die, and when investigated, they are found to contain memories of important historical events. They say that there is no smoke without fire. Likewise there is no tradition without historical fact, even though in the process of time the facts get covered over with the barnacles of human embellishment. And this appears to be true here.

315

The good news goes to Britain

There is one more clue we must establish before going into the story of Joseph of Arimathea. It is widely assumed that Christianity in England was founded by St. Augustine, sent there in 597 AD on a mission by Pope Gregory.

Nothing could be further from the truth! Augustine, after being in Britain for just three years, sent a letter to Gregory, in which he said:

> In the Western confines of Britain, there is a certain royal island of large extent, surrounded by water, abounding in all the beauties of nature and necessities of life. In it the first neophytes of catholic law, God beforehand acquainting them, found a church constructed by no human art, but by the hands of Christ Himself, for the salvation of His people.[8]

Well, however we take Augustine's words, amazingly enough **there is a fund of early documentary evidence** that Britain received the gospel of Jesus Christ soon after the resurrection.

One of Britain's earliest historians was the monk "Gildas the Wise". In 550, he penned the following lines:

> We certainly know that Christ, the true Son, afforded His light, the knowledge of His precepts to our Island in the last year of Tiberius Caesar.[9]

According to Roman history, Tiberius Caesar reigned for 23 years. His last year was 37 AD. Since the resurrection of Jesus was in 31 AD (see Chapter 17), then the gospel arrived in Britain just six years after Jesus rose from the dead.

The early Christian writer Tertullian (155 – 222 AD) declared:

> The extremities of Spain, the various parts of Gaul, the regions of Britain which have never been penetrated by Roman armies, have received the religion of Christ.[10]

Now this is an interesting statement, because Roman Britain had been established gradually from the days of Julius Caesar in 55 BC. But the regions of Devon, Cornwall and Somerset (known then as the Land of Dumnonii) had never been penetrated by the Roman armies. And this is further proof that the Christian message was already established on that "certain royal island" mentioned by Augustine, and which we now recognize as Glastonbury.

(But of course the whole area has long since been drained, so Glastonbury is no longer an island. However, much of the ground around Glastonbury is still below sea level, and becomes marshy in wet weather.)

Another lead comes from the Church Councils of Pisa (1409), Constance (1417), Sienna (1424) and Basle (1434), through whom it was written:

> The churches of France and Spain must yield in points of antiquity and precedence to that of Britain, as the latter church was founded by Joseph of Arimathea immediately after the passion of Christ.[11]

And Roman Catholic Archbishop Ussher (1550 – 1613) wrote:

> The British National Church was founded AD 36, 160 years before heathen Rome confessed Christianity.[12]

Mind boggling, isn't it? Another common misconception has come crashing down.

Here is history we never knew existed. So it WASN'T Augustine who introduced Christianity to savages in the 6th century!

Before we leave this point, here are three final quotations on the matter.

Sabellius, Roman Catholic prelate and theologian, who was excommunicated by Pope Calixtus in 220, writing in 250 AD, said:

> Christianity was privately confessed elsewhere, but the first nation that produced it as their religion and called it Christtian, after the name of Christ, was Britain.[13]

And then we have the written testimony of Maelgwyn of Llandaff, Lord of Anglesey and Snowdonia (450 AD):

> Joseph of Arimathea, the noble decurion, entered his perpetual sleep with his XI companions in the Isle of Avalon.[14]

Polydore Vergil (1470 – 1555), the learned Italian historian, living in England, also wrote:

> Britain, partly through Joseph of Arimathea, partly through Fugatus and Damianus, was of all kingdoms the first that received the Gospel.[15]

317

When Augustine was sent from Rome in the 6th century, Britain had already known Christianity for 500 years! Primitive, pure Christianity.

It was former American president Franklin D. Roosevelt who said, "All histories should be rewritten in truth."

Who was this Joseph?

Joseph of Arimathea. The man who gave Jesus his own personal tomb to use. The man who stuck his neck out to honor the hated Messiah. We have just noticed his name cropping up in histories of Britain.

Who was this man? And what was he doing in Britain?

Joseph of Arimathea was a Pharisee of some reputation in Jerusalem. He was a rich man, according to the New Testament – and one who could go privately to Pontius Pilate and make bold requests. Pilate knew him and respected him. And granted him leave to remove Yeshua's body from the cross and bury it in his own newly-cut sepulchral chamber. This was in accordance with existing Roman law[16] that a near relative could attend to the burial of a crucified man. It has been claimed that Joseph was a great uncle of Jesus.

However, that Friday was no ordinary day, and Pilate's temper had been severely frayed. Yet he entertained Joseph with all due respect and courtesy – and that from a Roman who admitted hatred of all the Jews.

The Jewish Sanhedrin, of which Joseph was a member, consisted of 71 members, all from the aristocracy. There were three orders of election: (a) the chief priests, (b) the elders, being the principal men in the community, and (c) the scribes. Joseph had been elected to membership of the Sanhedrin from among the eldership. The Vulgate Latin translates the word "Counselor" (applied to Joseph in the King James Bible), as "Decurion" (Mark 15:43), a title which had a special place in Roman society, suggesting the position of Town Counselor, or Senator of a Municipium or Colonia.

But the Greek text of Mark 15 speaks of Joseph as an "honorable counselor" that is, a man of high esteem. The Latin reads "Nobilis Decurio", meaning a nobleman, a member of the aristocracy. Matthew says he was "a rich man from Arimathea".[17]

318

It could be that he was "head man" of that whole region, which according to the *Onomasticon*, an ancient record of place names, is identical to Ramathaim-Zophim, in the hill country of Ephraim.

This is enough to show us that this man was no ordinary Pharisee, but a man of substance, position and honor among his peers in Jerusalem, and one who was in fairly constant touch with the Procurator, Pontius Pilate.

Joseph declares himself

We also know that Joseph was a secret follower of Yeshua. He did not want his sympathies known. Perhaps he felt he could be more useful that way. He would certainly lose his position if it were known that he believed in Yeshua.

But after that rush Thursday night trial of Yeshua, Joseph was in shock. Then, as Yeshua died the next afternoon, Joseph could remain silent no longer. He "came out into the open".

Cast adrift in a boat

After he gave his tomb for the placement of the body of Yeshua, the Jewish religious leaders wanted their revenge. Of that we can be sure.

And the report that Joseph was soon imprisoned may well be true, though we owe this report to a 4th century document only.

In the persecutions that broke out in Jerusalem against the followers of Yeshua, we know that Saul of Tarsus (another Pharisee, and also a member of the Sanhedrin) took a leading part. It is likely that Saul hounded Joseph mercilessly.

Several medieval traditions agree that Joseph was cast adrift on a boat, from which oars and sails had been removed. We do not know the origin of these accounts.

One could see this as an act of Saul, who, rather than bring down ignominy on his own head for arraigning such an august company of disciples, decided secretly to commit them to the mercy of the waves. In this way he would not have been responsible for their fate.

Let us draw together some of the threads. It is clear that Joseph was a rich man, possibly from his involvement in the tin trade.

Joseph's association with the tin business would probably have been connected with the Israelites of the tribe of Asher who worked in Cornwall.

According to ancient records, the inhabitants of the region conversed in Greek and had a highly sophisticated way of life. Celts and Israelites, these were no savages, but people who had built up a contact with most other places in the known civilized world through their trade.

Ultimately Joseph was to become the "patron saint" of tin miners, and his memory is still vivid in the minds of Cornishmen to this day.

When archaeologists find a few fragments of a broken pot, and try to assemble it, they are usually able to assess exactly what the missing parts looked like because of the pattern. In the same way historians are able to assess missing information by a similar process, though not with such great accuracy.

Others exiled with him

Do we have any further information in the records?

One snippet comes from the pen of Cardinal Baronius, who asserts that he obtained his information from ancient documents in the Vatican Library. (We do know that many important documents have been hidden away here, which ought to be public property.)

Baronius quotes Frederic Mistral (1859) and earlier (unnamed) sources, saying:

> These were the names of the castaways – Joseph of Arimathea, Mary the wife of Cleopas, Martha, Lazarus, Eutropius, Salome, Clean, Saturninus, Mary Magdalene, Marcella (maid to the Bethany sisters), Maximin, Martial, Trophimus, and Sidonius.[19]

But a good number of other sources from early times (which I have not personally seen) state emphatically that Mary the mother of Jesus also accompanied Joseph.

John the apostle, who, after the crucifixion, was to care for Mary as though she were his own mother, was apparently unable to fulfill this task when on apostolic missions. After ministering at

Ephesus, he had entrusted her to Joseph of Arimathea, who was reportedly Mary's uncle and sole surviving relative.

Voyage to Marseilles

Another ancient manuscript contains the following account of the castaways' journey from Palestine to France:

> Leaving the shores of Asia, and favored by an east wind, they went round about, down the Tyrrhenian Sea, between Europe and Africa, leaving the city of Rome and all the land of Italy to the right. Then happily turning their course to the right, they came near the city of Marseilles, in the Viennoise province of the Gauls, where the river Rhone is received by the sea. There, having called upon God, the Great King of all the world, they parted, each company going to the province where the Holy Spirit had directed them, presently preaching everywhere, 'the Lord working with them, and confirming His word with signs following'.[20]

The records show that Joseph of Arimathea, together with his band of castaways, landed at Marseilles in the south of France.

Other sources tell us that this was the center of evangelism of the apostle Philip,[21] who became a dear friend of Joseph.

On to Britain

Another source states that:

> From Massilia (Marseilles) Joseph and his company passed into Britain... preaching the gospel there.[22]

John Capgrave, a voluminous writer of English history, quotes an ancient manuscript which asserted that:

> Philip sent from Gaul a hundred and sixty disciples to assist Joseph and his companions.[23]

Ancient sources stated that Joseph stayed in Glastonbury until the death of Mary fifteen years after arriving in Britain. On the basis of this chronology, she would have died in 51 AD. She was said to be buried in Glastonbury.

After the passing of Mary, Joseph is recorded as having returned to France for a few years, then again to Britain to work and minister until his death on July 27, 82 AD at the grand age of 98.

Most of Joseph's companions eventually returned to France. And French historical records are replete with traditions and mentions of each one, where they worked, how they lived and how they died. Lazarus, for example, became Bishop of Marseilles, living there for seven years before he died in 41 AD.

In this chapter we have tried to paint a picture of Joseph – the man who gave his own tomb to Yeshua. We have done this from available evidence. Some may consider it highly conjectural. So be it.

We prefer to deal in FACT. And this much we can say with fair certainty: Joseph DID come to Britain. And the Christian gospel WAS first brought to Glastonbury. It is an interesting sidelight to our overall story.

But back now to our day. Let's resume the story of our dig site in Jerusalem.

CHAPTER 30

THE OBSTRUCTIVE BISHOP

As the excavation continued, a series of events transpired that, to put it mildly, were remarkable.

On occasions, as many as ten persons would be working on the site.

Permission to continue work rested in the hands of a bishop.

At the particular time in question, Ron was working at the site alone, when word came from the bishop:

"YOU ARE NOT TO CONTINUE."

This news was shattering. A penetration of this site was crucial to the continuance of the project.

Ron told some dedicated friends back home. They began to pray. The prayer went something like this: "Lord, if that bishop is going to hinder your work, would you please remove him?"

A week later the man dropped dead. Within a month, a new Director was appointed. And this gentleman sent word:

"YOU MAY CONTINUE."

Digging – but no cave

... It was November, 1980. The team had now been toiling for nearly two years. Between other commitments, they could come here to excavate for only a few weeks at a time, several times a year.

Yet, some wonderful finds had been made. And these they had reported in detail to the authorities.

While excavating outside the cliff face, the team continually found pottery and other objects. But once inside the cliff face, they found nothing — no sign of human habitation.

A few artifacts deemed of no significant value, Ron was permitted to keep.

However, the object of their search continued to elude them. The work was exhausting and slow. And Ron was getting anxious.

One evening, the boys sat finishing their meal.

Danny spoke.

"So, we've explored the entire cliff face. There's no sign of a cave or tunnel. What do we do now?"

"If the Ark is in that location," replied Ron, "it will surely be hidden in a cave. I feel 'impressed' that we should just break through the rock of the cliff face."

"I agree," responded Ronny.

"But there's a problem," Ron conceded. "Do you realize how hard that rock is? It would be extremely difficult work. We'd have to use hammers and chisels."

Danny was deep in thought. After a while, he spoke again. "OK, I'm ready. I think we should go ahead and try to break through, anyway."

So it was decided. After all, breaking through the cliff face was the only option left. They would begin next day.

To their relief, it wasn't long before they broke through the rock into an open cavity. Gradually they enlarged the hole. Behind it there appeared a cave.

The men crawled through the opening. Soon they were standing inside a cave about 15 feet high and of a similar width.

Inside Mount Moriah

"Just think of it!" exclaimed Danny. His face expressed the wonder. "We are this moment standing **inside** Mount Moriah!"

But the glimmer would soon fade. If now they expected something worthwhile for their pains, it was not to be.

Over the past two years, they had been outside, in front of the cliff, burrowing into the earth – and uncovering artifacts and structures almost daily. Now they were inside the mountain, in this cavern – and it was empty. No sign of human activity.

It was disappointing. But keep exploring they must.

In one of the extremely tight tunnels

Inside Mount Moriah

It turned out that this cavern was just a very small part of an extensive honeycomb of natural caves and tunnels inside the mountain.

The next year would be occupied, on and off, exploring many of these cavities. But there was no clear evidence of any human presence. To increase the difficulty, these tunnels were not all connected with one another. So many hours were spent chiseling through the cave walls, searching for adjacent tunnels. Each time the men found such tunnels, they were empty.

The following winter, as the third year drew to a close, the men headed from their homes back to Jerusalem. Although it would be cold outside, they knew that the cave system retained a year-round constant temperature.

The "promise"

But Ron was beginning to wonder if he was wasting his time. Had he misinterpreted what he was supposed to do? As a

Christian, he believed that God answered prayer. And now he prayed in earnest to know what to do before starting this trip. As he prayed, he sensed a strong impression that he would find the Ark of the Covenant on that trip. Ron believed with all his heart that this was an assurance from One who could make it happen.

However, things could not be worse. They had spent many months hammering and squeezing through holes and tunnels, in vain, it seemed. By now they had twisted through about 90 feet of tunnels.

As 1981 came to an end, they all began to develop a fever and slight chills due to the dust they had inhaled in the confined tunnels. Ronny had to be sent back to the States on Christmas Eve because he was so ill. And Danny had to follow on New Year's Eve.

Ron was running a temperature of 102 degrees. But he was far more persistent. Or stubborn. He was determined to keep working.

Each year the team comprised many locals, who hauled off tons of earth and debris. A condition of the team's being permitted to excavate was that they must completely restore the above ground area before they left.

One of the young locals who had proved very honest and trustworthy we shall call "Rafat", to protect his and his family's identity. He was an Arab, 27 or 28 years of age. Since this young man was small and slender, he was a perfect candidate for squeezing through the tight tunnels of the excavations.

Underground scout

Exploring every "nook and cranny", the team members would follow each new tunnel. If and when they found a small opening, Ron would enlarge it enough for Rafat to crawl through. Rafat would go ahead, check it out and report back everything he saw.

They followed one particularly difficult passageway which took them through a "chimney". This continued straight up to connect with a tunnel.

This tunnel proved to be so tight that Ron had to exhale just to wriggle through. He had to stop to breathe, but when he inhaled, the passageway was so narrow, he could not fill his lungs completely.

Emerging into a wider area, Ron saw a tiny opening in the wall of the passage.

Directly in front of the hole was a stalactite about 16 inches long. It almost appeared to be "guarding" the hole.

He cracked off the stalactite (and ended up taking it home where he still has it today). Examining the stalactite, I happened to sniff at it and found that it retained a pleasant, sweetish smell.

Pressing his face close to the small hole, Ron could see nothing. So time was taken to enlarge the hole, so as to peer through. No use. All he could see with the aid of his flashlight was a chamber filled with stones.

The stones were of fist size and larger. They were piled up to within 18 inches of the ceiling. There appeared little promise of anything here.

But Ron's plan on this trip was to leave no possibility unexplored. So he enlarged the hole enough for Rafat to crawl through.

Terror in his face

Moments after crawling through the tiny opening, Rafat came tumbling back. He was in a frantic state.

"What's in there? What's in there?" he cried. "I'm not going back in there!" He was trembling and shaking. In his eyes was sheer, complete and utter terror.

"What did you see?" demanded Ron.

"I didn't see anything," he cried.

Whatever his experience, it was stark and real, since he left that chamber, and the entire cave system, never to re-enter. He would continue to assist Ron from time to time, above ground. But that was all.

What was it that Rafat had sensed?

Never would Ron have given that chamber another look, had it not been for Rafat's terror. Now Ron was cautiously excited. He took his hammer and chisel to expand the hole.

Then he crawled through.

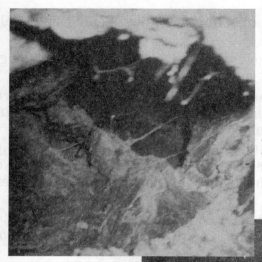

*The small hole into the chamber
just after Ron removed the
stalactite and before he began
to enlarge it.*

*The stalactite that
guarded the chamber*

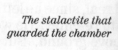

CHAPTER 31

SECRET CHAMBER

Only 18 inches' clearance. That's all he had. Ron lay on his stomach, inching forward with nothing but the flashlight in his hand.

With Rafat's reaction throbbing in his head, Ron purposely looked at his watch. It was 2.00 pm, Wednesday, January 6, 1982.

Under the rocks

The beam of light shone forward over the massive pile of rocks. Something shiny under a gap in the rocks caught his eye.

He began to move the rocks one at a time. It was slow, tedious work. And just under the rocks were planks of dry-rotted wood. And beneath them some dry-rotted remains of animal skins. When he touched them, the skins turned to powder.

The animal skins were laid over a gold-veneered table with a raised molding around its side. The molding comprised an alternating pattern of bells and pomegranates.

His heart raced. In a moment, the truth flashed into his brain. This was one of the items of furniture from Solomon's Temple.

The space was so cramped here, he could not uncover the whole table. But for a long time he examined it closely. Eventually Ron Wyatt concluded that this was the Table of Shewbread described in the book of Leviticus... and made in 1446 BC.

There were several other objects in the chamber, as well.

Earthquake crack in the ceiling

With adrenalin racing through his veins and with mounting anticipation, Ron scanned the chamber to see what else he could see, which wasn't much.

He shone his torch around over the stones and then up to the ceiling. Ahead, something caught his interest. It was a crack in the ceiling, on which a black substance was deposited.

A stone case

Slowly and painfully, he crawled over the rocks to the other end of the chamber.

There he saw a stone case extending through the rocks. It was a thin-walled case, similar to those used in ancient times to contain objects.

The stone lid was cracked completely in two and the smaller section moved aside, creating an opening into the stone case. (Illustration: Jim Pinkoski)

It had a flat top. This stone lid was within four to five inches of the ceiling. And it was cracked completely in two. The smaller section of the cover was moved aside, creating an opening into the stone case.

He could not look inside because the top was too close to the ceiling. Yet he knew what was inside. The cracked part of the lid where it was open, was directly below the crack in the ceiling. And the black substance had fallen from the crack into the case. He knew this, because some of it had splashed onto the lid.

The meaning of it

It was at this time that the pieces quickly came together. Instantly it dawned on Ron what had happened here.

That crack they had found outside in the elevated cross-hole (now many feet above him)... here was the end of that crack, right here in this ceiling. And the black substance was blood.

It was an instant impression. Now Ron realized what had happened here nearly 2,000 years ago. Overwhelmed with emotion and double pneumonia, Ron passed out.

It was 2.45pm when he came to – a mere 45 minutes after entering the chamber.

But he had become the first modern witness to the most awesome event in history.

Now in his waking thoughts Ron realized why the team had needed to do those three years of excavation **first** – before finding this chamber. If they had not first of all discovered the niches and the post-holes, with the crack running across the back one, he wouldn't now have "put two and two together" and realized the full implication of what now lay before him.

Eager to **see** what lay within the stone coffer, he felt great frustration, and complained, knowing that although the Ark was **there**, right in front of him, he could neither see it, nor could he think of a way in which it might be brought out into the daylight.

Promise fulfilled

Yes, the promise that Ron would find the Ark of the Covenant on this trip, he now believed was honored, even though he did not set eyes on it. In his frustration and complaining, Ron sensed another VERY strong "impression": "I only promised that you would FIND it. It will come out when the time is right."

Right here, it ought to be said. One should be careful not to dismiss experiences of this kind out of hand. A living relationship with one's Creator is something that cannot be explained, but only experienced. I know my wife Josephine has experienced such vivid and specific impressions – and they have been proven correct. I can testify to similar experiences, though not always so dramatic. Many others will be able to relate to this. (See Appendix B)

The condition of the chamber, completely full to within 18 inches of the ceiling, made it impossible for Ron to do anything else. He could not foresee any possible way to bring anything out, unless the original entrance through which the objects had been taken into the chamber, was found.

Ron eased himself back out of the cave and through the small hole, to retrace his way through the tortuous complex of tunnels.

Then he sealed the passageway with a stone. Anyone looking along the passageway would think it came to an abrupt end. However, Ron could easily remove the stone when he returned.

The archaeologist did not report his experience to anyone at that time. His mind was still whirring with all that had transpired. He needed time to think. His plan had been to find the Ark and bring it out... but now that appeared impossible.

Attempt to photograph

He made several other trips back to the site, with cameras. By inserting a long pole through the opening at the top of the stone case, attempts would be made to photograph the Ark.

A Polaroid camera was brought in. The photos turned out foggy.

A 35 mm camera was brought in. The photos turned out foggy.

A video camera was brought in. The pictures again turned out foggy.

The photos were taken looking over the shoulder of the first cherub, toward the other one. But in each case, after development, a strange effect was noticed. In front of the cherub (which he could see clearly) there was, as it were, a golden mist obscuring the view. So he concluded that he simply wasn't supposed to take any photographs.

As Ron's wife, Mary Nell, puts it, "He later understood why: at that time, he was much freer with sharing his information and this could have caused a lot of serious problems if some of the 'unsavory characters' he came in contact with over the years had **seen** evidence that this solid gold object **really** existed. Remember how Noah's wife's grave was plundered?" [1]

You're right, Mary Nell. In the next chapter, I shall relate the story of an encounter with one such character.

Perhaps a passage from Scripture is applicable here:

> He holdeth back the face of his throne, and spreadeth his cloud upon it.[2]

(Not forgetting that the Ark, symbolic of the divine "Throne" had once been sanctified with the Divine Presence, as his earthly "Throne".) Another text:

> It is the glory of the Lord to conceal a thing.[3]

Three of those involved in the Ark of the Covenant dig have also been with me on other expeditions.

One of them, Bob Murrell, has helped on the Ark of the Covenant dig three times. Although Bob and Ron have not always agreed on methodology, still there is one thing about this project that Bob would not dispute. He has seen enough evidence to be certain that the Ark of the Covenant is there.

And now I can testify, so have I.

Report to Israeli authorities

Ron made several more trips into the chamber. Eventually he reported to the authorities what he had found.

Perhaps not able to believe what Ron told them, or perhaps recognizing the problems that could arise were it made known, his superiors told him not to tell anyone about this discovery.

Alas, it was too late for that, since Ron had already told a few people, he confessed.

Realizing that "what is done is done", they then ordered him not to reveal any more details than he had already revealed. For this reason, we cannot be as specific in relation to what follows.

Evidence handed over

Some time later, Ron was able to present something from the excavation to the authorities. What he presented convinced them that he had indeed found some items from the First Temple.

The Israeli authorities then decided to test public reaction. (We shall recount that event in a later chapter.)

Verifying the presence of the Ark

On one of his subsequent entries to the chamber, Ron took a "trinkle drill" used by orthopedic surgeons, as well as a colonoscope (an instrument used to peer inside a human body). He wanted to be sure that the Ark really was inside that stone case.

To his dismay, the drill would not penetrate the hard stone of the case. So he had to resort to his star-tipped stone chisel and hammer.

He hit the tip a little, then turned the bit. Then hammered again, and turned.

He kept doing this until he had a hole about five eighths of an inch wide in the stone case.

Through this small hole he inserted the colonoscope. This had a powerful light source. He guided it down, rotating the lens until he saw what he recognized as the bottom of the crown-molding around the top of the lid, the Mercy Seat. Then he saw the flat golden side.

It should be appreciated that the colonoscope has limitations in allowing one to view only a small area at a time. Also the latitude of rotation was small. So Ron could not see a great deal. However, he saw enough to KNOW this was the Ark.

Depth of the crack

On a future expedition, attention would focus on the two cracks. These cracks – one in the ceiling and one in the lid of the stone case – were in line. The crack came down through the rock, leapt as it were through the air, then started again. Rather odd, I thought.

It was decided to investigate the crack in the ceiling.

" Rafat, let's get the metal tape measure," suggested Ron, "and see if this comes out anywhere."

And so, while the young Arab sat up on the ledge outside, Ron entered the chamber... and began to push the rigid metal tape up through the crack in the ceiling.

It came out at the left-hand side of the elevated cross-hole.

The other man caught hold of it to show it had come through. They discovered that the crack extended through 20 feet of solid rock.

Items in the cave

The chamber itself was 22 feet long by 12 feet wide at one

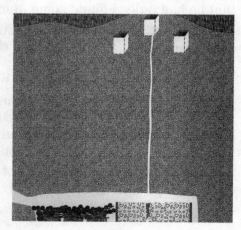

Illustration: Peter O'Connor

336

end. The other two sides followed the line of the cliff face, narrowing the chamber in one corner. The height of the chamber was about 8 feet, with the ceiling fairly flat.

The objects in the chamber that could be confidently identified were:

- The Ark of the Covenant in the stone case
- The Table of Shewbread
- The golden Altar of Incense
- The Golden Censer
- The 7 branched Candlestick holder. (This latter object did not have candles, but tiny, bowlike golden oil lamps built into the tips of the candlestick.)

Other objects in the cavern were:

- A very large sword, 5 feet 2 inches long
- An ephod
- A miter with an ivory pomegranate on the tip
- A brass shekel weight
- Numerous oil lamps
- A brass ring. (This appeared to be for hanging a curtain or something similar.)

The very large sword may have been the one belonging to the giant Goliath, used by David to cut off Goliath's head, and which David laid up in the tabernacle,[4] but was later transferred to the Temple. It bears no markings by which to identify it. At 5 feet 2 inches long, it is quite a size to handle. David must have been supremely strong. David's predecessor, King Saul, a man head and shoulders above his fellows, had offered

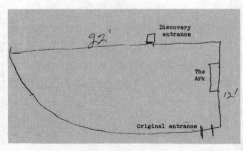

An original plan of the cave

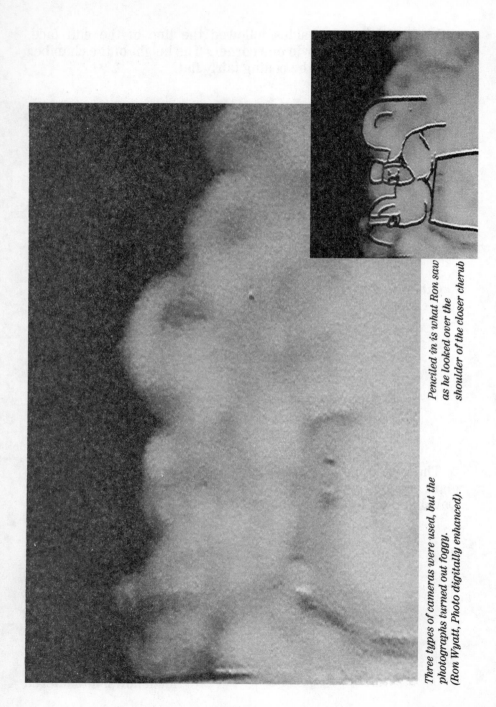

Penciled in is what Ron saw as he looked over the shoulder of the closer cherub

Three types of cameras were used, but the photographs turned out foggy. (Ron Wyatt, Photo digitally enhanced).

In ancient times, the Shekinah light rested over the Ark of the Covenant. (Picture: Jim Pinkoski, adapted by Peter O'Connor)

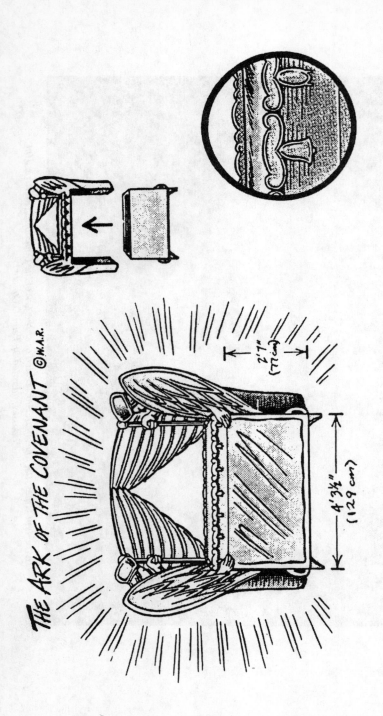

THE ARK OF THE COVENANT ©W.A.R.

2'1"
(77cm)

4'3½"
(129 cm)

Drawings: Jim Pinkoski

David his own armor to try on. and from this one adduces that David also was tall. He never said Saul's armor was too large, but rather that he had not tried it, was not accustomed to it. Apparently, David was physically on a par with Saul. In this case, his wielding of Goliath's sword, as well as the souveniring of that sword, seems reasonable enough. Maybe this sword **was** Goliath's, after all.

All these objects were covered by dry-rotted, dark-coloured animal skins, on top of which were dry-rotted wooden timbers, and finally large rocks piled over everything.

The Ark of the Covenant

The Ark is described in the twenty-fifth chapter of Exodus[5]. It was made of wood overlaid with gold. The Mercy Seat and cherubim were one solid piece of gold.

Various ancient accounts describe the cherubim wings as being raised above or level with their heads. Yet the word translated "upward", "on high" or "above" (Hebrew *lema'lah)* in Exodus 25:20 and 37:9 actually indicates that the wings were spread **horizontally** near their heads.

On the page opposite is Jim Pinkoski's rendering of what Ron saw in that cave chamber. One wing of each cherub is thus outstretched, with the other clasped by the side.

At this point I hear someone say, Those figures don't look like angels. My answer is simply, How do you know? Have **you** ever seen an angel?

Certainly, what we see here does not conform to prevailing notions of how the Ark - or cherubim - looked.

Our ideas, remember, are based only on what our artists have imagined. The center sketch shows how the Mercy Seat fits over the Ark, which contained the tablets of the Ten Commandments.

The sketch in the circle is a close-up of the crown molding around the edge of the Mercy Seat. This is approximately 2 to $2^1/_2$ inches high. It comprises alternating bells and pomegranates. The Mercy Seat, about $3^1/_2$ inches thick, may be of wood covered by thick gold plate. And the golden cherubim, if not made of wood, are

341

This oil lamp was just inside the chamber. The design in the center shows a goat or ram on its hind legs eating from a grape vine.

probably hollow, since the two acacia wood carrying poles would have snapped off in attempting to lift an Ark that was too heavy. At present, there is no way of telling. The Mercy Seat looks like solid gold.

It is believed that the tables of stone are still **inside** the Ark, under the Mercy Seat.

In the back "side" of the Ark is a small cubicle. Only during a subsequent visit into the cavern, after the stone case was removed, would this become visible. When Ron caught sight of this, his heart almost skipped a beat. The cubicle still contained four scrolls... presumably the original "Book of the Law" which Moses himself wrote - the first five books of the Bible. The books of Exodus, Leviticus, Numbers and Deuteronomy were there.

"Perhaps Genesis is there. I don't know," recalled Ron, after an examination. "Maybe it's rolled up with one of the others. They are written on split leather scrolls. They are still in wonderful condition, almost as if they'd been made yesterday. They are written on soft leather."

Just as the shoe leather of the Israelites did not wear out in the desert, so has this leather remained in perfect condition and shows no deterioration.

Lamps show breeze direction

The big question, however, was this. Since it had taken the team so long to get to the cavern, how on earth did Jeremiah or his priestly helpers do it? They probably had very little time in which to secrete all of those Temple vessels into this cavern.

It was quite obvious that there **had** to be a different way in. An easier way. And that the entrance had been subsequently sealed.

That original approach tunnel Ron had to find.

Until now, Ron had concentrated on the Ark and the upper areas of the chamber. He had come away without exploring the floor. Now he would re-enter. And down there close to one wall of the cavern he was to find something unpretentious – a total of seven oil lamps.

Obviously the visitors had left these behind.

Later, my heart was to thud with excitement as I held one of the lamps, examining it closely. It was very ornate, depicting a goat or a ram standing on its hind legs, eating from a grape vine. It displayed Assyrian characteristics, which is consistent with the cultural influence in Judea at the time just prior to the Babylonian siege of Jerusalem.

Ron noticed something as he stood by the lamps. The soot on the lamps and the rocks was all to one side... in one direction.

Then he caught his breath. And simply stared. That soot was showing the breeze direction! Very clearly! Here was the direction of a breeze that came through here 2,500 years ago. A breeze that must have followed the priests into the approach tunnel.

This was just the clue that...

He turned toward the wall, trembling now... half afraid to look lest he be disappointed...

He spread the beam of his flashlight across the stone wall of the cavern, searching, back and forth...

He began probing... On this side of the chamber there must be a false wall...

His heart skipped wildly...

Yes! Yes! YES!... there it was... a plug of rocks closing up the wall!

Was there a tunnel behind it? He **had** to find out...

CHAPTER 32

"THERE'S NOTHING DOWN THERE"

He was puffing. It was tough work. But it began to give. He was actually moving the rocks.

Ron's heart was throbbing madly. He had removed enough rocks. He held the flashlight high and directed the beam through.

There was a void!

He kept removing rocks. Soon there was enough room.

He clambered through. With his flashlight, he could see that this was a tunnel. It was large. But from which direction had those men of Jeremiah's day come, when they brought the Temple objects into the chamber?

Could this tunnel be traced to its source?

His heart skipping wildly, Ron turned left from the hole in the wall. He made it just a few steps... and was blocked. He turned the other way. After a short distance, that also was blocked. The tunnel extended in both directions. But each direction was barricaded to the ceiling with rocks.

Those men who came through here 2,500 years ago had been very careful to ensure the chamber would not be easily found.

You can pass the Ark of the Covenant chamber and not even know there is a man-made entrance into it.

Ron climbed back through the hole into the chamber. Disappointed, he eased himself back up onto the rocks that still covered the precious Temple artifacts. He wriggled along over the rocks, his back again touching the ceiling of the chamber. Then,

345

pushing himself through at the other side, he retraced the tortuous route through the endless maze of cavities that twisted back and forth and upward to the daylight.

The ancient access passage had been blocked in both directions by the Temple priests. **That** had to be **the** way in.

He must find the entrance to that tunnel.

◆◆◆◆◆◆

One day, during the excavation, a well known United States evangelist stumbled upon the diggings.

Believing the man to be honest, Ron told him what he was searching for and even invited him down into the cave. The visitor made big promises of assistance.

Later, after Ron had gone home to America, a team of people associated with the evangelist came to the site, telling the authorities that they were with Ron's expedition and that he would join them in a few days (which was untrue).

They entered the cave system and began digging.

Suddenly the cave walls collapsed upon them. They were almost buried alive. They quickly packed up and went home.

That whole collapsed system had to be re-excavated. It made a lot of extra work for the team.

"Let's get out"

Some time later we sat, six of us, in a room in the Jerusalem Hotel.

"Jonathan," began Dane, a cameraman on my team. "I know a certain man. And perhaps I should add, he's not noted for his truthfulness. But he declares he went in with Ron to look at the Ark of the Covenant - but there was nothing down there."

"That's right, Dane," I said, recalling the facts.

"You mean it's not there now?"

"Oh, **it is** in the chamber still."

"Well, how come, when that man went down..."

"Let me tell you what happened."

◆◆◆◆◆◆◆◆

346

"Mr Wyatt, I wish to help your project."

The smartly dressed man with a polished front indicated he would love the world to sit up and take notice.

Ron was moved by the man's apparent sincerity.

"But first," pressed the man, "I'll have to see this precious Ark for myself."

It was settled. They would fly over to Jerusalem. Ron, the man and his two sons.

Well, they rested at the hotel, that night after they arrived. And the next morning they headed for the excavation site.

The man was bubbling with enthusiasm. He was talking a lot. As they entered the cave system, it came out.

"This Ark," enthused the man, "must be worth a fortune. Hundreds of millions of dollars. When I start promoting it, we'll all be very rich, in no time!"

Ron stopped. He stared at the man in unbelief. But said nothing.

"Why are we stopping?"

"This way," said Ron.

In a little while they found themselves in a rather large cavern.

The man looked around it. The walls, the ceiling, the floor.

"It's empty!" he exclaimed.

"Yes," was Ron's response. "Come on, let's get out."

Ron had led him deliberately into a side chamber. To Ron, the Ark was a holy object. He did not want a fortune seeker on the team.

Ron was learning the hard way how important it was to be careful with whom he shared his information. Honest, and by nature a very trusting person, he expected others to be the same.

The tunnel sealed

This and other incidents led the team to seal the tunnel which led to the chamber. It would be impossible to get any large object out of the chamber through that passage, anyway.

Search for original passage

We have just related how, before permanently sealing the team's excavation tunnel, Ron had re-entered the Ark chamber to see if it was possible to find the original approach tunnel. And we noted how he opened up the original entrance into the chamber and discovered the very large tunnel on the other side extending in both directions. This tunnel appeared to be natural. But chisel marks suggested it had been artificially enlarged.

Unfortunately, the passage was blocked off in both directions with large stones.

The question was, Which way had the Temple priests come in?

Simple reasoning would have it that the Ark and other Temple treasures had begun their journey from the Temple, inside the city.

Now they were in this chamber under the Calvary escarpment, away down below ground level.

Although the Temple Mount and the city itself were honeycombed with tunnels, Ron did not know of any that headed in this direction.

Where had those men entered this tunnel? From somewhere inside the city? Or was the entrance just outside the city's northern wall somewhere?

Ron sat alone for hours, trying to collate all the information in his head.

"Zedekiah's Cave"

One thought kept surfacing.

He had read that, away back in 1854, a physician by the name of Barclay was walking in this same general area. As he passed the Damascus Gate, his dog, running ahead, suddenly vanished. Dr. Barclay called and whistled. At first there was no response. Then he heard muffled barking coming from the direction of the city wall. He turned to scan the area close to the wall. Then he saw it – a deep hole. His dog's bark was emanating from that hole. In this manner was "Zedekiah's Cave" rediscovered.

This vast cavern spreads under the streets of the Moslem section of Jerusalem. Beginning at the dry moat which cuts Mount

Moriah into two segments, it extends 750 feet long and 325 feet wide at the maximum point. The average height is almost 50 feet.

It was cut out anciently – perhaps during the First Temple period – as a stone quarry. But its existence was not well known. In fact, it was totally sealed and shut, probably for fear of enemies using it to penetrate inside the city.

Indeed, so little was known concerning it, that most authorities considered there was no entrance into the city from the quarry.

The darkened area shows the underground quarry known as "Zedekiah's Cave". the Moslem cemetery (top, north of the quarry) can also be seen. The "Calvary" escarpment is the darker line extending along the side of the cemetery.

"Zedekiah's Cave" — the darker sections are the stone pillars left in place... all stone except for one.

The accompanying diagram shows the layout of this underground quarry, the dark areas representing the rock pillars left in place to support the ceiling, like the pillars left in a coal mine. As the mine is progressively worked until the coal has been taken out, the miners eventually retreat and remove the pillars of coal. Often the mine will cave in after this.

Zedekiah's Quarry retains the pillars, so the buildings and streets above are not at risk of collapse.

It was here that Ron resolved to commence his search.

He came in and began a careful examination of the quarry. Soon one thing bothered him.

Having worked with Ron on several locations, I had observed his deftness at linking together seemingly unrelated pieces of data to discover things that most people would miss.

Some critics had found it difficult to accept that one man could make several important discoveries that had eluded other

349

archaeologists and scholars. However, it should be understood that when the Lord selects a man for a particular task, He qualifies him with gifts to match the need.

I had found Ron to be unrestricted by the impediments of conventionally trained scholars who often recited glibly what it was fashionable to believe. Rather, Ron was blessed with good old-fashioned common sense.

Ron's first question whenever he embarked on a new project was to ask himself, What is the easiest way to do it with the least effort?

Now, as he examined the massive quarry carefully, something bothered him.

Here he was, underground. And this quarry extended very deep into the mountain. What an enormous task it would have been to bring all that stone out of the quarry, to outside the city, then lug it back through one of the northern gates and into the city! That didn't make sense.

He asked himself, Wouldn't it have been easier to cut the stone out of the other quarry across the street, the open one, rather than manipulate it out of this cavern?

What would **you** have done if you were in charge of those ancient stonecutters? Put yourself in their shoes!

To Ron there was an obvious solution. Since the quarry was right underneath the Old City, why not cut a hole through the quarry ceiling and simply haul up the rocks into the city? That's what **he** would do. And if **he** could think of it, then why not some of those ancient stonecutters?

It became more obvious, as he thought about it.

Yet to date no one had found an entrance linking the quarry with the city above it.

This thought now nagged at Ron so insistently, he determined to search for one. It was as he lay, trying to sleep, that the decision was made. And from that moment he could hardly wait till morning.

Back into the cavern he went. He began to examine the rock pillars. One by one...

This took some patience. But it was worth the effort. Sure enough, he found a pillar that was **not** of stone. Rather, it was a colossal mound of earth and debris - material that must have been carried or poured down into the quarry from outside. It was foreign material, piled up, he believed, to the ceiling and filling up a hole in the ceiling. On the surface, it would look like normal ground.

His heart – his whole body – was ready to leap for joy.

Whether a stone plug had been cut to seal that hole or whether it was simply filled with packed earth, he did not know. There was no way to go up on ground level and examine it. Buildings covered the area. But Ron was convinced of this: the hole was there.

A tunnel from the quarry

Now his mind was racing.

Just suppose there was a tunnel from down here in the quarry, running toward Skull Hill?

Could those men of Jeremiah's time have taken the Ark and the other Temple treasures, brought them to this hole and lowered them down into the quarry? And then, through the tunnel to their present location?

It was time to look for tunnels...

And he found one!

Boulders and overhanging rock hid it almost completely from view. Well, what he did find was an opening into the quarry wall that was sealed with a number of large cut rocks. And it was heading in the right direction.

Big problem, however. It was a long way from the Skull Hill excavation site. If this was the tunnel those ancient priests had taken, it could be a mammoth job clearing such a long tunnel.

The time: 7th century BC

More than a century ago – in the late 1880s to be more precise – the underground quarry was systematically surveyed and documented by Charles Clermont-Ganneau, a Frenchman. He plotted every inch, so to speak, of this enormous cavern, drawing sketches, maps and diagrams.

*Sketch of the etching found in
"Zedekiah's Cave" near the tunnel
entrance (Charles Clermont-Ganneau)*

*Sketch of cherub
from the palace in
Samaria*

He found etched in the rock a representation of a winged creature with a lion's tail and body and a man's head with a long, flowing beard. On the head was a strange-shaped hat. The etching was removed by chiseling around it. Then it was carried off to the Palestine Exploration Offices in London.

When the Frenchman's sketch is compared with that of a cherub from the Israelite palace in Samaria (see sketches), there is seen a similarity in basic features.

According to authorities who specialize in such things, the style of the etching in the quarry indicated that it was to be dated to approximately the 7th century BC when Israel was under the cultural influence of Assyria. This would place it in the period **before** the Babylonians destroyed Jerusalem. The time frame was correct for the period in which the Ark was hidden.

Just suppose this concealed tunnel **was** the passage through which the Ark was borne to its resting place. This etching – did someone etch this cherub as a symbol "guarding" the tunnel entrance?

(Remember Eden? How at the entrance were cherubim, blocking the way in? [1])

352

The etching **was** located near the blocked entrance. Just a thought.

Some time later, sub-surface interface radar would be used. And the result was encouraging.

Up on street level, the equipment was able to detect a tunnel-like void running at a depth of perhaps 20 feet under the road. It ran from the direction of the underground quarry. But on account of the distance to the Skull Hill excavation site, as well as to the presence of buildings now occupying much of the area, it was impossible to follow the "void" to its final destination.

The radar was now brought into the underground quarry. It revealed a void behind the stone blocks.

Thus encouraged, the team removed some of the blocks. And sure enough, behind them was a passage way. Unfortunately, after several feet, it was blocked again with large rocks and earth. It appeared that someone had tried to camouflage the fact that it was a plugged tunnel and make it look like natural earth and rocks.

What was to be done? This tunnel would be extremely long. The very thought of having to clear it out was forbidding.

Would it be better to keep working within the original excavation site under Mount Moriah – and try to find the main tunnel from that end?

By now Danny's and Ronny's construction careers back in the United States, as well as other responsibilities, were making it difficult for them to keep dashing back to the Middle East.

Ron would bring others into the team...and they would re-enter the Skull Hill cave system.

Mary Nell Wyatt by the tunnel entrance after Ron had first opened it (Photo: Ron Wyatt)

CHAPTER 33

THE "MAN" WHO KNEW

It was October 1988, and after a break of several seasons, weather-beaten archaeologist Ronald Wyatt was back in Israel to resume excavation.

There had been a complete turnover of personnel within the Department of Antiquities. Policies had also changed. Permits to excavate here were difficult to obtain, even for institutions, while for individuals the rules were even tougher.

Notwithstanding, the team was now in Jerusalem. Ron went to apply. His permit to excavate the Ark of the Covenant site was, he had been told years earlier, permanent. But now it wasn't looking good.

After the application went in, they waited three weeks.

"Let's go down to the Mediterranean," said Ron to the team. So off to Ashkelon they went. Ashkelon was the site of an ancient Philistine city. It has quite a decent beach. I found it a good place for swimming. And that's exactly what the team did.

It was while in the water that Ron stubbed his toe on something. Closer inspection proved it to be the rim of a large Canaanite burial pot. Others were also found to be nearby.

The great Kathleen Kenyon had bulldozed through the whole Roman level here searching for the Canaanite burial site – yet no one had thought of looking just a few hundred feet out in the water.

When the find was brought to the notice of the appropriate authority in Jerusalem, he was delighted. An "accident" had reopened the way...

Ron got his permit to excavate in Jerusalem!

Descending the 25 foot shaft into the open chamber (Photo: Ron Wyatt)

356

The planks which form the "floor" in the main cave chamber. In the previous photo, Ron is standing on these planks. The plank at his shoulder level is to help with the descent and also to set the buckets of rocks (which are being removed) upon. The buckets are then hoisted up through the hole by a rope to several men posted at various levels in the crooked shaft, and finally passed up to the "above ground man". This plank is seen resting in the hole Ron and the boys chiseled into the cliff-face in December, 1981, when they first discovered the cave system. Below these planks, it is 40 feet straight down. (Photo: Ron Wyatt)

Back into the Skull Hill cave system

With the tunnel from the quarry end solidly blocked, the search for an entrance into the tunnel from the opposite direction was the remaining option.

Work now switched back to the cave complex inside the Golgotha hill.

Radar was brought in to help detect voids behind solid rock walls. Within the cave system, there was one particular location where Ron **knew** he was only so many feet away from the Ark of the Covenant chamber. However, getting through many, many feet of solid limestone from point A to point B was easier said than done.

Numerous were the false leads. Ron had been in here before, although without radar. And, as before, there were small holes and even jagged shafts that dropped up to 25 feet **straight down.** With just thin planks to stand on (brought in years earlier by the team). And below the planks, 40 feet down, a gap to another cavern.

Twisting and turning, trying to conform the body to the narrow shaft, was enough to completely disorientate one. Some areas were so tight... it seemed impossible to even measure anything.

Where necessary, buckets of rocks were removed with several men posted at various levels, hoisting the buckets by rope to the "above ground man". The "bucket brigade" sometimes consisted of ten of more people.

Back to "Zedekiah's Quarry"

The team also went over to the underground quarry. Ron crawled in through the tunnel entrance there, and came again to the pile of big stones that blocked further advance. He began to remove the rocks and debris. The "bucket brigade" went to work again. Each man passed the buckets on to the next, to be dumped by the last man.

It was just an ordinary day. But it would be remembered. Suddenly, while they were working, Ron was struck with a feeling of impending disaster. "Guys," he shouted, "I've had this impression. I don't know what's going to happen. But I think we'd all better pack up our gear fast and get outta here."

Everyone raced to get the equipment out. And just as they started walking away through the quarry, there was a loud booming and a thud. It came from the tunnel area. A huge rock in the tunnel ceiling had come crashing down just where Ron had been sitting.

Next day they broke up the boulder and continued clearing. However, the debris now seemed to be endless.

"Let's leave," said Ron.

They replaced the blocks. And for now that would have to be it. Whether the tunnel was blocked all the way, who could tell? Was it even the correct tunnel?

Sometime later, Danny would come back to the tunnel, and while there he would pick up a Roman coin with Tiberius stamped on it. That indicated that the tunnel had been opened in Roman times, then resealed.

Digging straight down

Many long hours would be spent lying awake at night. The frustrating thing was not being able to get at the Ark.

Maybe there was an easier way. And then the thought came, Why not open up the chamber from above?

As a last resort, an attempt would be made to dig and drill a shaft through the solid rock into the Ark chamber.

This would be a colossal undertaking. An awful amount of work would be required. And it could be quite dangerous if the shaft should cave in; it could damage some of the objects in the chamber. Or, after such an enormous effort, they could even find they had missed the chamber.

Nevertheless, it would be attempted. Toward the end of one trip to Israel, after the main excavation team had left for home, Ron and two others began the shaft.

They now used jackhammer drills.

Several trips to the site would follow, during which they managed to get through about ten feet of solid limestone.

But the end appeared nowhere in sight. Frustration grew from the tremendous effort and expense that appeared to yield no results.

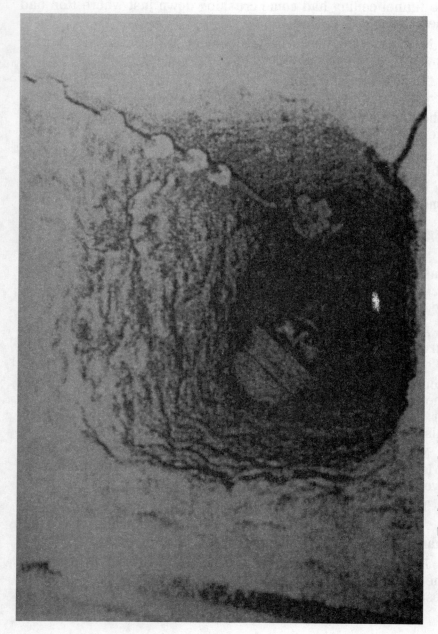

The shaft straight down into the solid rock inside the cave system (Photo: Ron Wyatt)

And then came the crunch, a trip for which Ron had to fork out all the expenses. He was close to $8,000 down the tube. And for no apparent results.

A sense of unworthiness

Of all projects he had undertaken, it was on this particular one that Ron's sense of unworthiness was most ever-present. He was vividly reminded of the biblical examples of men who accomplished a work for God but at some time or other failed in some manner. As when Moses defaulted on a divine command and it cost him the privilege of leading the Israelites into the promised land.

It was now 1992. Almost ten years since he first found the Ark in the chamber. Ron felt that his efforts since then didn't seem to be paying off. Was he being taken off the job and didn't know it?

The "man" who knew

Then Ron had an experience that changed his life.

With the team was a colleague whose trustworthiness had not been tested so it was decided not to investigate the region of the cave where the Ark stood.

One was drilling the shaft. Ron was down in the excavated trench in front of the cliff face. He was changing the paper on the radar scanner. The third man was sitting close by in the shade of a large bush eating his lunch.

Suddenly there was heard a voice above them.

"God bless you in what you are doing."

Ron wheeled around and saw, high up behind him, a tall, slender man with dark hair. He wore a robe and head covering similar to that worn in biblical times, except it was all pure white.

"God bless you for what you are doing," said the stranger.

Ron was startled. He hadn't told anyone. Virtually nobody knew what he was doing.

Ron tried to make polite conversation. "Are you from around this area?" he asked.

There was a pause... Then, "No." And more silence.

"Are you a tourist?" queried Ron.

"No," was the reply. And more silence.

Then the stranger said, "I am on my way from South Africa to the New Jerusalem."

Ron was so startled he couldn't speak, but just stared at him.

Once again the stranger spoke, "God bless you for what you are doing here."

He then turned and walked away.

After a moment, the team member who was eating lunch – but who couldn't see the visitor on account of the bush – shouted, "Ron, do you think we've been talking to an angel?"

Ron opened his mouth. "At least..." And his words died.

He was stunned.

Regaining his composure, Ron stumbled up the bank and questioned the locals who worked along the **only** path anyone could take into the area.

"Did you see him?" Ron shouted.

"Who?"

"That man!"

Nobody had seen anyone of that description either enter the area or leave.

The workmen and the vendors along the only entrance path, Ron knew well. There was no doubt about it. The stranger in white had been seen by no one else.

Ron was glad his lunch-eating companion had at least heard the conversation. At least he knew for sure that it had really happened.

That night he ran to the phone to tell Mary Nell, back in the USA. As he spilled out the story, his voice was still shaking with excitement.

Mary Nell says of that conversation, "I remember his call like it was yesterday. Ron is very lowed keyed. He never acts excited or angry. His voice rarely gives away his true feelings. But I knew something had happened even though his voice was calm. He explained that, just hours earlier, he had silently given up, frustrated, tired and simply worn down. He had lost his belief that he was working within the Lord's will. And then there was this conversation! It was heard by the other man as well, so he knew for sure that it really happened."

Just when he was worn down, and about to give up...

THEN THIS STRANGER APPEARED!

Whether Christ or angel, the experience was enough to encourage Ron that his efforts had **not** been in vain... and that he **was** still in God's will.

I can tell you that from that moment onward nothing has ever damped Ron's zeal or belief in that or any other project.

•••••••••

To prepare you for the rest of the story, I suggest that we now flash back... back to the prodigious events that occurred on this very spot long ago. Events most extraordinary, that would soon emerge as the catalyst for a modern, earth-shaking piece of news.

Are you ready?

CHAPTER 34

NO TURNING BACK

WARNING!

Up to this point, we have presented FACT after FACT in a continuing investigation of the search for the Ark of the Covenant.

The next four chapters will be different. They are **not** part of our investigation. Some readers may be offended by the contents of these chapters. They may prefer to skip them and recommence at Chapter 38.

For other readers, these chapters will be helpful in providing a background to the feelings of the people involved in the big event that possibly fulfilled the blood symbolism of the Ark of the Covenant.

The interaction between three convicted men, the emotions of friends and enemies, as recorded by eyewitnesses that day 2,000 years ago. The thoughts, emotions and internal struggle of the man who was allegedly about to fulfill his prophetic role as a sacrifice. What would be passing through such a man's mind?

WARNING. Go to Chapter 38, or read at your own risk. No responsibility taken.

•••••••••

It was **not** crucifixion that killed Yeshua.

Let me explain.

365

On Thursday night the 13th of Nisan, the evening before the crucifixion, Yeshua went with his disciples to the Gethsemane Garden on the east side of town.

The Passover moon, broad and full, shone in a clear sky.

As they neared the garden, the disciples noticed a change come over Jesus. He became sad and silent. They had never seen him like this. His form swayed as if he were about to fall. He seemed to be suffering under the pressure of some terrible burden. But they dared not question him about it.

They entered the garden.

"Pray for me," he asked them. Then he went a few paces further in among the trees.

They did pray for a while. They had never seen him so distressed.

Now he dropped down among those cypress and olive trees and began to pray.

He had predicted his own death. He had said that he would lay down his life – and that he would rise again on the third day.

The Garden of Gethsemane

Now it was time. Jesus was about to take upon himself the world's sins, to be punished for them. He had never sinned. To him sin was totally repulsive.

Now he began to feel it – the tremendous weight of retributive justice that should fall on a lost world; the utter anguish that lost man would feel at the last judgment. The agony began.

The disciples heard him groan in deep anguish. They heard his heartbroken cries to the Father to "let this cup" (whatever that meant) "pass from me." Then, overcome with weariness, they slept.

Yeshua wakened them. He begged them to pray with him. And they tried. But their eyes were heavy, and the day had been long. Again they slept.

Once more Jesus was seized with agony. He staggered back into the grove. His anguish grew more intense. He broke out in a cold sweat. And with the sweat, drops of blood oozed from his pores. He fell again to the earth.

Stretched out on the ground, he pleaded with God to find an easier way to save the human race. He did not want to be crucified. Was there no other way to save mankind? Even now, he could decide not to go through with it.

Jesus had approached the consummation of his work a conqueror. He had been victorious in every detail of his life, in every crisis. Each step he had gained the victory over the powers of darkness. Now he was buffeted with a force the like of which he had never experienced.

"Oh my Father, if it be possible, let this cup pass from me. But, if this cup may not pass from me, unless I drink it, Your will be done."

His whole life had been leading to this hour. But now his human nature staggered under its horror.

But it was the world's guilt that he was assuming as his own that was the real burden.

Now his face expressed the horror of it, a depth of anguish no man could realize. He began to feel that sin was so offensive to God that he would soon be separated from his Father forever. The gulf was so broad, so black, so deep, that his spirit shuddered before it.

As Jesus felt his unity with the Father broken up, he feared that in his human nature he might be unable to endure the coming struggle with the powers of darkness. That he might not be able to bear the guilt and the separation from the Father.

Jesus longed for companionship, but he again found his disciples sleeping. Their eyes were heavy. They stirred ... saw his face marked with bloody sweat, but understood nothing.

Returning to his former spot, Jesus collapsed, overcome by horror of a great darkness.

"Oh, my Father, if this cup may not pass from me..."

Three times he had uttered this prayer. Three times his human nature shrank from the last crowning sacrifice.

In that hour, the powers of darkness pressed upon him. The temptation to give up became strong. Why should he die for a world that didn't even want to be rescued? Why not let man pay for his own sins?

As Yeshua wrestled with the temptation to turn back, the fate of the whole human race trembled in the balance.

But no. If they were to be reconciled to their Creator, he must take the shock within himself of that reconciliation.

Even if it meant that he would go down to a grave from which there would be no resurrection.

"Nevertheless, Father, not as I want, but as you will."

He realized that the human race would be lost unless he agreed to die. He would keep his promise.

As Jesus felt the crushing weight, the horror, of the sins of the world descending upon him, the agony grew unbearable.

The sufferings of the human race rushed before him. The overwhelming power of sin. The helpless cries of a doomed world. And his decision was made. He would save man at any cost to himself.

Having made the decision, he fell dying to the ground. The death process for our sins had begun. After this, Jesus would have soon died even if they had never put him on the cross.

The blood-sweat of agony, when the circulatory system breaks down under extreme mental anguish, is a first sign of approaching death, which will follow within a matter of hours.

The disciples awoke. They heard his groans. And they saw a heavenly being, dispatched to his side, strengthening him.

A peace now rested upon his brow, blood-stained as it was. He had just tasted the sufferings of death for every man and woman.

The arrest

Yet already the sound of an approaching mob shattered the silence. One of his own disciples had betrayed him. They had come to arrest Yeshua of Nazareth.

The betrayal by Judas

For a moment, divinity flashed through his countenance. The leaders of the mob staggered back.

At that moment, he could easily have walked away. But he stood there. And let it happen.

He would permit them to bind him, torture him, put him on trial, condemn him and execute him. He submitted without protest.

Yet Jesus was hardly a helpless victim. He knew he could call a squadron of angels to his side, if he wished. They could have swooped from the Throne of his Father in an instant.

IT WAS NO ORDINARY EXECUTION. Jesus sacrificed himself. Men in their wickedness might choose to crucify him, but it was he who gave himself into their hands to do it.

Before the mob, he now stood tall and straight, ready for what lay ahead.

"I lay down my life for the sheep," he had said. "No man taketh it from me, but I lay it down of myself. I have power to lay it down, and I have power to take it again."[1]

Led to be executed

It is Friday morning. A little after 8 am.

A vast crowd follows Yeshua from the courthouse to Skull Hill.

The news of his conviction has spread throughout Jerusalem, and people of all classes and ranks flock toward the execution spot.

The priests and council men have been bound by a promise not to molest Yeshua's followers if Yeshua himself were to be caught. Many believers join the crowd.

As Jesus passes the court gate, the cross is laid upon his bruised and bleeding shoulders.

Two robbers are to suffer death at the same time with Yeshua. And upon them also are crosses placed.

Jesus, faint from his recent ordeal of an all-night mockery of a trial, finds the cross too heavy.

All night he has taken no food or drink. He has agonized in Gethsemane Garden in conflict with satanic forces. He has endured the anguish of betrayal by one of his own disciples, and has seen the remaining members of his little band forsake him and flee.

He has been taken before Annas the ex-high priest, then to high priest Caiaphas, then to Governor Pilate, then to King Herod and back to Pilate.

From insult to renewed insult, from mockery to mockery. Twice tortured by the scourge. All that night there has been scene after scene.

Jesus has not failed. All through the disgraceful farce of a trial he has borne himself with firmness and dignity.

But now, after the second scourging with the whip, when the cross is laid upon him, human nature can bear no more.

He falls fainting beneath the burden.

The crowd shows no pity. They taunt him because he cannot carry the heavy cross.

Again the burden is laid upon him. Again he falls fainting to the ground.

His persecutors are puzzled to find anyone who will bear the humiliating load. The Jews themselves will not do this, because the "defilement" will prevent them from observing the holy Passover feast. Not one of the mob that follows him will stoop to bear the cross.

For a third time he staggers under it. The cross crashes to the ground. Cruel whips lash out at him.

Screams of horror ring out from some of the women who have known him. Their sick and their suffering he has healed. They now wonder at the hatred of the crowd toward him. Their own hearts are melting and ready to break.

Jesus looks upon them. Their sympathy awakens in his heart a deeper sympathy for them.

A prophecy

With a soft smile, he turns to them. "Daughters of Jerusalem, weep not for me. But weep for yourselves, and for your children."

Jesus is looking ahead to the time of Jerusalem's destruction. In that terrible scene, many of those who are now weeping for him, will perish with their children!

The stranger

At this time a stranger, Simon, from Libya in North Africa, coming in from the country, meets the crowd.

He hears the taunts and sour jokes. He hears the mocking shout, "MAKE WAY FOR THE KING OF THE JEWS."

He stops in astonishment at the scene.

And as he looks on with compassion, they seize him and place the cross upon his shoulders.

Simon has heard of this man Yeshua. His sons are believers in him. But he himself is not a disciple.

The bearing of the cross is a turning point in his life. He will in time to come be ever grateful for this twist of events.

Disciples in despair

Come to think of it, Jesus' own disciples might have come forward and offered to carry the cross. But fear holds them back from any demonstration of allegiance to him.

Some disciples follow the crowd in bitter sorrow. They call to mind Yeshua Messiah's triumphal ride into Jerusalem only a few days earlier.

Then they had followed him, crying, "Hosanna in the highest!" They had strewn their coats on the ground. And palm branches.

They had thought that he was about to take the kingdom and reign as a physical prince over Israel! They had pressed close, wanting to be seen with him.

How changed the scene! How blighted their prospects!

Now they are stricken with fear and despair. Slowly, sadly, they follow at a distance him who has been disgraced and humbled.

And who is about to die.

CHAPTER 35

THE EXECUTION BEGINS

At length they reach Skull Hill. Place of death.

The centurion stops... and orders the crosses to be set in the rock, where deep holes have already been cut.

The crosses carried by the thieves are now thrown down by them, by one with a curse, by the other with a sigh – as he anticipates the agony he is to suffer upon it.

Yeshua's cross is taken by three soldiers from the back of the Negro and cast heavily upon the rock.

The centurion orders his soldiers to clear a semi-circle about the place where the crosses are to be planted with their spears.

Crucifixion is a Roman death, a form of capital punishment, reserved for criminals. And it serves as a graphic warning to all people.

Crucifixion is an excessively brutal way to die. They strip a convict naked and flog him till his chest and back are in ribbons. Then they arrange his legs uncomfortably and drive blunt nails through his ankles and wrists into a wooden frame.

The Jews, who have crowded near in eager thirst for their victim's blood, edge back slowly and reluctantly before the sharp points of the Roman lances against their chests.

Now the Roman soldiers can get on with their work. It is a terrible work they have to do. And though it is part of the routine of their life, they must hate doing it, especially when their prisoners fight and struggle.

First, a drink

Before they start, they offer each man a drink of wine containing drugs. The effect will not last long, but it will just deaden the beginning of the pain.[1]

The two thieves gulp their drink thankfully. But Jesus refuses his. He wants to keep his mind as clear as he can. His faith must keep fast hold upon God. This is his only true strength. To becloud his senses will give the powers of evil an advantage.

Then the nails

The first robber, upon seeing the man approach with the basket containing the spikes and hammers, scowls fiercely upon him – and glares defiance.

He is instantly seized by four savage-looking Parthian soldiers of the Roman guard and stripped naked, then thrown upon his back onto the cross.

The struggles of this athletic man are so violent, that it takes six persons to keep him held down upon the arms of the cross.

The legionnaire feels for the depression at the front of the wrist.

One of the crucifiers, with bare and brawny arms, presses one knee upon the arm and drives a heavy, square wrought-iron nail in through the wrist and deep into the wood, by three quick and powerful blows with his short, heavy-headed hammer.

The prisoner gnashes his teeth as the nail enters the quivering flesh.

Quickly the soldier moves to the other side and repeats the action. He is careful not to pull the arms too tightly. Some flex and movement will have to be allowed.

The cross is then lifted into place.

Then both feet are lapped together. The left foot is pressed backward against the right foot. With both feet extended toes down, a long, sharp spear-nail is driven through the arch of each, into the timber, leaving the knees flexed.

A shriek, mingled with curses, testifies to the agony of this wretched man. Thus secured he is left, bleeding and writhing.

The blood-stained crucifiers, with their baskets, cords, hammer and spikes, now approach the other robber.

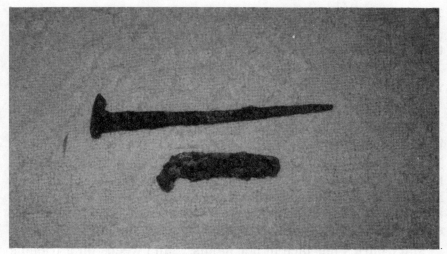

Crucifixion nails

He, too, wrestles in their hands. After much resistance, his arms are thrust back and nailed to the cross.

When the centurion gives orders to bind Jesus also to the cross, the four soldiers lay hold upon him, remove his robe and begin to strip him of every garment.

But Jesus makes no resistance.

The mother

The mother of Yeshua is there.

Her heart is still throbbing with hope that Yeshua will work some mighty miracle and deliver himself from his murderers.

Again her heart sinks as she recalls the words in which he had foretold the very scenes that are now taking place.

She looks on with agonized suspense. Will he permit himself to be shamed like this? Must she witness his shame and sorrow, without even supporting him or bathing his forehead?

She watches him thrown onto the wood. The hammer and nails are brought.

A few of the disciples stand at a distance. Their hearts faint.

But his mother is bowed with agony almost beyond endurance.

"Oh, don't let me hear the crashing of the nails into your feet and hands. My son, my son! Oh, prove to your mother that you are a true prophet!"

"What's all that wailing?" snaps one of the priests. "Who is that woman?"

"The mother of Yeshua," answers someone.

"The mother of the blasphemer? Let her be accursed!" he cries in a savage tone.

"You see, woman, what is the end of bringing up an impostor to blaspheme Yahweh and the Temple. You wretched woman. Your hopes and his have today miserably died! So die all false Christs and false prophets! You see, if he were the Messiah, he would not stand there and be crucified like a common evil-doer!"

Mary buries her face in her hands... and weeps on a friend's shoulder.

As some disciples bear her from the scene, they can hear the awful preparations... the rattling of the hard cord as they bind him to the cross... and the low, eager voices of the four busy crucifiers... then the ringing of the spikes being taken from the basket... then a moment of silence and suspense.

Next comes the sickening blow of the hammer!

A shriek bursts from the soul of the mother. It echoes far and wide among the tombs of Skull Hill, only to be broken by the crashing of the spikes, as they are driven through the bone and muscle of his tender flesh.

Jesus? He murmurs not, but groans in agony. The piercing nails, tearing his tender flesh, make it quiver. And his face, though calm and serene, turns pale, And large drops of sweat stand on his brow.

Jesus hears his mother's shriek and a deep sigh escapes him.

Pity and forgiveness

While the thieves are cursing their executioners, this Jesus , in his agony, makes no murmur or complaint.

There is no pitying hand to wipe the death-dew from his face. Nor words of sympathy. Nor his disciples' loyalty. Instead there is ridicule.

While the nails are being driven through his hands and the sweat-drops of agony are forced from his pores, from the pale, quivering lips of the innocent sufferer, a prayer of pardoning love is breathed for his murderers:

"Father, forgive them, for they know not what they do!" [2]

His mind passes from his own suffering to the sin of his persecutors – and the terrible retribution that will be theirs.

No curses are called down upon the soldiers who are handling him so roughly. No vengeance is invoked upon the priests and rulers, who are gloating over the accomplishment of their purpose.

Jesus actually pities them in their ignorance and guilt. He breathes only a plea for their forgiveness, "for they know not what they do".

Should they know that they were putting to torture the One who had come to save the sinful race from eternal ruin, they would be seized with remorse and horror.

However, willful ignorance does not remove guilt. It is their privilege to know and accept Yeshua as their Savior. And some of them will yet do so. Others, by stubborn refusal, will prevent Yeshua's prayer being answered for themselves.

It strikes me that, in a broader sense, that prayer includes all of us.

Upon all rests the guilt of the Son of God's death. To all, forgiveness is freely offered. "Whosoever will" may have peace with God... and inherit eternal life.

His cross lifted into place

As soon as Jesus is fastened to the timber, it is raised above the ground by strong men, and with violence thrust into a hole in the rock two feet deep.

This causes most intense pain. The shock brings his whole weight upon the nails in his wrists. It tears and lacerates them, nearly dislocating his shoulders.

The first thief faints from pain at the shock caused by the setting of his own cross. The second, cool and defiant as he has been, utters a loud cry of agony. But Jesus makes no moan – though his deathly pale appearance shows how inexpressible is his torture.

377

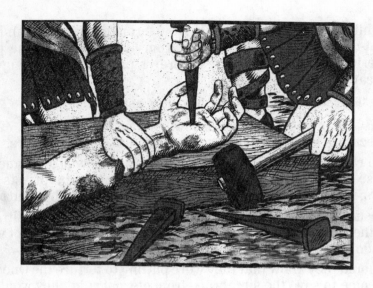

Sketch: Jim Pinkoski

It is 9 am .[3]

The three crosses have now been fixed and raised, with the "feature criminal", Yeshua of Nazareth, in the midst on a level several feet higher than the others. This is the chief place of disgrace.

Now the centurion pushes back the crowd so that the criminals can be left to die.

Someone begins sobbing. "Oh, what a fearful death for Yeshua! For him whom we knew so well. I still love him... although he has deceived us."

They know he might linger on for days, dying slowly... exposed to the fierce sun by day and the chilly winds of night. While above him will hover on steady wings the savage birds of prey, impatient for their feast.

As he slowly sags down with more weight on the nails in the wrists, excruciating, fiery pain will soon shoot along his fingers and up his arms to explode in the brain. The nails in his wrist will put pressure on the median nerves.

In pushing himself up to lessen this stretching torment, he will have to place his full weight on the nail through his feet. So again he will feel the searing agony of the nail tearing through the nerves between the bones of the feet.

The time will come when the arms will fatigue. Cramps will sweep through the muscles, knotting them in deep, relentless, throbbing pain.

With these cramps, he will eventually be unable to push himself upward to breathe. Air will be drawn into his lungs, but to exhale will be difficult. He will then be fighting to raise himself, so as to get even one small breath.

Gradually, carbon dioxide will build up in the lungs and blood stream. Cramps will partially subside. Spasmodically, he might push himself upward to exhale and bring in life-giving oxygen.

Hours of this limitless pain, cycles of twisting, joint-rending cramps, intermittent partial asphyxiation, searing pain as tissue is torn from his lacerated back, as he moves up and down against the rough timber.

Then another agony begins: a deep, crushing pain deep in the chest, as the pericardium slowly fills with serum and begins to compress the heart.

It is now almost over – the loss of tissue fluids has reached a critical level. The compressed heart is struggling to pump heavy, thick, sluggish blood into the tissues. The tortured lungs are making a frantic effort to gasp in small gulps of air.

He can feel the chill of death creeping through his tissues. Finally he can allow his body to die.[4]

That is what lies ahead.

All this is recorded in Scripture with the simple words, "And they crucified him."[5]

What kind of love is this that Jesus is willing to go through this, with each of us in mind?

He could call 10,000 angels from his Father to rescue him, but he willingly endures the agony for each one of us.

The long hours

The sun is high, now, and the heat is adding the misery of thirst to the other torments of the crucified men.

The hours will seem long, and some of the soldiers sit down on the ground to pass the time as best they can.

They divide the prisoners' clothes amongst them.

In spite of the blood and dirt that stains Yeshua's robe, they can see what a beautiful garment it is. It was given to Jesus; it was a gift. They gamble for it.

The mockery

Yeshua's enemies vent their rage upon him, as he hangs on the cross. Many priests are present at the execution, to witness the climax of their bloodthirsty plot.

What men to lead the nation! How cruel, heartless and utterly devoid of mercy and pity are they, gloating at the suffering of their victim!

Luke records the event:

> And the people stood beholding. And the rulers also with them derided him, saying, He saved others; let him save himself, if he be the Christ, the chosen of God.[6]

Jesus , in agony and dying, hears every word.

As the priests scream, "He saved others; himself he cannot save. Let Christ the king of Israel descend now from the cross, that we may see and believe," Yeshua could do just that.

But it is because he will not save himself that you and I will have hope of pardon and favor with God. If Jesus now saves himself, he will forfeit the power to save others. The plan of rescue will have been broken.

Though they know it not, those Jewish leaders give utterance to a profound truth. Jesus' refusal to save himself is the supreme demonstration of divine love.

It is precisely because Jesus chooses not to save himself at this moment, that he will be able to save others.

As Jesus has gone through the experience in the Gethsemane Garden, and now as he hangs upon the cross, Satan spares no device, however cruel and false, to shake the Deliverer's hold on his Father's love and overruling providence.

"He trusted in God; let him deliver him now, if he will have him: for he said I am the Son of God." [7]

Several times during his remarkable, brief career as Messiah, the voice of God had been heard proclaiming Yeshua as his Son. This had occurred at his baptism and again at his transfiguration experience just before his betrayal. The Father had spoken, witnessing to his divinity.

But now the voice from heaven is SILENT! No testimony in Jesus' favor is heard. Alone he suffers abuse and mockery from wicked men.

In their mockery of the Messiah, the men who profess to be the expounders of prophecy are repeating the very words which the old writings had foretold they would utter on this occasion.[8]

Yet, in their blindness, they do not see that they are fulfilling the prophecy.

But the most startling scenes are yet to come.

"For indeed a death by crucifixion seems to include all that pain and death **can** have of horrible and ghastly - dizziness, cramp, thirst, starvation, sleeplessness, traumatic fever, tetanus, shame, publicity of shame, long continuance of torment, horror of anticipation, mortification of untended wounds - all intensified just up to the point at which they can be endured at all, but all stopping just short of the point which would give to the sufferer the relief of unconsciousness.

"The unnatural position made every movement painful; the lacerated veins and crushed tendons throbbed with incessant anguish; the wounds, inflamed by exposure, gradually gangrened; the arteries - especially at the head and stomach - became swollen and oppressed with surcharged blood; and while each variety of misery went on gradually increasing, there was added to them the intolerable pang of a burning and raging thirst; and all these physical complications caused an internal excitement and anxiety, which made the prospect of death itself - of death, the unknown enemy, at whose approach man usually shudders most - bear the aspect of a delicious and exquisite release."

Frederick W. Farrar, *The Life of Christ*. Dutton, Dovar: Cassell and Company, 1897,p.619

CHAPTER 36

TWO THIEVES

The crosses of the two thieves stand one on each side of Jesus, but lower down and a little forward of him.

They have heard the taunts of the priests, and half crazed with pain, they cast the same at him.

One of them, under his suffering, only becomes more desperate and defiant.

The pain becomes more than he can bear, and he cries out, "If you are the Messiah, save yourself and us. If you did raise a man once from the dead you can surely keep us from dying!"

Then he rails at that Man in the middle, because the pain goes on.

"You are a vile wretch, if you have power as a prophet and will not use it for me when you see how heavy I am of body. My great weight is torturing me. It's burning and tearing at every joint. You're evil!"

The other thief speaks up. This man is not a hardened criminal. He was led astray by bad company. But he is probably much less guilty than many who are standing by the cross abusing.

Some time ago, he had seen and heard Yeshua. And he had been persuaded by his teaching. However, the priests and rulers had dissuaded him.

Seeking to stifle the conviction in his heart, he had plunged deeper and deeper into wrong-doing, until he was caught and arrested. Now, tried as a criminal, he is condemned to die.

In the courthouse and on the way to Skull Hill, he has been in the company of Jesus. He has heard Governor Pilate declare, "I find no fault in him." He has noticed Jesus' "godlike" bearing and his pitying forgiveness of his tormentors.

On the cross, he sees the religious leaders sneering and abusing Jesus. He sees their wagging heads.

He hears the other thief's rebukes to Jesus.

Among the passers-by he hears some others defending Yeshua. He hears them repeat his words and tell of his works.

Now the conviction comes back to him that this is indeed the Messiah.

The cursing and muttering of the other thief is suddenly intolerable to him.

"Stop it!" he cries. "Don't you fear God? You are equally guilty. Who are you to condemn?"

The dying thieves have no longer anything to fear from man.

But there presses upon one of them the conviction that there is a God to fear... a future to cause him to tremble.

And now, all messed up as it is, his life history is about to close.

"Do you not fear God?" he cries, "seeing you are in the same condemnation? We suffer justly for our crimes, and today we receive the due reward of our transgressions; but this young man has done nothing wrong."

There is no question now. No doubts.

When first sentenced for his crime, the thief had become hopeless and despairing.

But now strange thoughts spring up. Tender thoughts. He calls to mind all he has heard of Yeshua... how he has healed the sick and pardoned sin. He has heard the words of those who believed in Yeshua and followed him weeping. He has seen and read the title that was to go above Yeshua's cross. He has heard the passers-by repeat it – some with grieved, quivering lips; others with jesting and mockery.

The Spirit of God illuminates his mind. And little by little the chain of evidence is joined together.

"We suffer justly for our crimes, and today we receive the due reward of our deeds; but this man has done nothing wrong." [1]

An honest admission

This thief is honest to the point of making a candid admission of his guilt.

Significantly, he now reflects the attitude that is necessary to receive mercy from the Lord. A sense of one's need is, we're told, the first condition of rescue for eternal life.[2]

This thief, as the minutes drag by – minutes that seem like hours – does begin to understand something. And what he understands is the difference between himself and the Man beside him!

But he does not stay bogged in the filth of his own sin, helpless and despairing. He wrenches himself out of it. And though the movement is an added torture, he turns his head toward Yeshua, to look at him.

I do not know for how long he looks. But during the silence between this cry of repentance and the cry of love that follows, he travels a long way.

(Remember, men and women do sometimes travel quickly and far when they are suffering. Further, perhaps, in ten minutes of great pain, than in ten years of ease.)

Looking at Yeshua of Nazareth, he knows at last what he wants, and has always wanted.

He wants just this very splendor of love that is beside him and upholding him, this Man whom they mockingly call the King of the Jews.

He wants to be with him always.

In Yeshua, bruised, mocked and hanging on the cross, he sees the Lamb of God that takes away the sins of the world.

Hope is mingled with anguish in his voice, as the helpless, dying nobody casts himself upon a dying Savior.

"Lord, remember me," he cries, "when you come into your Kingdom."

The promise

Jesus turns his bleeding head. The thief sees tears sparkling in his eyes.

Jesus is deeply affected... and smiling, in his pain. While a glittering drop dances down his beard and breaks into liquid diamonds upon his body.

He says, "You are accepted, my child." And then, quickly, the answer comes. Soft and melodious is the tone, full of love, compassion and power:

"Truly, I tell you today, you shall be with me in paradise."[3]

At this, the other thief curses the prophet aloud. He gnashes at him with his teeth, with looks of demonic hatred.

But the thief who has repented now seems to rise inexpressibly happier, and superior to his sufferings.

Thinking only of others

For long hours, insults and mockery, jeers and curses, have fallen upon the ears of Jesus.

With longing heart, he has listened for some expression of faith from his own disciples. He has heard only the mournful words, "We trusted that he was the one who should have delivered Israel."

How sweet, then, to his ears is the expression of faith and love from the dying thief!

While the great leaders of the nation and church deny him – and even his own followers doubt him – the poor thief, on the brink of eternity, calls him Lord.

In his humiliation, naked in public on the cross, Jesus is glorified.

Bystanders are arrested as they catch this conversation. He who in all other eyes appears to be conquered is a Conqueror.

They can exercise power over his human body... they can pierce his head with a crown of thorns... they can strip from him his clothes and quarrel over dividing them... but they cannot not rob him of his power to forgive and cleanse from sin.

He has become the sin-bearer.

His enemies have positioned his cross in the center, between the two thieves, to indicate that he is the greatest criminal of the three.

And they unwittingly fulfill an ancient prophecy: "He was numbered with the transgressors."[4]

It's true, you know. Even the most unselfish people, when they are suffering, find it hard to think of anything but their own pain.

But throughout his ordeal, Jesus is thinking of the people about him!

"Forgive my murderers."

And now the thief.

Heavenly beings, unseen by the crowd, are also watching this historic event.

With amazement, they behold the unlimited love of Jesus, who, suffering the most intense agony of mind and body, thinks only of others.

As the eyes of Jesus wander over the crowd below, one figure arrests his attention.

His mother has returned to the terrible scene, supported by the disciple John.

She cannot endure to remain away from her son. And John, not knowing when the end will come, has brought her again to the cross.

In his bodily pain and mental suffering, Jesus does not forget his mother. He sees her standing there, at the foot of the cross. He well knows her distress.

Looking down at his mother and John, his two best beloved, he has thought about them and planned for them.

They will be lonely. But he thinks of a way to comfort them.

Looking into her grief-stricken face, and then upon John, he says to Mary:

"Woman, behold your son. John, behold your mother." [5]

Thus he provides for her that which she most needs – the tender sympathy of one who loves her because she loves Jesus.

And from that hour, the disciple John takes her to his own home.[6]

While the crucifixion continues...

The crucifixion scene, according to the new evidence

CHAPTER 37

ACT OF LOVE

A fatal experiment wiped out millions.

... and killed the Man who invented the remedy.

Millions of unaware victims will die this year. Millions will be saved by the remedy.

HOW SAFE ARE YOU?

••••••

The story of that experiment, we related in Chapter 4. The experiment was the thing we call... SIN.

And the remedy was the death of the Innocent One.

Why the need for the cross?

Mary Anne looked perplexed.

"It does bother me," she said "It seems like it was just a gimmick."

"What do you mean?" I asked.

"Well, if he was about to die anyway, then why allow himself to be nailed publicly to a cross? I almost feel sorry for those priests. It's like God willed it, so they had to act their guilty part. Like they were victims of fate."

"I understand," was my reply. "But let's be clear on this. Jesus' enemies were not victims of fate or of prophecy. They didn't have to do what they did. Jesus had done everything possible to save them from this terrible deed. But they **freely chose** their course of

389

action. **And God overruled it to His purpose**. He did this in two ways."

Two that I could think of. I shared these with Mary Anne. And they're worth repeating now.

Firstly, AS UNDISPUTED EVIDENCE THAT THE SACRIFICE HAD BEEN MADE.

The agony of a **public** death meant that witness of it could be borne without the shadow of doubt. It was to become the pivot of history.

Consequently we know more about the details of those hours leading up to and during the death of Jesus than we know about the death of any other one person in all the ancient world.

In the tenth century Apaplus wrote:

> We have found in many books of the philosophers that they refer to the day of the crucifixion of Christ.[1]

And elsewhere we have cited statements from Tacitus, Josephus and the Jewish Talmuds, relating to this event.

Secondly, THE CROSS WAS OVERRULED TO REACH MEN'S HEARTS.

The cross became God's chosen means of winning men and women to His love.

Shame... or triumph?

To anyone watching the event, it was a disaster. Jesus had failed.

On the other hand, if he really **was** the Messiah, choosing to die on man's behalf, one could draw several startling conclusions.

1 – Sin must be a tremendously important matter.

Sin **required** Jesus' death. And he died because sin was **curable.**

When does a doctor operate? When there is hope! Certainly not when it is hopeless! So sin is neither hopeless nor incurable, otherwise he would never have died. For sin to be grappled with successfully, God Himself must come right into it.

2 – The cross proved God's love.

390

His death answered the question as to whether the Father and Son had sufficient love for mankind to exercise self-denial and a spirit of sacrifice, so that humans could be saved.

The spotless Son of God hung upon the cross, his flesh lacerated with whip strokes; those hands that so often reached out to help people, now nailed to wooden bars; those feet so tireless on errands of love, spiked to the cross; that royal head pierced by a mock crown of thorns; those quivering lips shaped to the cry of woe.

And all that he endured: the blood drops that flowed from his head, his hands, his feet; the agony that racked his frame; the unutterable anguish that filled his soul for lost man...

It was for me... and you.

He who calmed angry waves and walked the foam-capped billows, who made devils tremble and disease flee, who opened blind eyes and called dead men to life... offers himself upon the cross as a sacrifice.

And this from his love to us!

He endures the penalty of divine justice for your sake... and, mine. His death proves his love.

What a triumph!

3 – It proved who it was that cared.

For thousands of years, the forces of evil had been in a tussle for the control of the human race.[2]

It was claimed by the prophets that behind man's rebellion were evil entities. They had denied God's truthfulness and His concern for His subjects. Having initially rebelled against the government of heaven, they had been cast out. Rather than destroy them there and then (which could have been misunderstood), God decided to fight the rebellion with LOVE.

Lucifer, their leader, it was held, had shifted his battlefield to planet Earth – and led our first parents into rebellion.

"Go it alone," he urged. "Be independent. You don't need God."

And we fell for it.

When the rebellion began, it had seemed incredible that sin could be as dangerous as God said it was.

But when the universe saw the centuries of hatred, heartache and death on planet Earth, they began to understand. They watched Lucifer's (Satan's) kingdom in operation.

Then they saw God's Son enter this enemy territory to save mankind. He lived and suffered with us – showing us by his example how to overcome.

Then he went to the cross. That showed the value God had placed upon men and women. It was the ultimate evidence of God's great love.

But Satan's unquenchable hatred toward the Son of God was revealed in the way he carefully planned the betrayal, mock trial and shameful crucifixion.

This opened the eyes of the universe to his true criminal character. Heavenly beings were horror-stricken that Lucifer, a former one of their number, could fall so far as to be capable of such cruelty. Now every sentiment of sympathy or pity which they ever felt for him in his exile was quenched from their hearts.

So there is Lucifer, professing to be clothed in celestial light – yet with envy he exercises revenge on an innocent Person, against the divine Son of God who has, with unprecedented self-denial and love, come from heaven and assumed the nature of lost mankind.[3]

Now Satan appears hideous! He has committed such a horrible crime against heaven, that heavenly beings shudder with horror.

The last link of sympathy with him is broken. He is finished, as far as the inhabitants of other worlds are concerned.[4]

He has revealed his true character as a liar and a murderer.[5]

Lucifer is discredited. Jesus Christ is vindicated.

What a triumph!

4 – It satisfied divine law and established it as unchangeable.

The death of Jesus was a convincing argument that the law of God was as unchangeable as His Throne.

The fact that God's own Son, the surety for man, was not spared, testified that the divine law, which had been violated, could not be altered to save the sinner.

No, the violation of that law must meet the penalty, death. Therefore, the justice of God must put to death His beloved Son who stood in the wrong-doer's place.

The law must stand as firm as the Throne of God – although the earth shake and the whole creation tremble – as the Son of God dies in agony.

Justice demands that sin be not only pardoned, but that the death penalty must be executed The very purpose of Jesus' death was to secure pardon for the law-breaker, without destroying the law.

The death of Jesus is the mightiest evidence of the holiness of the law of God.

In the days of the Persian empire, the monarch Darius labored strenuously, feverishly, to save Daniel from the lion's den. But there stood the "law of the Medes and Persians which alters not."[6] The majesty of law, the very stability of the government, demanded that the sentence be executed, or else the throne itself would be imperiled.

Even so, had there been another way to vindicate the sovereignty of divine law, Jesus need not have died.

But infinite love and wisdom could devise no other plan, since to abolish the law would have immortalized sin.

The royal law must stand unshaken, even though it cost the life of the beloved Son. The law and justice of God – all-holy – are established.[7]

What a triumph!

The grandest drama of all

When I finally grasped the grandeur of this event, I realized that beside it all the wisdom of earth's wisest men sank into insignificance.

Just think of the immensity of the drama!

The co-Creator gave himself as a ransom. He laid off his royal robe. He laid aside his kingly crown, and stepped down from his high command over all heaven, and took upon himself feeble human flesh.[8] And as if that were not enough, he so abased himself as to suffer the excruciating pain of the cross, at the hands of people he had created.[9]

It is a mystery that he did it. And it is a mystery that God so loved the world as to permit His Son to make this great sacrifice. Science is too limited to comprehend this event. This mysterious and wonderful plan of rescue is so far-reaching that philosophy cannot explain it. The most profound reason cannot fathom it.

Indeed, this was the most daring rescue mission of all time.

For many years I lived as an unbeliever. There are readers who, like myself, will be able to relate to the following true experience of yet another skeptic.

George Vandeman recounts this story of an unbeliever who rescued an orphan boy from a burning building.

"Having lost his own wife and child, he desired to adopt the lad. Christian neighbors were skeptical about the wisdom of placing the boy in an infidel home. But the applicant won his case when he held up his hand, badly burned in the rescue of the lad, and said, 'I have only one argument. It is this.'

"He proved to be a good father, and little Bobby never tired of hearing how Daddy had saved him from the fire. And he liked best to hear about the scarred hand.

"One day with his new father he visited a display of art masterpieces. One painting interested him especially – the one of Jesus reproving Thomas for his unbelief and holding out his scarred hand.

"'Tell me the story of that picture, Daddy', the little fellow pleaded.

"'No, not that one.'

"'Why not?'

"'Because I don't believe it'.

"'But you tell me the story of Jack the giant-killer, and you don't believe that.'

"So he told him the story. And Bobby said, 'It's like you and me, Daddy'. And then he went on, 'It wasn't nice of Thomas not to believe after the good Man had died for him. What if they had told me how you saved me from the fire and I had said I didn't believe you did it?'

"The father could not escape the sound reasoning of a little child. He had used his own scarred hand to win a small boy's heart.

Could he continue to resist the scarred hand of the Man who had died for him – and say he didn't do it?" [10]

It has to be the mightiest argument of all, that cross on Skull Hill.

The scarred hands of Yeshua. Hands that were wounded in his encounter with the forces of evil – so that you and I could live!

And now we return to the crucifixion site...

THE CROSS WAS HIS OWN

They borrowed a bed to lay His head
    When Christ the Lord came down;
They borrowed the ass in the mountain pass
    For Him to ride to town;
BUT THE CROWN THAT HE WORE AND THE CROSS THAT HE BORE
    WERE HIS OWN – THE CROSS WAS HIS OWN.

He borrowed the bread when the crowd He fed
    On the grassy mountainside;
He borrowed the dish of broken fish
    With which He satisfied;
BUT THE CROWN THAT HE WORE AND THE CROSS THAT HE BORE
    WERE HIS OWN – THE CROSS WAS HIS OWN.

He borrowed the ship in which to sit
    To teach the multitude;
He borrowed a nest in which to rest
    He had never a home so rude;
BUT THE CROWN THAT HE WORE AND THE CROSS THAT HE BORE
    WERE HIS OWN – THE CROSS WAS HIS OWN.

He borrowed a room on His way to the tomb,
    The Passover lamb to eat;
They borrowed a cave for Him a grave,
    They borrowed a winding sheet;
BUT THE CROWN THAT HE WORE AND THE CROSS THAT HE BORE
    WERE HIS OWN - THE CROSS WAS HIS OWN.

                 L.M. Hollingsworth

CHAPTER 38

BLACK NOON

It was high noon on Friday, the sixth day of the week, the fourteenth of Nisan, 31 AD.

Suddenly the sun went dark. But this was no eclipse: the darkness smothered the land for three long hours.[1]

Historians would write that the darkness reached to the very heart of the empire, in Rome.

Close outside Jerusalem, on a ledge of a hill shaped like a skull, a figure on a public stake was dying... BUT NOT FROM CRUCIFIXION.

The events leading up to his death were bizarre.

The attendant military commander, a tough, seasoned skeptic, was heard to exclaim, "Truly this man was the Son of God."

Hours earlier, the Roman governor had declared publicly, "I find no fault in this man," and, tremblingly succumbing to the public clamor, washed his hands of the affair.

The accused was condemned by a Jewish religious court. Not for any criminal act – indeed, hard as they tried, they had found no fault with his life on any score – but for the fact that he had claimed to be God. HIS TRIAL AND EXECUTION WERE FOR ONE THING ONLY – HIS IDENTITY!

And today several eerie things had happened.

◆◆◆◆◆◆

For the past three years this enigma of a man had shaken Israel. Never had there been such a life as this.

397

But he had also predicted his own death. He had said that he would lay down his life as an atonement for the world's sins, then rise again the third day.

Now he hung on a Roman cross. The cross was a symbol of their sun worship. By nailing Jesus to the cross, they said in effect, "We cannot have mercy on this criminal. Oh, god of the sun, we commit his soul to you."

Mysterious darkness

The fiery orb climbed directly overhead.

Suddenly the sun was blacked out.

For three hours a mysterious darkness hung over the land.

This darkness, witnessed by so many, would require a naturalistic explanation from those who did not want to believe.

In 52 AD, the Samaritan-born historian Thallus was to write a history, now lost, but cited by other writers. One of these, Julius Africanus (c. 221 AD), states:

> Thallus, in the third book of his histories, explains away this darkness as an eclipse of the sun – unreasonably, as it seems to me.[2]

The first century historian Phlegon, in his *Chronicles*, confirms that:

> During the time of Tiberius Caesar an eclipse of the sun occurred during the full moon.[3]

Could this have been a natural eclipse? No way. And here's why. For one thing, eclipses do not last three hours. Minutes, at the most. But this darkness continued from noon till three in the afternoon. Three hours.

And something else. The date was Nisan 14 – two weeks after the new moon. That means, it was about full moon, when the moon could not possibly eclipse the sun – being in the opposite part of the sky.

Philopon writes:

> And about this darkness... Phlegon recalls it in the *Olympiads*... he did not know from his sources about any (similar) eclipse in previous times... and this is shown by the

398

historical account itself of Tiberius Caesar. (De. opif. mund. II. 21). [4]

He dies alone

In that darkness, Jesus was alone.

And what anguish! He was giving up everything – his heavenly home, his own Father, even life itself – for them. The sneering ones around the cross – he loved them still. But where were his disciples?

The prophet Daniel had said it all: he was to die "not for himself", but for others – "and shall have nothing" [5] – no people, no place, no recognition, no kingdom, no followers. Not even his clothes. Stripping him naked was the ultimate shame. Deprived of everything.

Through long hours of agony, Jesus had been gazed upon by the jeering crowd. But now, while he drank the last dregs of the cup of divine displeasure, now, from the gaze of the curious crowd, he was mercifully hidden by the mantle of darkness. The silence of the grave seemed to have fallen upon the countryside. Breathless heat. The stillness of earthquake weather.

A nameless terror gripped the crowd that was gathered. The cursing ceased. Some trembled.

The darkness persisted. Lightning occasionally flashed, illuminating the cross and the victim. At first, priests, executioners and the mob began to wonder if their time of judgment had come.

Eventually, some regained their composure and moved out. Others remained, speaking in whispers. An undeniable dread was upon each mind. The overspreading darkness was as unaccountable as it was frightening.

A woman was heard to exclaim, "This is his power! He has produced this miracle."

"Perhaps we'll see him come down from the cross," breathed another.

A few more attempted to grope their way back to the city.

And now only the soldiers remained close to the cross, duty-bound to stay. As well as those who most loved Yeshua.

The two thieves were heard sobbing, then muttering in delirium as the high fever of great pain muddled their minds.

But from the center cross came only silence.

In the darkness Jesus was alone. He was passing through the deepest and most dreadful part of his agony. So great was the anguish that his physical pain was hardly felt.

The dreadful thought was pressing upon him, "Even your Father in heaven won't want you now. All this guilt you have chosen to take upon yourself has doomed you. You are finished."

Throughout his life Yeshua had been telling people the good news of his Father's mercy and pardoning love. Salvation even for the worst of sinners, he had said. But now, with the terrible guilt he was bearing, he could not see the Father's forgiving face.

How the divine Father must have suffered with His Son! One can imagine Him pressing close in the darkness, longing to intervene. But He must hold back and let the penalty be paid. What a price was paid for your rescue and mine! The Innocent Ones were the victims.

Jesus, the sin-bearer, endured the wrath of divine justice against sin. Now, as God strikes sin, He strikes His own Son. The guilt of every wrong committed on this planet presses upon his soul. In the place of the wrong-doer, the Son of God suffers the penalty.

Alone Jesus endures this anguish to save us from it. He feels the black despair which the lost rejecter of rescue will feel on the final judgment day... the torment of separation from one's Creator... the torment of the damned, when they realize that, by their own choice, they are God-forsaken and lost forever.

"My God, my God" – Jesus' cry pierces the darkness – "why have you forsaken me?" [6]

Since eternity they have been together – closer than siamese twins.[7] Throughout his life on earth, every morning while it was still dark, Jesus has been rising to spend hours with his Father, to gain strength in prayer for his work among humans.

Now, in the darkness, it seems that even his heavenly Father has deserted him. The hope of rising from the tomb a conqueror now seems a distant illusion. Despair tells him that his separation from his Father will be permanent.

Now it appears that he is going down to a grave from which there will be no resurrection. So that these men and women around the cross can receive the joy of life in a new world and the company of the Father, he himself must give up life forever.

"My God, my God, why have you forsaken me?"

Unutterable anguish fills his soul at the hiding of his Father's face because of the world's sin upon him.

The Rescuer's heart breaks with that cry. He has borne all that even he can bear.

He was counted a law-breaker, that he might release us from the penalty of the law. The guilt of every person since Adam was pressing upon his heart. It was this sense of sin, which he was bearing as man's substitute – it was the terrible revealing of God's displeasure against sin, which made Jesus' suffering so bitter, and crushed out the life of the Son of God.

In preparing this chapter, I have reflected deeply on the implications of this for me personally.

Rescue was that day purchased for me by the suffering and death of the Son of God.

It can be mine – and yours – to accept gratefully. But no one is compelled to yield. If I disregard it, that's my choice – and at the end I shall receive my wages. I will have lost a life of eternal happiness for the fleeting pleasures of the sin disease now.

What value our Creator has placed upon each person!

The darkness disperses

The end was approaching... The darkness lifted from the oppressed spirit of Jesus. He revived to a sense of **physical** suffering, and in a faint voice, called, "I thirst."

Those words were simple as those of a child, words that his mother must have heard so often when he was a little boy. It was as the **human** son of Mary that he said, "I thirst."

The light was coming back. And the soldiers, looking at him, could see his face again. And see that he was dying.

Strong men lived sometimes for days upon the cross, and it must have astonished them to see this strong young man approaching his end after only a few hours.

Even the most brutal of men are pitiful to the dying. And one of the soldiers fixed a sponge to a hyssop stalk, and, dipping it in a pot of vinegar, stretched it upward to the parched lips of the convict.

Such an opiate had been given to the first thief, whose swollen tongue protruded. He drank it with a sort of mad thirst. The other man, also, gladly assuaged his burning fever with it. And soon afterward both of them had sunk into insensibility, hanging unaware of their situation, showing no other signs of life than the heaving of their chests and from time to time, the involuntary twitching of the muscles.

But Jesus, having at first refused this, and retaining his senses in all their clearness, had suffered to the full. Now he took the free gift of love which the soldier brought him.[8]

But as the soldier did so, the priests mocked at Yeshua's agony. The last opportunity to relieve his sufferings they refused. "Let be," they said, "let us see whether Elijah will come to save him."

In silence the watchers awaited the climax of the fearful scene.

The sun shone forth. But the cross was still enveloped in darkness.

Priests and rulers looked toward Jerusalem. The dense cloud had settled over the city. And over the plains of Judea.

You might call that symbolic. The Light of the World was withdrawing his beams from the once-favored city of Jerusalem. Fierce lightnings of judgment would soon be directed against the fated city.

But eternal rescue had now been made possible for those who chose it. "That's why you – and I – are safe in his hand," writes George Vandeman. "That's why we can sleep tonight, unafraid, knowing that He will be very, very careful with our little world." [9]

♦♦♦♦♦♦♦♦

Did you know that this whole event had been witnessed by prophets 500 years earlier? Did you know that 40 prophecies came true during a 24 hour period?

In the very next chapter we shall consider a handful of them. If I'm not mistaken, you should find this captivating.

CHAPTER 39

STARTLING PREDICTIONS

"Rabbi, what have we done?"

Mark was totally distraught. "You're our leaders. I believed in you."

"Don't stand there, man, where everyone can see you. Come in!"

David ben Uzzah ushered Mark into his living room.

"Right, sit down." The rabbi and Mark had grown up together. They remained close friends. But Mark's assertions sounded like madness.

"I tell you, it was predicted," Mark cried. "It's in here."

"What are you saying? **That we've assassinated the Messiah?**"

The events of that weekend were witnessed by many simple, honest people.

Subsequently, some of them, priests included, would be driven to search for themselves into the prophecies concerning the Messiah.

It would be found that prophecies of the Deliverer spanned some 4,000 years.

Any ordinary reader of the prophetic writings could follow the gradual progress of the divine revelations.

They would discover that the simple outlines of the first promise became progressively more detailed as the Divine Mind inspired different writers. Each new prophet was like a painter who uses the brush to put in details – until at last the word painting was

403

finished and the full picture of the coming Messiah stood out perfect and complete.

Did you know that the whole life story of the Messiah – his coming to earth, and when he would come – was written hundreds of years in advance, in the Old Testament?

Nowhere else in the world do you find a man whose biography was written before he was born.

A few introductory predictions included these:

1 – The Coming One would be a descendant of Abraham the Semite.[1]

2 – Of Abraham's two sons, the Messiah would come from "the seed of Isaac".[2]

3 – Of Isaac's children, we should look for the Coming One to appear through "the seed of Jacob". [3]

4 – The prophecy narrowed it still further. Of Jacob's twelve sons, the Deliverer would be born of the tribe of Judah.[4]

5 – Of all the families in Judah, it would be through the family-line of Jesse that he would come.[5]

6 – Jesse had at least eight sons. Now a prophecy eliminated all of them except one – David. The Messiah was to be a descendant of King David.[6]

7 – He was to be born in Bethlehem – and a particular Bethlehem at that. You see, there were two towns called Bethlehem. There was Bethlehem of Zebulon, 70 miles to the north in Galilee; but this was not where the Messiah would be born. The prophesied place was "Bethlehem Ephratah... in Judah".[7] So now God eliminated all the cities in the world, except one, for the entrance of the Promised One.

8 – He was to come BEFORE the Temple was destroyed and the Jews finally exiled.[8] The time factor was clearly given. The Messiah had to come **while the second Temple was still standing.**

When the Second Temple was being built by Zerubbabel, many sorrowed over the fact that it was inferior to Solomon's Temple. But the prophetic compensation to those who sorrowed over that inferiority was that the glory of the latter house should exceed the glory of the former house,[9] since the Messiah would come to that second Temple.[10] He had to come BEFORE the destruction of that Temple – or the prophecy would fail.

The fulfillment of any single prophecy would prove little. But it is the combined strands of 332 distinct predictions which would eventually form an unbreakable rope of evidence – and make Jesus' claims absolutely indisputable.

The Final 24 hours

There were 500 years of prophecy fulfilled in 24 hours. In those 24 hours, no less than 40 prophecies came true!

Let's take a look at five of them.

His betrayal

It was prophesied that:

a) He would be betrayed by a friend.

b) He would be sold for 30 pieces of silver.

c) The money would be cast down in the Temple.

d) It would end up in the hands of a potter.

These details were given no less than 500 years before the events.[11]

In fulfillment, one of Yeshua's close disciples betrayed Yeshua. The priests paid Judas 30 pieces of silver. Later, when Judas saw that Jesus was going to make no effort to save himself, he returned the money to the priests, then went out and hanged himself. The priests discussed among themselves what to do with the returned money. Someone suggested it be put into the treasury.

But they decided to purchase a potter's field in which to bury strangers. And you realize that if they had put the money into the treasury, the Scripture would have been broken, because it said that the money would be used for a potter's field.

They finally decided to do the very thing the prophet said they would do.

Death by crucifixion

Here is the prophecy: "They pierced my hands and my feet." [12]

Crucifixion was practically unheard of when this prophecy was written (c. 1000 BC) – and even after it became the accepted method of capital punishment, then rope, not nails, was often, if not usually, employed to fasten victims to the rough beams.[13]

The prophecy said his hands and feet would be pierced.

They would cast lots for his robe

"They divide my garments among them, and for my clothing they cast lots."[14] This prophecy seems to be contradictory until we discover what really happened.

Jesus' clothing was given to the soldiers. They tore and divided the four pieces, but when they came to his robe, "they said... Let us not tear it, but cast lots for it, to decide whose it shall be."[15]

About 150 AD, Justin Martyr, addressing his "Defense of Christianity" to the emperor Antoninus Pius, referred him to the governor Pilate's report, which he believed was preserved in the archives in Rome. Referring to the soldiers dividing Jesus' garments and casting lots for his robe, he adds:

> .. and that these things were so, you may learn from the 'Acts' which were recorded under Pontius Pilate.[16]

His bones would not be broken

"He keepeth all his bones: not one of them is broken."[17]

Toward the end of the crucifixion day, a command was given to break the legs of Yeshua and the other two men. Those two were still very much alive, so their legs were broken. "But coming to Jesus, when they saw that he was already dead, they did not break his legs." [18]

Quite simply, the reason the Jewish Council wanted the legs of the convicts broken, was to hasten death. It was Friday and the Sabbath would soon begin. They did not want these men hanging on the cross over the Sabbath day.

The soldiers came to the first thief, on one side of Jesus, and broke his legs. Then to the thief on the other side, and broke his legs.

You may wonder, Why did they go to convict no.1, then to no. 3? Why on earth did they bypass Yeshua who was in the middle? Why not simply go 1-2-3?

May I suggest a reason. Could it be that the two thieves were easier to reach? That the soldiers left Jesus until last for the simple reason that he was further back on a ledge four feet higher than the others? (See Chapter 22).

But when they came to Jesus, he was dead already – so they did not have to break his legs.

Here again our archaeological discoveries dovetailed with the biblical account perfectly.

Think about it. If Jesus had been sold for 50 silver pieces, instead of 30, or if the priests had used the money for some other purpose, or if Jesus had been bound to the cross rather than nailed, or if the soldiers had divided his garment equally among them, or if his legs had been broken – then you might have reason to question Jesus' identity. But the precise fulfillment of the prophecies speaks for itself.

Notice another prophecy:

Death with the wicked, burial with the rich

"They appointed his grave with the wicked (plural), but (he was) with the rich (singular) in his death", or "when dead".[19] In the original Hebrew, "the wicked" is in the plural, and "the rich" in the singular number!

As a final insult, Yeshua's enemies wished to bury his corpse among criminals – a purpose which was defeated in a truly marvelous way. Joseph of Arimathea, a rich man, was so shaken by the drama that he requested Jesus' body and placed it in his own personal tomb. Does this not indicate the hand of an overruling Providence bringing to pass the fulfillment of a most improbable prediction?

Acted them out?

It might be objected that, knowing the prophecies, Jesus deliberately acted them out.

Such an objection might seem plausible until one realizes that many of the prophecies were totally beyond human control, such as place of birth, manner of death, people's reactions (spitting, mocking, and so on), piercing of his side, not breaking his bones, manner of burial, and others. There's no way an impostor could have acted out all these.

Just coincidence?

So, perhaps it was just coincidence that these things happened?

Coincidence? In *Science Speaks*, Peter Stoner shows that coincidence is ruled out by the science of probability.

Stoner says that, taking just eight of these prophecies,

> ...We find that the chances that any man might have lived down to the present time and fulfilled all eight prophecies is one in 10^{17}. That would be 1 in 100,000,000,000,000,000. [20]

Stoner illustrates this staggering probability in this way:

> If we take 10^{17} silver dollars and lay them on the face of Texas, (they will) cover all of the state two feet deep. Now mark one of these silver dollars and stir the whole mass thoroughly, all over the state. Blindfold a man and tell him that he can travel as far as he wishes, but he must pick up one silver dollar and say that this is the right one. What chance would he have of getting the right one? Just the same chance that the prophets would have had of writing these eight prophecies and having them all come true in any one man, from their day to the present time, providing they wrote them in their own wisdom.

Stoner considers 48 prophecies and says,

> We find the chance that any one man fulfilled all 48 prophecies to be 1 in 10^{157}.

(That is 1, followed by 157 zeros.)

The Executive Council and a committee of members of the American Scientific Affiliation examined Stoner's manuscript. They declared his mathematical analysis to be

> based upon principles of probability which are thoroughly sound and Professor Stoner has applied these principles in a proper and convincing way.[21]

The prophecies irrefutable proof

Though Jesus' life, words and miracles may all stamp his mission as divine, if you want irrefutable proof that Yeshua was who he said he was, it is to the Old Testament prophecies that you must turn. If he doesn't measure up to the prophecies, it matters not how many miracles he worked.

Explain it as you will, these prophecies and dates do fit exactly with the life of Jesus and nowhere else. The events have been fulfilled perfectly and wonderfully.

The noted British soldier, General Gordon, was one who turned to the Bible regularly for practical help in his everyday life. He claimed that "Christ in you is the golden key that unlocks the Bible."

In Khartoum, Sudan, he was captured by the Moslems. They presented him with a robe and ordered him to put it on, deny Jesus Christ and profess Islam.

Gordon scanned the horizon for any sign of the expected relief army. Seeing it approaching, he acted. First he tossed the robe into the river. Then he faced the spears.

Within half an hour his head was strung up with a hole through it.

It did not matter to him. He had a hope.

Paul wrote:

> I know whom I have believed and am convinced that He is able to guard safely my deposit, entrusted to Him against that Day.[22]

✦✦✦✦✦✦

My investigation of the facts would lead me into a rabbi's office.

I had a question for him. And he revealed something that I just have to share with you...

409

The Temple veil was suddenly ripped from top to bottom. (Sketch: Darren Hunter)

CHAPTER 40

SURPRISE UNDER SKULL HILL

That afternoon in Jerusalem, a man clothed as a priest was about his Temple duties, preparing a lamb for slaughter.

It was the annual Passover celebration. And around 3 pm, in accordance with Jewish custom, the priests were to kill the Passover lamb.

But he was troubled. Something very strange was transpiring. Out on the hill to the north – on Skull Hill, the place of execution – an eerie darkness had fallen three hours ago. And it had spread far and wide, even over the city.

He tried not to be distracted by it. And continued his work.

Clothed in his gorgeous robes, the priest stood with lifted knife, ready to slay the lamb for the ceremony.

With intense interest, onlookers stood by.

Suddenly the earth shook. There was heard a loud, sharp ripping noise, from inside the building.

The priest got such a fright, the knife dropped from his trembling hand, and the lamb escaped.

In terror and confusion he rushed inside the first chamber. And looking ahead he saw that the massive curtain which separated the first room from the second, had been torn. As though by unseen hands, it had been ripped violently from top to bottom.[1]

The Most Holy Place, which was off limits to everyone except the high priest, now lay exposed to the view of all.

It was startling. The great veil had been torn not from the bottom upward as men might have done it, but from the top to the bottom. You could call it – if you dared – supernatural.

I understand Josephus says somewhere that the great veil of the Temple was 3 inches thick! It would have taken a team of bullocks to tear it!

Always cautious, I resolved to track down, if possible, whatever sources outside the New Testament were available.

An obvious help would be a Jewish rabbi.

I recall it was an Australian mid-winter Sunday afternoon- June 29, to be precise - that I went to the home of Rabbi Reubenzacks. The rabbi ushered me into a study crammed with books, mostly on shelves, but also in numerous piles neatly stacked along the wall.

I quickly came to the point. "Rabbi, do you know anything about the tearing of the veil of the Second Temple?"

The rabbi looked surprised.

I added, "It is supposed to have occurred early in the first century CE at the time of Passover."

Initially taken aback by the directness of the question, the rabbi recovered his composure, then guardedly, but with honesty, responded.

"Yes," he said, "there is an unwritten Jewish tradition that the veil was torn mysteriously at that time."

◆◆◆◆◆◆

Once the veil was torn, anyone who cared to peer into the Holy of Holies could now see for himself that the fabled Ark of the Covenant was missing.

"It is finished"

Outside the city, at that same moment the veil was torn, Jesus cried out:

"IT IS FINISHED!" [2]

From now on, Temple sacrifices would be meaningless. The symbol was meeting its fulfillment in the death of the Lamb of God.

The Messiah had completed the work his Father had given him to do.

It had been planned from the beginning of the world.[3] And every step in the plan of rescue had been completed according to schedule.

Lucifer had been unsuccessful in his attempts to overthrow the plan. Jesus' victory assured the salvation of mankind.

As Jesus in his death agony cried out, **"It is finished,"** a shout of triumph must have rung through the heavens. The great contest that had been so long in progress was now decided and Jesus was conqueror.

The fulfillment was almost startling. On the annual Hebrew Day of Atonement (Yom Kippur), the high priest would enter the Holy of Holies three times – once with a special incense offering and twice to sprinkle the blood of the sacrifices.

When he entered with the blood of the sacrificed animal, he would sprinkle the blood upon the Mercy Seat, which represented the Throne of God. After **three hours in the darkness** of the Most Holy Place, the high priest would come out with the empty basin, hold it up, and proclaim, **"It is finished."** Then the people knew that the sacrifice had been accepted by God and their sins were forgiven.

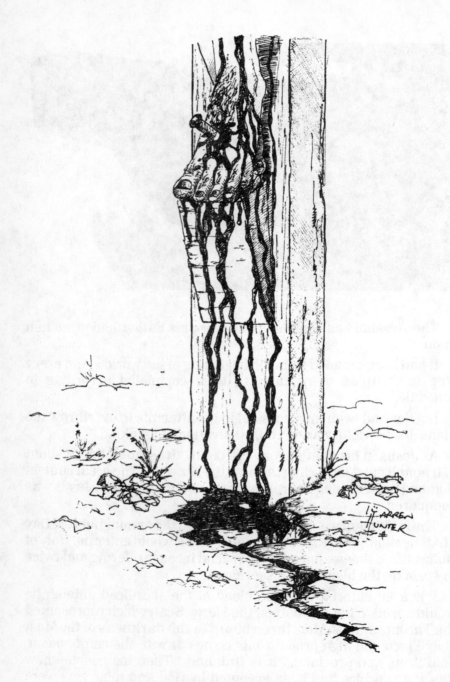

Sketch: Darren Hunter

414

Yeshua's **three hours in darkness** on the cross ended with the triumphant cry, "**It is finished**."

He had done all he could. We now had a means of rescue.

That did not mean that everyone would be saved. A parachute is manufactured and finished to the extent that it can save a pilot who bails out of a plane. But it still needs something... the action of the man to pull it open as he jumps. His part is also necessary. Although a parachute is **finished**, the pilot's part has yet to be finished, before he can be saved.

In the divine rescue plan, our individual response would be crucial.

Rock split open

Jesus gave one final cry with a loud voice,

"Father, I commit my spirit into Your hands." [4]

As he submitted himself, the sense of the loss of his Father's favor was withdrawn. By faith, Jesus was victor. He had now become conscious of triumph and confident of his own resurrection.

Immediately a fearful rumbling sound erupted from deep down in the earth. The ground shook violently and the rocks were split open.[5]

Jesus was dead.[6]

From the startled Roman centurion were forced the words, "Truly this man was the Son of God."

Death by crucifixion was a slow process. A victim could linger on for days. Those soldiers were a special despatch assigned to crucifixions. They were familiar with crucifixion scenes. They were shocked that Yeshua was dead already.

A spear thrust into his side

The priests wanted to be sure Yeshua was dead, so at their suggestion a soldier thrust a spear up into his side.

Notice carefully what happened next. The disciple John records it:

However, one of the soldiers pierced his side with a spear, and blood and water flowed out. I saw all this myself and

415

have given an accurate report so that you also can believe.
The soldiers did this in fulfillment of the Scripture that says,
"Not one of his bones shall be broken," and, "They shall look
on him whom they pierced."[7]

Did you notice? Out flowed two copious and distinct streams,
one of blood, the other of water. This was noted by those who stood
by.

It was when the semi solid dark
red blood poured out, distinct and
separate from the accompanying
watery serum, that they knew
Yeshua was, indeed, dead.

Here was startling evidence that
Jesus' death was not due to physical
exhaustion, nor to the pains of
crucifixion, nor to the spear thrust.
His heart had literally burst.

Two things – that sudden cry, uttered **"with a loud voice"** at the
moment of death,[8] and the stream of **blood and water** that flowed
from his side - declared that he had died of a broken heart. The
muscles of the heart may have been actually torn. It can happen
under intense mental strain.

Ah, there's more to this than meets the eye, when we look into it.

Blood and water: medical testimony

Some years ago, Dr. Walshe, Professor of Medicine at University
College, London, declared that in heart rupture the hand is carried
to the front of the chest and a piercing shriek uttered. Usually
death very speedily follows. Blood escapes into the cavity of the
pericardium (the heart sac), which sac has, in cases of rupture of
the heart, been found to contain two, three, four or more pounds of
blood accumulated within it, and separated into red blood and
limpid serum ("blood and water").

Recently, when I was in South Australia preparing to speak on
this subject, it was brought to my notice that controversial
theologian Barbara Thiering had attacked me on the grounds that
blood and water could not have flowed out of Jesus' side.

Since Jesus was dead, it was asserted, the blood would have
already clotted. Case closed!

However, I already had in my file the results of repeated observations and experiments made upon dead men by medical experts.

In 1957, A.F. Sava reported that he had experimented with cadavers less than six hours after death. These experiments proved that when a lance is thrust into the side of the chest, "fluid from the pericardium and the heart will 'flood the space around the lung rather than ooze its way slowly across the pierced lung' to the wound in the chest wall."[9]

Sava believed that in Jesus' case, blood and water would have gathered just inside the rib cage, between the pleura lining the chest and the pleura lining the lung. He also suggested that the scourging (flogging) a few hours before he was crucified was sufficient to cause an accumulation of bloody fluid inside the chest:

> Experience with severe chest injuries has demonstrated that non penetrating injuries of the chest are capable of producing an accumulation of a hemorrhagic fluid in the space between the ribs and the lung. This volume of bloody fluid varies with the severity of the injury and the degree of response to such an injury.... Such collections of blood in closed cavities do not clot. The red blood cells tend by their weight to gravitate toward the bottom of the containing cavity, thus dividing it into a dark red cellular component below, while the lighter clear serum accumulates in the upper half of the collection as a separate though contiguous layer.... From a purely anatomic-mechanical standpoint, therefore, the likelihood of hemorrhagic effusion between the lung and the ribs is far greater than a similar occurrence within the pericardial sac.[10]

In 1975, John Wilkinson, a medical missionary, analyzed and assessed various theories, and concluded that the issue of blood and water was due to "gravity and the vertical position of the body on the cross. Noting that blood remains fluid for some time after death, Wilkinson concluded that the lance must have pierced the lower part of the heart cavity. On the basis of his medical experience with severe injuries he agreed... that the 'water' originated in the pericardial sac. This fluid 'was thin, clear and colorless and quite distinct from the thick, opaque, red blood it accompanied.' The lance thrust released the fluid and, in

417

penetrating the heart, also released the blood, which came out first. It is probable that more watery fluid flowed out than blood."[11]

Dr. C. Truman Davis, a medical doctor who has meticulously studied crucifixion from a medical perspective, says that "an escape of watery fluid from the sac surrounding the heart" is evidence "not [of] the usual crucifixion death by suffocation, but of heart failure due to shock and constriction of the heart by fluid in the pericardium."[12]

Samuel Houghton, MD, the great physiologist from the University of Dublin, an authority on the physical phenomena accompanying death wounds, states:

> That rupture of the heart was the cause of the death of Christ is ably maintained by Dr.William Stroud; and that rupture of the heart actually occurred I firmly believe...The importance of this is obvious. It (shows) that the narrative in St. John xix could never have been invented; that the facts recorded must have been seen by an **eye-witness**; and that the eye-witness was so astonished that he apparently thought the phenomenon miraculous.[13]

John thought it, if not to be miraculous, at least to be unusual.

It had begun the previous evening, in Gethsemane Garden, when Yeshua sweated blood, as Luke the physician noted.[14] That's where the "great anguish" began, which was ultimately to snuff out his life.

Jesus did not die from nail wounds or the pain of crucifixion. Did he die of anguish from the massive weight of sins he had taken upon himself – and from the perceived abandonment of God because of those sins upon him? Was he slain by the sin of the world that he had chosen to bear?

This was not the ordinary death we all die, but the "final" death of separation from God. Jesus tasted that death, to save us from it.

Jesus literally, as well as metaphorically, died of a broken heart.

The same crack

In the earthquake, the rock was torn open. Immediately to the left of the center cross-hole, at the very base of that hole which held the cross of Yeshua, the rock was TORN OPEN.

Then, when the centurion thrust his spear up into Jesus' side, the two copious streams, one of blood, the other of water, flowed out. The average person has 4 to 5 quarts of blood. The blood and water flowed down his side... down his legs... and into the cross-hole.

The blood went right into that split in the stone. And it went down that crack and sprinkled onto the Mercy Seat of the Ark, that was buried in the cave approximately 20 feet below.

How do we know? Because the crack has been closely examined – and it shows copious amounts of blood having flowed down into it. It is still there. And it is human blood.

It is hard to shake off the feeling that a Divine Mind was orchestrating a series of events, here.

Firstly, it was arranged for the Ark to be hidden in that chamber some 600 years before Yeshua died.

During the siege of Jerusalem by the Babylonians in 587 - 586 BC, Jeremiah and/or some Temple priests had been motivated to hide the Ark of the Covenant in a cave chamber. They had absolutely no knowledge of the events which were to occur on that Friday in 31 AD.

Secondly, the Romans who hacked out the post-holes had absolutely no knowledge of what lay beneath their feet, nor that they were positioning the **central** hole in precisely the right place.

Thirdly, until Jesus had died, there was no way for blood to trickle down, because there was no crack.

But these amazing coincidences actually happened. Coincidences? Yes, because everything had to **coincide** exactly, for it to happen.

Doesn't it make you think? Who could have arranged it so?

And now, 2,000 years later, the One who knows neither haste nor delay, finally reveals the Ark of the Covenant just as we approach the next great intervention - the promised Second Coming. Something on that later.

My wife, who has been to the site with me, made a pertinent comment the other day. She said, "It's just like Him to do something unexpected. So that ultimately there will be no doubt as to why that Man died on that cross that day."

Yes, it's just like Him.

"For nothing is hidden, except to be revealed; nor has anything been secret but that it should come to light." So said Yeshua himself.[15] "For there is NOTHING covered that will not be revealed, and hidden that will not be known." [16] And it was also foretold, "Truth shall spring **out of the earth.**" [17]

Can it be said that this eventual Ark discovery was already planned?

Who REALLY chose the location?

I've been re-reading that story in Genesis chapter 22 concerning Abraham and his son trekking to Mount Moriah for their sacrifice. This time something hit me like a "lightning bolt". It was the discovery that **GOD HIMSELF CHOSE THE SPOT!**

Notice the account:

> Then God said, Take your son, your only son, Isaac, whom you love, and go to the region of **Moriah.** Sacrifice him there as a burnt offering on **one of the mountains I will tell you about.**[18]

One might ask, Why did the Lord instruct Abraham to take his son to "a mountain I will tell you about", and not to just any mountain? Was God trying to indicate that one day **His** Son was to be "sacrificed" on that very same mountain in the future?

Was He describing to Abraham how the Messiah would one day die?

As the significance of this and the comparison of Abraham and Isaac to God and His Son dawned on me, I read further:

> So Abraham called that place The Lord Will Provide. And to this day it is said, **"On the mountain of the Lord it will be provided."** [19]

Was the Lord telling us that, just as the ram was that day provided for Abraham in place of Isaac, so one day in the future God's Son would be provided in place of us? Was this a prophecy that the Messiah would one day be "sacrificed" or "provided" there for us, on that very same Mount Moriah?

Come to think of it, Jesus did declare:

Abraham rejoiced to see my day: and he saw it, and was glad.[20]

What did Jesus mean by that?

To the nation of Israel, the Lord had specified:

You may not sacrifice the Passover within any of your gates... but **in the place which the Lord your God shall choose**.[21]

Did you notice that? Since the Passover lamb was prophetic of the coming Messiah, it was to be sacrificed **outside** the gate **at a place which the Lord Himself would choose**.

The New Testament confirms that Yeshua was crucified outside the gate of Jerusalem.[22]

I hasten to suggest that his crucifixion site was AT A PLACE WHICH THE LORD HIMSELF CHOSE.

Divine Mind and its wonder working is beyond our finite minds to understand. No detail is forgotten in God's plans, already perfect.

And try to catch the wonder of this:

The **TEARING** of the **Temple veil** signaled that the earthly Temple sacrifices were now invalidated. In that same event, the Most Holy Place was exposed to view, so that it could be plainly seen that the **Ark of the Covenant was not there**.

According to the book of Hebrews, that torn veil symbolized the **flesh** of Jesus,[23] which likewise was **TORN** – on the cross.

Again, as the Messiah died, the **rock** below the cross was **TORN OPEN** for his blood.

Of course the Ark of the Covenant was not in the Temple, because the Lord God planned it to be **outside** the Temple, **"outside the gate"**, to receive the blood of Jesus.

How apt that this **"blood of the everlasting COVENANT"** [24] should fall upon the **Ark of the COVENANT! It was all so carefully arranged.**

Every detail pivots on the person of Jesus. He did not die at that location just because the Ark was there. Rather, it was the Ark that had to be positioned in relation to where Yeshua was appointed to die.

Sketch: Jim Pinkoski

We cannot discount the operation of a divine providence in this whole matter.

Two mountains of God

Did you know that the Bible designates two places on planet Earth as "mountain of God"? **Mount Sinai** is called "The mountain of God" [25] and **Mount Moriah** is designated "the mount of the Lord".[26]

Physically linked

Mount Sinai was a part of God's reaching out to mankind. He reached out to man with His **LAW**, the transcript of His own character... physically engraving it **with HIS OWN FINGER**. He instructed Moses to enshrine it within the Ark of the Covenant.

Later, on **Mount Moriah**, the Lord reached out to mankind with His **MERCY**, sprinkling the Mercy Seat of that same Ark of the Covenant **with HIS OWN BLOOD**.

The Lord reached out to us **PHYSICALLY, BOTH TIMES**. Both times **He physically left His impression**. God is spiritual. We are physical beings. To reach us, He used physical things... things we can understand.

What He had written at Mount Sinai – the truth of His law, the Lord ultimately placed under Mount Moriah – to forge a link.

"Mercy and truth are met together" [27] - the **truth** of God's law, and the **mercy** of God's love.

To receive the blood of His Son, He CRACKED THAT HILL WIDE OPEN so that the blood would go onto the Mercy Seat over His law.

"**Mercy** and **truth** are met together," says the psalmist under inspiration, "**righteousness** and **peace** have kissed each other." MERCY AND TRUTH MET TOGETHER on that Mercy Seat – when the violated law's demand for justice struck Jesus who had become "sin" [28] in our place – and we were granted God's mercy. Can you see it?

Everything from the past came together in ONE ACT.

And through his RIGHTEOUSNESS (his right-living life, credited to our account, individually, if we will accept it), we can be made at PEACE with our Creator, just as though we had never done wrong!

A massive quantity of blood

The Ark of the Covenant, with its Mercy Seat, sits a little more than 20 feet below the base of the cross-hole where Jesus' body was hung.

The fissure has been closely examined. It clearly took a massive quantity of blood.

Yes, I know. The question will be asked, After all this time, would not such evidence have been destroyed?

That thought did cross my mind. It was time to ask a few more questions...

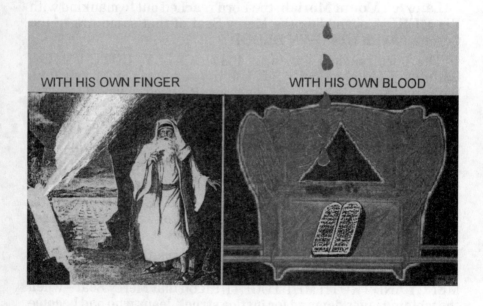

WITH HIS OWN FINGER   WITH HIS OWN BLOOD

CHAPTER 41

QUESTIONS

I had just come out of the shower when a loud rap on the door sent me scurrying for my towel.

"Time to eat!'" called Bob. "I can't wait another moment."

Our hotel in Jerusalem was modest. But the water was hot. Just perfect after a dirty day underground. By now, I had almost lost count of the times I'd been in this city. Jerusalem... home of the great kings, David, Solomon, Hezekiah. Old city of cobblestone alleys through which the Son of God had personally walked. The aura in Jerusalem was unlike any place on earth. Its smells, sights and sounds were endearingly special.

Today our team had separated. Ron had taken two young helpers up to the Galilee region to look over some places closely linked to New Testament events. Richard Reeves, Bob Murrell and I had gone down into a complex of elaborate underground tombs of the First Temple period.

We had undertaken a careful survey of these, taking detailed measurements of outer and inner chambers, as well as smaller recesses. Our findings confirmed that the standard measure in use during the First Temple period was the 20.6 inch cubit. This find was significant to some of our other projects.

That evening, we found ourselves reclining in the basement restaurant of our hotel. It was a small room. And the subdued lighting, augmented by taped Arabian music, set the mood for pleasant relaxation. This had become our favorite spot, where we could unwind at the close of a physical day.

425

The first fragments of news concerning the Ark of the Covenant find were already arousing intense interest in our respective home countries.

But there was some information not to be revealed. This was a most sensitive issue and one must be aware of the problems that it could generate for the political leaders of Israel. We intend to touch on those later.

I leaned forward to speak to the man who had first found it.

"A couple of questions, Ron," I began.

"Fire away, Jonathan," he responded.

Wouldn't the blood wash away?

"What do you think, Ron? About that rock over at the crucifixion site. It was cracked open, right? Well, shouldn't the blood in that crack have disappeared, by now? Surely it would only take the next shower of rain after the crucifixion, to wash that blood away!"

"A fair question," drawled Ron. "But remember what we found in the top of the 'post- hole' which had held the cross?"

"The plug?"

"You've got it. There was inserted that tightly fitting large, squarish rock. It had been covered in travertine. You've seen it."

"Yes, there were actually finger handles on the two sides where you could put your fingers under it to lift it up. I've examined it a few times."

The stone plug was 13 inches by 14 inches in width and approximately 4 inches thick.

"I guess the intent of that plug was to prevent horses or people from tripping into the hole."

"You've said it," said Ron approvingly. "And it would also prevent debris from falling in when the holes were not in use."

He looked thoughtful now, recalling the day when that discovery was made.

"But the ultimate result of this sealing of the holes — all of them — was that when we removed the plugs, the holes were found to be empty. So the plug in the cross-hole obviously helped to preserve anything that was under it. And the plug itself was in position under several feet of debris, as you know."

Underneath that plug, everything was well protected. That made sense.

The cross-hole used again?

In the candlelight, I glimpsed a twinkle in the big American's eye. He was enjoying this. It was close to his heart. He turned to Bob and then back to me. "I think Jonathan's got another question."

"As a matter of fact I have. Suppose that cross-hole was used for later executions. Have you thought about that? How can we know that the blood in the crack of the rock is that of the Lord Jesus?"

"OK, Jonathan, let's tie all the strands of evidence together. For starters, the big earthquake split in the rock. This may well have rendered that particular cross-hole quite unsuitable for any further crucifixions. In any case, there are writings which state that soon after Jesus' crucifixion, the method of death by crucifixion in Jerusalem was abolished."

"Abolished?"

"That's right. You see, it resulted from the scenes which took place at his death. The inhuman conduct of the mob, the unexplained darkness which veiled the earth, and the agony of nature displayed in the tearing of the rocks, the lightning flashes and so on. It struck those people with such remorse and terror, that the cross, as an instrument of death, soon fell into disuse."

"But what about AD 70?" I objected. "When the Romans destroyed Jerusalem, weren't there crucifixions then?"

"True enough, Jonathan," droned the archaeologist. "There was a brief time when mob power seized control and crucifixion was revived."

"But for those intervening years..."

"More crucifixions on that site? I think not! And then..."

"Joseph!" I cut in.

"Joseph?" asked Bob, now taking an intense interest in the discussion.

"Yes, Joseph of Arimathea! " I exclaimed. "A member of the Sanhedrin, wasn't he?"

427

Ron nodded. I continued.

"A very rich man. Just think about it. He had been a secret follower of Jesus and never openly supported Jesus. But now suddenly Jesus had gone... He was a rich man. Wouldn't he do everything in his power to safeguard the site... the crucifixion site? After all, he took the body and placed Jesus in his own nearby tomb! Then, now that the Lord had risen, wouldn't Joseph try to secure the site with the only remaining evidence of his beloved Lord — the cross-hole with the blood? Wouldn't it be most precious to him? A precious reminder of that awesome event?

"You're right," said Bob. "If I were Joseph, I sure would keep a bold and jealous protection over that crucifixion site. And we know now that some first century Christians did just that. They enclosed that very site with a stone building. It would be natural to do something like that."

"I'm glad you guys are catching on," smiled Ron. "But I want you to know there's better evidence, now. Real, tangible." His voice dropped.

Bob leaned sideways, straining his ear.

"I have recently done a DNA analysis of that blood in the crack... of the last person to spill his blood at that site. Once this information can be made public, it will be conclusive."

"What are you saying?" I asked.

"It will be shown, guys, that the last blood that flowed down into that split rock was most unusual blood. It was not the blood of your ordinary man."

I stared hard at Ron. He continued.

"Apart from that, Jonathan, anyone who is knowledgeable of how particular God was concerning the way the Ark of the Covenant was treated, will know that the Lord would not permit the blood of a random individual to sprinkle in such a remarkable way onto the Mercy Seat."

"When will the blood analyses be made public?"

"Probably fairly soon. If anyone wants to know more, just ask them to watch and wait."

The blood of Abel speaks of it

After I had reported on the blood in my newsletter, *Update International* of May 1996, a lady in Western Australia, Carolyn Higgins, was reading the book of Genesis concerning the first human death. Adam and Eve's first son Abel was murdered by his own brother, Cain.

After this, the Lord confronted Cain – and the book of Genesis picks up the story:

> He said: What have you done? Listen! Your brother's **blood** is crying to me **from the ground**, and now you are **cursed** from the ground that has **opened** its mouth to receive your brother's blood from your hand.[1]

That word "cursed", Carolyn realized, ultimately referred to the penalty of eternal death which Cain brought upon himself by his sin - and to which we are all condemned.

And then it struck her! The Scripture actually linked the shedding of Abel's blood with the shedding of Jesus' blood! Carolyn noticed this statement in the New Testament:

> And to Jesus, the mediator of a new covenant, and to the sprinkled blood that tells of better things than that of Abel.[2]

And another passage said concerning Abel:

> He being dead yet speaketh.[3]

Carolyn had recently read a book by a man called Bullinger, which pointed out that the first occurrence of a word in the Bible bears some significance or lesson:

> These are always important. The ancient Jewish commentators call special attention to them and lay great stress upon them, as always having some significance. They generally help us in fixing the meaning of a word or point us to some lesson in connection with it.[4]

Now, the above passage in Genesis chapter 4 is the first reference to **blood** – and the **opening of the earth to receive it**. Carolyn wondered could this bear significance in relation to the earth opening up to receive Jesus' blood – the blood that dripped down through the earthquake crack onto the Mercy Seat?

429

The blood that speaks **out of the earth**, like Abel's blood? Carolyn was so excited by the idea, that she just had to write to me about it.

Blood on the Mercy Seat

On January 6, 1982, Ron Wyatt first entered the chamber containing the Ark of the Covenant and numerous other things that we believe are the rest of the furnishings constructed at Sinai by God's explicit directions for the earthly sanctuary.

Upon the Mercy Seat, he found what looked to him to be dried blood. Today, we know that this is blood and that it is human. We believe it is the very blood of Jesus.

This concept was entirely new to us. Yet, as we consider the matter, how more precisely could it have happened to show the world that the symbol was fulfilled perfectly?

More on Daniel's prophecy

My research then zeroed in on the messianic prophecy recorded by Daniel. In speaking of the Messiah and what he would accomplish by his death, Daniel wrote:

> Seventy weeks are determined upon thy people [the Jews] and upon thy holy city [Jerusalem] to finish the transgression, and to make an end of sins, and to make reconciliation for iniquity, and to bring in everlasting righteousness, and to seal up the vision and prophecy, and to **anoint the most Holy**.[5]

"TO FINISH THE TRANSGRESSION"

According to Daniel's prophecy, all kinds of sins - transgression, sin, and iniquity - are to be finished by virtue of the Messiah. (There is a clear parallel here to the three categories of sin listed in the Jewish sacrificial system.[6])

The word "transgression" means a deliberate violation of the law, or willful disobedience.

The word "sin" means "missing the mark". Man is born a slave to sin and no matter how hard he wills or tries, he will fall short of the divine mark.

430

"Iniquity" is simply seeking our own way. The primary meaning of iniquity is not an act but a condition. As a result of man's fall, man by very nature is spiritually "bent", so that the driving force of his very nature is love of self.

"TO MAKE AN END OF SINS"

The original word for "sins" is translated in Scripture as "sin offerings" 116 times.

Messiah's death would potentially save the world from its sins,[7] as well as bring an end to ceremonial sin offerings. Paul speaks about him as having to "**put away sin** by the sacrifice of himself."[8] For through him, expiation for all sins will be provided for.

"TO MAKE RECONCILIATION FOR INIQUITY"

There would be "laid upon him the **iniquity** of us all",[9] so that we, the alienated, could be reconciled to our heavenly Father. That is the meaning of atonement - AT-ONE-MENT. God would love us enough to offer to us his Son, "**reconciling** the world to himself."[10] The Messiah was to bridge the gulf of man's separation from God.

"TO BRING IN EVERLASTING RIGHTEOUSNESS"

"My righteous servant shall justify [make righteous] many," said the prophecy of Isaiah.[11]Jeremiah adds, "And this is the name whereby he shall be called, THE LORD OUR RIGHTEOUSNESS."[12] The Messiah's death would be the basis for making us right in God's eyes. "By the **righteousness** of one... shall many be made righteous," notes Paul.[13]

"TO SEAL UP THE VISION"

The fulfillment of the events in Daniel's 70 week prophecy will authenticate that prophecy.

I found that the Hebrew phrase **qodesh qadashim**, here translated to read "most Holy", is the very same phrase as "Most Holy Place".

Variant readings of this passage say "anoint a most holy place" (RSV) or "consecrate a most holy place" (Moffatt).

The term is also used many times to denote objects in the Most Holy Place.

It is a term used freely through the book of Leviticus to characterize **things** and **places**, but is NOWHERE applied to PERSONS.[14]

In the sacrificial system, once a year the high priest would enter into the Most Holy Place and **anoint the Mercy Seat** of the Ark of the Covenant by sprinkling animal blood upon it. Having established this, I then read that Messianic prophecy of Daniel 9:24 again:

> Seventy weeks are determined upon thy people and upon thy holy city, to finish the transgression, and to make an end of sins, and to make reconciliation for iniquity, and to bring in everlasting righteousness, and to seal up the vision and prophecy, and to **anoint the most Holy**.

It will be seen that all of the first five particulars were **fulfilled on earth at Jesus' death**.

So the question kept nagging at me, why not the sixth one? Why not, **"anoint the most Holy"** also?

I then underlined four words in this passage. Four Hebrew words with their English equivalents:

- pesha' = **transgression**
- chatta'th = **sin**
- 'awon = **iniquity**
- kaphar = **reconciliation** (or atone).

And what was significant about them? The **only** other place in Scripture with the same combination of these four words was in Leviticus 16 relating to Yom Kippur (Day of

432

Atonement). Nowhere else. **Only** in that one place. Thus Daniel 9:24 was linguistically a statement of Yom Kippur.

And what happened on Yom Kippur? It was the **only** occasion the high priest would drop **physical blood onto the Mercy Seat**.

So, here it was, all in this one passage: transgression, sin, iniquity, reconciliation – **and** "anoint the most Holy".

The symbolic rites of Yom Kippur involved sacrifice, intercession, cleansing and judgment. The **blood sacrifice** met its fulfillment at Golgotha (Skull Hill). An end times application of the Yom Kippur symbolism will be touched upon in a later chapter.

In the light of our discovery under the crucifixion site, may I now suggest that Jesus' anointing of the Mercy Seat under the cross-hole is a possible - as well as reasonable – fulfillment of the prophetic phrase "anoint the most Holy"?

In the ancient services, anointing was accomplished by both oil and blood.[15]

Since **anointing** was symbolic of the cleansing and covering accomplished by Christ's blood, it would be perfectly consistent for the fulfillment, in reality, to be the ANOINTING of the central object of the Most Holy Place **by the only substance in the universe which can ever REALLY cleanse and purify** – the blood of the Messiah.

Radio "debate"

It was a magical evening. In our log cabin, I sat unwinding, staring out at the moon-cast shadows on the front garden. A sudden tingling of the phone aroused me. Reaching for the hand piece, I heard an English voice on the line.

"This is UCB radio," said the voice, pleasantly. "Are you ready? You'll be on air in ten minutes."

A few months had rolled by since my latest British seminar tour. UCB, which beams across Europe to a potential audience of 40 million homes, had organized an on-line "debate" between Jonathan Gray and a skeptic. We would go to air for one hour.

The skeptic (we shall call him Clive) was an amiable sort of fellow and the "debate" turned out to be more of a discussion.

He had his questions, or objections, if you like. My job was to give the answers.

Depiction on the Arch of Titus in Rome, of items brought from Jerusalem

The gentleman announced that he had several "curly" questions to offer.

Curly? Not really. We had just about heard them all, by now.

He brought up our claim that a number of items from Solomon's Temple were lying in the Ark cavern – in particular the seven-branched Lampstand. This he strongly challenged.

"When the Romans destroyed the Second Temple in 70 AD," insisted Clive, "they took that Lampstand. Yes, it is depicted on the Arch of Titus, along with other booty taken to Rome. So how on earth can it be in your cave?"

Good question. Clive had done a little homework.

My explanation to Clive was that the priests of Jerusalem had given to Titus "two lampstands similar to those deposited in the Temple"(Josephus 6:388). Not our original, you see.

When the Ark of the Covenant vanished from the First Temple, so did the Lampstand and some other Temple treasures. They were not recorded among booty taken to Babylon, nor listed among items brought back from Babylon for the Second Temple. (We dealt with this in Chapter 12.) So it appears they were not in the Second Temple which was looted and burned by the Romans.

Moreover, many Jewish scholars insist that the 7-branched Candlestick depicted on the Arch of Titus can hardly be the original, since its octagonal base is shown to have graven images, contrary to the law of Moses who built the original. (This fact is further elaborated upon in Chapter 2.)

"The Candlestick on the Arch of Titus doesn't show what you say," retorted Clive.

"Oh yes it does. Just take another close look at it."

◆◆◆◆◆◆

With that, we now return to the physical discovery in Jerusalem. And the man who found the Ark, Ron Wyatt.

Here comes a man – not qualified, some would allege. And right under the noses of the professionals, he achieves a world scoop. That's mud in your eye!

Why Ron Wyatt? Why not somebody with multiple doctorates and a host of other letters after his name?

This is where the game gets vicious.

CHAPTER 42

VICIOUS MEN

"Come, I'll show you the markings," whispered Mehmet.

I did not know it at the time, but this man carried a gun under his jacket.

"Come," he said, "Come."

But instead of leading me to the place promised, Mehmet and his henchmen skirted that area, then hustled me away from it.

We passed the giant twelve foot altar which overlooked it all – and KEPT GOING!

Up on the hill, beyond the big altar, Ron had seen human bones – and a skull with hair still on it, which dogs had been devouring. This man, Ron believed, was a killer. It was up this same hill that Mehmet was now luring me.

Did Mehmet suspect I knew? Suddenly I had a sinking feeling.

Mehmet had been robbing graves. He had been in league with a man who sold treasures on the Istanbul black market. If he thought I knew...

Now I was sure he suspected it.

"How far is it?" I asked.

"Just 100 meters," was the reply.

We covered that distance and I grew apprehensive. There was a rock with some markings on it, but the grave marker would not have been brought up here.

"How far now?" I pressed.

"Come," he said.

"How far?" (He had said a hundred meters.) "How far is it?"

"Just one kilometer more," said the man. "Come."

I recalled the earlier plot to get Ron into these same hills and kill him.

It was time to act – fast. I turned to my Kurdish friend Sayim.

"Tell him the sun is getting low. We must turn back."

I wheeled around - and sped downhill.

Sayim followed. We leapt into the car and sped off.

In archaeology, there can be moments that you would like to skip. Like this day recently, in Turkey. All in the task of checking out Ron Wyatt and his claims.

Why not known earlier

As intimated earlier, when Ron Wyatt claimed in 1982 to have found the Ark of the Covenant, this claim was not immediately made public. In fact Ron had told only a few of his associates before the host government requested that he keep certain details confidential for the time being.

So well was the secret kept that it was not until 1991 that I learned of Ron's claimed discovery. I was naturally skeptical of such a claim and decided to do a thorough investigation.

I expected to quickly disprove the claims of Ron Wyatt. However, after intense investigation and repeated visits to the dig sites, I was overwhelmed by the evidence uncovered.

Yet there remained questions concerning the man himself. What were his motives in all this? For years he had worked tirelessly with his two sons, been captured by terrorists in Turkey and imprisoned by Arabs in Saudi Arabia.

This real-life "Indiana Jones" had got himself beaten, kidnapped, almost killed a few times. Why was he doing it?

For Fame?

More recently, Wyatt had been accepting invitations to speak publicly and his discoveries were becoming better known.

Such exposure ensured that any who were critical of his work would begin to voice their objections.

After one public seminar a man accosted the convenor of the meeting. "That was a great performance," he sneered. "But that chap Wyatt has made it all up to draw attention to himself."

The convenor found Wyatt leaning against the stage. He relayed to him what the critic had said.

Ron turned and bent down to face the convenor. His voice was almost at a whisper, as tears formed in his eyes. "Arthur," he said, "How could I do such a thing? What would I say to my Lord when I meet Him face to face?"

"I saw the agony on his face," reported Arthur.

Ron Wyatt was enduring a great deal of mockery and outright accusation by "specialists" in various fields, people who ought to know better.

It was one thing to disagree, and to simply say so, stating the grounds for disagreement; and quite another to mount a campaign to vilify a man, to assassinate his character.

"Why you?"

It was October, 1992, that I had first confronted the big, bearded American face to face.

His claims were not moderate. The discoveries he was claiming were unashamedly bold. It seemed impossible that ONE MAN could discover so many of THE MOST SOUGHT AFTER RELICS ON EARTH.

"If what you are saying is true," I had told him, "then this is a world phenomenon."

"Jonathan," he had chided, "the credit is not to me. Its all to God."

"But why are you doing it?" I asked. "Three or so trips a year must cost you a packet."

The anaesthetist father of three straightened up and eyed me squarely. "Jonathan it's not for treasure. I take the Bible LITERALLY and go after evidence that will prove His interventions in history... evidence that will vindicate Him."

"But why **you**? You've had no formal training in archaeology!"

"That's right."

439

"Surely there are better qualified men. Men with strings of letters after their names. And archaeologists who have been for years in the field. So why were **you** permitted to be the first person to see the Ark?"

"Jonathan, I don't know why the Lord would choose someone like me." And as he said that, there were tears in his eyes.

"Maybe because I'm willing to work for Him."

It was a crazy question, really. Who are we to question God's wisdom and choice?

It could also be asked, Why did the angels who came to announce Christ's birth bypass the Jewish Sanhedrin, the leaders of the nation? Why did they announce such an important event to a bunch of humble shepherds?

But isn't that how the Lord always works?

What strange methods has God used throughout history! Just read again the *"Peculiar strategy"* section of Chapter 9. Time after time, by violating all the rules of war, God made it plain that there was no way the Israelites could have won the victory. He Himself was at work.

And today through Ron Wyatt He violates all the rules of archaeology - to prove that not man but He, has done it.

"Ron, some clever men are against you. They are saying that if it was true, they would have found it, and not you."

The fact was, Ron Wyatt had achieved a coup right under the noses of the experts. And they didn't like it.

"He's an amateur"

Horror of horrors, he was an "amateur"! How was it that he, a rank amateur, had succeeded beyond the wildest dreams of any archaeologist in history?

So what? Some of the world's great archaeological discoveries had been made by amateurs.

When Heinrich Schliemann said he'd discovered Troy, the scientific community snubbed him. For years!

And there was John Lloyd Stephens who discovered wondrous things among the Mayan ruins of Central America. Another amateur.

It was Champollion the "amateur" who got Egyptology going!

One could say that our knowledge had deepened more through the efforts of amateurs like Fawcett, Schliemann and Heyerdahl, than through the efforts of franchised experts.

Why Wyatt? Well... why not Wyatt?

A few sneering scientists would find in Wyatt's discovery an impediment to their atheistic philosophy. And among all the wise owls of stereotyped learning, many would pooh-hoo and hoot. They would be content to sit in their air conditioned offices and pontificate criticisms, hoping that because of the dignity of their office and prestige people would accept their words as final. But if the Ark of the Covenant was meant for discovery in our day, it would indeed be the most wonderful of all possible finds.

In all fields, there are two classes - the professionals (the "experts", if you like) and the amateurs. Both are very human, very fallible.

A living "expert" today is not the solid object he appears to be, but is really almost entirely empty space, a series of holes joined together by French knitting. That is to say, the expert is as human as the rest of us.[1]

The cause of science is not served by automatic ridicule of men like Schliemann, Heyerdahl and Wyatt.

Any person who so behaves is an enemy of science. He might be listed in *Who's Who*, but he doesn't know what's what.

Qualifications? Degrees? Ron Wyatt's work bore evidence that he was **qualified** by the most important **degree** required, the degree of COMMONSENSE. And the only **distinction** he wanted was in service to others.

He smiled.

"God sure uses simple things to shame the wise. But I can say that there is no one on earth who could be more grateful than I am to be allowed to work on this project."

It's always been so, I thought. Paul expressed it so well:

> Not many wise men after the flesh, not many mighty, not many noble, are called: But God hath chosen the foolish things of the world to confound the wise; and God hath chosen the weak things of the world to confound the things which are mighty; and base things of the world, and things

which are despised, hath God chosen... That no flesh should (boast) in his presence.[2]

"How do you finance it?"

I recall having asked Ron that nagging question, "How do you finance all your expeditions?"

"For the most part, out of my own pocket," he had said. "I sold a farm. We now live in a rented house, and own nothing except the equipment for our research, and two vehicles. I work in hospital for half the year to earn money. Then I use the rest of the year for archaeological research, mostly at my own expense."

Why not found before?

Why hasn't the Ark been found before?"

"It is my belief,"said Ron, "that we are living in the last days of this planet's existence as we know it. And that Christ is coming very soon. God is going to bring human history to a close with a tremendous show of His power. So, in this age of skepticism, just before it happens, He is going to reveal these previously hidden evidences to give proof that His past interventions were real. He was keeping it for now."

"There's a prophecy that He will do something that will call non-believers (Gentiles) to Him, and that He will show them that He really is the Lord."

I had later found the reference.. The Lord had spoken it through Jeremiah, the same man who was credited with having organized the hiding away of the Ark. This is what he had written:

> The Gentiles shall come to you from the ends of the earth, and shall say, **Surely our fathers have inherited lies**, vanity, and things wherein there is no profit... Therefore, behold **I will this once cause them to know**, I will cause them to know my hand and my might; and they shall know that my name is THE LORD.[3]

"He hasn't done this yet," said Ron. "And He says clearly 'this once' He will do it. We believe that the things He has revealed through this work and others in the field of biblical archaeology will be a big part of this event. There are almost 6 billion people on this planet, and for the first time in history, a large number of those people can be reached through television satellites and mass

442

communications. We have instant translation capabilities, as well. Technology is such that, when it is God's time, He can get this information throughout the entire world. I truly expect this to happen soon."

It suddenly struck me. Too many professors and clerics were currently denying the truths of God's word. This IS the age of skepticism. What better a time than now for the Lord Himself to bring to the man in the street the evidence he needs to know, and to believe!

Ron spoke quietly. "That's why I have been allowed to find these things, not for my benefit, not for my glory, but for God's purposes."

And as I listened, I sensed the truth in what this man was saying. His whole manner was focused God-ward. For a moment, I sought to praise him. He quickly demolished that pedestal. And that's how it should be. Even the Messiah made himself a servant. And his followers should not seek attention for themselves.

The opposition

"What about the skeptics?"

That was a tame question. Some men were positively infuriated with Ron. The attacks were vicious, including character assassination. And they were issued by men of high standing and repute who could not tolerate the fact that an **amateur** could achieve such notable success.

The emotions aroused seemed to have cost some of them a temporary loss of faculties. From their ivory towers poured trite objections which displayed their awesome accumulation of logic!

In the campaign to vilify a man, professional jealousy was showing through, even on the Internet. Not a Christian act, if one was to judge.

Was I mistaken in sensing that the anti-Wyatt hysteria, the HATRED welling up against this man and his work, seemed almost hysterical?

There had been historical parallels to such a reaction. In the first century, the leaders of God's "chosen" Church of Israel tried to persuade everyone that the resurrection had not occurred – so that the ordinary people would not know. The **feverish and urgent attempt** to cover up the true story before the news could spread,

443

strongly indicates that an opening of the tomb had only just occurred.

Had human nature changed? Today, certain Christian leaders were rushing desperately to tell us that the Ark had not been found.

The discovery claim might be mocked. It might be denied. But they were at a complete loss to disprove it.

Yes, I had been a skeptic. But had done something about it.

Of course, having gone in with my eyes open, having seen the sour grapes and the vitriol against Ron, I knew what to expect.

Once I was convinced, there arose within me a burning desire to vindicate the truth at whatever cost. So I had joined the cause, accompanying Ron to various expedition sites, leading my own independent expeditions, and sharing the news with the world.

My wife had joined me in placing all we possessed on the line. We no longer had any real estate, or medical insurance.

As our work was to grow in strength, we would become the focus of similar attacks. No problem. We would simply pray for our opponents, committing them to the Lord.

And how was Ron reacting?

"Attitudes," observed Ron, "are influenced by parents and environment. And later we may find we've picked up some wrong ideas. That's often hard to face. So the least I can do is show some understanding. Jesus died for these individuals too."

Over a number of years, I had come to know Ron well. He was a humble, honest man. One sensed that he had spent many hours in deep study and prayer. Here was a man trying to follow the "still small voice" of his Master.

Both Ron and Mary Nell were demonstrating a genuine Christian spirit toward those who chose to attack them. They would not bite back, but just get on with the important work they had to do.

Both had one determination: to serve God and establish the truth of His written word. Obedience had brought a rich reward, not for self, but for all mankind.

The greatest disappointment

"What's your greatest disappointment, Ron?"

He and Mary Nell, Josephine and I were strolling past the lake near their Nashville home.

"My greatest disappointment," reflected Ron, "is not being able to get back in and see the Ark."

Not yet, anyway.

When this book is released, critics will follow one another, ad libbing their objections like sheep. We know that. And it is healthy, because it will help the news to spread like wild fire.

May I share with you a statement we received in the post the other day, which was penned by someone a hundred years ago. It is so true:

> In every age God's chosen messengers have been reviled and persecuted, yet through their affliction the knowledge of God has been spread abroad. Every disciple of Christ is to step into the ranks and carry forward the same work, knowing that its foes can do nothing against the truth, but for the truth. God means that truth shall be brought to the front and become the subject of examination and discussion, even through the contempt placed upon it. The minds of the people must be agitated; every controversy, every reproach, every effort to restrict liberty of conscience, is God's means of awakening minds that otherwise might slumber.[4]

And that is precisely our experience. As the news spreads, the criticism acts as a catalyst. And the public is overwhelmingly POSITIVE toward the discovery.

That includes open minded and well educated men of letters. Honest men who have the good grace to be elated at the possibility of the find..

········

One should not be surprised if, on occasions, field archaeology becomes physically dangerous. But when simply reporting to an audience puts one's life at risk, now that's something else!

Read on...

Oh, but first …

When this book was being written, we planned to omit the information in Chapter 43. However, Josephine and I both began to receive strong impressions that it ought to be revealed. The more we tried to squash those impressions, the more guilty we felt. It was only when we promised the Lord to tell it as it was, that peace of mind came.

We later understood why.

Firstly, documentation of Jesus' sufferings at the hands of the religious leaders of his day – even to naming the attackers – is a biblical principle. Would one wish that Matthew, Mark, Luke and John had "covered up" these details? For purposes of credibility and accuracy, revealing of names is necessary.

Secondly, not only did Jesus suffer, but he stated that those who upheld the truth on his behalf would suffer persecution. Thus the apostles of Jesus documented their own experience of suffering – as did Christians throughout history – for the encouragement of those who should follow. People who have faced persecution report that the "Ambush" chapter has encouraged them to remain strong and endure.

Thirdly, the question arises, Why do some religious leaders ("holy men"?) oppose the news that the Ark is found – if, in fact, it is a God-given discovery? Chapter 43 will demonstrate that leaders are as human as the rest of us, and often have their own agendas – that one ought not to trust in man, but in God.

CHAPTER 43

THE AMBUSH

"Get him! Stop him... whatever it takes!" The word was out. Get Jonathan Gray - and his fellow speakers. And when we arrived at the airport, they were waiting.

It was about to get nasty...

Perhaps I should explain something. These discoveries - of the Ark of the Covenant and other items - are evidences of dramatic interventions in history by God Himself. I have no doubt that over the centuries the forces of evil would have dearly loved to destroy these evidences before they could be rediscovered. But a hand has protected them for their final role as God's great attention-getters.

Now, just suppose that an historic feud was in progress between the forces of good and evil.

Unable to destroy these evidences, would not the enemy put out fakes or decoy discoveries so as to minimize the impact of the real thing when it should come to light? And would not the genuine be attacked, using every dirty trick necessary? And just think how more plausible might the opposition seem, should it be orchestrated from of all unexpected places within the church itself?

First I should tell you that I present seminars on the discoveries only when and where invited, and that I never charge a speaking fee or solicit funds. Income is derived from the distribution of books and videos.

Anonymous circular

However, on February 2, 1996, an anonymous "Statement" condemning my work emanated from the headquarters of the only denomination ever to put out literature against me. It was from the office of the Seventh-day Adventist (SDA) church in Wahroonga, New South Wales, Australia.

The anonymous sheet complained that "Gray works.... soliciting funds... This is money that could be put to better use" and it directed members throughout the South Pacific to "not support his meetings."

Interestingly, I had neither spoken against this church, nor asked its members for funds. For that matter, the SDA component of my total audience would not even average one per cent. It turned out that a widening rift had been developing within the SDA group on a number of issues. The church's financial woes were reaching catastrophic proportions, growth was stagnant, and a hierarchy had become entrenched which sought to control each individual congregation, rather than represent them as it had been elected to do.

Into such a situation had come the discoveries, breathing fresh life into the hearts of millions in many countries. Men and women of all religious persuasions – and none – were sharing the *Surprising Discoveries* videos and books with zest. In the case of the SDAs, both laypersons and clergy were doing this without permission from Wahroonga. The leadership was losing control. And this pushed a handful of officials into a near panic.

And so was circulated the "Statement". Its author claimed that we had said things in our videos that we certainly never said. This anonymous one page document graced with fourteen untruths was traced to one Gerhard Pfandl at the SDA office.

Pfandl was pleased to take the credit for it. His arrogant tone surprised me.

Once the fallacies in his "Statement" had been exposed, however, Pfandl protested that he had only "edited the statement". The contents had been fed to him by his colleague David Down, an SDA cleric who also edited a magazine on archaeology. For many years Down had been considered the spokesman for his church on archaeology.

However, now, as he was coming toward the end of his career, something **big** was happening: a new wave of discoveries. His people were rising up and excitedly talking about them. But he was not a part of the action. How would you expect him to react?

Down was reportedly a genial sort of man. But this matter was striking close to the nerve. Cynical at first, he soon became positively infuriated!

He saw only one option. And that was to squelch the Ark of the Covenant discovery claim and kill the growing public interest in it once and for all.

In this widely circulated "Statement" to his members, Mr. Down wrote:

> There is a cave beneath Gordon's Calvary but it is occupied by a wholesale banana merchant. He knows nothing of this discovery.

The dear man was probably sincere in his interrogation of the surprised banana merchant. But had Mr. Down first come to us, he could have saved himself so much sweat. Our underground chamber has not moved; it remains, as ever, a good distance away in the opposite direction!

Down's banana cave we know well. Located on street level, it is open to any stray cat that chances to wander in. You would hardly hide valuables in it.

In the "Statement", Mr. Down then went on to say:

> Claims that it has been spirited away by the Israelis are without foundation.

How we loved this man! His assertions gave us some good laughs. And that is good for the soul.

The reader will know by now that the Ark of the Covenant is still firmly reposing down in the cavern. No one has spirited it away.

This man, bless him, had not invested the means, time or energy, nor risked his life, to determine the truth. And he had **never** approached us. When seminar organizers asked if he had examined our reports, he responded, "I'm too busy." When tour promoter Nancy Hardy invited him to attend a seminar and see for himself, his excuse was, "I have no time."

And now came a flood of reckless and careless statements for which, somehow, he **did** find time. "Anyway, it's all rubbish!" he told an inquirer. The poor man demonstrated that he had no knowledge of what he was saying, and even less concern for the truth of the statements.

So it was that when Down's bosses called for a report, they published it, believing he had made a thorough investigation.

Character assassination

To add weight to the Down-Pfandl circular, their communications colleague Ray Coombe added his own note, which he faxed for British consumption. Many years ago, he wrote, Gray had resigned from public life "under unfortunate circumstances."

When a gentleman in Wales asked Coombe, "what were the unfortunate circumstances?" Coombe wrote back, titillatingly, "I do not wish to give further details... as it involved a moral indiscretion."

"But whose moral indiscretion was it?" pressed the Welshman. "Gray's moral indiscretion, or someone else's?"

From his air-conditioned Wahroonga office, Coombe finally confessed, "I do not have any information on the details and I prefer to leave it that way. It is not necessary for me to be concerned with events that transpired many years ago, and it does not affect my assessment of Jonathan now. I have no reason to infer guilt or blame on anyone... Thank you for the catalogue of (Wyatt/Gray) materials that you have supplied. Do you know if there is a local source or distributor here in Australia?"

The Welshman's head was reeling. He wrote to us:

> I note that all criticism of the R.Wyatt/J.Gray team is severe, yet, when challenged, a far more conciliatory tone is apparent in replies. This is a strange phenomenon! I sent him the UK list of videos/books available. How can the books/videos be criticized when he doesn't know how to get hold of them in Australia? This is another strange phenomenon, surely?

Attack backfires

In response to the Wahroonga outburst, one of their own pastors wrote:

It is a shocking commentary on the modus operandi of the South Pacific Division that it could in any measure countenance such blatant deceit as that emanating from Pfandl's office.

Tom... New South Wales

If the Wahroonga "heavies" hoped to stifle interest in the discoveries, their attempt was to prove a colossal flop. Interest simply exploded.

One observer wrote:

I am sorry that there are men in high places who are so stupid. Your work won't stop. It's got too much of a hold now. It's going in leaps and bounds. The Lord is moving. I can feel it.

Gwen... Victoria

Another of their followers wrote to them in this manner:

I regard it as a reckless and irresponsible document, in which truth has taken a very low priority.

Anybody who has gone to the trouble of checking on the work of Jon Gray in various parts of the world will be greatly impressed by the overwhelming success of his efforts.

Among the visitors to his seminars are Buddhists, Moslems, atheists, Roman Catholic priests, Communists, and just about every type of person with or without any religious belief.

These meetings all have one thing in common - there are many conversions of life, and many people who were unbelievers are converted to God.

This work obviously has God's blessing, and it is NOT going to fail.

For the church leaders to bitterly attack these men and their earth shaking claims and activities, is sheer folly. It can only alienate more and more people from the church.

There is NO excuse for broadcasting false statements when so much evidence is there to be seen and examined by all.

Albert Biddle, Queensland

451

How little did we suspect what lay ahead...

The Warning

On November 24, following Sydney seminars, I flew north to Papua New Guinea, to present the archaeological discoveries there.

Convention organizers had warned me that, triggered by ten murders in one weekend in Port Moresby alone, a 9 pm curfew had been imposed. One would hardly have guessed, however, the source of the violence soon to be encountered.

First stopping over to present a talk at the Moresby University, I flew the next morning to the northern coastal town of Madang, where a week-long open air convention had been organized at the Lutheran village of Yabob. With me were convention organizer Geoff Whitehouse, a pleasant guy with a disarming smile and a charming Papua New Guinean wife; Abdulla Ahomed, a dynamic speaker from Zimbabwe; and Australian speakers and newly-weds Peter and Cathy Date.

We were honored to stay in a new bamboo thatched house. "A village family has just built it," we were informed. "Haven't occupied it, yet. They want you to be first." Standing on stilts, which permitted cool air to circulate below, the building looked elegant. It was expertly framed, with a tall, steep roof. We were to sleep on floor mattresses under mosquito nets, but would enjoy the luxury of electricity and a wooden kitchen table and stools hand made.

Outside, within a bamboo enclosure, cold showers would be enjoyed by filling a bucket with water and splashing oneself with one hand whilst rubbing with a bar of soap in the other.

It was to become a daily ritual: a breakfast of bananas, coconut, mango and papaya. Since papaya seeds contained quinine, we would each mix in a spoonful of seeds as a precaution against malaria from the ever-present mosquito. The fruit salad disguised the taste!

The convention venue filled an enormous clearing, flanked on three sides by a tropical forest and on the fourth by a river. Ideal for an instant tent town! Most of the space, however, would be occupied by the audience, seated on the grass under the stars. A stage had been erected on stilts at one end.

452

To attend, some had actually walked, I was told, up to 600 kilometers. Increasing steadily, the audience would swell by week's end to an estimated 2,000.

I was warned upon arrival that the meetings had been denounced by local SDA leaders under the jurisdiction of the Australian hierarchy. From the pulpit, members were urged to break up the meetings. There were even threats to kill.

A truckload of thugs was reported to have arrived on the first night. However, the crowd was so immense that the thugs had second thoughts on the matter, and merely listened to the address. Some of the would-be trouble makers were impressed by subsequent meetings they attended.

Others decided it would be easier to attack individuals after the crowd had dispersed.

They waited.

Nevertheless, the animosity was such that one SDA worker at the town water works cut off the water supply to this Lutheran village for two days.

The programs proceeded as scheduled. With the use of an on-site generator, the discoveries were presented each evening, illustrated by color slides. Half of those attending were new Christians, drug addicts, some of the worst criminals and street people. There were also members and pastors of various denominations. Audience reaction was electric. Some described the information as "life-changing".

On the fourth night, heavy clouds emptied their reservoir of water upon us. Nobody moved. We simply covered the projector and continued. Thoroughly soaked, no one complained. After all the rain was warm. And they would not have missed the program.

As a matter of fact, the next morning I heard of a young lady who, undeterred by the imminent birth of her child, had traveled all the way from the highlands to attend. Her baby - a girl - had been born in a tent. From then on, the mother received a persistent stream of young visitors to her tent. In a day or so, both mother and daughter were up and about.

It was Sunday, December 1, the final day of camp. And Geoff shuffled out of his room looking a little bleary-eyed.

"Man, that Ark of the Covenant presentation last night!" he yawned, cheerfully. "Do you know, I was up about all the night. I went around the tents. Nobody wanted to sleep. They just wanted to talk about it."

Geoff sat on the bench. "By the way, Jonathan, what time's your plane?"

"10.20.," I replied.

Then I'll take you and Abdulla to the airport around nine,"said Geoff. "Is that OK?"

Geoff worked for a mining company. Today he faced a grueling three hour drive along a pot-holed road to the highlands. He considered we would be safe in the waiting room until our plane took off.

◆◆◆◆◆◆

Ambush

The Land Rover bumped its way for ten minutes along a narrow road lined with frangipani, coconut palms and mango trees, turned in through a gate and braked beside the waiting room door. The terminal was a low, modest looking structure. The passenger area would be about the size of a large house. Several rows of seats faced the check-in counter.

"Good-bye, chaps," he waved. "Hope to see you again. Safe trip, now."

"So long, Geoff."

Abdulla settled onto one of the seats. I plopped down beside him and looked at my boarding pass. We were going out on a Fokker F28; Flight PX129, to be precise, operated by Air Niugini.

At first we did not notice them. Several men were standing at the end of the row, watching us. Then it happened.

Suddenly a man snatched my bag containing "discoveries" evidence, as well as the manuscript for this book.

"My bag!" I shouted.

Ahomed stared at me in shock.

No time to talk. I ran out through the door of the terminal building, which opened onto the small car park. It was mostly empty. Just a few people were standing around. I paused momentarily to survey the scene. And then I spotted him. Outside the gate, a man was racing across the road, headed for a side road. The bag was swaying from his left shoulder.

"Thief! Stop him! Stop him!" I called to observers. They all just stood, some in the car park, others on the road outside. I ran through them.

"Stop him!" I shouted. And kept running.

The bag snatcher was a hundred or so yards ahead. He was now along the side road, running fast. And then something weird happened. The man slowed and just plopped down the bag in the middle of the road. He didn't need to; he was so far ahead of me.

Still running, I barely glimpsed the group of other men standing there.

I was now perhaps ten paces from the bag. Suddenly my skull took the impact. It felt like a blow from a 4- by 6-inch block of timber, flat against my head, from behind. It was so violent, it sent me reeling leftward.

The thought came rushing, "I'm losing consciousness." I knew that should I fall to the ground, these men would kill me.

"Must go on. Must go on," I thought ... and felt a surge of energy to go forward and reach for the bag... just seconds away.

Retrieving the bag, I turned.

Then it resumed. Blows to the head. Heavy and hard. From behind...from the left... And I suddenly realized it... these were stones!

Perhaps eight or nine natives dressed in Western style shirts and trousers. This was organized and I was helpless to escape...

By some miracle, I felt NO PAIN.

Unexpectedly, the attack stopped. A thug with a stone as large as a baseball suddenly dropped it at my feet. The assailants just stood and looked at me, as I walked through them.

I strode back to the road that ran in front of the airport. I crossed it and entered the car park. Ahomed stood, shaken, in the terminal doorway. He turned with me, back inside, and we took our seats in the waiting room.

I hardly spoke. Abdulla was deathly silent.

We examined the bag and its contents. By a miracle, nothing was missing.

"How are you?" asked Abdulla, after a pause. He was grave.

"There's no pain. Abdulla, I felt no pain! Can you believe that?"

Not even bruises or marks. Just one ugly eye full of blood, enough to scare a kid, like something out of a horror movie. Otherwise no visible signs.

"Did an angel intervene?" the examining doctor back in Australia would later ask.

Minutes later, some of the attackers entered the airport and began poking Abdulla, slapping and threatening him.

"Write down your name!" shouted one who was better dressed than the others. The man sported a clean, white shirt and well-pressed trousers. He sounded well-educated. He had the bearing of a leader. "Write down you name!" he screamed.

Abdulla scrawled his name on a sheet of paper.

The other squinted at it. "Yes, you're another we're looking for," he roared. "Because you're breaking up our church. We don't want you here!"

All who attended the Madang convention would be aware that at no time was a presentation made that criticized the SDA church or its leadership, nor any attempt made to encourage the breaking up of that church.

Again the thugs poked, slapped and threatened him.

Abdulla arose and moved to the check-in counter. "Where's your security?" he demanded.

"Quick, come in here," urged an official. "You can hide till the plane goes."

Now the thugs vented their anger on me. The well-dressed leader shouted, "What happened to you on the road is because you are breaking up our church. We don't want you here."

"Are you an SDA?" I asked.

"Yes. We don't want you here!"

"Friend, I feel only peace toward you."

"Don't you come back!" he screamed.

"Well, my brother, I love you and if you ever come to Australia, my door is open to you."

The thugs slowly backed off.

The trap

The iron fist policy of control emanating from the Wahroonga SDA "heavies" was to result in fiercer violence three days later.

When fellow speaker Livingstone Kul and many of his laymen returned to Goroka in the highlands, Wahroonga-linked church leaders mobilized hostile feelings against them.

About 7am on December 4, fifteen to twenty leaders and others gathered on the main road outside the house where Livingstone and his laymen were guests.

"Livingstone Kul!" shouted one man.

Kul appeared in the doorway.

"Livingstone, we would like to hear about the Madang meetings," the man called. "Would you come outside and tell us the good news?"

Only too willing to share their joy, Kul and his laymen came out.

But it was a trap. Too late, Livingstone and his friends saw them...and froze. Suddenly, from the bushes, materialized more men. And a vicious attack began.

"Let's get outta here!" cried Livingstone. He and his men wrestled, struggling to break free.

They were punched, kicked and beaten. One was struck unconscious. He was to end up in hospital. Several laymen received gashes to their faces, bleeding noses and significant bleeding all over. Afterwards, some would not be able to eat, due to painful jaws and teeth and swollen lips.

Wrenching free, Livingstone and his friends made a dash down the road.

"Head for the church," he shouted. The men were running. Their assailants followed, hurling sticks at them.

"Quick, in here," panted Livingstone. "We should be safe inside. They'll respect the house of God." Beaten and dripping with blood, they staggered inside the building.

The mob burst in...

Livingstone was near the pulpit.

"Get him!" screamed one fanatic. They rushed upon him, and there beside the pulpit punched and kicked him to the floor. Livingstone lay groaning. Several laymen, themselves in pain, came to his rescue, and the mob dispersed. Kul's friends carried him back to the house, stationing guards at the door.

By this time, the whole village of Bena had gathered around. While the crowd watched, one Wahroonga-linked attacker stood and, pointing to the laymen's church, defiantly announced, "My name is ... I am going to burn down this building."

Many of those standing around were not SDAs. They were crying. "Don't! Don't do it!" they pleaded. "You're supposed to be Christians. Don't burn down the church."

But to no avail. The man lit a match. The church burned to the ground.

Mission accomplished, the SDA church officers left.

"Let's go after them," said someone. He was a new Christian, recently converted from a violent life.

"No, no," called Livingstone and other laymen. "We must pray for them, that God will forgive them."

"Be joyful," shouted Livingstone, through a swollen mouth. "Like Peter, Paul and others who have gone before, please rejoice, all of you, that we have been counted worthy to suffer for our Lord."

Within days, I made telephone contact with Livingstone. In high spirits, he threw out the challenge. "Next year we'll organize seminars in every city," he announced. "We want you to come back!"

◆◆◆◆◆◆

I looked into the bedroom.

"Come here, honey," she called.

"What are you doing?"

Josephine was on her knees. "Just join me," she asked. I went down beside her.

458

"Dear God," she began, "Thank you for bringing my husband safely back. Thank you for giving us a part to play in the discoveries. Please forgive those men, for they do not know what they are doing."

She arose and beckoned me to follow. "Out here. Come on!"

Josephine unrolled a mattress under the crinkly willow tree in the back garden.

"Lie down, Jonathan," she smiled impishly. In a plastic yellow bucket she was kneading a big mass of brown stuff. Potter's clay. "This will relieve any congestion," she soothed, plastering some first of all on the cover sheet over the pillow. "OK, pop your head in it." She wrapped my head all around with the mud pack and burst out laughing. "You handsome guy," she kidded.

"Now comes the hard bit... two hours a day for fourteen days. Think you'll survive it? And I'll put a comfrey poultice over that eye. And the aloe vera drops. In just a couple of months you should have one hundred per cent vision again."

Dear wife, she knew exactly what to do. Natural remedies were her specialty.

"Has the doctor reported back on the electro-encephalogram?"

"Yes, the brain waves were normal."

"No problem, then. Any internal damage will heal of itself." Tell me, Jonathan, what do you think will happen after this?"

♦♦♦♦♦♦

The cover up

Coombe was sitting on a volcano about to blow its top. At SDA world headquarters in Maryland, U.S.A., undersecretary Athol H. Tolhurst turned pale. News of the murder attempts had hit the Internet. There were members who demanded, "Will those church officials be disciplined?" Alarmed, Tolhurst rushed off a fax to Australia.

"Don't blame us!" cried public relations man Coombe.

Relieved, Tolhurst assured his inquirers, "...it was not the officials of our Church who did this. It was ex-Adventists who beat these two men." (Letter to a Mr & Mrs Heinrich, February 4, 1997)

At home, Josephine sat perusing the faxes.

"I can't believe this!" she exclaimed. "A fax from Coombe to a Ron Taylor, complaining that those reporting the attacks had failed to come to the Wahroonga Conference office for the true information. Then, on the very next line he writes that he does not have the information, anyway. He moans, 'We face the difficulty of getting information from our leaders in PNG.' See, he's virtually wiping his hands of it. The hypocrite!"

"Darling, you know these things don't bother me. Leave him to God."

She smiled. "Sure. But one of those 'hit' men will eventually boast to someone. Mark my words. Then just see if Mr Coombe and Company can suppress the truth!"

The deceit exposed

Coombe didn't know?

Geoff Whitehouse shook his head. Fully six weeks earlier, on December 12, he had confirmed by letter to SDA president Jessley Farugaso and to his Australian boss (Wahroonga's representative in Papua New Guinea), Brad Kemp, that "Elders and Deacons led the group of church members who beat and kicked Livingstone" and burned down the church building. Whitehouse lived in the area and knew the people. Mail from PNG to Australia, I should tell you, takes barely a week.

Clearly, Coombe and his "heavies" saw Livingstone as a threat in PNG. This gentle-natured man was, horror or horrors, a "dissident", and "independent", said Coombe - a dissident, I might add, whose life would soon be in danger again from church leaders.

The shock revelations continued. On January 17, 1997, a full six days before Coombe's fax pleading ignorance, Harold Peiko, one of my Madang seminar interpreters, announced in a public letter that the attempt upon Jonathan Gray's life had been "led by the Madang-Manus (SDA) Conference Treasurer." During the camp, wrote Peiko, the same man had dropped by and acted friendly. In the end, this man had played "Judas".

Surprise confession

Roll on March 18. It was 7.10.am. I was at Sydney International Airport, preparing to board a Qantas Boeing 747-400 to Johannesburg, for the start of an African lecture tour. But first, a last-minute phone call to my wife.

"Honey," she squealed, "you won't believe the fax I just got. One of the 'ambush committee' has confessed!"

"What!"

"Just listen to this..."

"Sweetheart," I cut in, "there's a postal counter here. Let me see if they have a fax machine."

I left the receiver dangling, spoke quickly to an attendant, then retrieved the mouthpiece. "Here's a number. Why don't you fax that thing through to me?"

The boarding sign began flashing...

Church leaders implicated

Flight attendants had just served orange juice. Unzipping my cabin bag, I reached for the document. The two signatories were a Bisho Bigorah and Harold S. Peiko. But it was the opening paragraph which grabbed my attention:

> The attack on Ahomed and Gray at Madang was planned and organised by the leaders of the Madang Manus local Conference [paid leadership] of the Seventh-day Adventist church.

Here was a confession from the deacon of that church:

> I was present at an urgent board meeting called by the district Pastor to discuss the means they could employ to harm the two visiting speakers. I was sorely afraid in the middle of the meeting, because the district Pastor who chaired the meeting that late night behaved unusually. Often, at certain times of the discussions, the Pastor would stand up and would shout. He would show his fist, then he would punch the empty air, and he would hit the table.

> All the leaders acted out their part in the attack. The Secretary of the Conference [in command of numerous SDA

461

churches] used walkie talkie to monitor Jonathan Gray's and Ahomed's movement.

The youth director led and mobilised the youth and Path-finders, along with the leading Pastors of the Conference church and laid in ambush for them at the airport.

Would-be murderers praised

From his Wahroonga office, Gerhard Pfandl had thumped the order: Don't support Gray! Stop him getting through to our followers! This directive reached Papua New Guinea.

Confessed the deacon:

> After the incident at the airport, the Treasurer of the Conference publicly admitted and boastfully told both the PNG laymen and the Conference church members that he was the first person to play and act like Mohammed Ali on Jonathan Gray. The Treasurer also stated that **the Union Mission [Wahroonga's direct agents], praised them for the good work done on their behalf**.

The Wahroonga octopus had extended its tentacles into PNG.

"The reason for the assault on Jonathan Gray," wrote Geoff Whitehouse, "would appear to be the 'sin' of presenting slide presentations on the archaeology of the Bible."

Of course, this was the very thing the Wahroonga "happy trio" hated. In his fax, Coombe admitted the attacks, but why worry? Jonathan Gray had been, he said, "preying upon vulnerable groups."

No wonder the hysteria whipped up by Wahroonga had been translated into a murder attempt!

The revelations kept coming. In his public letter, Harold Peiko revealed that after I had left the country, "conference leaders and members searched everywhere for Livingstone Kul, Harold Peiko, Tepi Yaato, and Geoff and Lydia Whitehouse to kill us. But fortunately," added Peiko, "the Lord led us out of the country." (How each one left the country, just in time, is another story.)

Livingstone came to Australia. After his return to Papua New Guinea, he wrote, on January 12, "At present I am living in fear because some of them want to take my life. They are even threatening other lay members. **You will soon hear of blood shed in PNG."**

Coming Storm

Certainly one could have no brief against the sincere members of the SDA organization. Rather it was a handful of "heavies" in one geographical division of the world, whose motives, actions and influence might well call for investigation. Strangely enough, one could pity such men in their turmoil. Even love them, pray for them. One could be grateful that nobody had so far been killed. But it might not be long. The Wahroonga men should have good reason to be shaking in their boots.

Today one was hearing the rumblings of a coming storm. It was emerging within all groups of people. In a manner reminiscent of the early centuries, men, women and children will be persecuted at the instigation of religious leaders who seek control over what the masses will hear. It will be considered divisive to share the good news without their prior authorization.

In any case the Down-Pfandl-Coombe debacle with their outburst against the discoveries had now, contrary to their hopes, ignited a fire among their lay people that shall not be quenched.

As one man phoned to assure us, "The more intense the opposition, the greater must be the value of the work that is being done."

Among all peoples, the discoveries were getting set to explode with a power that might well shake the world.

••••••

The next question is, How do the Israelis feel about the discovery? Somehow I knew you'd ask that...

CHAPTER 44

ON A KNIFE EDGE

"Me? You're asking Me? There's no way I'm going in there."

"Well... **somebody** must do it."

"And you can count me out, too!"

"You too? What's wrong with you guys? Are you a bunch of school girls?"

"You can forget me too. I'd rather resign!"

"Oh, come on now. It can't be that dangerous."

"No thanks. Anything else but this."

"Three of you – strong and tough... You're all scared, aren't you? Dan... will you..."

Dan Barhart was a Doctor of Archaeology. Bright, keen and well-read. He also lectured at the Hebrew University. And he had written a book or two.

This was the year 1989. Dan was in charge of the Jerusalem district this year.

Dan ran his eyes around the room, resting them in turn on each man. You could feel the tension. Three chickens, he thought, his mouth twisting into a smile.

"Dan... ?"

"Sure, you can count on me. I'm not afraid to go in."

The following morning Dan headed toward the dig. He had on some old gear. An outfit that could get torn or dirty and it wouldn't matter.

He pushed aside the barrier and peered in.

"A piece of cake," he decided. "Scared? Scared of what? Today I shall see the Holy Ark."

Dan pulled out his flashlight and headed in. He had not got three steps toward the tunnel system. Suddenly his legs and back didn't work. He fell to the ground, groaning.

Dan lay on a bed for two weeks... in agony. Two weeks to think. Two weeks to relive each second. Two weeks to wonder...

"I can't believe it," he kept mumbling to himself. "Whatever happened?"

A well educated man, Dan Barhart knew well the story of the Ark. Certainly, there was no doubt something had happened to him. Thank God, at least he was alive.

Some time later, while visiting the United States, Dan would meet Ron Wyatt again. And they would recall the episode. "You know, Mr. Wyatt," he would say, "I've never had trouble with my back before. And I've never had trouble with my back since."

After that, he gave up any idea of going in to view the Ark of the Covenant.

So now the Antiquities officer with whom Ron was liaising permitted Ron to continue his work alone. And for a considerable time, knowledge of the find would be kept more or less secret.

By the time of the final visit into the chamber, the stones, rotted timbers and skins had been largely cleared away, and even the stone case that surrounded the Ark itself was removed.[1]

At last Ron was able to make a video of all the furniture. For the moment this remains classified. Nevertheless I believe the time is near when this video footage will be released for all to see.

The excavation hole was now to be sealed. In any case, the Temple treasures could not be brought out through such a maze of narrow cavities.

••••••

Government reaction

In recent days, I have often been asked, "How do the Israeli authorities react to the find?"

I shall speak frankly. From the information I am able to acquire, it is evident that the authorities do not know how to handle this discovery.

They have a right to be nervous. And I can think of two reasons. The first is political.

Some time ago, a permit was granted to some Israelis to undertake an excavation under the Temple Mount. After a short while, it was reported that workmen had been seen lugging crates into the excavation tunnel.

This aroused the curiosity of the authorities. They sent men in to investigate. It was found that the tunnel penetrated to a spot close under the Dome of the Rock... and high explosives were being set in position, presumably to blow up the place.

If you didn't know, the Al Aqsa mosque and the Dome of the Rock, together named the **Haram al-Sharif**, comprise the third most important place for the Moslem people.[2]

Just think what sabotage of that site could do! It might well provoke an Islamic **Jihad**, a "holy war".

The Israeli government desires to maintain good relations with the Arabs. It does not want to disturb the peace with the Arabs.

There are extremists who believe the Dome of the Rock sits illegally on the old Temple Mount. That does not make them extremists. However, it is reported that these men would feel quite safe in provoking a war just to get the mount – if they knew they had the Ark of the Covenant "on their side".

It is remembered that during the period of the ancient Judges, before Solomon's Temple was built, the Israelites would take the Ark with them into battle. And they were victorious.

467

Dome of the Rock in Jerusalem (Photo: Jonathan Gray)

468

Well, not always. It depended upon their faithfulness to the Lord. There was nothing inherent in the Ark itself that brought them victory. Their help came from the Lord.

Nevertheless, there are some modern religious extremists who would not hesitate to provoke a war in order to secure the old Temple site and build a Third Temple – if they could lay their hands on the Ark, believing its very possession would render them victorious.

One can understand why the Arabs are set on thwarting any future archaeological efforts in this vicinity. As a matter of fact, they have sunk some deep concrete pillars around the southern wall to prevent further digs.

When Ron provided some evidence of the discovery to the authorities, they devised a plan to "test" the water, so to speak. They sought to determine public reaction to a possible announcement of the discovery of the Ark of the Covenant and to a possible building of a new Temple.

The result was a bloody clash and many deaths.

The morning of Monday, October 8, 1990, would go down in history as the "Temple Mount massacre". An ultra-conservative Zionist group known as the Temple Mount Faithful marched up to the Moghrabi Gate, holding aloft a large banner which bore a Star of David and an inscription in Hebrew which read:

TEMPLE MOUNT - THE SYMBOL OF OUR PEOPLE IS IN THE HANDS OF OUR ENEMIES.

The demonstrators hoped to enter through the gate to the Temple Mount itself, march to the Dome of the Rock and there lay a cornerstone for a proposed Third Temple.

This had been the location of the First and Second Temples, of course.

To the Arabs also, the Temple Mount is a site of tremendous importance. It has been a special place to Moslems ever since work began on the Dome of the Rock in the 7th century AD.

The situation was loaded with political dynamite.

In almost no time, an estimated 5,000 militant Arabs amassed inside the walls of the Temple Mount, armed with stones to hurl down upon the approaching marchers.

The Moghrabi Gate through which the zealots planned to pass is not only a mere 150 yards from the front porch of the Al Aqsa Mosque, it also penetrates the southern end of the Western Wall of the mount. The exposed exterior of this wall, known as the Wailing Wall, is most important to Jews. It is, in fact, the single most important Jewish holy place.

This wall is actually part of a retaining buttress built in the late first century BC by Herod the Great, which escaped demolition by the Romans in 70 AD.

It had always been a symbol for Jews scattered over the world.

After the Six Day War of 1967 a large plaza was cleared in front of it and the site dedicated as a formal place of worship. Today, Jews from all over the world gather here to lament that they have no Temple.

However, the Israeli authorities have banned Jewish worship on the Temple Mount itself and restricted access above and below ground. This area remains under the exclusive control of the Moslems.

But to continue our story...

As the Zionist procession attempted to enter through the Moghrabi Gate, the thousands of Arabs began to rain down showers of stones – not only upon the demonstrating zealots, but upon the heads of Jews praying at the Wailing Wall.

This sign states that access to the Temple Mount is restricted.

The result was catastrophic. Eleven Israeli worshippers and eight policemen were injured, while 21 Arabs were shot dead and 125 seriously injured.

Again, on September 24, 1996, as on so many previous occasions, the simmering hostility exploded.

The government had been employing workers to construct a new tourist tunnel in Jerusalem, to cope with the tourist flow in the Via Dolorosa area. Workmen had been digging secretly under the Moslem quarter, enlarging an old tunnel that ran from the Western Wall to the Via Dolorosa.

As they were about to break through at one end, the word got out. The excavation, you see, was close to the Al Aqsa Mosque. A crowd of Arabs rushed to the site and starting throwing stones.

The rioting, by week's end, had cost the lives of some 70 people.

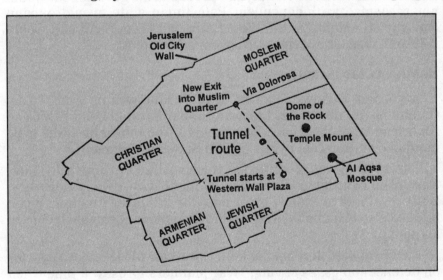

So we have Jewish extremists... angry Palestinians.. and a third potentially explosive factor... the Ark of the Covenant find.

U.S. News and World Report put it well:

> In a land torn by competing historical claims, archaeology is a weapon.[3]

While the authorities (and by this I mean a handful of tight-lipped officials) know of the Ark's location, they have decided that the matter is too politically volatile for them to go public. An official announcement could provoke "premature" action by fringe groups wanting to build a new Temple.

Government officials regard this as a critical issue, in which the safety of the people must come first.

In view of the prospect of a negotiable peace in the Middle East, the present actions of the government are deliberately against any disclosure of what it knows.

It was just one week after our 1995 Israel expedition that Prime Minister Rabin was assassinated. And the authorities were blaming one of those disaffected extremists.

Today, the Israeli government walks a knife edge.

Many believe that peace is possible, although, upon assuming office, Prime Minister Netanyahu promised his government would not recognize an independent Palestinian state, would expand Jewish settlements in the West Bank and Gaza Strip and would refuse to discuss sharing Jerusalem as a capital.

Death ray for Israel?

According to news reporter John Barala, writing from Tulsa, Oklahoma, a "**death ray**" laser weapon that had been denied to American forces because it was thought "**too inhuman**", was to be handed over to Israel by the United States government.[4]

The weapon was identified as the **Nautilus anti-missile** laser. The laser can destroy missiles in flight with deadly accuracy. However, there are many other uses for this laser weapon. It can be used also to immobilize and blind thousands of combat troops in an instant.

Barala quoted Jeremy Sackett, a veteran wire service reporter on defense topics, as saying, "War planners foresaw a time when the mere terror of a swiftly, silently gliding ray that melts – literally incinerates – the human eye would panic hostile troops and rout them without firing a shot."

And Dr. Vanessa Hughessen, a physicist specializing in arms-control studies at MIT said, "The potential is there. The Nautilus represents the ultimate combat technology. Properly engineered, it will destroy anything in its path."[5]

Israel, the "holy land" that so many of us love, is today on tenterhooks. The government is nervous. It does not want war. Neither do most of the people, whether Israeli or Arab.

But it is against this background that we must view the present official attitude toward the Ark of the Covenant discovery. It is potentially the most explosive object on earth... politically and religiously.

What the Secret Service agent knew

I recall a conversation I had with a gentleman who asked, "What if I were to write to the Israeli Government and ask them about it?"

My reply was, "They'll deny it, of course. Both the project and the man. That is how it has to be for the time being. And it would be naive of one to expect otherwise. In virtually every country, official denials of certain matters are standard procedure. And in such cases, almost all personnel in the department concerned are kept in the dark."

A classic example of the denials policy in action was seen in April,1995, after Channel 7 Radio in Israel broke the news that Foreign Minister Shimon Peres had met with the Pope with a proposal to place the Old City of Jerusalem under Vatican control.

Israel's Ambassador in Rome, Shmuel Hadas, and Peres himself, denied such a plan.

However, a copy of a telegram sent by Miriam Ziv to the Foreign Ministry in Jerusalem, outlining Peres' plans, surfaced and was printed in the *Hatzofe* newspaper.

Former Prime Minister Yitzhak Shamir told *The Jewish Press* that:

> ...this is similar to Peres' denial that there was ever a letter with promises to Arafat about Jerusalem and later the letter surfaced. **Now this telegram was revealed. Who knows what else they are concealing from the public?**[6]

Indeed. So to the gentleman who asked would the Israeli authorities admit the Ark find if he wrote to them, my reply was, "You would probably receive a letter that went something like this: 'We have no record of any archaeological permit having been issued to a Ronald Wyatt, nor does anyone in this office know him.

If Mr. Wyatt conducted any excavation in Jerusalem, it would have been done illegally.'"

"And what about Jonathan Gray?" (This has already occurred. Self-appointed antagonist David Down has said so.)

"Don't know him. Never heard of him." And we smile.

Has human nature changed? On January 17, 1883, General Gordon observed in a letter to his sister:

> The present-day governors, like those at the time of Christ, continue to be corrupt and are preoccupied with political expediency.[7]

Occasionally one bumps into an official who admits that not all is being told.

Following a 2½ hour presentation on the Ark of the Covenant to an audience in Auckland, New Zealand, a member of the audience introduced himself to me as an Israeli ex-Secret Service agent. He raised the subject of Rabin's assassination and said, "I have information that Rockefeller initiated the act and that Israeli Secret Service men were implicated. It was called 'Operation Champagne'. But let me tell you this: your lecture on the Ark of the Covenant has just filled in missing gaps in what I already knew."

What did this man already know? With the pressure of a crowd around us, there was no opportunity to continue the conversation.

Attitude of religious leaders

Many great rabbis of the past and present have rejected, on religious grounds, any search for the Ark.

The Ashkenazi Chief Rabbi, Rabbi Unterman, was quoted as saying:

> What will happen, if, as a result of the archaeological excavation, you find the Ark of the Covenant, which Jewish tradition says is buried in the depths of the earth?[8]

The rabbi said that it was precisely such a discovery that he feared. Since the children of Israel today are not "pure" from the viewpoint of Jewish religious law, they are forbidden to touch the Ark of the Covenant. Hence it is unthinkable to even consider excavating until the Messiah comes![9]

Such concern about the Ark does reflect orthodox thinking. Since the destruction of the Second Temple, all Jews have been considered to be in a state of ritual impurity. This condition is supposed to end only with the coming of the Messiah.[10]

Strong opposition to archaeological work could, therefore, be expected from some Jewish religious authorities. This still represents a potential obstacle to bringing anything out from the cavern.

Lubavitcher rabbis have said, "What will you do with it if you find it? Will you bring tourists to look at it? You had better leave it closed until its time will come."

Attempt to reveal the location

I have always considered discretion and respect for a host government's wishes to be important in such matters.

A number of times, Ron and I have discussed the ramifications of the discovery. Unfortunately not all have been discreet.

Over the years, five different people lost their lives at the very time they were attempting to interfere with or even halt the excavation.

One man stumbled upon the discovery when he noticed the team members coming and going from the excavation. He began to ask questions.

This man, a young British tourist, soon found out what was going on and was determined to learn the precise location.

As Ron entered the hotel on this particular night, the man approached him again. "Will you show me where is the Ark of the Covenant?" he urged.

"I don't know you," was Ron's reply. "Why should I reveal it to you?"

But the gentleman was not to be put off. Each day he kept pestering the archaeologist to tell him the location.

Failing to elicit this information, the man resorted to watching. One morning as Ron left the hotel early, the man darted from behind his hiding place and followed him at a distance. He found out the location.

Ecstatic, he made his next move. He himself would tell the world.

He went to a phone box and called the media. He informed them that he would conduct a press conference the next day, in which he was to announce "a great discovery". The conference was scheduled for nine in the morning.

As the crew members came in from the diggings that night, the man intercepted Ron.

"Mr. Wyatt," he announced, "Tomorrow I shall tell the world."

"You can't do that!" exclaimed Ron. "It's too sensitive!"

"This is something the whole world needs to know," he insisted.

"We are sworn to secrecy on the location," said Ron. "Cancel your news conference."

"Too bad!" he thundered. "I'm going to do it anyway."

That night, the team members changed their flight booking and left early.

The press conference was scheduled to take place in a nearby alley, a relatively secluded place.

The next morning, when the journalists arrived, they found the man lying in the alley in a pool of blood. There was a bullet hole in the back of his head. He had been shot by a single sniper's bullet. The lane was swarming with mounted police, soldiers and medical units.

"Arab extremists," said the newspaper. No further explanation was given.

That was back on April 27, 1986. The situation has not changed.

Another reason for the clamp

We have noted already that both Arabs and Israelis would prefer that some diggings didn't take place. This is the case whether they be religious leaders or political. But not just leaders.

I suggested there might be two reasons why the discovery of the Ark of the Covenant was a hot issue. The first was political. The second is religious.

Just think of the repercussions within Judaism if it were to be officially announced that the Person who was crucified at Skull Hill on that historic Passover Day, branded by Jewish church leaders as an impostor, had actually spilt his blood on **THEIR** Mercy Seat? What would that do to Judaism?

Yes, the Jewish people may be excited about discovering the Ark of the Covenant, since that is the most important piece of furniture for their Temple.

But the last blood to flow onto that Ark was the blood of Jesus Christ, a so-called impostor. Can they take the blood of animals again and sprinkle it on that Mercy Seat? They have a decision to make.

Every Jew will have to examine his or her faith and decide whether Yeshua is the Messiah or not. That has the potential to shake world Judaism.

The Israeli political climate is so volatile that, in the eyes of some, the government's very survival could depend on maintaining the status quo. And for this reason alone, there are many who would not welcome a further destabilizing of the scene.

Sealed up

When the authorities ordered the crew to seal up the entrance to the excavation tunnel leading to the chamber, we knew that absolute confirmation of our story would be impossible for the present.

Bob Murrell was among those who constructed a steel door to close off the entrance. And several feet of earth were piled over it, to disguise the location.

The cross-holes also were covered over with timber and gravel since the authorities did not want them revealed.

Meanwhile the government has placed a clamp on some information concerning the discovery. And we shall not go against the host government.

Currently, therefore, we are unable to present all collected data on this subject. We only ask that the reader watch and wait until that time when it will be made public.

Certain rabbis may have had some influence in this decision, believing that the secret of the Ark belongs to the future time of redemption and the Messiah's appearance. They may fear that a premature disclosure of the facts could possibly delay these events.

No matter how wonderful and exciting would be the display of the items in that cave, it seems likely that this will have to wait a while longer.

And what has happened to Rafat, the young Arab man ?

Rafat now lives outside Israel, and because of governmental visitor regulations he cannot re-enter the country. But he has conversed by telephone.

Meanwhile, the accumulated evidence must ultimately apply public pressure to international politicians. SHOULD THIS DISCOVERY BE KEPT UNDERGROUND FOR ANOTHER DECADE?

•••••••••

If you think that's the end of the matter for now, then I have news for you. Wonderful news.

Something else happened down there in the Ark cavern. And it's so amazing, you had better be sitting down!

And, as with other events in the saga, the timing was... PERFECT!

We shall devote most of the next chapter to it...

CHAPTER 45

BLOOD BATTLE

Before leaving the site for good, Ron took samples of the blood that had come down through the crack in the chamber ceiling. Within the crack itself, there was evidence that copious amounts of blood had poured down. Some blood was splattered on top of the split-open lid of the stone case enclosing the Ark. And blood had also sprinkled down onto the Mercy Seat.

The blood samples were taken from the lid of the stone case and from the crack in the cave ceiling.

Upon his return home to Nashville, Tennessee, Ron had the blood analysed. Through his work at hospitals, he had contacts. This simplified matters.

The dried samples were soaked in a saline solution for three days. Using an electron microscope, it was possible to find the chromosomal content of the blood.

The blood was found to be human, but **very** peculiar.

Could blood last so long?

We were back home in Australia. And it had to happen! I went to the mailbox - and there was a caustic letter ridiculing the very idea of the blood.

The man, bless his heart, was a doctor. Which should carry some weight? Blood, he asserted, deteriorates quite rapidly, especially at high temperature. Jesus' blood could have been quickly removed by bacteria or parasites such as cockroaches, who would eat it up readily.

"It just is absolutely not feasible that blood from the cross could have survived 2,000 years."

Sounds pretty shattering, doesn't it? Perhaps it's time to go home and forget the whole thing.

Not really.

I rang my friend in Oxleigh, England. "Arthur, see what you can find from your medical friends there, about the possibility of human blood remaining in a non-degraded state over long periods of time."

It would be a month before Arthur Eedle could fax me the results of his investigation. The fax came through at 7.15 am on Monday, November 4,1996.

"Jonathan," he said, "In point of fact there is no one here from whom I can obtain a definitive answer." He added that any opinion in the United Kingdom "would be pure speculation." Like the opinion of the dear doctor in Australia... nothing but speculation.

Only those with archaeological experience in the Middle East in specifically sampling mummy remains, for example, might be equipped to say anything of any value.

I recalled something that had come in the mail a little earlier - also from Britain.

It mentioned a Professor Steve Jones who, in 1993, published a book called *The Language of Genes*, in which he stated:

> In the infancy of human genetics, 20 years ago (that is, about 1972), biologists had a childish view of what the world looks like.[1]

How recent, indeed, is our ability to test the chromosomal content of blood!

Again, he says:

> Paternity can be tested beyond the grave. DNA is tough stuff, which can persist long after the death of its owner.[2]

He continues:

> The Egyptian Pharaoh Tutankhamun was buried about the same time as another mummy, Smenkhare. Their blood groups can still be identified. The pattern of gene sharing suggests that the two Pharaohs were brothers.[3]

480

How amazing, to be able to make such analyses, so long after the death of the individuals! Such tissue analyses were once thought impossible. In the light of this, who should dare pour scorn on the blood analysis that Ron had done in the laboratory?

It has been known for some time that Siberian mammoths died from suffocation by gases or drowning - a conclusion that is possible because after thousands of years their skin still remains congested with blood corpuscles.

A geneticist assured me that under certain conditions, such as freezing, blood could be preserved indefinitely.

I made contact with the skeptical doctor. I shall call him simply, P.D.

"P.D.," said I, "you postulated that the blood of the Son of God would be eaten by cockroaches or whatever. Let me explain to you this.

"At the crucifixion site, we are speaking of a cool chamber in the bowels of the earth suddenly linked to the cross-hole by a brand-new **sterile** crack in the rock, which receives the blood and is then sealed tight with a stone plug. A home for cockroaches? Let's get real!"

"It just is absolutely not feasible that blood from the cross could have survived 2,000 years."

One could agree with you... and add also that 'it just is absolutely not feasible' that the Israelites' shoes would survive without wearing out for 40 years. You believe the Holy Scriptures?"

"Of course."

"You remember, then, that the Hebrews wandered in the desert all that time, their shoes not wearing out? The Bible called it one of 'those great miracles'."

"W-well..." stammered the doctor, "scientifically it's impossible."

"Its good to hear from the mouth of a doctor that science has its limitations. But God has no limitations. Cannot He preserve something if He chooses? I understand, P.D., that you are a professing Christian?"

"Indeed I am."

"Then you will acknowledge the statement of Jesus that 'things which are impossible with men are possible with God?[5] 'With men it is impossible, but not with God: for with God all things are possible.'"[6]

It is fashionable to believe that current scientific opinion is the last word.

Yet one is reminded that in the cavern, in the back "side" of the Ark, sit four leather scrolls of the law, as fresh and supple as the day they were written upon. They show no deterioration. Amazing indeed. The blood on the Mercy Seat, and the scrolls of the law, in perfect condition. On the other hand the wooden beams and the skins which the Jews used to cover the other furniture have rotted away, degraded almost to the point of being mere dust.

The important things - precious items so valuable to the Lord - He has preserved intact.

It was about 5 am. Fresh and alert in the stillness of the early morning, I had spent the past hour mulling over these thoughts.

Suddenly Josephine called from the bedroom.

"Honey, come in! Listen to this!" She was sitting up in bed, a blanket over her shoulders, with the book of Leviticus before her.

"It says here that 'the life of the flesh is in the blood.' Chapter 17 and verse 11. Well?..."

"That's right," I confirmed. "But what are you getting at?"

"Hear me through, darling. I've been reading a prophecy concerning the coming Messiah[7] and it's quoted in the New Testament book of Acts: 'Thou wilt not leave my soul in hell, neither wilt thou suffer thine Holy One to see corruption.[8] Honey, do you see a connection?"

"I'm not sure," I said. "I need a stroll in the early morning air."

Outside was coal black. An almost eerie stillness. Above, the Milky Way floated brilliantly close. A gentle, cool breeze brushed my face. My mind began to churn...

> The life of the flesh is in the blood... neither will you permit your Holy One to see corruption.

Suddenly it flashed. "That's it!" I heard myself shouting, glad that nobody could hear me. "Yes, there **is** a connection. If this were the Lord's intention concerning His Son's flesh, that it should not decay or be corrupted, and if the life of the flesh is in the blood, might He not also have had a purpose in preserving remains of His Son's blood, not to be devoured by insects?"

Then I recalled what Ron had said after the microscope inspection of the blood from the cavern. There was movement in it. It was living blood.

The Messiah's body was changed into the glorious body on the third day, and his blood has remained in an uncorrupted state ever since.

One might ask, does the blood of Jesus Christ bear witness? It may be possible to take literally the Scripture which says:

> There are three that bear witness in earth, the spirit, and the water, **and the blood.**[9]

If we are to believe the Scriptures, Jesus Christ himself has gone to heaven, but the promised Holy Spirit is here... along with the other two, the water and the blood, bearing witness for him.

Whether the Lord preserved blood by freezing or simply by His WILL for 2 minutes or for 2,000 years...

The ancient Scripture declares:

> Is anything too hard for the Lord?[10] Behold, I am the Lord, the God of all flesh; is any thing too hard for me?[11]

Well, we at least know this: the blood **has** been preserved.

In a research report, Mary Nell had written:

> He had taken other specimens from along the crack where it extends through the bedrock adjacent to the cross-hole and I **myself** had been able to take a small sample, rehydrate it over a 3 day period, and view the red blood cells through the microscope. But even then, he never mentioned to me any actual lab analyses being done. Nor have I ever seen the other specimen. Therefore, all I can report here is what he has already said, as he has told me that when the time is right, he plans to have 2 unbiased geneticists go into the chamber, take their own samples, and each do his own independent analysis which will be filmed in progress.[12]

For my own part, I now know of a geneticist who believes in Ron's analysis to the extent that he is ready to go with Ron into that cavern, when the Israeli government permits, and perform an independent test of the blood.

Mary Nell adds:

> Again, this is Ron's plan - what HE hopes will occur - but, as with everything else, we do not know for sure exactly how, when or where everything will ultimately occur.
>
> But for now, he has nothing more to say on the subject. He learned from his experiences with Noah's Ark that even when he had the lab analyses filmed as they were done, there were those who came up with incredible reasons for discounting the results, such as saying that Ron "made" the specimen, etc.

Chromosome determination

As I revealed earlier, Ron Wyatt, in his tests, was able to find the chromosomal content of the blood. The blood was found to be human, but **very** peculiar.

Normal human blood has a total of 46 chromosomes. When a child is conceived, 23 chromosomes come from the mother and 23 come from the father.

One of these pairs is the gender determinant. For this pair, the mother always provides an "X" chromosome (so-called on account that its shape somewhat resembles the letter "X"). And if the father provides an "X", the child will contain the chromosomes "XX" - and will always be a female. But if the father provides a "Y" chromosome (shaped to some extent like the letter "Y"), the child will have a chromosome combination of "XY" - and will be male. The other 44 chromosomes (comprising 22 pairs) are known as autosomes.

All eggs produced by the female organism will be identical, containing "X" only. For her to produce a male offspring, the addition of a "Y" is necessary.

The blood analysis from the Ark chamber showed a total of only 24 chromosomes. Of these, 23 were derived from the mother. And there was one "Y" chromosome. This indicated that the blood belonged to a male.

No human blood like this had ever been known to exist. Nowhere on the earth!

The scientific term for this is "ploidy", or "haploidy". There have been known examples of females born with only half the normal chromosome count of 23, instead of 46, but never a male child. For a male to be produced, the father HAS to provide that distinctive "Y" chromosome!

Yes, I know. From the human standpoint it is impossible for a healthy human to survive with a greatly depleted chromosome count. In a normal human, 46 chromosomes would be needed for the cells to function. That is the verdict according to our present understanding of genetics.

And it was on this point that P.D. became a little upset.

"An open mind"

"I have an open mind," insisted the doctor. "But just tell me, what will happen to those people who have been introduced to the gospel news through so-called sensational discoveries, when one or more of them is proved conclusively to be false? Wouldn't that cause them to lose their faith?"

The man sat there, seething.

"P.D., you have just said you have an open mind," I replied. "That is commendable. But then you ask 'what will happen **when** one or more of the so-called discoveries is proved conclusively to be false? You said 'WILL' - not 'may'; 'WHEN' - not 'if'. You have pre-judged them already as false, you see. So where is your 'open mind'? But let me say, P.D., you are correct. There is certain to be an unfavorable backlash, but it will not be because of our claims. When the final evidence comes out, the back lash will be against those who publicly sought to denounce the finds, and suppress the truth. Just wait and see."

"But you don't have the qualifications in genetics," he insisted. "Nor the understanding to know about what you are speaking."

There are certain things about which one does not argue. My reply was simply, "Doctor, do you have the qualifications to know about what you are speaking in the field of archaeology?"

He didn't.

"And you know nothing about what we have been experiencing and finding on our digs. Make no mistake, God is a witness to what we have found."

485

Too depleted in male chromosomes to survive?

"That claim by Wyatt is totally laughable," he scoffed. "...that he has had blood analyzed and that the DNA contains only one set of chromosomes!! This is amateurism of the most stupid kind. Haploid human beings cannot survive." (The normal chromosome complement is called "diploid".)

On first thought, one might be tempted to agree with the good doctor. Such concepts do almost strain credibility. One is tempted to ask, Could it really have happened that a Man walked the earth with a normal chromosome count from his mother only - but not from a father?

On this point, I must share with you something that happened shortly after our late 1995 British tour.

My friend Arthur Eedle was sitting at dinner when the phone began to ring. It kept ringing insistently, until Arthur arose, walked across the room and picked up the receiver.

On the other end of the line was an excited friend of Arthur's, a retired Doctor of Medicine. He had become aware of Ron Wyatt's testimony concerning the chromosomes.

Being a cautious, scientific man, he found that this kind of claim disturbed him.

Was it possible, he questioned, for any man to have blood so depleted in male chromosomal content? Surely not!

However, being a man of Christian understanding - as well as of faith and action - he kept an open mind.

Not many days passed before he picked up the *New Scientist* for October 7 - printed just one week before we left England for our next Middle East expedition. And there on page 16 he found the following heading:

THE BOY WHOSE BLOOD HAS NO FATHER

He could hardly believe his eyes! The author, Philip Cohen, quoting an article by David Bonthron and his colleagues at Edinburgh University in *Nature Genetics* (Volume 11, page 164), explained that a certain three-year-old boy had been found whose white blood cells contained two "X" chromosomes, the signal for a female.

To cut a long story short, they went on to explain that the probable cause was a self-activating unfertilized ovum which had subsequently (after a short time) become fertilized in the normal way. The sperm would then have entered only a PART of the divided ovum, thereby creating this most unusual effect.

Bonthron believed that the boy's remarkable genetics depended on a number of highly unusual circumstances combining together, and occurring within a very short time window. "I don't expect we'll ever see another one," he said.

This was an incredibly rare condition. Such male chromosomal depletion for a **boy** was something which, until this case, would be considered scientifically impossible.

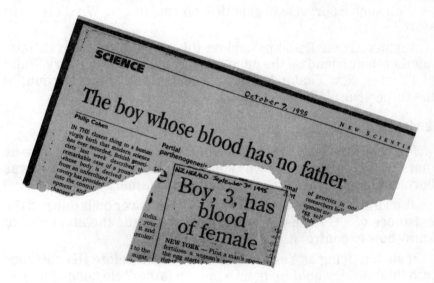

For three years this child was there with "impossible" blood and science did not know it. If the child had never come to the hospital, we would never have learned it was "scientifically possible".

Exclaimed Arthur's friend, "It's a miracle that I should be given this information at this very time!" The doctor was so excited, Arthur could almost hear him jumping up and down on the phone.

The child's blood cells were totally without any male chromosomal input. Of course, his chromosomal complement was very different from that of the Man who died on Skull Hill, but it did present what Cohen called "partial parthenogenesis" (the biologist's term for Virgin Birth).

What was its significance? The similarity was such that it proved the possibility of a man existing with a total depletion in his male-derived chromosomal blood count.

With such a surprise in genetics, one might ask, What else is in store?

Just as Arthur Eedle passed on this news to me from Britain, another dear friend on the opposite side of the world, Barry White of Thames, New Zealand, forwarded me a newspaper account of the three year old boy.

A virgin birth?

For thousands of years the Scriptures have thundered out to us that the Man whose blood was spilt for the world on Skull Hill was born of a virgin - that is, he had no human father.[1]

Is a virgin birth impossible? I guess the answer boils down to the existence of a God all-powerful. One who made the atom should know how to control it.

If such a Being as Yeshua Messiah existed before His entrance into this world, would He need a human father? He needed only to take humanity through the vehicle of a human mother. A virgin birth would be natural for such a Being.

If God became man, then one would expect Him to have an unusual entrance into this life. Certainly **it is the only type of birth consistent with the identity and character** of such a Deliverer for a lost planet.

I now asked P.D., could he explain scientifically Jesus' miracle birth?

488

Come to think of it, wasn't everything about this Person a miracle? God becoming human flesh was indeed UNIQUE. You could call it an "IMPOSSIBLE" event.

The virgin birth of this Son of God was nothing less than a miracle. And the blood of such a miracle could be considered miracle blood!

Medical science, with all its wonderful advances, is unable to comprehend the way in which the Creator works. Often, if men cannot understand, they will say it is not true. In such matters we come face to face with a Creator's **ability** to do **anything** - and man's **inability** to comprehend.

A certain pride is mingled with the consideration of divine truth, so that men feel impatient and defeated if they cannot explain every portion of Scripture to their own satisfaction. It is too humiliating to them to acknowledge that they do not understand.

The most learned geneticist would be hard-pressed to predict the chromosomal composition of the blood of the Son of God.

We are considering here the reality of a God-devised plan for His Son to walk the planet, born of a virgin, and whose blood cells would comprise a total of only 24 chromosomes... 23 from an earthly mother, and one "Y" chromosome from God.

Impossible? Then answer me: Which is omnipotent - natural law, or the God who created natural law and can override it to His purpose?

To this would Jesus himself reply, "**Ye do err, not knowing... the power of God.**"[14]

There will be rejection from some "learned" men, not because it's not true. But because they can't comprehend it they will not believe.

"P. D.," I added, "we can theorize, argue and, quibble about this, but it will not alter one whit what has been discovered in that cavern."

"Forgive me," interjected P.D. in his helpful manner. "But I'll need to inform you of a few basic biological facts, Jonathan. Human red blood cells have no nucleus, and therefore no DNA. So DNA studies can only be done on white cells, which are only 0.16 per cent of the cells. This means that any dried blood sample contains an absolutely minute amount of DNA, so small as to be virtually undetectable unless a large volume of blood sample was taken."

"So how do you define 'large'? P.D., knowing nothing about Ron's blood analysis, you seem prepared to dismiss it out of hand."

"You will remember the Australian Chamberlain case?" asked P.D.

"Yes, I remember."

And who didn't? That case had been one of the most bizarre in legal history. On August 17, 1980, while the Chamberlain family were camping near Ayers Rock in Australia's central desert, their nine week old baby Azaria disappeared. Although no body was found, Lindy was accused of murder with her husband Michael an accessory-after-the-fact. A first inquest found that a dingo (wild dog) had taken the baby. A second inquest did not. A Darwin court later sentenced Lindy to prison, with hard labor, for life. After three years, she was set free. A Royal Commission effectively cleared the names of Michael and Lindy and the convictions were subsequently quashed.

In December, 1995, a third inquest presented an open finding, refusing to rule that a dingo caused the death of the Chamberlain baby.

Reporter James Oram (*Sun-Herald*, December 17, 1995) said that the coroner "had ample evidence to find that a dingo caused the death of Azaria Chamberlain. He chose to ignore it."

Described as one of the worst miscarriages of justice in Australian legal history, the Chamberlain case certainly had been one of the most talked about.

Who didn't remember it?

P.D. continued. "In the car was supposedly found splattered blood from the baby. Now remember, new-born babies have quite a few immature blood cells in their blood which do contain nuclei, and therefore much more DNA than an adult. Not only were the forensic pathologists unable to detect whose blood group it was, but, at the second inquest, their tests couldn't even be established to prove that the substance was even blood at all! And that 'dried blood' had only been in the car allegedly for a year or so."

P.D. sat back confidently, awaiting my response.

490

"Concerning that stain in the Chamberlain car, then, P. D., you admit that at the second inquest forensic pathologists couldn't even prove that the substance was even blood at all. So, on your own admission, my friend, it may not even have been blood! In that case you tread on thin ice if you try to use it to judge the validity of Ron's blood samples."

"Then supply me with the name of the laboratory which tested Ron's blood samples, its address, or preferably fax number, the date, or approximate date, the samples were sent, and any code number or name under which they were identified."

"P.D., dear man, you will learn the details at the same time as everyone else. There are details we have been sworn by the host government not to disclose yet. Meanwhile the lab does not want to be bothered by an avalanche of requests. You must watch and wait. There were persons in Jesus' day who were constantly demanding, 'Show me this, prove me this'. And who would not be convinced if one rose from the dead.

"And I should tell you something else, P.D., thousands of' hours have now gone into making sure that documentation is available to cover virtually every question we can legitimately answer. The most efficient use of our time, therefore, is not to stop and repeat the answers to each individual, but rather to refer you to the published materials."

"I understand," said P.D.

"So you have a problem with the blood? Whose problem is it? It's **your** problem, P.D. OK, give it to God. Is it a problem with HIM? Is anything too difficult for Him?"

Preserved for an ultimate witness

The blood was preserved and discovery not permitted until humanity had the technological means of determining its chromosomal content.

Genetics is a relatively new and rapidly developing science. What was science yesterday is fiction today. And much that is science today will be fiction tomorrow.

We might well wonder, IF the Lord intends that His Son's blood be shown publicly as having such unique characteristics that his humanity and divinity cannot be denied, will He arrange for this evidence to be presented in a manner that 'clever' men cannot explain away?

Even since Ron found the blood, genetic research has come a long way.

Sitting in the Wyatt lounge room one afternoon, we discussed what might occur soon.

Mary Nell leaned forward and confided:

"I really believe that God is preparing mankind for the ultimate proof - the proof that will not remain silent, but will shake the world."

Just a little longer...

Meanwhile, I had come to know the major players in this drama very well. Josephine and I had both seen and handled evidence which left no doubt in our minds regarding the integrity not only of the players but of the discovery itself.

Of this much one can say: **human** blood is on that Mercy Seat. **Special** human blood. **Unique** blood.

The blood and the Mercy Seat. Is this physical contiguity accidental? Or by design? You decide.

That "detour" was planned

In our home we live with the discoveries. We've experienced enough to know that the unexplainable is commonplace. The discoveries are the topic of conversation throughout the day, at meal times and even in bed.

As with Ron and other members of the team, there are times when Josephine and I just can't sleep. Such as the other night.

It wasn't the heat, the barking dog or the moonlight.

I was reflecting on the three years or so of seemingly needless detours in the search for the lost Ark. All that hacking, digging and circling about. Why wasn't the team led straight to the chamber?

Then something flicked on in my cortex and I began to see why.

Just think! If the original tunnel had been found first, the team would never have gone digging and found the cut-out niches, nor the cross-hole with the earthquake crack, nor the seal-stone of the tomb. Ron would have entered the Ark chamber and not recognized what had happened here.

The question arises, WHAT NOW? Is there a divine plan in the discovery of the Ark of the Covenant? Will something happen soon?

Are there any clues?...

WARNING!

At this point, with a mountain of facts presented, our archaeological quest concludes.

There now follows something of a different nature. Some readers may regard this as mere speculation and be offended by it. They may prefer to skip these next two chapters and proceed to the Epilogue.

However, other readers will be asking, is there a possible link between the Ark of the Covenant's timely discovery and events now looming under the New World Order? For such readers, we suggest a scenario of the future, biblically based, in which the Ark might well play a role. Please note that chapters 46 and 47 should be read in conjunction with Appendices G and H.

WARNING. You may choose to proceed to page 519 or read on at your own risk. Again, no responsibility taken.

CHAPTER 46

WHAT NOW?

"It left me spellbound," confided Jed Brewer. "In all my life I've never heard anything that made me cry like that."

Jed took another gulp of orange juice. "Believe me, only the mind of God could conceive it."

He had attended one of our recent Ark of the Covenant seminars. "Jonathan," he asked, "is everything still in the cave?"

Everything's still there," I answered," Just where Ron found it, completely hidden and very well guarded."

Will **all** those objects in the cave be shown publicly?"

"We don't know."

He looked disappointed.

"Well," I continued, "it is desired to excavate the entire area, to expose the site of the crucifixion and right down to the Ark chamber. But we don't know whether that will happen. Events **always** occur differently from our expectations. But we **do** believe that the Lord Himself will take charge and that the world will get to see the objects in that cave. We also believe that the tablets of stone will be brought out."

"Do you think the Israeli government will make a move soon?" Jed would like to know it all.

"I am in no position to say. But the information that is permitted to be revealed is already out. And this in itself is creating quite a stir. Let us ever remember that this Ark belongs not to man, but to God. It was the Lord who said, 'let them make **me** a sanctuary.' And all things in that sanctuary were patterned after the 'things in the heavens'.[2] Jed, if and when that Ark is brought out, it will be only with His permission. Not due to political expediency. Of that you can be certain."

Jed's eyes sparkled. "Jonathan, will the Ark – perhaps just the Ark – be brought out?"

"Again, we don't know, Jed. It is deep in the earth. To get it seems almost impossible without some divine intervention."

As we spoke, I recalled that in 1956 the waste ground at the foot of Skull Hill had become an Arab bus station. The Israelis now had a blueprint to move the bus station to a new location so as to develop the site into an Archaelogical Park.

"Could somebody get down there to destroy the evidence?" asked Jed. For a moment there was a flicker of horror on his face.

"Already, Jed, there have been men who tried to do what they shouldn't. And what happened to them... you've heard some of it."

"Will something happen soon?"

"I believe so."

"How long do you think it will be?"

"That's not easy to answer. But the whole world will see these things. Hopefully within a year or so it will be time to reveal the Ark of the Covenant cave to the entire world. When it's possible. Ron will return and re-enter that cave and take along with him a camera crew and one or more genetic scientists. We will see them take a sample of blood. And we shall see the test results of that extremely unique blood! Ron has already tested his own sample, and he knows what the results will be. Remember, Ron works as anesthetist in several hospitals, and he's seen lots of blood."

"What makes you think it will be so soon?"

"We can't be sure. But we're watching world events closely. And we'll know when the time comes. And Jed, it is possible that you will also see the Ten Commandments removed from the Ark of the Covenant cave."

"Will they go on display and travel around the world like the Tutankhamun exhibit? Do you think I'll actually get to see them in person?"

"I doubt whether the Ark will ever be moved from the cave. But the stone tablets of the Ten Commandments... that's different. They will be put on display eventually, I believe."

"In Jerusalem?"

"They'll probably be displayed in America."

"Why not Israel?"

"Its too sensitive an area. Who knows what might be triggered off? Look how violently some responded to the opening of a tunnel recently? And that was something minor. But this..."

Wherever the tablets go, one can be sure that Israelis would accompany them.

"Oh, about the cavern itself," prodded Jed, hopefully. "You still won't reveal its precise location?"

"This is a most sensitive issue, my friend. Just try to ponder the effect this discovery will have on the Jewish people. And the problems that it generates for the political leaders in Israel. There is information which cannot yet be revealed, for security reasons. Just be patient and await the time when we can do more. Hopefully, that may be soon."

Significance for the Jews

"About the Jewish people," pressed Jed. "What significance will the Ark of the Covenant have for them?"

"Rabbis have various opinions about that. One considered that the discovery would promote the building of a Third Temple. Another that it would signal the end of the Diaspora, the dispersion of the Jewish people. Another said it would be a clear signal that we are nearing the end of this age and the beginning of the messianic kingdom. Certain rabbis have believed that the Ark of the Covenant would be exposed at the time when the Messiah is to appear. Indeed, there is growing expectation that the Messiah will soon appear."

"I've been hearing about that," said Jed. "One segment of Judaism has been putting out prophetic newsletters, international newspaper advertisements, posters and the like."

"'You are referring to the Lubavitchers, a Hasidic Jewish group, probably."

"That was it."

Also I had recalled an interview reported in the *Jerusalem Post*. Menachem Brod, who was overseeing public relations and publications for the Habad Youth Organisation in Israel, announced to readers:

> Dear Jews, Moshiach is about to arrive! The dream of millions of Jews for centuries is upon us, and we all need to be ready for it.[3]

Of course, the true Messiah, Yeshua (Jesus Christ), had already come 2,000 years ago. Yet today, among Christians, there was also an expectation that he was soon to return. This was based on some 300 New Testament prophecies of the event.

The Ark for sacrifices again?

Jed scratched his chin. "What do you think, Jonathan? Will the Jews reinstate the sacrificial system when the Ark of the Covenant is revealed?"

"To that I'll say 'No', Jed. Jeremiah, who prophesied during the time of the Ark's disappearance, wrote:

> And it shall come to pass, when ye be multiplied and increased in the land, in those days, saith the Lord, **they shall say no more, The ark of the covenant of the Lord**: neither shall it come to mind: neither shall they remember it; neither shall they visit it; neither shall that be done any more.[4]

"This passage indicates that God will **never** return the Ark of the Covenant to the Jews for this purpose."

"It is not His will to restore animal sacrifices. Jesus, by his death, has done away with animal sacrifices. He has annulled them. He has abolished them. He has '**caused sacrifice and offering to CEASE**'"[5]

Blood on the Ark: the implications

Jed shuffled. "When the Jewish people learn that Jesus' blood was sprinkled on the Mercy Seat of the Ark, what do you think that will do?"

"I firmly believe this, Jed. To many Jews this will be a powerful revelation. As the Old Testament Scriptures are blended with the New in an explanation of the Lord's eternal purpose, this will be to many Jews as the dawn of a new creation, the resurrection of the soul. As they see the Christ of the gospel portrayed in the pages of their scriptures and perceive how clearly the New Testament explains the Old, their slumbering faculties will be aroused and they will recognise Jesus Christ, Yeshua, as the Savior of the world. Many will by faith receive him as their Deliverer."

Why discovered now?

"Why on earth," asked Jed, "hasn't the Ark been found before? Why now?"

"The answer may shock you."

"Fire away, then."

"I believe it's because we've arrived at the turning point of history - judgment time."

"Why do you say that'?"

"Well, Jed, there's an old biblical prophecy. The prophet John saw a vision of the future, concerning ...

> the time of the dead, that they should be judged, and that (God) should give reward to... small and great; and should destroy them who destroy the earth. [6]

"That's clearly speaking of the end times, Jed, when God is about to interrupt mankind's rule and take over this planet.[7] And in that context the prophet saw something else, as well:

> And the temple of God was opened in heaven, and there was seen in his temple the ark of his testament.[8]

"That's the **Ark of the Covenant** - the original in heaven."

"So what's the significance?"

Cause and effect

"Well, right through that book of Revelation a connection is shown between events in heaven and those on earth. And it does make sense. After all, if God has a rescue plan for His faithful ones on this planet, and if it is from His Throne in heaven that the plan emanates, then why shouldn't events planned in heaven have their effect on earth?"

Again Jed stroked his chin. "The mention of the **heavenly** Ark in the end times - could that be hinting at the importance of the

earthly Ark... that it might yet have a role to play in the divine purpose?"

The Ark in prophecy

"According to this prophecy, the heavenly Ark - the original - has something to do with an end times judgment period of planet earth."

Jed flashed a reply. "Yeah, haven't we all asked at times, why doesn't God step in and stop man's inhuman practices and avenge the wrongs? God sure is patient, even with the wrong-doers. But there has to be a time when everything will be made equal."

I looked at Jed. "Well, that does make sense."

"You know, Jonathan," sighed Jed. "The Scriptures repeatedly tell of judgment to come; that God has appointed a day when He will judge the world and every person will receive according to his works; [9] that we must all appear before the Judgment Seat."[10]

"What do you think Jed? What's the standard by which we'll be judged?"

Jed smiled. "Well, in this judgment time the **heavenly Ark of the Covenant** plays a role. And what's inside the original Ark? What else but the original - the heavenly original of the **law of God,** by which all are to be **judged**. [11] But there's also **mercy** - the Mercy Seat - for the forgiven."

As Jed spoke, I recalled that in the old Hebrew symbolism, the Ark of the Covenant was always linked to a day known as Yom Kippur, or Day of Atonement.

For the Jews, this was the great day of judgment, when every case was sealed. Notice this statement from a Jewish author:

> The Day of Atonement is the day of Judgment, and on that day... the Jew cries loudest and often for mercy.[12]

Phrases from the Jewish *Prayer Book for the Day of Atonement* include
-Justify us in the Judgment
-The Advocate in heaven
- He, the Ancient of Days, sits as Judge
-In the book of life, blessing, peace and good substance. May we be remembered and sealed by Thee. [13]

This is the Jewish concept of Yom Kippur.

So Yom Kippur - the only day that the Ark of the Covenant featured - was a symbol (or prophecy, if you like) of the **judgment time**.

One could say that its **sacrificial** aspect was fulfilled when the Messiah died. That was a complete and perfect act of **mercy**. But the **judgment** aspect comes at the end times. God's unerring justice is as real as the death Jesus died for us.

Getting back to that Hebrew prophetic symbol. The high priest completed his Yom Kippur work in front of the Ark of the Covenant, then came out from the Holy of Holies and announced, **"It is finished."** Today, the Messiah, as High Priest, represents us at the Throne of God, the heavenly Ark of the Covenant. And as he comes out, to return to earth as King of kings,[14] the announcement **"It is finished"** will be heard.

Looking into the future, the prophet John wrote:

> Then in heaven, the temple of God was opened and the **ark of his covenant** could be seen inside. Lightning flashed and thunder crashed and roared, and there was a great hailstorm and the world was shaken by a mighty earthquake.[15]
>
> And they gathered all the armies of the world near a place called, in Hebrew, Armageddon... and a mighty shout came **from the throne of the temple in heaven, saying, "It is finished."** Then the thunder crashed and rolled, and lightning flashed; and there was a great earthquake of a magnitude unprecedented in human history.[16]

"Whew!" whistled Jed. "if we are to believe the prophecies, this age will come to a dramatic and sudden end. History will cease to continue in the hands of men."

I might never see Jed again. He was talking about moving with his family into the country. Fresh air, quietness, home-grown food, all that.

And that brings us to the final chapter, where we postulate what Jed and his wife Elizabeth might be thinking a few years from now. And how the Ark of the Covenant may be destined to play a role....

CHAPTER 47

THE FINAL SHOWDOWN

It had been an upheaval for Jed Brewer, quitting his well-paid job as an engineer, uprooting from the house they had called home for eighteen years, leaving behind the beautiful landscaped garden Elizabeth had nurtured for so long.

The Brewers were now settled in a much smaller cottage in the mountains. They were growing their own food. And that was good. Most of their friends were not so fortunate. They had taken too long to cut all their strings in the city. And now they could not get out.

Jed peered out through the window. The helicopter was out of sight. But he could still hear it. The unmarked helicopter had been scouring the valley for a few days now.

Jed's mind was spinning as he tried to fit the pieces together.

Global control

First America had needed to be brought under the New World Order. The eventual takeover of the Executive, Legislative and Judicial branches had been carefully worked out by the planners. Law enforcement had been powerfully consolidated under one head, while the population as a whole was progressively disarmed. To enforce the coming New World Order legislation, the Constitution had needed to be circumvented and the media fed New World Order/ New Age Marxist propaganda.

This had taken many years, but eventually it had worked. And once America was brought under, after that it had been quite fast. The rest of the world had been easy prey.

The world had now entered a period of history like no other... a time where every move of every person on earth could be tracked and watched.

The whole thing had happened quite quickly..

In June, 1967, the Israelis for the first time in 1,900 years had reoccupied Old Jerusalem.

Jesus, in his epic prophecy concerning "the end of the world", had said, "Jerusalem shall be trodden down of the Gentiles (nations) until..."Jed reflected on this. That word "until" implied a CHANGE OF STATUS. "There shall be a change." Was divine prophecy giving warning by this event that the history of this world was coming to its climax and that the countdown had begun?

In 1971, in the United States, a group of informatics specialists had been assigned to develop a system of surveillance of all citizens in a manner neither obvious nor intrusive. Their recommendation was a national EFTPOS system. After this, the EFTPOS computer-linked method of purchase had come into wide use throughout the world.[2]

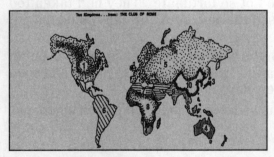

Ten Kingdoms...from: THE CLUB OF ROME

In 1975, the Club of Rome had produced a blueprint for a World Government, in which the whole world was to be divided into ten economic zones, with one person as a ruler of each region.

The emerging united Europe had been described by Enoch Powell, retired British statesman, as a reappearance of the old "Holy Roman Empire". This was seen as a move toward a New World Order.

At the time Jed had wondered. Would it be a new Roman empire over just Europe, or over the whole world? Now he knew!

On June 7, 1982, the United States and the Vatican, in "one of the great secret alliances of all time",[3] had agreed to undertake a clandestine campaign to hasten the dissolution of the Communist empire.

504

On December 27, 1989, the *Catholic Weekly* had revealed that behind the scenes the Pope and his men really did most of it.

In 1990, one-time Jesuit and Vatican insider had announced that, of the three contestants for world dominion (the papacy, communism and Western capitalism), the Pope held the trump card. He saw himself as the coming leader of the New World Order.[4]

In 1992, following the collapse of the USSR, its president Mikhail Gorbachev forecast a possible global government.

In 1994, the Vatican had signed an agreement with Israel to gain sovereignty over Jerusalem. The city would stay the capital of Israel, but would be administered by the Vatican. The city would have an Israeli mayor and a Palestinian mayor, both under orders from the Pope. Jerusalem would become a second Vatican. Jed now recalled a conversation he'd had at the time with Elizabeth. "You know, Jed, he's to plant his abode in Jerusalem just before God Himself interrupts human history." And she had added, "It's a prophecy nobody studies much."[5] Could it not merely have a symbolic religious fulfillment, but **also** a physical fulfillment?"

On July 18, 1994, cars traveling along Interstate 15, near Farmington, Salt Lake City, Utah, had their engines suddenly cut out. Four unmarked black helicopters were hovering overhead. Traffic was at a standstill for almost an hour. Drivers attempted to start their vehicles, but without success. Then, as if by magic, all the engines in the stalled vehicles were able to be started again. The four black helicopters were flying away in formation.[6]

With such technology eventually in place, roadblocks had become unnecessary.

In February, 1996, David Meyer in his *Last Trumpet Newsletter,* had written that the United Nations had set the date for the beginning of the New World Order as being the 6th day of the 6th month, 1999. "... they have picked the only year in this century that can be read in inverted cryptic. If you turn the number 1999 upside down, it reads 6661, or the first year of the era of 666 or the antichrist beast."

On March 23, 1996, Jack McLamb, head of Police Against the New World Order, had warned concerned Americans to get out of concentrated population places and prepare for what was coming.

Short-wave radio program hosts had warned Christians to do likewise. There had been a silent migration out of the cities.

As the New World order had developed, in each country local military forces had been phased out and United Nations forces phased in. A global taxation system had been imposed.

Eventually, a biometrically coded ID card had been introduced. The card identified by fingerprints, retina scans and/or DNA, every person in the nation. This provided the possibility of positive identification for the enforcement of oppressive laws. Those who submitted to the Biometric ID could be required to submit to all kinds of information in the process of qualifying as "citizens". Those who refused to submit had been immediately identified as "aliens", non-citizens, dissenters, subject to detention or deportation. It had become possible to scan an automobile driver's retina, as well as those of his passengers, identifying them personally at a distance as they approached.

Satellite linked technology had made it possible to track people, listen to their conversations at home and watch their movements. Surveillance of every citizen was now an integral part of the new global system.

Again Jed glanced out through the window. These events, he thought, were not necessarily the most important, but they stood out in his memory. And he sensed a common link between them.

One world economy

And there had been that titanic financial collapse. He could see it all clearly, now. The globalists had wanted control. And to achieve total control, it had been first necessary to bring the economy down – and then have their one-world monetary system to replace it.

The ruin about to burst upon the world had been sudden and unexpected.

Jed thought back...

That collapse just **had** to have been engineered. The stock market had closed at a record high on the Friday. Then on Monday it opened at a level fixed way down. Trillions of dollars had been lost by people all over the world. Property values had collapsed within days. Many farms were abandoned, leaving crops unharvested. Food shortages had followed. Then riots. And

506

violence. Petrol had dried up. Supplies couldn't get through to the cities. Martial law was imposed.

In a short time cash money had been removed and all transactions were now being made by a computer code system based on the number 666. Those who did not comply with the New World Order laws were being denied buying power.

The moneys of people, stored up as treasure for their last days, all were useless. They had no more value. Bank bills were flying in the car parking lots. And there was no longer any financial freedom.

One world religion

Then a single state religion, embracing all faiths, had been set up. Religious laws were being enforced – laws that although seemingly "good and moral", were contrary to the expressed word of God.

Some had thought it would never happen.

Jed didn't know a lot, but he felt the divine law should not have been tampered with.

This man-made alteration of the holy Ten Commandments showed two important changes. The **second commandment** of the Lord instructed mankind not to make images or statues, to bow down to them. But this command had been completely erased in the man-made version. The **fourth commandment** memorialized the creation of planet Earth and called mankind to acknowledge the sovereignty of the Creator. It spelled out God's requirements concerning His holy memorial of that fact, the Sabbath day. But in the man-made version most of that commandment had been eliminated – in order that man might do things to suit himself, instead of his Lord. And with one commandment (the second) eliminated, there remained only nine. So to compensate for this change, the **tenth commandment** had been cracked in two.

Jed pondered. Did it really matter? Of course it mattered! That morning, Jed had gathered his wife Elizabeth and his two teenage children around the table, to recite to them again the reasons why they had moved to the comparative safety of the country. It was so that they could serve their Lord without the financial and social pressure now being imposed upon their friends to conform to the new system.

THE LAW OF GOD

I

"Thou shalt have no other gods before Me."

II

"Thou shalt not make unto thee any graven image, or any likeness of anything that is in heaven above, or that is in the earth beneath, or that is in the water under the earth. Thou shalt not bow down thyself to them, nor serve them, for I the Lord thy God am a jealous God, visiting the iniquity of the fathers upon the children unto the third and fourth generation of them that hate Me; and showing mercy unto thousands of them that love Me, and keep My commandments."

III

"Thou shalt not take the name of the Lord thy God in vain; for the Lord will not hold him guiltless that taketh His name in vain."

IV

"Remember the Sabbath day, to keep it holy. Six days shalt thou labor, and do all thy work; but the seventh day is the Sabbath of the Lord thy God. In it thou shalt not do any work, thou, nor thy son, nor thy daughter, thy manservant, nor thy maidservant, nor thy cattle, nor thy stranger that is within thy gates. For in six days the Lord made heaven and earth, the sea, and all that in them is, and rested the seventh day: Wherefore the Lord blessed the Sabbath day, and hallowed it."

V

"Honor thy father and thy mother, that thy days may be long upon the land which the Lord thy God giveth thee."

VI

"Thou shalt not kill."

VII

"Thou shalt not commit adultery."

VIII

"Thou shalt not steal."

IX

"Thou shalt not bear false witness against thy neighbor."

X

"Thou shalt not covet thy neighbor's house; thou shalt not covet thy neighbor's wife, nor his manservant, nor his maidservant, nor his ox, nor his ass, nor anything that is thy neighbor's."

-Exodus 20:3-17

THE LAW OF GOD
AS CHANGED BY MAN

I

I am the Lord thy God. Thou shalt not have strange gods before Me.

(The Second Commandment has been omitted!)

II *(actually III)*

Thou shalt not take the name of the Lord thy God in vain.

III *(IV)*

Remember that thou keep holy the Sabbath day.
(The Sabbath Commandment has been radically altered!)

IV *(V)*

Honor thy father and thy mother.

V *(VI)*

Thou shalt not kill.

VI *(VII)*

Thou shalt not commit adultery.

VII *(VIII)*

Thou shalt not steal.

VIII *(IX)*

Thou shalt not bear false witness against thy neighbor.

IX *(actually X, first part!)*

Thou shalt not covet thy neighbor's wife.

X *(actually X, second part!)*

Thou shalt not covet thy neighbor's goods.

-The General Catholic Catechism.

Yes, God's law was important. It was given to protect man." Do and live." Jed had only hours ago read to his family their Lord's own words:

> What thing soever I command you, observe to do it: you **shall not add thereto, nor diminish from it**... whatever God does, it shall be forever: nothing can be put to it, nor anything taken from it: and God does it, that men should reverence before Him.[7]

Because God **could not change** His character or His law, Jed told his family, Jesus had had to die for us. And if God couldn't change it, then could man? It was binding forever.[8]

It was the changes in this law that had paved the way for a single state religion. Anyone could be comfortable with the way the Ten Commandments were now worded – anyone. Hindus would not be offended by the command against bowing to idols, because that was deleted. Nobody, whether Jews, Moslems or Christians, could be offended by the now vague fourth commandment. Even New Age people could go along with such a sanitized version of the Ten Commandments. So to be a dissenter was unreasonable. A dissenter would stand out like a sore thumb. He would be a menace to world unity.

When Jed had first heard it, the whole idea had seemed a distant illusion. Not for his time, anyway. Perhaps fifty years into the future.

Now it was a chilling reality.

Jed recalled a meeting he had once attended. It had been addressed by Dr. Kurk E. Koch, professor and lecturer at 100 universities in 65 countries. Dr. Koch's subjects of expertise included the New World Order, Occultism, Extreme Movements and Parapsychology. The doctor had given his assessment of the One World Government:

> The system will be made up of a single currency, single centrally financed government, single tax system, single language, single political system, single world court of justice, single head (one individual leader), **single state religion.**

He had further stated:

510

Each person will have a registered number, without which he will not be able to buy or sell; and there will be one universal church. Anyone who refuses to take part in this universal system will have no right to exist. [9]

A statement had also been issued by P.A. Dalvalle, president of the Defenders of the American .Constitution, and a retired Lieutenant General of the United States army:

The magazine, *Foy et Rai*, reported from the United Nations Organization in Geneva, Switzerland, that plans are worked out to dissolve the UN to make way for a World Tribunal which will seize all possessions and all savings and bank deposits. Every man, woman and child will receive a certain amount of money and a number. This money is already available and deposited in a bank just waiting for distribution. Everyone with a number will be employed either in the administrative, the commerce, the industrial or the agricultural branch. **This project and this plan provides for a single form of worship. The appointed day for all people will be Sunday. The number received, by the people will promise the right to buy or sell.**

At the end of this statement, a Christian arose and asked the speaker, "What happens to the minorities who will not accept this plan?" The Christian was told, "Their number will be canceled with a black line and they will be deprived of the right to buy or sell and will thus be forced to destruction."[10]

And now it was actually happening! Those down in the cities were the ones suffering! He had heard some had even been arrested and taken off to camps.

That night Jed and his family went to bed early. They were thankful that they had made the move in time.

Surprise witness

The next morning there was a furore on the news channels. Something was happening in Jerusalem. Some men were down in a tunnel, pushing toward Skull Hill. They were about to bring out the tablets of the Ten Commandments – the ones written by God and placed in the legendary Ark of the Covenant. It was all down there in the cavern. Hot news!...

A Jewish rabbi was being interviewed. This same man had once said:

Of all the treasures yet to be discovered, what could be more important, more fascinating, and more awe-inspiring than the Tablets of the Ten Commandments. No other archaeological find would have a greater impact on the destiny of man.[11]

Like the day Armstrong was headed for the moon, so now again the hours dragged by... and millions held their breath. The world was waiting...

And finally, as the cameras fell upon this wondrous sight, two stone tablets engraved as with a laser beam, words seen with clarity and sharpness... engraved with the very finger of God... the news went like shock waves around the world.

Literally now, some famous words were coming to pass:

The law shall go forth from Zion, and the word of the Lord from Jerusalem.[12]

However else one might understand this prophecy, thought Jed, one thing was certain, the physical tablets of the law were literally coming out of Jerusalem, out of that cave. It was exciting!

In enforcing its "spiritual laws", the New World Order was negating the law of God. The Psalmist put his finger on it:

It is time for thee, Lord to work: for they have made void thy law.[13]

Jed gazed out upon his garden. And reflected...

The **Ark of the Covenant** is thus named because it enshrines "the tables... **of the covenant,** the ten commandments".[14] It is the "**covenant** of the Lord".[15] "My **covenant** will I not break," He says, "nor alter the thing that is gone out of my lips."[16] (At Sinai, God had audibly spoken it to a whole nation.) Says the Psalmist, "he hath **commanded his covenant for ever.**"[17] Said Jesus, "Not one dot of an 'i' or crossing of a 't' will pass from the law till heaven and earth pass."[18]

Jed knew that things were pretty severe. But had heaven and earth passed? Not yet.

What a witness! Jed was trembling with emotion. Even now those tablets of the Ten Commandments were coming out as a witness. That meant that Jews, Christians and unbelievers alike, who had declared God's sacred law to be of no consequence, would now see it. They would have to be aware now, that they had been fighting against God. Even those who didn't know, before, now faced a choice.

Perfect timing!

Nobody wanted to work that day. Jed was excited. Elizabeth was excited. The kids were excited. So they just sat around talking. And all the time their thoughts kept returning to the Holy Land, where the stone tablets were now coming out.

The impersonator

"Say, Dad, about the Holy Land," mused Richard. "You know, before we came up here I heard our next door neighbor Mr. Sheppard say his dead aunt had appeared to him and prophesied that the world economy would collapse and that the next day the Messiah would arrive in the Holy Land."

"That was hardly his dead aunt, Richard."

"How do you know?"

"The dead just can't communicate with the living."

"Are you sure about that?"

"We're all here, are we not, because we've come to accept that the Bible is our Lord's word? So we live by it."

"Yes."

"Do you know what that word tells us? It says, 'The living know that they shall die: but the dead know not anything ...Also their love, and their hatred, and their envy, is now perished; neither have they any more a portion for ever in anything that is done under the sun.' 'Whatsoever your hand finds to do, do it with all your might, for there is no work, nor device, nor knowledge, in the grave whither you go.'"[19]

Jed paused to turn a few pages. He couldn't help noticing Richard's face.

"Wow!" uttered Richard. **"That's** in there?"

"And more, son. Listen to this. 'So man lies down, and rises not: till the heavens be no more, they shall not awake, nor be raised out of their sleep... his sons come to honor, and he knows it not; and

513

they are brought low, but he perceives it not.' 'He that goes down to the grave shall come up no more. He shall return no more to his house, neither shall his place know him any more.' It says also that 'the dead praise not the Lord' because their thoughts have perished.[20] You see, they are waiting in their graves for the resurrection day,"[21] said Jed.

"Then who was it that appeared to Mr. Sheppard? This person knew all the details of his life, just like his aunt did."

"Son, there's more to this universe than meets the eye. The Bible speaks of opponents who are not human – but are evil and powerful spirits.[22] They can even work miracles.[23] In mercy, their forms are beyond the light spectrum, so that we are not able to see them. Yet, by condensation, they are capable of becoming visible.

In spiritualistic seances they personate the dead to loved ones, playing a cruel hoax. And their messages contain information that supposedly nobody else but a loved one would know."

Who are the figures brought to light by spirit mediums? (Picture: Jim Pinkoski)

"But how can they know one's secrets? Oh, yeah, I suppose if they're like the guardian angels, all around, out of sight but watching us all the time... then I suppose they know as much as we do."

"Most interesting," called Elizabeth, coming back from the kitchen. "It wouldn't surprise me if, before this is all over, the devil himself would personate Christ. Jesus did say there would be persons staging a fake Second Coming. Where is that passage, dear?"

"I'll find it," mumbled Jed. He flipped through the well-worn book. "Here it is. Jesus himself gave the warning:

Then if anyone tells you, 'The Messiah has arrived at such and such a place, or has appeared here or there,' don't believe it. For false Christs shall arise, and false prophets, and will do wonderful miracles, so that if it were possible, even God's chosen ones would be deceived. See, I have warned you.

So if someone tells you the Messiah has returned and is out in the desert, don't bother to go and look. Or, that he is hiding at a certain place, don't believe it! For as the lightning flashes across the sky from east to west, so shall my coming be, when I, the Messiah, return. And wherever the carcass is, there the vultures will gather. [24]

Fantasy? Not quite. Jed recalled that a man called Texe Marrs had described this very scenario. In his book *Dark Secrets of the New Age*,[25] he revealed that the New Age movement expected the increasing earth changes to develop into utter world chaos. Then, at the time of a great earthquake in Jerusalem, the New Age "Christ" would appear on the Mount of Olives, and would proceed to become king of Jerusalem.

"Can you imagine it? A being of dazzling radiance... majestic... perhaps he appears on the Mount of Olives, and then enters Jerusalem, escorted by a vast procession of people."

Elizabeth closed her eyes, as though visualizing it. "The people prostrate themselves before him. He lifts up his hands and utters a blessing over them. His voice is melodious, soft and subdued. He speaks heavenly truths and heals sick people, just as Jesus did. Then he gives a blessing to the New World Order and says that all those who will not come together under its laws have no right to exist. Just think of the effect that would have!"

The 'big event'

"But Mum, how will we know it is **not** the Second Coming?" Kylie was troubled. "The whole thing seems so confusing."

"Honey, no sweat. According to the prophetic Scriptures, when Jesus Christ returns, the world is heading for the greatest spectacle in its history. The sky will light up from London to Los Angeles."

"And from Melbourne to Moscow," cut in Jed. "You know, kids, 'every eye shall see him.' And it'll be noisy. And he won't at that time set foot on the earth. That's the difference."[26]

"Wow! But it's going to get pretty bad for a while first, right?"

"No need to be afraid, though, chick. And I'll tell you why. The promise is that we won't starve. Our bread and water will be sure.[27] Yeah, we might suffer a lot. But stand for Him and He'll stand for you. Pretty wonderful, eh?"

Richard looked thoughtful. "You know, I saw something this morning. It was mighty cool, I thought."

"OK, spit it out," grinned Jed.

"The prophecy says, 'At that time shall Michael stand up, the great prince which stands for the children of your people: and there shall be a time of trouble, such as never was since there was a nation even to that same time: and at that time your people shall be delivered, every one that shall be found written in the book.'[28] Now, isn't that neat?"

※※※※※

And it gets better. Do you know, what happened that day above the Ark of the Covenant guarantees that the time is coming when this planet will be cleansed of evil, suffering, and yes, even death. A new earth will emerge. And there you and I will be able to fulfill ambitions we've not been able to reach now.[29]

There will be pleasant and invigorating things to do. No more fear of losing loved ones. We shall plant and build. Have perpetual intercourse with other worlds. And there will be endless wonders and mysteries to explore.

You can count on it.

Don't know about you, but I just can't wait to meet that Man who made it all possible. And you know what? I want to praise his matchless love for a world that did not love him!

Jed gazed into his garden. "Yes, it's all pretty wonderful!"

What Love!

I never really understood the significance of this for me personally, until one day I was standing on a curb, about to cross a street. Suddenly the realization hit home - and some long standing questions were resolved. These were questions that millions must be asking. So I shall lay them out here, with what I believe to be the correct answers.

1. **Does He really care about me?** ANSWER: God's never-ending love for you is far beyond your understanding. He loves you as though you were the only lost soul in the universe. He would have given his life for you if there had been no one else to rescue. YOU ARE PRECIOUS IN HIS SIGHT.

2. **How can I know God loves me?** ANSWER: He has DEMONSTRATED his love for you. Because He loved you so deeply, He was willing to see His only Son suffer and die, rather than be deprived of you for eternity. You will not be able to understand, but He did it, JUST FOR YOU.

3. **Did Jesus die for me personally?** ANSWER: Jesus died to satisfy the death penalty against you. His death would be accepted by God as full payment for all of a person's past wrongs.

4. **But how could he love someone like me?** ANSWER: Amazing wonder of wonders! His love is unconditional - whether you're a thief, adulterer or murderer. He created you. HE LOVES YOU.

YOUR PART IN THE RESCUE PLAN

Here's what to do:

1 – First realize the basic problem. You do need Jesus.

Remember, you're under the death sentence. And you cannot save yourself. You cannot be rescued without Jesus. He is not **A** way. He is **THE** way.

The Bible is quite explicit about the fact that if I do not recognize sin in my life, and do not turn with true sorrow for my sin to be washed clean of it, then I am at enmity with God.

So you've messed up your life? GOOD NEWS: Jesus wants you just **as you are** – no matter how filthy, how unlovely.

So ADMIT your need. Tell Him you're sorry. ASK for forgiveness. Jesus provides IMMEDIATE PARDON, freedom from guilt.

2 – We desperately need pardon. But we just as desperately need the POWER to **stop sinning**. Jesus is able to change you in this life and fit you for the coming new earth.

He can make a kind and attentive husband out of the town drunk.

Complete surrender of your will to Jesus will change the way you live. When the POWER of His Spirit floods into your life, **you will know peace and victory and constant happiness, no matter what happens to you.**

When God places His own character in people, He makes them as beautiful as a sunset, as enjoyable as the placid surface of a lake, as refreshing to others as a mountain stream or a waterfall. Yes, He can do that! He is the Creator!

3 – Feed your mind on positive books and tapes, and especially the Bible. For starters, read John's gospel over and over until the evidence overwhelms you. Ask God to help your unbelief and put into your life His resurrection power, and you will prove it for yourself!

4 – Associate with people who love Jesus, obey all His commands and are supportive.

5 – Be baptized.

6 – Like Jesus, reach out to those still lost and share His marvelous love. .

You can be sure of this... Jesus will become the best Friend you ever had - now and forever.

EPILOGUE

Wonderful as the Ark discovery is, there are aspects of the find which present numerous problems, not least of which is the position politically, in Israel itself.

Just reflect on this for a moment. Ron has worked in conjunction with only a **very few** officials in the departments of archaeology in Jerusalem. He has promised not to divulge any more information due to the grave security risks.

Numerous people are trying desperately to lever information from whatever source they can. And for many different reasons.

Some people are trying to discredit Ron, we believe, in order to stabilize the situation in Jerusalem. Others do so out of professional jealousy, as we have stated earlier. Yet others are concerned to establish the truth, because they are intent on building a new Temple in Jerusalem. And the Ark, they hope, would be the most treasured artifact to grace that Temple.

There are people with very keen interests whose religious persuasions are either Jewish, Christian or Moslem. And the mixture is an explosive cocktail.

From the Christian standpoint many people are so thrilled to hear about the discovery of the Ark, that all the surrounding implications are overlooked. This is so in countries where no back-lash would occur.

But in Israel the climate is quite different. That is why so much secrecy surrounds the find. Remember that it dates back to January 6, 1982. And only very recently has Ron suggested letting out further information.

So now you understand why we have deliberately **not** set out to produce all the evidence in our possession.

We cannot improve on the procedure adopted by the biblical John in relating the events of the crucifixion. When he recounted that "one of the soldiers with a spear pierced his side, and forthwith came there out blood and water" (John 19:34), all he could add was this: "He who saw it has testified and his testimony is true - he knows that he tells the truth - in order that you may believe." (v.35 Modern Language).

Although scientists might have cried "foul", because they could not be brought in to confirm his story, nevertheless his testimony carried the ring of truth.

We stated at the outset that the purpose of this book was simply to tell our story.

Requests to bring out and test more samples of blood cannot be acceded to, simply because the site is now sealed up, and no one is allowed to open it up. However, when permission is granted, it is planned to take two independent geneticists who will take samples and have it analyzed under strict supervision, so as to establish the truth of what is already known.

••••••

But coupled with the intrigue from the human point of view, one needs to remember that this piece of furniture was designed by the Lord Himself, kept under very strict control by the Levites, and attended by remarkable events.

As we have pointed out earlier, it is clear that the Lord Himself still owns the Ark - and still maintains a KEEN INTEREST in what happens to it.

QUESTIONS I AM ASKED CONCERNING THE ARK OF THE COVENANT

522

Appendix A

ZEDEKIAH'S QUARRIES (OR SOLOMON'S QUARRIES)

About eighty-five years ago a man named Barclay was walking round the walls of Jerusalem with his dog and a gun. When he came to the Damascus Gate he discovered that the dog was missing. He whistled, but the animal did not appear. Turning back he saw the dog crawling out apparently from beneath the city walls, where he had evidently made a find. He stood barking, asking his master to come and look at his discovery. When Barclay went over, he found that bushes, shrubs, and the debris of centuries concealed the opening to a cavern which ran under the walls and beneath the city.

Such a discovery in Jerusalem fires the imagination and encourages the wildest rumors. The Arabs believe to this day that in such a cavern the gold and silver treasures of Solomon, the Ark of the Covenant and the vessels used in the Temple sacrifices lie waiting to be found. This dream is not confined to the Arabs. I have heard several men, whose opinions claim respect and attention, say that they believe the Ark of the Covenant is hidden somewhere in the mysterious and quite unknown underworld of the Temple area.

So Barclay wisely said nothing and, returning on the following day with a search-party, widened the small hole into which his dog had jumped and entered the cavern. The torches of the search-party lit up a weird and terrifying scene. The explorers stood in a snow-white cavern, so large that its extremity was hidden in the darkness. One glance at the stone walls told them that it had been artificially made.

The torchlight was not powerful enough to penetrate to the end of the cavern. It was an immense excavation that ran on and on beneath the streets of the Old City.

It was soon realized that they had discovered Solomon's Quarries – called by Josephus the "Royal Quarries" – the quarries which, lost for nearly two centuries, had provided the stone for Solomon's Temple about nine hundred years before Christ.

I think these quarries are one of the most interesting sights in Jerusalem. They are neglected by the average sightseer, although every Freemason who visits Jerusalem is aware of them. Masons from all parts of the world hold lodge meetings there at night, when they will not be disturbed or observed, because they hold the theory that the builders of the Temple were the first Freemasons.

When I visited the quarries, an old Arab who sits at the entrance gave me a lantern and warned me not to fall down any of the frightful precipices, for Solomon's quarries are no place for the short-sighted or the stumbler.

Another Arab, working in the patch of daylight that penetrates the cave, was shaping paper-weights and small hammers such as chairmen use at meetings. These objects, when decorated with appropriate triangles and compasses, are eagerly bought by masonic visitors and find their way all over the world. Stones from the quarries are also exported to become foundation stones for masonic buildings.

I went into the darkness, swinging my lantern, and the path led steeply down into an enormous entrance cave like a buried cathedral. From this excavation wide, high passages led off in many directions. I pulled up sharply on the edge of chasms and, waving my lantern in the darkness, saw that the rock fell away to lower workings, to more distant and deeper caverns.

It has been estimated that in ancient times sufficient stone had been removed from these quarries to build the modern city of Jerusalem twice over. It is a peculiar and unusual pure white stone, soft to work but hardening rapidly when exposed to the atmosphere. The Arabs call these caverns the "cotton caves" because they are so white. Here and there, however, when I flashed my lantern towards the lower portions of the roof, I saw a number of black patches.

In one place I was near enough to see that they were large bats, hanging to the roof and waiting for the night.

On every hand I noticed the sign of workmen. With a feeling of awe and bewilderment, a feeling that I was dropping down through the very floor of Time, I knew that these workmen had been dead for nearly three thousand years.

Yet the marks made by the Phoenician stone-cutters when Solomon was king of Jerusalem were as clean, as sharp and, apparently, as recent, as the marks a man sees in the Portland quarries to-day.

The workmen had cut niches in the walls for their lamps. And it all seemed so new, so modern, that I had the odd feeling that it was lunch hour during the building of the Temple and that at any moment I might hear the returning feet of Solomon's quarrymen, kicking aside the chips and stones as they poured back to work.

I propped the lantern on a ledge of rock, and by the light of its candle I read the extraordinarily detailed account of the building of the Temple which you will find in the Second Book of Chronicles, chapter two, and the First Book of Kings, chapter five.

I suppose a modern architect could not, given the same number of words, create for us a more accurate and vivid picture of the plans, design, engagement of workmen, rates of pay, building, and furnishing of a great building, than is to be found in these chapters of the Bible.

Down in the darkness of Solomon's quarries, with the white dust of the stone on my clothes, the building of the Temple took on a reality that surprised me. It frequently happens in Palestine that some verse of the Bible, hitherto meaningless, suddenly unlocks itself, and one is left amazed by its minute accuracy. I realized the real meaning of a verse which must have puzzled many people. Verse seven, in the sixth chapter of the First Book of Kings, describing the building of the House of the Lord, says:

" And the house, when it was in building, was built of stone made ready before it was brought thither: so that there was neither hammer nor ax nor any tool of iron heard in the house, while it was in building."

I have always imagined that this verse meant that the Temple stone was quarried far away out of earshot of Jerusalem. What else could it have meant? But why should the writer of Kings have

525

stressed the obvious fact that distant quarrying could not be heard on Mount Moriah? Obviously the point of this verse is that the stone with which Solomon built his Temple came almost from beneath the Temple, yet **not a soul heard the cutting of the stones.**

In these quarries you can see how the stone was broken from the bed, how it was passed at once to the masons, who shaped and smoothed it – the floor is in places many feet deep in tons of chips – and how it went straight into the daylight ready to take its place in the building of the Temple.

No matter how earnestly those in the streets of the city above might have listened for the sound of hammers, they could have heard nothing.

Many stories are, of course, told of a mysterious underground passage which linked the quarries with the Temple. There is a widespread belief that the priests hurriedly hid the Temple treasure in these caverns when the Roman armies under Titus razed Jerusalem and the Temple to the ground. I do not know why treasure hunters should still think it possible to find these precious objects, for it is quite clear that many of them were carried through the streets of Rome when Titus celebrated his triumph. However, one earnest explorer some years ago probed for a secret passage - and found one! In order to reach it you have to bend down and crawl for a few yards into a narrow tunnel about three feet in height, and then you find yourself in another passage of the rock. You are at the extremity of the quarries now and moving under Jerusalem in the direction of the Temple Mount. Suddenly you come up against an ancient fortified wall. What it was for, who built it and when it was built, no one knows.

I left the quarries and went out into the blinding light of afternoon with the feeling that yesterday and to-day are one in the empty caverns where, it seems, the workmen of Hiram, King of Tyre, have just "knocked off" for a ten-minute break.

H. V. Morton In the Steps of the Master.
New York: Dodd, Mead and Co., 1934,
pp.62-66

Appendix B

WHEN THE CLOCK STRUCK 13

Some years ago, two men stood one night at the foot of the large clock in the city of Plymouth, England. At midnight, both of them observed that the clock had struck thirteen times.

Not long after this incident, one of the two men, Captain Jarvis, arose early one morning, dressed himself, and descended the stairs to the door leading to the street. Upon opening it, he was surprised to find his servant waiting for him with a saddled horse.

"I felt an impression that you needed your horse," he said, "and I could not go back to sleep. So I came and saddled it."

The captain was astonished, but said nothing. He mounted his horse and gave it free rein. The horse carried him to the edge of the river and stopped near the place where the ferryboat would dock to pick up passengers who wanted to reach the other side. His amazement grew when he saw the ferryman on the boat waiting for passengers. It was still very early in the morning.

"Why are you here so early today?" asked the captain.

"Sir, I could not sleep. I had a feeling that someone needed to cross the river."

The captain got aboard the ferry with his horse and they soon reached the other side. He again loosened the reins and the horse followed its nose. After a good ride, they arrived at a town. The captain inquired of a passer-by if anything of interest was happening there.

"Nothing sir, except the trial of a man indicted for murder."

The captain went to the courthouse, dismounted, and entered the courtroom just as the judge was asking the accused if he had anything to say in his own behalf.

"I have nothing to say, Your Honour, except that I am innocent, and that there is only one man in the world who can testify to my innocence, but I do not know his name or where he lives. Some weeks ago, that man and I were together in the city of Plymouth at midnight and both of us heard the clock strike thirteen times rather than twelve, after which we commented on the incident. If he were here, he would confirm what I have just said. But I do not nurture the slightest hope because I do not know where he is. "I am here! I am here," shouted the captain. "I am the man who was in Plymouth that hour and heard the clock strike thirteen times rather than twelve. The prisoner is speaking the truth. On the night of the murder, on the exact moment it happened, he was with me in Plymouth and we remarked to each other the fact that the clock had struck thirteen times at midnight." Thus the man's innocence was proven, and he was acquitted of the charge.

May I ask, who was it that arranged those events in such a manner that the two men should meet exactly at that hour? Who awakened the captain so early in the morning? Who roused the servant and constrained him to saddle his master's horse? Who guided the horse to the ferry? Who awakened the boatman and compelled him to go down to the river? And, who led the horse to the town in which the innocent man was going to be sentenced for murder? Finally, who influenced the captain to enter the courtroom at the right time? Who imparted these "impressions"?

Appendix C

NZ HERALD September 30 1995

Boy, 3, has blood of female

NEW YORK — First a man's sperm fertilises a woman's egg, and then the egg starts to create an embryo, right?

Yes, usually, but now scientists say they have discovered the first known human case of an egg that didn't wait for the sperm, a boy with genetically female blood.

Normally, sperm delivers a half-set of the father's genes to a half-set of the mother's genes in the egg. The embryo forms when the egg divides into two cells, each of which divides into two more cells, and so on.

But in the case of the boy, now aged 3, scientists believe the egg started dividing before the sperm showed up, said Dr David Bonthron of the University of Edinburgh in Scotland.

However, fertilisation still occurred, perhaps even before the egg had completed its first splitting.

This meant that the father's genes did not reach all the cells in the boy's body, including those that make white blood cells. So the boy's white cells contain only doubled copies of his mother's genes.

Skin cells from the boy, who was identified only as FD, contain the normal combination of his mother's and father's genes.

AP

Appendix D

RON WYATT - BIOGRAPHY

On June 20,1987, the Turkish government officially recognised the discovery of the remains of Noah's Ark in eastern Turkey with the dedication of Noah's Ark National Park. Nashvillian Ron Wyatt, an amateur archaeologist, was guest of honour at the ceremony, credited as the "discoverer" because it was his persistence throughout the years which finally resulted in the evidence which convinced the Turkish authorities of the authenticity of the site. Ron didn't "discover" the site. He read about it in a 1960 "Life Magazine" article which told of an American archaeological team that investigated the site in 1960 and pronounced it "of no archaeological interest". This article led to his profound belief that the site "most likely" contained the remains of Noah's Ark, a belief which was confirmed 17 years later when he first saw it in person.

An anaesthetist by vocation, Ron became interested in archaeology, history and all the sciences at the age of 15 and, through the years, read everything he could get his hands on concerning these subjects. His ventures into actual field work in the Middle East began in 1977, when his 3 children (whom he raised alone) were into their teens. His interest in archaeology was the direct result of his profound belief in the total accuracy of the Biblical account. Curiosity and the belief that evidences of certain Biblical events were most likely still in existence led to his ventures into "the field".

His own study had led him to conclude that many of the commonly accepted locations of Biblical sites were incorrect. Since that 1977 trip to Turkey, Ron has made well over 100 trips to the Middle East, working in Turkey, Israel, Egypt and Saudi Arabia. In addition to Noah's Ark, in 1978 he found the site of the Red Sea crossing with chariot remains on the sea floor; in 1984, he found the real Mt. Sinai in northwestern Saudi Arabia (Midian) which still contains the altar at the foot of the mountain, the Golden Calf altar, and so much more. He found 5 ashen cities - Sodom & Gomorrah being the most famous - which were permeated throughout with roundish balls of sulphur which were once on fire; and in 1982, he found the Ark of the Covenant in a chamber many feet below the present ground level - the only claim which he is unable to substantiate at this time due to restrictions placed on him by the authorities, but which he believes he will be able to make public in the future. He has also made other discoveries and is presently attempting to verify the remains of the Tower of Babel.

He has not sought the "approval" of "educated" scientists and archaeologists, but presents the evidences to those who are interested, that they may make their own decision. For this reason, he is severely criticised by the academic community, some of whom have fought vehemently to discredit both Ron and the evidences. However, Ron is of the belief that God would not preserve evidences of the Truth of His Word, the Bible, which would have to be "interpreted" or verified by others.

Ron has financed at least 95% of his work through his work as an anaesthetist, and he presently still works at 2 Nashville area hospitals. He has never sought publicity and prefers to work quietly. However, over the years, his "misadventures" have many times placed him in the headlines, such as in 1984 when he and his sons were imprisoned in Saudi Arabia for 3 months after being accused of being Israeli spies; and in 1991 when he and his team were taken hostage in eastern Turkey for 21 days.

In 1993, he formed "Wyatt Archaeological Research", a non-profit, non-denominational organisation dedicated to making these discoveries available in books and videos to "those that ask". "W.A.R." has provided publications and videos to missionaries of almost every denomination who are sharing the discoveries in almost every country of the globe. In February or March of 1997,

W.A.R. planned to reopen their museum in its new location south of Nashville, TN. At exit 27 on 1-65.

Ron has appeared on CNN; ABC's "20/20"; Good Morning America; CBS Morning News; Nightline; The Discovery Channel; the BBC; Japan's "Nippon"Network; The Voice of America (from Cairo); TBN's "Behind the Scenes"; and much more.

He firmly believes that these remains have all been preserved and hidden by the Hand of God until this time in earth's history to provide evidence of His Truth in the last days. Why was Ron "chosen" to make all these discoveries? He believes that it is humanly impossible for one person to find all of these things, no matter how "smart" or educated they may be, and therefore, in using someone average and without "professional" training, God ensured that people would know that these discoveries are "of God" and not man. And although some "leaders" and "educated men" have fought to keep these evidences from the world, the discoveries are daily accomplishing the work that the Lord meant for them to. The simplicity of the evidences of each discovery doesn't require that anyone seek out the "experts" to tell them if it is real or not. All that is needed is a desire to know His Truth.

1 Corinthians 1:27 - But God hath chosen the foolish things of the world to confound the wise; and God hath chosen the weak things of the world to confound the things which are mighty.

Appendix E

MORAL AND CEREMONIAL LAWS

In the Bible, God's law is called his will (Psalm 40:8), or COVENANT (1 Kings 8:21,9). This is the Ten Commandment law, also known as the moral law. Jesus' death established its validity and permanence. Thus it is linked to the eternal covenant of salvation. This law **defines sin. Jesus Christ saves** us from sin. Sometimes the expression "Old Covenant" and "New Covenant" are used in Scripture. The first is based upon mankind's futile attempt to honor the law in his own strength. Its fault is in the people, not the law. The second is based upon God's promise to place that same law in the heart, and empower each person to observe it (Hebrews 8:8-10).

It may surprise some to realize that although the Old Covenant has been superseded by the better New Covenant, the laws which formed the foundation for the Old are still valid under the New.

Acts of adultery were forbidden under the Old. Jesus showed us that thoughts of adultery are just as wrong, even if not so evident. The spirit of the law is just as binding as the letter, if not more so!

Not changed

The Covenant was sealed, made permanent, by the death of Jesus Christ. A covenant, a testament, a will, cannot be changed or added to after the death of the one giving it. To anyone who might say that a change was made in memory of the resurrection or any other event after the death of the Lord, Paul the apostle answers:

"Just as **no one can set aside or add to a human covenant that has been duly established,** so it is in this case." Galatians 3:15 NIV)

That is, once the salvation covenant was confirmed at Calvary, nothing could be changed or added to it.

ANGLICAN CHURCH

Thirty-nine Articles of Religion. Article 7 reads:-

"Although the laws given from God, by Moses, as touching ceremonies and rites, do not bind Christian men, nor the civil precepts thereof ought of necessity to be received in any commonwealth; yet notwithstanding, no Christian man whatsoever is free from the obedience of the commandments which are called moral."

METHODIST CHURCH

"Methodist Episcopal Church Doctrines and Discipline," Article 6, page 23:-

"Although the law given from God by Moses as touching ceremonies and rites, doth not bind Christians,... yet, notwithstanding, no Christian whatsoever is free from the obedience of the commandments which are called moral."

PRESBYTERIANS

"Confession of Faith," chapter 19, articles 2 and 5:-

"**The moral law** doth forever bind all, as well justified persons as others, to the obedience thereof: and that not only in regard to the matter contained in it, but also in respect of the authority of God, the Creator, who gave it. Neither doth Christ in the gospel any way dissolve but much strengthen this obligation."

Also from the Larger Catechism, Questions 93 and 98:-

"Ques. What is the moral law?

"Ans. The moral law is the declaration of the will of God to mankind, directing and binding everyone to personal, perfect, and perpetual conformity and obedience thereunto.

"Ques. Where is the moral law summarily comprehended?

"Ans. The moral law is summarily comprehended in the Ten Commandments, which were delivered by the voice of God upon

534

Mount Sinai, and written by Him on two tables of stone; and are recorded in the twentieth chapter of Exodus."

Also in "Confession of Faith," chapter 19, article 3:-

"Beside this law, commonly called moral, God was pleased to give to the people of Israel, as a church under age, ceremonial laws, containing several typical ordinances, partly of worship, prefiguring Christ, His graces, actions, sufferings, and benefits: and partly holding forth divers instructions of moral duties. All which ceremonial laws are now abrogated under the new testament."

LUTHERAN

"Shorter Catechism":-

"Ques. Are we under obligation to keep the moral law?

"Ans. Yes, because it is founded on the nature of God, and cannot be changed; it is of universal application, which was impossible with respect to the ceremonial and civil laws. Christ demands obedience to His law."

"Ques. Are we under obligation to keep the ceremonial, or church, law of the Jews?

"Ans. No; the ordinances which it enjoined were only types and shadows of Christ; and when they were fulfilled by His death, and the distinction between the Jew and Gentile was removed, the ceremonial law was abolished, because it was no longer necessary."

As late as August 2, 1926, the Lutheran Herald published in Australia, said:-

"The moral law, or the Ten Commandments, is defined in our Lutheran Catechism as follows: 'They [the Ten Commandments] are the holy will of God, or the law wherein God tells us how we are to be and what we are to do and not to do.' There is no controversy in the Christian churches regarding the fact that this law is binding upon all men for all time.

"The ceremonial law consisted of laws which pertained to the religious life and worship of the Jews, having no intrinsic value in themselves, but only in as far as they prefigured the person and work of our Lord Jesus Christ and the blessed fruit of His redemption. They consisted largely of divine precepts respecting meat and drink, various sacrifices, feasts, holy days, seasons, and ceremonies which were performed in the temple, the end and aim of which was to point to the promised Messiah... The ceremonial laws lost their meaning with the coming of Christ and the completion of His work of redemption. The moral law, however, will retain its value as long as the earth exists."

ROMAN CATHOLICS

"Catholic Dictionary" of Addis and Arnold, p. 204, art. "Commandments of God":

Two questions about the commandments must be mentioned, the former of which concerns the binding force, the latter the division and arrangement of the decalogue. As to the former question, the Council of Trent defines, against antinomian heretics of ancient and modern times, that the ten commandments bind the consciences of all mankind, Christians included. "If anyone says that the ten commandments have nothing to do with Christians, let him be anathema." "If anyone say that a man, though justified and ever so perfect, is not bound to observe the commandments of God and the Church, let him be anathema." The reason on which this obligation rests is manifest. God did not give a new law to Moses; He only republished a law written originally on the conscience of man, and obscured by his sinful ignorance. The ten commandments, then, did not begin to bind when proclaimed to the people of Israel, and they have not ceased to do so now that Christ has done away with the Jewish law.

Sess. vi. De Justif.con.19,20.
Cat.Rom III 1, 3.

THE SALVATION ARMY

Mrs. Booth, the wife of the founder of the Salvation Army, in her book entitled "Aggressive Christianity"says:- "I find frequently... a total misapprehension as to the meaning of the apostle, and a total confounding of the moral with the ceremonial law. Now, always mind, when you read anything about the law, to examine and find out which law is meant, whether it is the great Moral Law, which never has been, and never can be abrogated; or the Ceremonial Law, which in Christ certainly was done away. Mind which, because your salvation may depend upon that point. If you make a mistake there you may be lost through it; therefore, be very careful."

THE BAPTISTS

Baptist "Church Manual":

"We believe that the Law of God is the eternal and unchangeable rule of His moral government; that it is holy, just and good."

Two distinct laws

The Ten Commandment Law. Where Placed: "and thou shalt put into the ark the testimony which I shall give thee." Exodus 25:16. "And he took and put the testimony into the ark, and set the staves on the ark, and put the mercy seat above the ark." Exodus 40:20.

The Ceremonial Law. Where Placed; "That Moses commanded the Levites, that bore the ark of the covenant of the Lord, saying: Take this book of the law, and put it by the side of the ark of the covenant of the Lord your God." Deuteronomy 31:25, 26.

Jesus Christ "nailed to his cross" the "handwriting of ordinances," taking it out of the way. God had used those sacrificial ordinances to teach the children of Israel about the infinite sacrifice that the Lord of glory would accomplish on Calvary. When Jesus died on the cross, they lost their purpose.

This ceremonial law was written by Moses in a book, or scroll (Deuteronomy 31:24) which could be rolled together from each end. However, so sacred was the Law of God (the Ten Commandments - God's testimony), that no man had any part in writing it. God wrote it Himself.

Here we see that the Ten Commandment Law was placed INSIDE the Ark; and the ceremonial law, or law of rites, was placed by the SIDE of the Ark, indicating that they were two distinct and separate codes of law.

THIS IS SIGNIFICANT. One set of laws (the sacrificial) was to be put aside. The other (the moral) was to remain.

Appendix F

Plea for Owner of Solomon's Temple Relic to Identify Himself

The best archaeological sleuths in Jerusalem are stumped. Ever since BAR publicized the only surviving relic from the Solomonic Temple (see "Probable Head of Priestly Scepter From Solomon's Temple Surfaces in Jerusalem," January/February 1984), the archaeological cognoscenti in Jerusalem have been trying to identify the owner of the beautiful ivory scepter head carved in the shape of a pomegranate and inscribed with the legend "Belonging to the Temple of the Lord [Yahweh], holy to the priests."

The result: No one knows who owns it or where it is being kept. No one except the owner, that is, and perhaps the Jerusalem antiquities dealer who handled the sale. If he knows, he won't tell his best friend.

We can only plead with the owner to identify himself—or at least to allow the Israel Museum to display the inscribed ivory pomegranate anonymously, so that the public can view this beautiful relic, which can now be seen only in BAR's

lifelike color photographs.

The Israeli Attorney General and the Director of the Department of Antiquities should also look into the situation. Is it legal for a private individual to keep to himself a priceless artifact like this, which is part of the heritage of all Israelis and of the millions of visitors who could view it in the Israel Museum? If it is legal, should it be? Perhaps the Israeli law should be changed. In any event, the Israeli authorities should be investigating. We will continue to report to our readers as matters develop.

Artifact Found From Solomon's Temple. The first artifact from the Jewish temple built 3,000 years ago by King Solomon has been obtained by Israel. The artifact is a tiny ivory bell-shaped figure with four spikes. The Jewish Testament refers to the artifact as a pomegranate, reports Religious News Service.

Written on the pomegranate is an inscription in Hebrew that reads: "My heart with God holiness for priests." Israel paid $550,000 for the pomegranate to a seller who remains anonymous.

ARCHAEOLOGY

▶ Ivory Pomegranate

The ivory pomegranate pictured at right is the only known surviving artefact from King Solomon's temple in Jerusalem. It is dated to the 8th century B.C.

An inscription on the pomegranate, "Holy to the priests to the House of the Lord," links the pomegranate to the first temple, according to archaeologists.

Appendix G

**The Parliament of the
Commonwealth of Australia**

The following are excerpts from Parliamentary Paper No. 173/1986 commissioned for study by the Australian Commonwealth Government, entitled: "Toward a cashless society?"

It is presented as an item of interest only.

1.13.2 The ability of EFTPOS to provide information could also be used. If it were used universally, EFTPOS could provide **unobtrusive means for the surveillance of all actions involving purchases.** This could be achieved through using computers to **amass individual profiles of consumer spending, including times.**

A.1.15 **In 1971, the Centre for Strategic and International Studies at Georgetown University (USA) assigned a group of informatics specialists to develop a system of surveillance of all citizens in a manner neither obvious nor intrusive;** their recommendation was a national EFTPOS system. A vivid illustration of the way in which this would work was foreseen, perhaps playfully, in 1984.

DAILY SURVEILLANCE SHEET – CONFIDENTIAL – JULY 13, 1984

SUBJECT: John Q Public, 4 Home Street, Anywhere, USA, Male, Age 40, Married. Electrical Engineer.

PURCHASES: Wall Street Journal, $1.00; Breakfast, $2.25; Gasoline, $6.00; Phone (111 1234), $.25; Phone (222 5678), $.25; Lunch, $4.00; Cocktail $1.50; Bank (cash withdrawal), $200.00; Lingerie, $135.67; Phone (111 8769), $.85; Phone (869 1111), $80; Bourbon, $12.53; Boston Globe, $.50.

COMPUTER ANALYSIS

Owns stock (90 per cent probability)

Heavy starch breakfast – probably overweight. Bought $6.00 gasoline. Owns VW. So far this week subject has bought $25.00 worth of gasoline. Obviously doing something besides driving 9 miles to work. Bought gasoline at 7.57 am at gas station 6 miles from work. Subject probably late for work. Third such occurrence this week. Phone No 111 1234 belongs to Joe Book. Book was arrested for illegal book making in 1970, 1978 and 1982. No convictions. Phone No 222 5678 belongs to expensive men's barber shop specialising in hair restoration. Drinks during lunch. Withdrew $200.00 cash. Very unusual since all legal purchases were made using Uniform Federal Funds Transfer Card. Cash usually used for illegal purchases. Bought very expensive lingerie. Not his wife's size. Phone No 111 8769 belongs to Jane Doe. Phone 869 1111. Reservations for Las Vegas (without wife). Third trip in last three months to Las Vegas (without wife). No job related firms in Las Vegas. Will scan file to see if anyone has gone to Las Vegas at the same time and compare to subject's phone call numbers. Purchased Bourbon. Third bottle this month. Either heavy drinker or much entertaining.

FACT: The EFTPOS system has now been put into operation in Australia; all the technology is in place to track every person's movements.

Appendix H

THE "TIMES OF THE GENTILES" FILLED FULL

Certainly some events almost shriek out the demand to conceive of something besides bland coincidence. The sudden return of the Jews to Palestine after almost 2,000 years seems to be something of this sort.

For thousands of years, the Jew has wandered about on earth, despised and rejected, bruised and beaten, yet all the time wandering on.

He has seen far-flung empires crack and crumble, and mighty peoples dwindle to zero. Egyptian, Canaanite and Philistine; Assyrian, Chaldean and Persian; Greek, Roman and Saracen... all these and more have marched over him in pride – only to fall and die by the wayside.

But he, the Jew, still lives on.

What the Jewish return to Israel does NOT mean

Dramatic indeed was the restoration of the nation of Israel in 1948. And many Christians mistakenly permitted themselves to believe that God had re-instated the national entity as His agency. It should be understood, however, that since the Jewish period ended 1900 years ago, no nation is privileged above another. Since Jesus' sacrifice, there is no salvation, nor any eternal homeland, except for individuals who cooperate with Jesus in his plan to save them.[1]

541

The Jewish nation has, by its own efforts, attempted to reinstate itself... and this has been providentially permitted.

However, there IS a prophecy that we should all be watching with special care. Read it very slowly and carefully.

In the twenty-first chapter of Luke, Jesus foretold what was to come upon Jerusalem, and with it he connected the scenes which were to take place in the history of this world just prior to his return in majesty.

"The end – when?"

"This Temple will be totally destroyed," announced Jesus. (And we related the story of that event in Chapter 18.)

"This magnificent Temple?" they asked. "What you have prophesied must be the end of the world! When will the Temple be destroyed?"

"In this generation," he replied.[2]

"And what shall be the sign of your coming and of the end of the world?"

You see, it was a double-barreled question.

And the answer was plain and clear.

"When you shall see Jerusalem surrounded by armies, then know that its desolation has come near.... they (the Jews) will fall by the edge of the sword, and be led captive among all nations; and Jerusalem will be trodden down by the Gentiles, until the times of the Gentiles are fulfilled."[3]

"Fulfilled"

"Fulfilled" or "FILLED FULL" – what does that mean? Here is a HOT CLUE from the Bible. We shall consider this in three stages:

1 – THE AMORITES

Originally, the Israelites were restrained from taking over the land of Canaan (Palestine), because the wickedness of the existing Amorite inhabitants was said to be "NOT YET FULL".[4]

Even when the Amorite "cup of iniquity" was "full" and the Israelite Exodus took place, the Lord in His mercy still gave the

Amorites about 40 years' probation while the Israelites wandered in the wilderness, not permitted to displace them.

2 – THE JEWS

Later, Jesus told the Jewish nation that their allotted time was coming to an end because "You have **FILLED UP** the wickedness of your fathers."[5] "Therefore the Kingdom of God shall be taken from you and given to others who will bring forth the fruits of it."[6]

Even after the times of the Jewish nation closed, yet, in God's mercy, time lingered almost another 40 years for the individual Jew who worshipped in the synagogues, until the Roman destruction of Jerusalem in 70 AD. They had the opportunity to decide whether they would accept the decision of their hierarchy concerning Jesus as the Messiah, or whether they would accept the proclamation of the gospel that Jesus of Nazareth was indeed their Savior.

When Jerusalem was finally destroyed, it had had its day of grace – its time of visitation.[7]

3 – THE GENTILES

Could it be that the same principle applies today, on a wider scale? That the "Gentiles" (the world's nations) WILL ALSO HAVE AN ALLOTTED TIME AND A CERTAIN EVENT WILL MARK THE CLOSING OF THAT PERIOD?

Jesus had just said, "O Jerusalem, Jerusalem, you have had your day -your time is up."[8] Now the Gentiles take the stage, but their time will also come to an end. Will they not, in like manner, be rejected?

"Jerusalem shall be trodden down by the nations until..."

The word translated "trodden down" is a present participle of the Greek verb *pateo*. The force of the present tense is that Jerusalem was to be **continuously trodden down until** the times of the Gentiles would be FILLED FULL. This has been true. From 70 AD until 1967 only Gentile (non-Jewish) nations controlled Jerusalem.

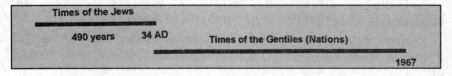

Times of the Jews

490 years   34 AD   Times of the Gentiles (Nations)

1967

543

Intended literally

In giving general signs that would apply to both the destruction of Jerusalem AND the end of the world, Jesus spoke **literally**. Signs in the sun, moon and stars were to be taken literally. The **armies surrounding Jerusalem** were to be understood **literally**. And the statement **"Jerusalem shall be trodden down of the Gentiles**, until the times of the Gentiles be fulfilled" – this also was given in **literal** language.

There is an hermaneutic principle or guideline: The Bible must be understood according to the plain, obvious and literal import unless a figure of speech is employed. When the plain sense of Scripture makes common sense, then seek no other meaning.

My experience over several years in a number of archaeological projects has reinforced this view: that the Scripture can be taken literally. Very much so.

To mention Jerusalem in prophecy is not to consider Jerusalem as the holy city of God, nor the nation of Israel as once more His chosen people. Daniel said that would end. [9] However, this fact does not exclude an equally important consideration that events in the history of Jerusalem can still fulfill Bible prophecy. For example, Jerusalem was NOT the holy city of God in 70 AD, YET the destruction of the city by Titus did fulfill the prophecy which Jesus had given – and the surrounding of the city by Cestius' troops in 66 AD was a sign to the Christians to flee the city.

This is crucial to bear in mind: **The same city that was surrounded by Roman armies is THE SAME CITY which is to be trodden down by the Gentiles (nations) until the times of the Gentiles be fulfilled.**

What went wrong in 1948 ?

Despite 80 million Arabs against them, the 2 to 3 million Israelis have won all three wars. The Israelis won, of course, their very first war, in 1948.

Yet, despite the amazing prowess of the Israeli troops, the ancient city of Jerusalem remained still in Arab hands.

Victorious as were the forces of Israel in every other part of Palestine, they FAILED TO TAKE the most dazzling objective of all.

Mysteriously they were held back from achieving this most prized goal, this culminating triumph, as though by an unseen hand.

What could be the reason?

ONLY THAT THE "TIMES OF THE NATIONS" WERE NOT YET FILLED FULL! Jerusalem was kept out of their reach. Because... Jerusalem was to **be freed from the domination of the Gentiles** only at the closing of the times of the Gentiles.

1967: The countdown?

In June, 1967, Israel's four Arab neighbors – Egypt, Jordan, Syria and Lebanon – invaded, with the avowed intent to wipe out Israel. In a lightning six-day war, tiny Israel defeated them – and for the first time in 1900 years reoccupied Jerusalem – the Jerusalem of which Jesus spoke.

LEBANON

SYRIA

Sea of Galilee

Tel Aviv

OLD JERUSALEM

JORDAN

Dead Sea

ISRAEL Before 1967

EGYPT

Was that retaking of Jerusalem a sign that the end of the Gentile period had begun.? That the cup of wickedness among the world's nations was now FILLED FULL?

Was the retaking of Jerusalem after 1,900 years a sign-post? Did it serve notice that the nations of the earth – the Gentiles – have filled up the cup of their iniquity? That the stage is set for the final scenes of this world's history, and the final struggle between truth and error?

Then, in 1980, the entire Jewish government - the Supreme Court, the Knesset, the office of both the President and Prime Minister - was moved to Jerusalem. This was done on July 30 of 1980. The prophecy of Jesus had met its fulfilment - literally.

Jesus had said "... until the times of the Gentiles be fulfilled."

That word "until" – can you see – implies a CHANGE OF STATUS. "There shall be a change."

Granted, the Palestinians still worship on Jerusalem's Temple Mount. But it is the Israelis who exercise the authority permitting them this usage. It is ultimately not the Arabs, but the Israeli government with its seat in Old Jerusalem, who decides whether the area is off limits to the Jewish religious population. As I strolled past the government buildings Israeli soldiers stood with their guns ready.

By the retaking of Jerusalem, did divine prophecy give warning that the history of this world was coming to its climax and that the restitution of all things was at hand? THAT THE COUNTDOWN HAD BEGUN?

Notice the prophecy in its physical context:

> And **when ye** shall **see** Jerusalem compassed with armies, **then know** that the desolation thereof is nigh...For these be the days of vengeance, that all things which are written may be fulfilled...And they shall fall by the edge of the sword, and shall be led away captive into all nations [*ta ethné*]: and Jerusalem shall be trodden down of the Gentiles [*ethné*], until the times of the Gentiles [*ethné*] be fulfilled. And there shall be signs in the sun, and in the moon, and in the stars; and **upon the earth** distress of nations [*ethné*] with perplexity; the sea and the waves roaring; men's hearts failing them for fear, and for looking after those things which are coming **on the earth**; for the powers of heaven shall be shaken. And then shall they see the Son of man coming in a cloud with power and great glory. And **when ye see** these things begin to come to pass, **know ye** that the kingdom of God is nigh at hand. Verily I say unto you, this generation shall not pass away, till all be fulfilled. Heaven and earth shall pass away; but my words shall not pass away. (Luke 21:20-33).

Several points should be noted. Luke passes by with only a mention of the "signs" in the sun, moon and stars. (Compare with Matt. 24:29 and Mark 13:24-45) He focuses Jesus' prophecy "upon the earth" emphasizing "the nations" [*ethné*] whether translated in the KJV - "nations" or "Gentiles". He speaks of their "times" and "distress" with "perplexity." In two instances, Luke has Jesus stressing - "When you see" then "know ye." The first, when the

546

armies surrounded Jerusalem, then they were to know that its destruction was nearing. We can ask - did that generation which saw this sign fulfilled live to see the destruction of the city? Likewise, Jesus said, those who see the end of the times of the nations and the events connected with it, that generation will not pass away till all be fulfilled.

What this means to you

Could it be said that if one cannot see that Jerusalem is an exceptional sign of the times, one places oneself in the same category with the Jewish religious leaders of old who knew how to 'discern the face of the sky' but could not discern the obvious 'signs of the times.'?[10]

It could be suggested that there is a distinct **parallel** in the closing of the times for the Jewish nation and the closing of the times for the world's nations (the Gentiles). Let's recapitulate.

The Jews: When the Jewish nation rejected the divine covenant, destruction did not follow immediately. Time still lingered for the individual Jew. He could still decide whether to follow the decision of his leaders against Jesus, or whether to accept Jesus as Lord.

THEN FOLLOWED THE PHYSICAL DESTRUCTION OF JERUSALEM, some forty years later.

The nations: Today, although most nations operate without reference to divine will, we are still free as individuals to do some very serious thinking.

Is literal Jerusalem a sign today, as for the Christians in 66 AD, just a few years before its destruction?

If so we now stand between these two events – the Jerusalem sign, and the return of Jesus.

Economic stress

Notice the prophecy again:

"Jerusalem shall be trodden down of the nations, until the times of the nations be filled full... And there shall be... upon earth distress of nations, with perplexity."[11]

When the times of the nations are fulfilled, they come into distress with perplexity.

The Greek word translated "distress" is *sunoche*, which means "imprisoned", "in the narrows, or straits". The added phrase "with perplexity" (*en aporia*, from the same root as *aporeo,* "to **have no way out**"), conveys the picture of nations unable to meet the demands placed upon them, including financially, with the inability to solve the monetary stress.[12]

According to Jesus' prophecy as recorded by Luke, the ending of the "times of the Gentiles", or nations, is closely associated with the "distress of nations, with perplexity".

Interestingly, THE SAME YEAR which introduced the closing period of the closing of the times of the nations (1967) is also the year which MARKED THE BEGINNING OF THE FINANCIAL WOES OF THE NATIONS.

In this context I cite C.V. Myers, described by Gordon Tether in the *London Financial Times* as "the well-known Canadian Financial expert."[13]

Myers stated that since 1967:

> ...things have gone from bad to worse; the US$ has been devalued; inflation has undermined world confidence in money; and now the bankruptcies come.[14]

Again, Myers wrote:

> From all that I have observed of international (monetary) conferences **since 1967** I do not believe that any conference is going to come up with any workable answer. It seems that the situation will just continue to deteriorate....
>
> All brains are stunned. They see no answer.... Therefore I can only see as the end product... a total collapse.
>
> Recently D'Estaing observed: 'The world is unhappy. It is unhappy because it doesn't know where it is going, and because it senses that if it knew, it would discover that it was heading for disaster.... It is actually the recognition of **a permanent change**.[15]

Myers continues to cite **the year 1967** as the base year for the beginning of the monetary perplexities which have gripped the nations since then.[16]

In *Newsweek,* in an article on the tax revolt, it was stated:

Since 1967, the value of the dollar has declined 47.6 per cent, and the average American working family is now barely better off in real dollars than it was a decade ago.[17]

The connection, it appears, is inescapable:

• THE END OF THE TIMES OF THE NATIONS, and

• THE BEGINNING OF THE "DISTRESS OF NATIONS".

Jesus linked them.

But the date when history will be interrupted, nobody on earth knows.

1 Galatians 3:7,28,29; Romans 2:28,29; 9:6-9; 1 Peter 2:9

2 Matthew 23:32-38; 24:34; Mark 13:30; Luke 21:32

3 Luke 21:20,24 RSV

4 Genesis 15:16

5 Matthew 23:32-35 (Free translation)

6 ch. 21:18-20,43 (Free translation)

7 Luke 19:43,44

8 Matthew 23:1-39

9 Daniel 9:24

10 Matthew 16:3

11 Luke 21:24,25 (Free translation)

12 Moulton and Milligan T*he Vocabulary of the Greek New Testament*

13 *London Financial Times*, June 28 1974

14 *Myers' Finance and Energy.* Special Issue July 4, 1974, pp.2,3

15 Ibid., March 11, 1975, pp.1,2

16 Ibid., May 24, 1976

17 *Newsweek* June 19, 1978, p.21

Appendix I

TYPE AND ANTI-TYPE

Mercy and truth

Says the psalmist concerning God's heavenly Throne:

> Justice and judgment are the habitation of thy throne: **mercy and truth** shall go before thy face. [1]

And in Jesus' death which occurred on earth:

> **Mercy and truth** are met together; righteousness and peace have kissed each other. **Truth shall spring out of the earth; and righteousness shall look down from heaven.**[2]

1 – **Mercy and truth** met when Jesus spilt his blood. The **truth** of his law, which we had broken, making us sinners; and the **mercy** he granted to us through his death. They **met together** when he sprinkled his blood on that Mercy Seat over that law.

2 – **From the earth shall spring forth truth** – when the Ark and the tablets of the Ten Commandments can be revealed to all the earth.

3 – Today "the Lord our **Righteousness**"[3] looks down from heaven, as he advocates his blood on our behalf before his Father. Here are some questions we have been asked:

1. BLOOD SPRINKLED IN HEAVEN?

QUESTION- Since the earthly sanctuary was patterned after the original in heaven, and since blood was sprinkled inside the earthly sanctuary, then wouldn't Jesus have taken his blood to be offered in heaven?"

550

ANSWER: In heaven, Jesus does not **spill** his blood but he is our Advocate there. He **pleads** our case. He still bears the memorial wounds of his death for us on earth. It is the effectiveness of his blood shed for us on earth that qualifies him to be our Intercessor in heaven. The blood was spilt on earth. The mediation is in heaven. "For Christ is not entered into the holy places made with hands, which are the figures of the true; but into heaven itself, now to appear in the presence of God for us. "[4] "There is one God, and one **mediator** between God and man, the man Christ Jesus."[5]

It is the fact of his blood shed for us on earth "once for all" that qualifies him to represent us in heaven. The blood bears "witness on earth."[6]

The symbol	The fulfillment
* Many lambs	* One Lamb of God
* Various kinds of sacrifices	* One all-embracing sacrifice
* Many sacrificial days	* A sacrifice on one day
* Blood shed many times	* Blood shed only once
* Blood shed in the courtyard, outside the sanctuary	* Blood shed on earth, outside heaven

"But this man, after he had offered **one sacrifice for sins for ever**, sat down on the right hand of God;... For **by one offering he hath perfected for ever them that are sanctified**. Now where remission of these (sins) is, **there is no more offering for sin**."[7]No blood spilt in heaven.

2. TYPE (SYMBOL)VERSUS ANTITYPE (FULFILLMENT) VIOLATED?

QUESTION: Since Jesus died to fulfill the Passover symbols, **at which time** (in the symbol) no blood was sprinkled on the Mercy Seat of the Ark of the Covenant, wouldn't Jesus' sprinkling of his blood on the Mercy Seat **at that time** be a violation of the symbol?

In the Hebrew services, blood was sprinkled on the Ark only on the Day of Atonement (September-October), not Passover day (March-April).

ANSWER: At Jesus' death, **in one simple act**, Jesus Christ demonstrated the very **heart** of the message embodied in all those complex sanctuary ceremonies. Jesus' blood, shed for every

551

sinner, spilled onto the Mercy seat, which covered the law of God. By breaking that law, we had all become sinners, subject to death. So Jesus' death – an act of mercy – set us free. That blood dropping onto the Mercy Seat over the law – that's the whole gospel in one simple act!

The Ark of the Covenant was a **composite symbol of the entire sanctuary system**. "All the sanctuary ceremonies reached their consummation at the Ark. It thus stood for him who is 'the end of our faith' (1 Peter 1:9), the center of our devotions, and the object of our search... The blood-soaked Mercy Seat was the central Throne of the Shekinah, or presence of the gracious and merciful God, and the goal and focus of His saving activity... On the many stages of Israel's journey from Egypt to the promised land 'the ark of the covenant of the Lord went before them...' (Numbers 10:33-36) The Lord provided food and water, rest and a safe haven, as long as His people cherished the Ark as the heart of their encampment."[8]

Would the types (symbols) be violated if Jesus' blood, at the time of the Passover, flowed onto the Mercy Seat of this Ark? It is true that the various feast days all had their own particular significance, representing different prophetic events. Yet they all had one thing in common: sacrifices were made on each of them. The priests shed blood in sacrifices **many** times. But Jesus did it "ONCE".[9] The one death of Jesus once and for all embraced within itself the deaths of every sacrifice slain in the entire Hebrew religious year.

"Many times" versus "once": the Scripture tells us that in this **detail** the 'type' or symbol cannot fit; it is **'not the very image'** of the real event it signified.[10]

In the symbol, the many sacrifices of lambs, goats and bullocks all prefigured, the ONE sacrifice of ONE Person, the Messiah, ONCE FOR ALL.

In the symbol, sacrificial blood was sprinkled on the altar of burnt offering, the altar of incense and also on the Ark of the Covenant's Mercy Seat. But all these were fulfilled ONCE FOR ALL when Jesus' blood was sprinkled on just ONE place, ONCE - the Mercy Seat.

The **time** of the year that Jesus' blood went onto the earthly Mercy Seat is not crucial here. Jesus was not required to spill it on the calendar Day of Atonement. The symbols of the animal blood that had been shed on **all** these days of the year, he had to fulfill **in ONE act.** It says 'Christ was ONCE offered.'[11]

All the detailed prophecies concerning the Savior's death had to be accomplished IN THAT **ONE** ACT.

So it is that our High Priest in heaven today can plead our case at the heavenly Mercy Seat by virtue of his blood spilt **ONCE** on earth.

Not an exact correspondence

An exact correspondence between the ancient symbol and the reality was not physically possible.

For one thing, it took **two** separate entities – both a lamb and a priest – to symbolize the one Messiah, first as the dying One, then as our resurrected Mediator in heaven.

Jesus could serve both as our Lamb and as our High Priest, because he returned to life after his death.

No lamb or other sacrificial animal could illustrate the resurrection. For that reason, both an animal **and** a human priest were required – one to symbolize his death, and the other his post-resurrection work as our Advocate.

Something else. The earthly priests were many in number, but Jesus ministers on our behalf continually, since he lives forever.

The **contrast** of the symbol and the fulfillment is **greater** than the likeness. The only way it can be made congruent is to recognize that the earthly symbol was 'an example', however imperfect, of the heavenly.[12] It would be an error, and unscriptural, to try to make every detail correspond precisely.[13]

Bridging the gap – earthly to heavenly

It is well to bear in mind also that once the veil of the **earthly** Temple was torn from top to bottom, in the divine plan it was "no more". At that moment the earthly priest's office ceased to exist. From now on, Jesus Christ was to take over. Nevertheless Jesus' function in the heavenly Temple had not yet commenced.

So there was this **interim period** when God, in His own brilliant manner **forged a link** between the earthly symbol and the heavenly ultimate.

And here is how He did it. To function as our High Priest above, Jesus must first offer the sacrifice outside that heavenly Temple. So this appointed High Priest sprinkled the blood – his own blood – a ONCE ONLY act of God to demonstrate direct the whole purpose of Jesus' death.

One item of the sanctuary had been preserved for that purpose – the Ark of the Covenant. So the blood spilled onto the Mercy Seat, demonstrating God's mercy to us, the law-breakers.

Thus the spilt blood (a prerequisite for Jesus' mediation in the heavenly Temple) went onto the most holy object of the **earthly** system – forging the LINK from the one to the other. Physically.

3. DID GOD'S PRESENCE LEAVE THE ARK?

QUESTION: When the glory of the Lord left the Temple (seen by Ezekiel), doesn't it follow that God's presence left the Ark? So would it not be pointless for Jesus to sprinkle his blood on the Ark if God's presence had left it?

ANSWER: The Lord's glory left the Temple just before the Babylonians destroyed the Temple. The Ark also left the Temple just before the Babylonians destroyed the Temple. It seems possible that the glory departed from the Temple when the Ark departed. The Scripture says God's presence left the Temple.

In the earthly sanctuary services, sin-laden sacrificial blood was never **carelessly** permitted to **just flow** onto the ground. Some of it was always taken by a priest and applied, in the case of individual offerings, onto the horns of the altar of sacrifice in the courtyard, and in the case of sacrifices for corporate sins, onto the horns of the altar of incense in the Holy Place.

Then the "clean" blood shed on the Day of Atonement came to these altars via the Most Holy place (where the Ark reposed), to cleanse the two altars where the sin-laden blood had been applied (See Leviticus chapters 4 and 16).

The earth has been defiled and for the time being the earth is controlled by evil forces. However, the Lord preserved one thing free from contamination – the Ark. It was the earthly "Throne" of God. It was holy and He kept it so. Thus it was upon this earthly Throne of his Father that the blood of the Messiah fell.

The fogginess of the Ark of the Covenant photographs taken by each of three cameras was **not** due to faulty cameras.

4. TOUCHING THE ARK TODAY

QUESTION: Is it safe to touch the Ark today? What would happen if you tried?

ANSWER: We all know, don't we, what happened in the long ago if someone tried to touch the Ark. (See Chapter 1)

That was because the Ark was a symbol of God's presence. God is holy and unholy man cannot approach into His presence. In those days, the people were forbidden to look upon it.

Even in recent times, when it was photographed, the pictures turned out foggy. And one might ask, Could it be that the Lord even now does not intend that it be seen by the world... at this present time?

Over the years, many unsavory characters have attached themselves to the search – men motivated by greed or self-interest. Suppose that such men were to catch a clear glimpse of the shimmering gold of the Ark, just what might they attempt then?

The Bible states, of course, that the Shekinah glory departed from the Temple before it was destroyed by the Babylonians. It is also true that once the Lord places His blessing upon something, that blessing remains forever.[14]

What would happen if one touched the Ark today? My personal feeling would be that unless one was chosen for the job, it would be advisable not to try and find out.

1   Psalm 89:14
2   ch. 85: 10, 11
3   Jeremiah 23: 6
4   Hebrews 9:24
5   1 Timothy 2:5
6   1 John 5:8
7   Hebrews 10:12,14,18
8   Hardinge, Dr. L. *With Jesus in His Sanctuary*. American Cassette Ministries, Book Publishing division,1991, pp.185-186,190-192
9   Hebrews 7:27
10   ch.10:1
11   ch. 9: 28
12   ch.8:5

13 One obvious observation between what is revealed of the heavenly Most Holy Place where "the judgment was set and the books were opened "(Daniel 7:9,10) and the Most Holy Place of the earthly type is that **a structural comparison is incongruent.**

In the earthly Tabernacle the high priest entered, on the Day of Atonement, the Most Holy Place which was but 10 cubits square. (The Most Holy Place of Solomon's Temple was a 20 cubit cubicle.)

A vision given to Daniel reveals a judgment set in a vast Temple room capable of accommodating the entire angelic host.

In the earthly, while the curtains of the Tabernacle were embroidered with the symbolism of cherubs, the emphasis on the service of the high priest on the Day of Atonement was that he should enter that sacred enclosure **alone** (see Exodus 26:1; Leviticus 16:17).

 THE CONTRAST OF THE TYPE AND ANTI TYPE IS GREATER THAN LIKENESS and can only be made congruent if we accept the dictum of Hebrews 8:5 that the priests served "unto the example and shadow of heavenly things."

14 l Chronicles 17:27

Appendix J

THE CLEFT IN THE ROCK

557

REFERENCES AND NOTES

Biblical texts:

- Most texts are from the *King James* Version

- Texts credited to JB are from the *Jerusalem Bible*. London: Eyre and Spottiswoode, 1968

- Texts credited to GNB are from the *Good News Bible*. American Bible Society, 1976

- Texts credited to RSV are from the *Revised Standard Version* of the Holy Bible. Division of Christian Education, National Council of Churches of Christ in the USA

- Texts credited to NASB are from *The New American Standard Bible*. The Lockman Foundation, 1975

- Texts credited to NEB are from *The New English Bible*. The Delegates of the Oxford University Press and the Syndics of the Cambridge University Press, 1970

- Texts credited to ML are from *The Layman's Parallel Bible, Modern Language Bible*. Grand Rapids, Mi.: Zondervan Bible Publishers, 1975

- Texts credited to NIV are from the *New International Version Holy Bible*. New York Bible Society International, 1978

- Texts credited to LB are from *The Living Bible, Paraphrased* Wheaton: Tyndale House Publishers, 1971

Some other ancient texts:

Ancient writers such as Josephus, Strabo and Herodotus can be researched in the following sources:

- Herodotus *The History*. David Green (trans.) Chicago and London: University of Chicago Press, 1988

- Jones, H.L. (ed.) *The Geography of Strabo*. London: Loeb Library, 1940

- Josephus, Flavius *Josephus, Complete Works*. Translated by William Whiston. Grand Rapids, Mi.: Kregel Publications, 1960

Chapter 1 Too Hot to Handle

1   2 Samuel 6:6,7

2   "Cast four gold rings for it, to be attached to its four feet, two rings on one of its side walls and two on the other." *Tanakh* Philadelphia, New York and Jerusalem: The Jewish Publication Society, 1988, p.123 (on Exodus 25:12)

"And thou shalt cast four rings of gold for it, and put them in the four feet thereof: and two rings shall be on the one side of it, and two rings on the other side of it." *The Holy Scriptures According to the Masoretic Text* (English translation) Chicago: The Menorah Press, 1988 (on Exodus 25:12)

3   Exodus 28:34,35. 1 have so far been unable to track down the source for the Jewish tradition concerning the rope attached to the high priest's ankle.

4   Leviticus 5:15

5   Leviticus 10:3

6   Habakkuk 1:13

7   Numbers 4:15

8   Numbers 7:9

Chapter 2 Lost... But Where?

1   II Maccabees, ii, 4-8

2   In its "Introduction to the Books of Maccabees" the *Jerusalem Bible* concludes that Maccabees was probably written around 63 BC.

3   *Catholic Encyclopedia, 1907*, art. "Ark". While the books of Maccabees are included in the Roman Catholic Bibles, being classed as apocryphal, they are excluded from most Protestant Bibles.

4   "Tom Crotser has found the Ark of the Covenant - or has he?" *Biblical Archaeology Review*, May/June 1983, p.68

5   Ibid.,pp.68,69

6   Ibid., p.69

7   Hancock, Graham *The Sign and the Seal*. London: Mandarin Paperbacks,1993

8   Gray, Jonathan, private files

9   Exodus 37:1

10   Leon Ritmeyer, in *Locating the Original Temple Mount,* reports that, according to Middot, the pre-Herodian Temple Mount in Jerusalem has been found. If the shorter 18 inch cubit had been used, each wall would be only 750 feet long, but they have been found to be over 850 feet long conforming to the 20.6 inch cubit measure.

Since Moses was raised and educated in Egypt, he would undoubtedly be using the Egyptian cubit. The royal Egyptian cubit was 20.6 inches.

At the base of Mount Sinai in Arabia, 12 pillars mentioned in the Scripture as having been erected by Moses there (Exodus 24:4) were found in 1985 by Ron Wyatt, still there but now buried for most of their height. These, too, were found to be cut to the measurement of the 20.6 inch cubit.

In January, 1994, Richard Rives, Bob Murrell and the author carefully surveyed some underground tombs of the First Temple period, north of the Old City of Jerusalem.

These included outer and inner chambers, as well as tomb recesses. We discovered that these were built to the standard measure of the 20.6 inch cubit. This shows that the 20.6 inch cubit was in use right through to the First Temple period.

11   Matthew 12:37

12   Hancock, *The Sign and the Seal.* op. cit.

13   Ezekiel 8:6; 11:22,23

14   "Ark of the Covenant: Not in Ethiopia", *Biblical Archaeology Review*, Nov/Dec 1993, p.78

15   Josephus, Flavius *Wars of the Jews.* 7: 148-150

16   *Talmud Hag.* 26b,27a

17   Deuteronomy 4:16-25; 5:8

18   Josephus, 6: 388

19   Ibid., p.555

20   Yoma 5:2

21   Vilnay, Zev *Legends of Jerusalem: The Sacred Land,* Philadelphia: The Jewish Publication Society of America, 1973, Vol.1, pp.ll,l2

22   2 Chronicles 35:3

23   ch.36:l9

24   Ezekiel 8:6; 11:22,23

25   2 Kings 24:13; 25:8-16; Jeremiah 52:17-23

Chapter 3 Into Dark Tunnels

1   Holman, A.J. *Bible Lands. 1*903

2   2 Kings 20:20

3   Lewis, David Allen *Prophecy 2000.* p.176

4   Price, Randall Interview with Rabbi Goren, Tel Aviv office. January 24, 1994. *In Search of Temple Treasures.* Eugene, Or.: Harvest House Publishers, 1994, ch.10

5   Gray, Jonathan, private files

6   *Petah Tikvah magazine* April-June 1995

7   Price Interview with Rabbi Getz, January 25, 1994. Ibid.

8   Ibid.

9   *The Apocalypse of Baruch,* 6:7-10

10   *The Apocryphal New Testamentt.* Oxford: Clarendon Press, 1989, pp.843,844

11   Ibid., see "Introduction to the Syriac Apocalypse of Baruch", particularly p.837

12   Revelation 11;15-19

13   Hebrews 8:1-5; 9:23,24

14   Ezekiel chs. 42 to 46

15   ch.41:22 ; 44:16

16   Barala, John *Today the Bible and You.* Tulsa, Okl.: August 1996, Editorial

17   Ibid.

Chapter 4 Daring Rescue Plan

1   Goetz, Delia, and Morley, Sylvanus G. *Popul Vuh.* From the Spanish translation by Adrian Recinos. Norman, Okla.: University of Oklahoma Press, 1950

2.   Tomas, Andrew *We are Not the First.* London: Sphere, 1978, p.13

3   Gray, Jonathan, private files

4   Gray, private files

5   Soddy, Frederick *Interpretation of Radium.* London: John Murray,1909,p243

6   Kramer, S.N. *Sumerian Mythology.* Philadelphia: 1944, frontispiece. For corrections made after additional fragments of the same story were found see Kramer, *Journal of the American Oriental Society*, vol.88 (1968) ,p.109.

7   For example, the Adapa Myth and the Gilgamesh Epic. A translation of the Adapa Myth made by E.A. Speiser is found in J.B. Pritchard, ed., *Ancient Near Eastern Texts Relating to the Old Testament*, henceforth abbreviated to ANET, 3rd ed. Princeton, N.J., 1969, pp. 101-103. A translation of the Gilgamesh Epic made by Speiser is found in ANET, pp.72-79. See especially, pp.88,90 and 96.

8   These principles can be recognised in a series of questions which a Mesopotamian text contains that tries to find the causes for the inexplicable fact that man lived under a divine punishment:

"Has he estranged the father from his son or the son from his father?

Has he refused to set a captive free?

Has he said yes for no or no for yes?

Has he used false scales?

Has he accepted a wrong account?

Has he set up a false landmark?

Has he broken into his neighbor's house?

Has he come near his neighbor's wife?

Has he shed his neighbor's blood?"

(L.W. King, *Babylonian Religion and Mythology.* London: 1899, pp.218,219)

The Egyptian Book of the Dead was a document that one took with him to the grave, attached to his body. It was intended to serve as a valid passport for the other world and assure its bearer admittance there. Of a long string of negative confessions the following are typical:

"...I have not committed evil.

...   I have not stolen.

...   I have not been covetous.

...   I have not robbed.

...   I have not killed man.

...   I have not damaged the grain measure.

...   I have not caused crookedness.

...   I have not told lies.

...   I have not been contentious.

...   I have not practiced usury.

...   I have not committed adultery.

(John A. Wilson in ANET,p.35).

9   King L.W. *Babylonian Religion and Mythology*. London: 1899, p.212

10   Jeremias, Alfred *Das Alte Testament im Lichte des Alten Orients*, 4th ed. Leipzig: 1930,p.99

11   Prescott, W.H. *Conquest of Mexico*, vol. 1. London: J.M. Dent and Sons Ltd., 1948,p.380

12   Seiss, Joseph A. *The Gospel in the Stars*. Grand Rapids, Mich.: Kregel Publications, 1982,p.11.

13   Ibid., p.33

14   Ibid., p.48

15   Seiss *The Great Pyramid: A Miracle in Stone*. New York: Harper and Row, 1973, p.66
Davidson, D. *The Great Pyramid: Its Divine Message*. London: William and Norgate, Ltd., 1936, pp.369,528

16   Cooper, David L. *Messiah: His First Coming Scheduled*.Los Angeles: Biblical Research Society, 1939,p.5

17   In the book of Genesis, it is stated that when Adam and Eve, the progenitors of the human race, fell from innocence, that God promised that one termed "the seed of woman" would ultimately crush the "serpent's" head, but not without himself being wounded (Genesis 3:15). I believe that we have in this promise the first suggestion of a virgin birth - "seed of the woman" without a man. Indeed, this is how the ancient races evidently understood it. This, the world's oldest prophecy, was passed on by Adam and Eve to all their descendants - a prophecy of a Deliverer.

In Egypt, the child-god Horus, known also as "the seed", is portrayed as standing on the head of a crocodile and as bruising serpents in his hands.

Nearly all Jewish commentators, with isolated exceptions, receive this as real history, and agree that the prophecy is messianic in character.

In the Targum Pseudo Jonathan on Genesis 3:15 the seed of the woman (interpreted as her faithful descendants) will smite the serpent's head "and you will wound them in the heel. However from them there will be a remedy, but for you there will be none, and in the future they will make peace with the heel **in the days of the king, Messiah.**"
(J.N.D. Anderson, *"The Resurrection of Jesus Christ"*, *Christianity Today*, March 29, 1968, p122)

Another Jewish source comments: "The Messiah shall restore the good state of the universe which is disturbed by the fall of man." (*Bereshith Rabba*, Ch. xii; *Bamidbar Rabba*, ch.xiii; Targum, Jer. i on Gen.3:15)

After pronouncing this prophecy, God provided them with animal skin garments. The skins they now wore were **not** from a naturally dead animal, as there had been no death until now; nor were the skins from an animal killed for food. (The use of animal food was sanctioned only after the Great Flood.) No, these were the skins of animals slain for sacrifice.

This is the inauguration of the system of sacrifices, planned to be, in years to come, a constant and vivid reminder of the terrible cost of sin. This was the message: one day the innocent Deliverer will sacrifice his life to pay the penalty for man's wrong-doing. The Lord will "cover"man's sins with His own robe of right doing, so that man may be counted as though he had never sinned. There are a number of biblical passages which illustrate this concept. (Psalm 32:1; Isaiah 64:6; Zechariah 3:3-5; Revelation 19:8)

Adam and Eve's first two sons were Cain and Abel. At the close of the appointed season (the time for the sacrifices, which were part of a regular series), the younger brother brought a lamb as a sacrifice, according to instructions. However, Cain found the shedding of blood revolting and chose instead to bring an offering of fruit, a substitute. Abel demonstrated faith in the Coming One. Cain refused. He argued, he disbelieved, he disobeyed. He thought that anything was good enough.

When Abel's offering was accepted and Cain's rejected, Cain flew into a rage - and his brother lay dead. (Genesis 3:21; Hebrews 11:4; 9:22;12:24)

Subsequent biblical history tells of faithful patriarchs continuing the sacrificial ritual. In particular, Noah (Genesis 8:20) and Abraham (ch.22:7-13).

18   Compare Acts 3:18-26; Jude 14,15

19   Hebrews 13:20 Compare Revelation 13:8

20   The "everlasting covenant" may be understood as, firstly, the eternal LAW, principle or
      standard by which God's kingdom operates, its humanized form being known as the
      Ten Commandments (Exodus 34:28; 1 Kings 8:21); and secondly, as including the divine
      plan to restore mankind into the spiritual image of God and into harmony with that
      universal law which is a transcript of God's own character (Hebrews 13:20; Romans 8:4;
      2 Corinthians 5:17; Colossians 1:27 ; Revelation 14:12).

Chapter 5 Fire God of the Amazon

1   Gray, Jonathan *Dead Men's Secrets* P.O.Box 3370, Rundle Mall, Adelaide, South Australia
      5000, 1996, pp.14-21

2   Faber, George Stanley *Origin of Pagan Idolatry*. London: F. and C. Rivingtons, 1816, Vol.
      I, preface

3   Horn, Siegfried H *Records of the Past Illuminate the Bible* Washington, DC.: Review and
      Herald Publishing Association, 1975, p.12

4   Davidson, I , and Aldersmith H. *The Great Pyramid: Its Divine Message*. London:
      Williams and Norgate, Ltd, 1936, p.526

5   Ibid.

6   Stewart *The Witness of the Great Pyramid* London: The Covenant Publishing Co. Ltd,
      1928, pp.64,65

7   Budge, E.A. Wallis *The Book of the Dead* London: British Museum Publications, 1920

8   Budge *The Gods of the Egyptians*. New York: Dover Publications, 1969 (reprint of the
      1904 ed.), Vol. I, p.32

9   2 Corinthians 4:4; Revelation 12:9

10   Budge, p.38

11   Faber, pp.495,496

12   Ibid., pp.472ff

13   Johnston, Thomas Crawford *Did the Phoenicians Discover America?* London: James
      Nisbet and Co., Ltd, 1913, p.179

Chapter 6 "Sacrifice Your Son"

1   Wright, G. Ernest *Biblical Archaeology*. Rev. ed. Philadelphia, 1962

2   Genesis 12:1-3

3   ch.22:11,12 Free translation

4   vv.8,14

5   John 8:56

Chapter 7 Escape at Midnight

1   Gray, Jonathan *Update International* PO Box 3370, Rundle Mall, Adelaide, South
      Australia, 5000, No.4, November 1993 to January 1994,p.1

2   Deuteronomy 28:1,13

3   v.12

4   Velikovsky, Immanuel *Ages in Chaos*. New York: Doubleday and Company, Inc., 1952,
      pp.25ff

5   Exodus 12:30

6   v.33

7   ch.14:21

8   ch.15:8

9   Velikovsky, p.43

10   Exodus 14:9

11   *Strong's Concordance.* See also Gray, *Update International,* No.15, May to July 1996, p.7

12   Exodus 9:16

13   ch-31:18

14   Isaiah 56:7 Compare Zechariah 8:20-23

15   Ezekiel 5:5 RSV

16   On God's schedule for the Jew, see Exodus 19:4-7; Deuteronomy 7:6,7, 9; 28:1-7,9,12-14

17   Deuteronomy 28:1-14

18   ch.28:15-68 Compare Jeremiah 18:9,10; Hosea 9:17

19   Galatians 4:25 Exodus 35:29 ; 37:1

Chapter 8 Covenant of Blood

I   Exodus 25:8

2   Psalm 77:13

3   I am indebted to Gar Baybrook for these illustrations and the explanation. Gar Baybrook, *Gospel in the Sanctuary.* Payson, Arizona: Leaves of Autumn Books,1989, pp.4,5

4   Exodus 25:8

5   Isaiah 53:7

6   *The Jewish Encyclopedia,* art., 'Atonement, Day of"

7   Numbers 5:6-8

8   Leviticus 17:11 The symbolic transfer of guilt from the sinner to the sacrificial animal is mentioned in Leviticus 1:4 - "And he shall put his hand upon the head of the burnt offering; and it shall be accepted for him to make atonement for him."

      Then the transfer of guilt was recorded in the sanctuary when the blood of the sacrificial animal was sprinkled on the horns of the altar - "The sin of Judah is written.. upon the horns of your altars." (Jeremiah 17:1) The blood in the sanctuary constituted a record that sin had been atoned for.

9   Leviticus 6:25,26

10   ch.10:17

11   Numbers 7:89

12   Exodus 25:22

13   Isaiah 66:1

14   Psalm 11:4; 20:6

15   Exodus 25:20; 37:9

16   1 Samuel 4:4; 2 Samuel 6:2; 2 Kings 19:15; Psalm 80:1; 99:1; Isaiah 37:16

17   1 Chronicles 28:2; Psalm 132:7,8

18   Exodus 34:28 Compare I Kings 8:21,9; Exodus 25:16,21,22;32:15,16

19   Psalm 97:2

20   1 John 3:4

21   Psalm 89:14

22   Isaiah 59:1,2

23   Leviticus 16:2,14,15

24   In the New Testament, Jesus the Messiah is spoken of as being our "propitiation" for sin (Romans 3:25). The original Greek word for "propitiation" has the same meaning as the word translated "mercy seat" in this context (see Hebrews 9:5). As our "mercy seat" Jesus interposes himself as the object of God's justice, but also provides his self-sacrifice as evidence of God's love.

25   ch.9:23

26   ch.8:5 RSV

27   Psalm 11:4; 18:6; 102:19; Isaiah 6:1; Revelation 11:19

28   Exodus 25:8-9,17-18,20,40 (emphasis added)

29   1 Chronicles 28-11,18-19 (emphasis added)

30   Deuteronomy 31:9-11,24-26

31   Exodus 16:32-34; Numbers 17:10

32   2 Chronicles 5:10; 1 Kings 8:9

33   Philo, *De Vita Mosis* 2:97; Josephus, *Antiquities of the Jews 3*:6.5.138; 8:4.1.104

Chapter 9 Why were the Canaanites Evicted?

1   1 Samuel 5; 6:1-12 LB

2   Faber, George Stanley *Origin of Pagan Idolatryy.* London: F. and C. Rivingtons, 1816, Vol. 3, pp.467,468

3   Deuteronomy 32:7,8

4   Unger, Merrill F. *Archaeology and the Old Testament* .Grand Rapids, Mi.: Zondervan Publishing House, pp.74,75. Note 3: *Manual of the Ancient History of the Near East,* Vol. II, p.219

5   Genesis 15:13-16

6   Henry M. Morris, expressing a Christian viewpoint, suggests: "Even the Canaanite children that were slain were possibly better off (many Christians believe that little children dying before the 'age of accountability' are safe eternally in Christ on the basis of His atoning death, which paid for their innate sin from Adam, and the lack of deliberate sin at their age), while the adults had descended to such depths of idolatry and depravity as to be irreclaimable." - *Science and the Bible.* Harpenden, Herts., UK: Nuprint Ltd, 1988,p.99

7   Exodus 23:28

8   Joshua 6:20

9   Garstang, John *The Foundations of Bible History;* Joshua, Judges. London: Constable, 1931, p.146

10 Joshua 6:24

11 2 Chronicles 20:15-22

12 Judges 7:16-18

13 Joshua 10:11-14

14 v.13

15 Matthew 7:2 GNB

16 1 Kings 8:42,43

17   Maxwell, Lawrence *God's Plan for our Planet*. Warburton, Victoria, Australia: Signs Publishing Co., undated, p.30

Chapter 10 Solomon's Fleet Mystery

1   Isdale, M.A. *The River Thames*. Thames, New Zealand: Thames Star Print, 1967. M.A. Isdale is a respected local historian.

2   Waddell, L.A. *Phoenician Origin of the Britons, Scots and Anglo-Saxons*. London: Williams and Norgate, Ltd 1924, p.220 (P.H.E. 2.146)

3   *Maha-Barata*, Indian epic of the Great Barats. Book 1, ch.94, sloka 3738

4   Waddell, p.1, quoting, Rig Veda Hymn

5   Ibid., pp.156,175

6   Ibid., pp.144-149. Haberman, Frederick *Tracing Our Ancestors*. Vancouver 2, BC: British Israel Association, 1962, pp.92-112

7   Waddell, pp. 385-393

8   Johnston, Thomas Crawford *Did the Phoenicians Discover America?* London: James Nisbet and Co., Ltd, 1913,pp.70-104,289. Compare with Jonathan Gray's *Dead Men's Secrets*. Adelaide, South Australia (P.O. Box 3370, Rundle Mall, South Australia), 1996, pp.77-81

9   Herodotus *History of Herodotus*. iv:42 Edited by George Rawlinson. London: Murray, 1875

10   Irwin, Constance *Fair Gods and Stone Faces*. London: W.H. Allen, 1964, pp.228,229,235

11   Strabo (H.L. Jones transl. i.3.2)

12   Bradley, Michael *The Black Discovery of America*. Toronto: Personal Library Publishers, 1981

13   Fell, Barry *America BC: Ancient Settlers in the New World*. London: Wildwood House Ltd , 1978, p.88

14   Bancroft, H.H. *Works of Bancroft*. San Francisco: A.L. Bancroft & Company, 1883, Vol. V, pp.64-65

15   Honore Pierre *In Quest of the White God*. London: Hutchinson & Co. Ltd 1963 (Transl. from the German by Oliver Coburn and Ursula Lehrburger), p.207. A more accurately fixed date for Solomon's reign is 971 to 931BC.

16   Hansen, L. Taylor *He Walked the Americas*. Amherst, Wisconsin: Amherst Press, 1963, p.209

17   Cited by Violet Cummings in *Has Anybody Really Seen Noah's Ark?* San Diego Ca.: Creation-Life Publishers, 1982, p.264

18   Bancroft *Nat. Races* iii.270

19   1 Kings 10:27

20   v.22 See also Ezekiel 27:12, which mentions tin.

21   Heeren *Historical Research*. Quoted by Johnston, pp.127,128

22   1 Kings 9:28; 10:11

23   Genesis 10:29,30

24   Josephus, Flavius *Antiquities of the Jews* vi.4

25   Johnston, p.131

26   Ibid., p.130

27   Ibid., p.132

28   Ezekiel 27:12

29   Jonah 1:3

30 2 Chronicles 20:36

31 Brugger, Karl *The Chronicle of Akakor*. New York: Delacorte Press, 1977, p.58

32 Fontaine *How the World Was Peopled*. Cited by Bancroft, Works of Bancroft: Vol. v, p.65

33 Johnston, p.248

Chapter 11 Into the Unknown

1   Pliny, v.37

2   Herodotus, iv.59

3   Strabo, i.493

4   Johnston, Thomas Crawford *Did the Phoenicians Discover America?* London: James Nisbet & Co., Ltd, 1913, p.151

5   *Encyclopaedia Brittanica, 1985*, art. "Polynesians"

6   Bancroft, H.H. *Works of Bancroft*. San Francisco: A.L. Bancroft & Company, 1883, Vol.1II, p.457

7   Johnston, p.69

8   Brasseur de Bourbourg *History of Native Civilisations*. Vol. I, p.17

9   Morley, Sylvanus Griswold *The Ancient Maya* Rev. by George W. Brainerd Stanford, Ca.: Stanford University Press, 3rd ed,1956, pp.77,78

10 Bancroft, Vol. V, p.91 note

11 Rivero and Tschudi *Peruvian Antiquities*. New York: George P. Putman & Co., 1857, pp.9,10

12 Johnston, p.31

13 1 Kings 6:7

14 v.22

15 Horne, Alexander *King Solomon's Temple in Masonic Tradition*. Wellingborough: Aquarian Press, 1972, p.219

16 Ibid.

17 Deuteronomy 27:5; Joshua 8:31

18 Ginzberg, Louis *The Legends of the Jews*. Philadelphia: Jewish Publication Society of America, 1909, vol.I, p.34 and vol. IV, p.166

19 Ibid.

20 Ibid., vol.1, p.34

21 Ibid.

22 Ibid.

23 Islamic traditions concerning the shamir are reported in Alexander Horn's book, *King Solomon's Temple in the Masonic Tradition*, p.165

24 1 Chronicles 28:2

25 ch.22:7-10

26 That is, 20 cubits by 20 cubits by 20 cubits, as stated in 1 Kings 6:20. The cubit used was the 20.6 Hebrew-Phoenician cubit. (See Chapter 2, Note 10)

27 2 Chronicles 3:8 informs us that 600 talents of gold were used for this purpose. Since an ancient talent weighed approximately 75 pounds, then 600 talents would total 45,000 pounds. See also 1 Kings 6:20,22,30

28 2 Chronicles 3:9

29   Bancroft, Vol. III, pp.452,453 See also Johnston, pp.258-260

30   2 Chronicles 9:23

Chapter 12 Jezebel, Seductress

1   2 Kings 9:33

2   Dollinger, Johann Joseph *The Gentile and the Jew in the Courts of the Temple of Christ;* translation of his "Heidenthum und Judenthum" by N. Darnell. London: Longmans, Roberts, and Green, 1862, Vol.1, pp.425-429

3   Ibid.

4   2 Kings 17:16,17

5   Hebrews 11:32-38

6   Jeremiah 11:11,12

7   Micah 4:9,10

8   Deuteronomy 28:36

9   2 Kings 24; 25; 2 Chronicles 36:5,6,9,10

10   2 Kings 25:8-10,13-16; Jeremiah 52:17-23

11   Jeremiah 52:19 JB

12   ch. 27:18-22 JB

13   Ezra 1:7-11

14   In the nineteenth century, a writer claiming inside knowledge made this statement: "Among the righteous still in Jerusalem, to whom had been made plain the divine purpose, were some who determined to place beyond the reach of ruthless hands the sacred ark containing the tables of stone on which had been traced the precepts of the Decalogue. This they did . With mourning and sadness they secreted the ark in a cave, where it was to be hidden from the people of Israel and Judah because of their sins, and was to be no more restored to them. That sacred ark is yet hidden. It has never been disturbed since it was secreted." (E. White, *Prophets and Kings,* p.453) "The precious record of the law was placed in the ark of the testament and is still there, safely hidden from the human family. But in God's appointed time He will bring forth these tables of stone to be a testimony to all the world against the disregard of His commandments." (Manuscript 122, 1901)

15   *Life of Jeremiah,* 11-19

16   *Paralipomena of Jeremiah* 3:5-19

17   *4 Baruch*

18   Jeremiah 25:8-11; 29:10-14

19   Isaiah 44:28

20   Ezra 1:2; 4:3; 5:13; 2 Chronicles 36:20-23

Chapter 13 The Prophecy and the Rabbis' Curse

1   Daniel 9:24

2   vv.25-27

3   Slotki, J.J. *Daniel, Ezra, and Nehemiah,* p.77a

4   Leviticus 25:8

5   *Lamentations,* Soncino ed. , p.65, note 3

6   *Yoma* 54at Soncino ed., p.254, note 6

7   *Nazir* 32b, Soncino ed., p.118, note 6

8   Leeser, Isaac *The Twenty-Four Books of the Holy Scriptures.*(1853), on Daniel 9:24,25; p.1243, notes 47,48

9   Daniel 9:25 RSV

10   Ezra 7:1,7,8

11   vv.11-26

12   ch.6:13-18

13   Bright, *A History of Israel* p.372

14   Around 520 BC, a governor "beyond the River" by the name of Tattenai (whose name is recorded on a cuneiform tablet) investigated the Jewish Temple rebuilding project which had now been under way for 16 years. As a result, he wrote asking Darius to check the Persian archives to see whether indeed the Jews had been given permission from Cyrus to rebuild the Temple.

      Darius responded with a thorough search and recovered a memo of Cyrus' decree (Ezra 6:1-5). He then issued the requested information (vv.6-12) in a new decree confirming that of Cyrus (ch.4:1-12).

      No mention was made by Cyrus, Darius or Tattenai of rebuilding the city itself, but only of rebuilding the Temple.

      While individual dwellings were erected here and there around the ruined capital, no evidence exists that the city proper was rebuilt as a result of Cyrus' and Darius' decrees. As late as 519 BC, Zechariah was still promised in a vision that plans would be laid for the reconstruction of the city.

15   Ezra 6:14 NASB

16   Ezra 7:24-26

17   ch.6:14

18   After Ezra arrived in Palestine in the 5th month of the 7th year of Artaxerxes's reign, he implemented the decree. Since, in old Jerusalem, the Jewish months were numbered from spring to spring, the 5th month fell between mid-July and mid-September on our calendar (depending on the timing of the Jewish New Year's day in a given year). The 5th month of the 7th year of Artaxerxes fell in late summer or early autumn of 457 BC The decree was implemented soon afterward.

19   Ezra 10:9

20   ch.9:9

21   Nehemiah 1:1-4

22   ch.2:5

23   v-7

24   v.8

25   ch.6:1,2

26   vv.15,16

Chapter 14 Messiah's Appearance Foretold

1   Daniel 9:25 NASB

2   Slotki, J.J. *Daniel, Ezra, and Nehemiah*, P.78

3   Matthew 3:2

4   Luke 3:15

5   Hengstenberg, E.W. *Christology of the Old Testament* (reprint; McDill AFB, FL, 1973) 2:824-825 von Lengerke, C *Das Buch Daniel* (1835) p.410.

The Septuagint (LXX) interprets the "weeks" in all instances in v.25-27 as "years" (ETE) and "times" (KAIROI).

6   *Testament of Levi* chaps. 14-16

7   Beckwith, Roger T. "Daniel 9 and the Date of the Messiah's Coming in Essene, Hellenistic, Pharisaic, Zealot and Early Christian Computation," *Revue de Qumran* 40 (1981): 521

8   Epiphanius, *Ilanarian,* "The Drugchest, a Refutation of all Heresies," Tertullian, "De praescriptione haereticorum"

9   Beckwith, p. 525

10   John 1:19,20

11   chs.6:14; 7:40

12   Matthew 3:2

13   John 1:29 GNB

14   Isaiah 53:7

15   John 19:7

16   Mark 1:15

17   John 1:41

18   Luke 4:18-22

19   ch.3:1,2

20   Bruce, F. F. T*he New Testament Documents. Are They Reliable?* London: Inter Varsity Press, 1974, p.90 (emphasis supplied)

21   McDowell, Josh *The Resurrection Factor*. San Bernadino Ca.: Here's Life Publishers, Inc., 1981, p.9

22   Tishri 1, Rosh Hashanah, was calculated to follow the new moon of either September or October. A king's "first year" was considered to be the interval between the day he began to reign and the arrival of the following autumn New Year's Day. Jewish clerks and those of some other eastern Mediterranean countries began to date documents by a new emperor's "first year" as soon as they heard the news that he had begun to reign.

      Tiberius' second year thus began in Palestine on New Year's Day in September or October, 14 AD even though he had been in power no more than about two months.

      Even today in some eastern lands, children are considered to be a year old in the year of birth and to be two years old on the subsequent New Year's Day - even if that New Year's Day comes only a day or two after a child is born. Interestingly, although many Palestinian coins from various years of Tiberius' reign have been found, archaeologists have not found one Palestinian coin dated to his "first year". This absence of "first-year" coins can be explained by the extreme shortness of Tiberius' first year.

23   On account of the fact that Jesus was baptized quite soon after John began to preach and that between Jesus' baptism and his first Passover (in the following March-April) he spent 6 weeks in the wilderness, gathered disciples here and there, and also attended a wedding feast, we may safely conclude that he was baptized within the year 27. The prophecy concerning 69 weeks (483 years) to the anointing of the Messiah at his baptism in 27 A.D was fulfilled with astonishing accuracy.

24   Galatians 4:4

25   Daniel 9:27

26   Malachi 3:1

27   **To "MAKE" a covenant?:**

      If Daniel had wished to state that a covenant would be **made**, why did he not use the ordinary Hebrew idiom for such a thought? Instead, he used a verb based on the Hebrew root **gaber** - which connotes "to prevail' (to persist, to predominate, to win, to have real success. See, for example, Genesis 7:18; 49:26; Exodus 17:11; Lamentations 1:16)

One "week" still future?

Many people think this 70th week of Daniel's prophecy is still future. But note the text itself: "Seventy weeks are determined upon thy people and upon thy holy city."(Daniel 9:24) The Hebrew verb translated **"are"** is **SINGULAR.** The importance of this being singular, is that the term **"seventy weeks"** is **PLURAL,** while the verb is singular. The singular verb indicates that the 70 weeks is to be treated as ONE UNIT. Therefore the last week of the 70 cannot be considered as separated from the rest and cannot be placed somewhere in the future.

Origin of the false theory concerning an evil man who will "make" a covenant with the Jews:

After the Protestant Reformation, the Roman Catholic Council of Trent was convened to counteract Protestantism. The Protestant charge that the Pope was Antichrist was upsetting the church.

Two Jesuits wrote books to counter the Protestant attack. One said that the "Antichrist" was in the past. The other Jesuit, named Ribera, said the "Antichrist" had not yet appeared, that he was still future. Ribera used Daniel's "70th week" to promote his view.

The Jesuit book by Ribera sat on the shelf for about two hundred years, until Rev Samuel Maitland, the librarian to the Archbishop of Canterbury, picked up a copy and read it. He subsequently wrote a commentary on the Bible - the first Protestant commentary to put the Antichrist in the future. It took about 400 years for Ribera's "Antichrist" theory to catch on. But today most Protestants have imbibed it.

28   Four annual Passovers occurred during Jesus' public ministry (between his baptism during September-October 27 A.D and his death during March-April 31 A.D) See John 2:13; 5:1; 6:4; 13:1

Jesus baptism to first Passover...	½ year
to 2nd Passover...	1 year
to 3rd Passover...	1 year
to 4th Passover...	1 year

TOTAL   3½ YEARS

29   Matthew 26:28 RSV

30   Daniel 9:27

31   Acts 2:38,39

32   ch-3:25,26 RSV

33   ch.6:7

34   Mark 16:20

35   Hebrews 2:3

36   Daniel 9:26

37   Isaiah 53:3-8 Concerning Isaiah chapter 53, the Jewish writer Abarbanel writes: 'Jonathan ben Uzziel interprets it in the Targum of the future Messiah; and this is also the opinion of our learned men in the majority of their midrashim. (cited by David L. Cooper, *Messiah: His Redemptive Career"*Los Angeles: David L. Cooper, 1935, p.90)

A similar confession comes from Alshech, another famous Jewish writer of the sixteenth century: "Our rabbis with one voice accept and affirm the opinion that the prophet (In Isaiah 52:13 to 53:12) is speaking of King Messiah." (Ibid., p.90)

The eminent commentator David Baron wrote that "the Messianic interpretation of this chapter was almost universally adopted by Jews, ...one of whom says... that in truth 'it was given of God as a description of the Messiah, whereby, when any should claim to be the Messiah, to judge by the resemblance to it whether he were the Messiah or no." (Ibid., p.90)

Many Jews would be amazed to find in their own prayer book this statement: "Our righteous Anointed [Messiah] is departed from us: horror hath seized us, and we have none to justify us. He hath borne the yoke of our iniquities, and our transgression, and is wounded because of our transgression. He beareth our sins on his shoulder, that he may find pardon for our iniquities. We shall be healed by his wound, at the time that the Eternal will create him (the Messiah) as a new creature. O bring him up from the circle of the earth. Raise him up from Seir, to assemble us the second time on Mount Lebanon, by the hand of Yinnon." *(Prayer Book for the Day of Atonement,* as translated by Dr. A. Th. Phillips, p.239. Bloch Publishing Company)

One might ask, Did the Jewish sages of old know all this concerning the Messiah when they wrote the prayer books? The Answer is obvious. **They must have known!** They are citing Isaiah chapter 53.

38   Daniel 9:26

39   Daniel 9:26 RSV This rendering of the passage is likewise seen in the marginal reading of the King James Version.

40   v.27 "Oblation" refers to offerings. Cereal, or grain offerings were frequently required, either along with or at least at the time when an animal was offered.They consisted sometimes of a baked loaf or of ingredients for making a loaf (see, for example, Leviticus 2:1-11; 6:14-19, etc.).

41   See Note 27

42   Maxwell, Mervyn *God Cares,* Vol. l. Mountain View, Ca.: Pacific Press, 1981

43   Ephesians 2:13-15 Compare Hebrews 9:8-10

Chapter 15 Born into Danger

1   John 1:1-3,14; Hebrews 1:1,2; Colossians 1:16

2   Matthew 4:8,9; John 12:31; 14:30; 16:11

3   John 3:16

4   Babylonian *Sanhedrin* 43a - "Eve of Passover", 95 - 110 A.D

5   Schaff, Philip *The Person of Christ.* New York: American Tract Society, 1913, p.133

6   Justin Martyr *Apology* 1.48 - c.150 A.D

7   John 1:48-53

8   1 Peter 2:22

9   1 John 3:5

10   John 8:46

11   Luke 23:22,41,47

12   Mark 14:55,56

13   Morton, John *Man, Science and God,* London: Collins, 1972, p.161

14   Whale, Dr. J.S. *Christian Doctrine.* London: Cambridge University Press, 1941, p.104

15   Thomas, W.H. Griffith *Christianity is Christ.* Chicago: Moody Press, 1965, p.11

16   Stott, John R.W. *Basic Christianity.* Downers Grove: Inter-Varsity Press, 1971, p.36

17   Ramm, Bernard *Protestant Christian Evidences.* Chicago: Moody Press, 1957, p.169

18   Schaff *History of the Christian Church.* Grand Rapids: William B. Eerdmans Publishing Co., 1910 Reprinted from original, 1962, p.110

19   Wells, H.G. *Outline of History.* Garden City: Garden City Publishing Co., 1931, pp. 535,536

20   Ballard, Frank *The Miracles of Unbelief.* Edinburgh: T & T Clark, 1908, p.251

21   Al-Imran, v.45

22   Mead, Frank (ed.) *The Encyclopedia of Religious Quotations,.* Westwood: Fleming H. Revell, undated, p.57

23   Latourette, Kenneth Scott *American Historical Review.* LIV, January 1949, p.272

24   Latourette *A History of Christianity.* New York: Harper & Row, 1953, p.44

25   McDowell, Josh *Evidence That Demands a Verdict* - Vol. I. San Bernardino, Ca.: Here's Life Publishers Inc., 1986, p.129

26   John 8:12

27   Mark 13.31

28   John 5:21

29   v.27

30   ch. 3:36

31   ch. 10: 30

32   ch. 3: 16, 34, 35

33   ch.17:5

34   ch. 8: 58 In the encounter during which Jesus declared, "Before Abraham was, I AM", he had warned, "I said therefore unto you, that ye shall die in your sins: for if ye believe not that I AM, ye shall die in your sins." (John 8:24) (The word "he" is supplied in the King James Version.) It is at this point that many today need to pause and do some serious thinking . The self chosen designation of himself as the I AM is not an accident nor incidental. He is the I AM, the self-existent One; and the I AM, the ever-existent One. Moffatt well translates this sacred name simply as the Eternal.

35   Exodus 3:14

36   Luke 22:69

37   John 5:17,18

38   ch.5:23; 10:30,38

39   Matthew 4:7; John 10:33; 20:28,29

40   John 5:27-29

41   Lewis, C.S. *Mere Christianity.* New York: The Macmillan Company, 1952, pp.40,41

42   Ibid.

43   Schaff *The Person of Christ.* New York: American Tract Society, 1913, pp.94,95

44   Schaff *History of the Christian Church,* 8 vols. Grand Rapids: William B. Eerdmans Publishing Co., 1910 Reprinted from original, 1962, p.109

45   Lecky, William E. *History of European Morals from Augustus to Charlemagne.* New York: D Appleton & Co., 1903, p.8

46   Isaiah 49:7; 53:3; Daniel 9:26

47   Matthew 7:13.14

Chapter 16 "His Blood Be On Us"

1   John 1:11

2   ch.19:14,15

3   Matthew 27:25

4   This tradition was passed down over the centuries.

5   Mark 15:22

6   v.25 (the "third hour" of day time)

Chapter 17 A Planned Time to Die

1   Daniel 11:20

2   v.21

3   v.22

4   ch.9:25-27

5   Tacitus, Annals, lib. xv. cap.44

6   Luke 3:1; 23:24

7   John7:30

8   ch.2:4

9   ch.7:6

10   Matthew 26:18

11   John 17:1; Matthew 26:45

12   Romans 5:6

13   Exodus 12:3

14   v.6

15   Abrabanal, Don Isaac Commentary on the book of Daniel, entitled *The Wells of Salvation,* 1497

16   *Shemot Rabbah* 15:12

17   *Peshachim* x

18   Luke 23:52,53

19   1 Corinthians 11:24

20   Revelation 2:17

21   Matthew 26:2 RSV

22   Mark 14:1,2

23   Babylonia *Sanhedrin* 43a - "Eve of Passover."

24   Leviticus 23:5

25   Josephus, Flavius. *Antiquities of the Jews,* Bk. 14, ch.4, sect.3

26   Matthew 27:45-50

27   Gray, Jonathan private files

28   Clarke's *Commentary*

29   John 20:31

Chapter 18 The Woman Who Ate Her Son

1   *Tractate Yoma* 39b

2   Isaiah 1:18

3   Daniel 9:26

4   Matthew 23:38

5   ch.24:1,2

6   Matthew 23:36; 24:34

7   ch. 24:15

8   Matthew 24:15 Compare Daniel 9:26,27

9   Matthew 24; Mark 13; Luke 21

10   Deuteronomy 32:18-21; Isaiah 65:1-5

11   Acts 7; 9:1-18; 13:46

12   ch. 17:6

13   Colossians 1:23

14   L. Taylor Hansen *He Walked the Americas.* Amherst ,Wisconsin: Amherst Press, 1963, pp.14-21,203,205,208

15   Jesus' discourse was given in reply to a double-barreled question concerning both the destruction of Jerusalem and the end of the age. There is good reason to believe that his reply is applicable to both events and that the same signs apply to the latter days, in which history is to be repeated.

16   Matthew 24:15-19; Luke 21:20-24

17   Josephus, Flavius *Wars of the Jews,* Bk.2, ch.19, sect.7

18   Matthew 24:20

19   vv.17,18

20   v.21; Luke 21:22-24

21   Leviticus 26:25

22   Josephus, Bk. 5 ch.13 (an amalgam of excerpts from several sections)

23   Deuteronomy 28:54

24   Josephus, Bk. 5, ch.10; Bk. 6, Ch.3 (an amalgam of excerpts from several sections)

25   Deuteronomy 28:49-57; Leviticus 26:29

26   Josephus Bk.6, ch.3

27   Deuteronomy 28:49,50 Compare Daniel 8:23

Chapter 19 The End Approaches

1   Milman, *The History of the Jews* Book 13

2   Mark 13:1,2

3   Josephus, Flavius *Jewish War* 6. pp.236-253; translation by H. St. J. Thackeray in Loeb Classical Library

4   Ibid.

5   Matthew 24:34; Mark 13:30; Luke 21:32; 23:28; Matthew 23:32-38

6   Luke 21:24

7   Deal, Colin *Armageddon and the 21st Century* . North Carolina: Colin Deal, 1988, p.47

8   Josephus *Wars of the Jews* 6:4.5

9   Ibid., 6: 5.1

10   Ibid., 5:10:5

11   Genesis 49:10; Micah 5:1-3; Haggai 2:7-9; Daniel 9:25-27

*JACOB'S PROPHECY (Gen-49:10): The essence of this prophecy is that the Scepter of authority and tribal independence shall not depart from Judah, nor a lawgiver from between his feet, until Shiloh (that is, the "Man of Peace") come - and to him will be the obedience (the submission, the homage) of the peoples.

To put it another way, government functions shall not pass from the tribe of Judah, it shall not cease from being a state, until Shiloh comes. HE SHALL APPEAR BEFORE the Jewish state shall be utterly destroyed.

That Shiloh is the coming Messiah was recognised by almost all Jewish expositors.
 - The Targums, or Chaldee Paraphrasis of Jerusalem, renders this prophecy "until the time when King Messiah shall come."(E.C. Ettmann, *Messianic Evidences,* Melbourne, Australia: Presbyterian Women's Missionary Union, undated, p.18)

-Onkelos (60 BC): "until Messiah comes, whose is the kingdom.'"

-The Talmud: "Shiloh is reckoned among the names of Messiah."

 - The Targum Pseudo Jonathan on Gen-49:lla states: "How noble is the King, Messiah, who is going to rise from the house of Judah."
Judah never lost its "tribal staff" or national identity during the 70 year captivity in Babylon. It still possessed its own lawgivers or judges even while in exile (Ezra 1:5,8).

Two signs to occur soon after Messiah's coming would be

1- removal of Judah's scepter or identity

2- suppression of her judicial power.

The first stage of the scepter's removal occurred when Herod the Great, a foreigner, took the throne.   Some time later, the Sanhedrin lost the power to pass the death sentence.
 -The Talmud itself admits that "a little more than forty years before the destruction of the Temple, the power of pronouncing capital sentences was taken away from the Jews." (*Talmud*, Jerusalem, Sanhedrin, fol.24, recto.)

 - Rabbi Rachmon says: "When the Sanhedrin found themselves deprived of their right over life and death, a general consternation took possession of them; they covered their heads with ashes, and their bodies with sackcloth, exclaiming: 'Woe unto us, for the scepter has departed from Judah, and the Messiah has not come!'"
Finally, in 70 AD, Judah lost her autonomy and national life; the scepter of ecclesiastical sway departed from Judah, and the Jewish people were banished from the Holy Land as a result of the wars of 70 and 135 AD For nearly 2,000 years they became a scattered people.

According to this prophecy, the Messiah would have to come before the destruction of the Temple and the final exile of the Jews.

Did he, and had they somehow missed him?

*MICAH'S PROPHECY (MICAH 5:1-3)
It was known that Messiah was to come out of King David's house. In Micah's time the monarchy flourished in the capital city, Jerusalem, so it would be natural to expect Messiah to be born there.

But, contrary to such expectation, Micah said he would be born in tiny Bethlehem, a village so insignificant that it counted almost for nothing in Judah.

The prophet thus foresaw the fallen condition of the Davidic dynasty - no longer able to perform government functions but retired to private life living in obscurity.

Since the Davidic dynasty did not lose its power until the Babylonian siege (606-586 BC), we should expect the Messiah to appear after this date.
Micah predicts three events:
 1 - Verse 1 foretells the Roman siege and collapse of the Jewish nation (which occurred in 70 AD

 2 - Verse 2 foretells the birth of Messiah in Bethlehem of Judah.

 3 - Verse 3 foretells the nation's age-long dispersion, declaring that as a consequence of Messiah's birth, God would give up the nation of Judah until the end time.
The word "therefore" which introduces verse 3 shows that Messiah's birth (v.2) precedes God's rejection of the nation (v.3), and that the siege (v.1), fulfilled in the Roman occupation of 70 A.D" was connected with this.

577

To put it another way, Micah's prediction of the Roman siege of Palestine and the collapse of Judah (v.1) is in a most intimate manner connected with the birth of Messiah (v.2). And Judah's age-long dispersion (v.3) is the outgrowth of these two events.

Therefore, of necessity, Messiah will be born prior to the extinction of the Jewish national life in 70 AD He will be born in Bethlehem. (From 135 A.D, the Jews were not permitted to live in Palestine, nor to own any property there.)

Interestingly, the ancient Jews accepted this as a messianic prophecy.
- The Chaldean paraphrase of verse 2 reads: "from thee Messiah shall go out before me."

- In the Talmud, verse 3 is applied to the fact that the Messiah was not to come until the hostile kingdom had spread over the whole world (Yoma 10a) or else over the whole land of Israel (Sanh.98b)

- Similarly, Micah 7:6 is applied to the messianic times in Sanh.97a and in Sotah 49b; also in Midr. on Cant.11,13.

*HAGGAI'S PROPHECY (HAGGAI 2:9)

Messiah will appear while the Second Temple is standing. "I will shake all nations, and the desire of all nations shall come; and the glory of this latter house (temple) shall be greater than of the former, saith the Lord of hosts." He is the One for whom all nations are longing.

The "latter house" is the Second Temple, which will be built to replace the former Temple destroyed by the Babylonians.

The Second Temple was destined to stand until 70 AD. So Messiah must come before this date.

*DANIEL'S PROPHECY (DANIEL 9:25-27)

Daniel is more specific: he predicts the precise year of Messiah's appearance, and a succession of events which will culminate in the destruction of Jerusalem and the Temple.

Messiah, then, must come before the collapse of the Hebrew nation and the dispersion of its people throughout the world

Either he came prior to that time, or the Hebrew Scriptures have been broken. One cannot believe the latter. All evidence shows that God fulfills His word literally.

12 *Talmud* Bab., Sanhedrin, Chap.4, fol.37, recto. This statement was made by the Sanhedrin when they found themselves deprived of their right over life and death, a few years before the destruction of the Temple.

13 Genesis 5:29

14 ch.10:25

15 Matthew 1:21

16 Luke 1:31

17 For example, in Isaiah 12:2 we read: "Behold, God is my salvation (yeshu'ah)." For a discussion on this subject, see *The 490 Year Prophecy,* by S. Howard SAN Enterprises Inc., PO Box 623,Thorsby, AL 35171, USA Also Arthur E. Glass, *Yeshua in the Tenach.* Cincinnati, Ohio: Messianic Literature Outreach, P.O. Box 37062

18 Habakkuk 3:13

19 *Prayer Book for the New Year.* Translated by Dr. A. Th. Phillips, revised and enlarged, p.100 Hebrew Publishing Company

20 Isaiah chs. 48-53; Daniel 9:25,26; Psalm 110:1,2

21 Cooper, David L. *Messiah: His Redemptive Career* Los Angeles: David L. Cooper, 1935, p.74

22 Anstey, Martin *The Romance of Bible Chronology.* London: Marshall Brothers Ltd, 1913, p.283

23   Newton, Sir Isaac *Chronology of Ancient Kingdoms Amended,* p.357

24   Davidson, D and Aldersmith, H. *The Great Pyramid: Its Divine Message* Vol. I London: Williams and Norgate, Ltd, 1936, pp.348-350

25   Leviticus 26:25

26   Daniel 9:27

27   Luke 19:43,44 paraphrased

28   Matthew 23:38

29   ch.24:15; Daniel 9:26,27

30   Talmud Sanhedrin 97-b, translated in the Babylonian Talmud ed. by Isidore Epstein. 35 vol. London: The Soncino Press Ltd, 1935-1952, p.659. This statement from the Talmud says: "The Targum of the Prophets was composed by Jonathan ben Uzziel ... He further sought to reveal by a targum (the inner meaning) of the Hagiographa, but a Bath Kol went forth and said, Enough! What was the reason? - Because the date of the Messiah is foretold in it." (*Megillah* 3a, pp.9,10 Soncino Press. Footnote 2 on p.10 says: "The reference is probably to the Book of Daniel.")

31   Josephus, Flavius *Antiquities of the Jews* Vol. 2, Bk. 10, ch.11, sect.7

Chapter 20 Holocaust

1   Micah 3:12; Jeremiah 26:18

2   Porter, Josias Leslie *The Giant Cities of Bashan.* London: T. Nelson and Sons, 1865, p.19

3   Deuteronomy 28:62

4   v.68

5   Josephus. Flavius *Wars of the Jews.* VI, 8, 9

6   Leviticus 26:33; Deuteronomy 28:25

7   Leviticus 26:33,36,37,39; Deuteronomy 32:24; 28:66,67

8   Hosea 9:17

9   Deuteronomy 28:65

10   Michelson, Arthur U. *Jesus Before the Bar,* preface

11   Deuteronomy 28:37; Jeremiah24:9

12   Leviticus 26:44; Jeremiah 46:28

13   Luke 21:24 "Gentiles"= "nations" (Compare Matthew 6:32 with Luke 12:30)

14   Deuteronomy 28:12

15   Leviticus 26:8

Chapter 21 The Search

1   Luke 21:24

2   2 Chronicles 35:3

3   2 Kings 25:13-15

4   v.1

5   2 Chronicles 26:15

6   Genesis 22:2; 2 Chronicles 3:1

7   John 19:17,20; Hebrews 13:12

8   Matthew 27:33; Mark 15:22; Luke 23:33; John 19:17

9   Quintillian, *Declarations*

10   John 19:17-20

11   Luke 23:38

12   Matthew 27:35-37

13   Linguistic expert Larry A. Hartman notes: "The word ' epi' should always be translated as 'on'; however this doesn't mean that it will always take a physical meaning as an object being physically placed 'on' something or someone. It can also be used in the figurative sense, an example of which occurs in Acts 1:26, 'and the lot fell on (epi) Matthias.' In this passage it is clear that nothing physically fell on Matthias, but that it is used figuratively to indicate that Matthias picked the unique lot. This is how 'epi' is used in Mark, Luke, and John, in the figurative sense, not the physical sense. In these passages the point which the author intends to make is the indication of which person was accused, not the physical location of the accusation." Personal letter to Jonathan Gray.The preposition "epi" may take either Genitive, Dative, or Accusative case in the noun following it. In John, it is the Genitive, and grammarians tell us that the word can then legitimately be translated "over" rather than "on".

Chapter 22 Gruesome Discovery

1   Acts 7: 57,58

2   Mark 15:29; Matthew 27:39

Chapter 23 The Link

1   John 19:41,42

2   Gray, Jonathan, *Update International*. Newsletter No 8, November 1994 to January 1995, p,3

3   Gray, private files

4   John 19:42

5   v.41

6   Matthew 27:60

7   v.57

8   John 20:5. The doorway, now enlarged was originally lower, requiring that one stoop in order to enter.

9   Luke 24:1-4

10   John 19:41

11   Matthew 27:60

12   John 19:41

13   Isaiah 53:9-11 - "And he made his grave with the wicked, and with the rich in his death; because he had done no violence, neither was any deceit in his mouth. Yet it pleased the Lord to bruise him; he hath put him to grief: when thou shalt make his soul an offering for sin, he shall see his seed, he shall prolong his days, and the pleasure of the Lord shall prosper in his hand. He shall see of the travail of his soul, and shall be satisfied: by his knowledge shall my righteous servant justify many; for he shall bear their iniquities."

This text specifically refers to what Jesus Christ would accomplish on earth and where **he would be buried.**

My dear friend and colleague Ron Wyatt comments:

"He was buried in a rich man's tomb, but what about His grave being "with the wicked"? Approximately 50 feet from the Garden Tomb to the left as you face the tomb, is located a large complex of tombs that belonged to wealthy Jews. One of these is hewn to the exact dimensions of the Holy and Most Holy chambers of Solomon's temple. The royal Egyptian cubit is used (20.6 inch = cubit). There was a brass box recessed into the floor that now, we were told, has been stolen, and the chamber cut into the stone floor left behind is exactly the dimensions of the table of Shewbread (20.6 inches wide by 41.2 inches long, or one cubit by two cubits!) The burial crypt in this chamber is of the size and position of the Most Holy place! This would imply that the owners and users of this tomb considered themselves equal to God. How much more wicked could one get - to be buried only a few feet from this blasphemous tomb is certainly being "with the wicked".

This complex of tombs to the north west of Joseph's (Christ's) tomb were hewn into the face of the dry moat that was cut across the ridge of Mount Moriah. This was done to make the north wall of Jerusalem less vulnerable to attack. The tombs were hewn in a north-west to south-east progression. It is obvious that these were the tombs of the wealthy and priestly class. They were hewn during the first temple period and used until the Babylonian captivity. During the captivity, the portable ossuary was introduced and used, as revealed in the ancient Jewish records.

These stone boxes were of a size to contain the bones of one individual and were designed to make it possible for the bones of the Jews to be transported back to Jerusalem and interred in the family tomb. The families who owned these tombs began using them upon their return from the captivity and they were used through the Persian and Greek periods. In some cases, the tomb entrances were sealed with slabs of stone bearing Greek inscriptions and some researchers present this as proof that the tombs date from the Greek period This view fails to take into consideration that such a tomb, and such a choice location was a matter of pride for the family, and they, of course, would have their inscriptions updated to the most popular and widest read language as newer members would die and be interred there.

The Garden Tomb is located in the next available position, immediately south east of these first temple period tomb complexes. There would be no need for the old, rich and priestly families to hew other tombs. No Jew wished to be buried anywhere but in their ancestors' tomb. Foreign kings had their tombs hewn near the highest points around the city; as higher indicated greater importance. The Garden Tomb location is the obvious first choice for the burial of "the new-rich" of Christ's time. And Joseph of Arimathea was just such a person. Bible scholars and believers have no doubt that he had his tomb hewn by Divine Providence just at the right time to allow for the fulfillment of the Isaiah prophecy about Christ's burial." - *Wyatt Archaeological Research Newsletter No. 4* , July 1993, p.16 .Nashville, TN.

14   Matthew 27:60

15   vv.62-66

16   vv.60,66

17   ch.28:2

Chapter 24 "The Dead Man's Alive"

1   Albright, William F. *Recent Discoveries in Bible Lands.* New York: Funk and Wagnalls, 1955, p, 136. See also, Albright in an interview for *Christianity Today,* 18 Jan. 1963; Albright *From Stone Age to Christianity.* Baltimore: Johns Hopkins Press, 1946, p.23

2   Acts 26:26

3   ch.4:20

Chapter 25 Who Stole the Body?

1   Luke 23:56;24:1

2   Matthew 27:63-66

3   ch.28:2-8

4   Josephus, Flavius *Antiquities of the Jews,* Vol. 3, Bk.18, ch.3, sect.3

The full text says: "Now there was about this time Jesus, a wise man, if it be lawful to call him a man; for he was a doer of wonderful works, a teacher of such men as receive the truth with pleasure. He drew over to him both many of the Jews, and many of the Gentiles. He was (the) Christ. And when Pilate, at the suggestion of the principal men among us had condemned him to the Cross, those that loved him at the first did not forsake him; for he appeared to them alive again the third day; as the divine prophets had foretold these and ten thousand other wonderful things concerning him. And the tribe of Christians, so named from him, are not extinct to this day."

5   Scaliger, Joseph In the Prolegomea to *De Emendations Temporum*, p.17

6   Mark 15:45-47

7   v.43; Luke 23:50

8   McDowell, Josh *Evidence That Demands a Verdict.* San Bernadino, Ca.: Here's Life Publishers, Inc., 1986, pp.212,213

9   Isaiah 53:7-11

10   Matthew 27:62-66

11   ch.28:12-15

Chapter 26 Did His Friends Steal the Body?

1   Matthew 28:15

2   Acts 18:2

3   This is in the Cambridge library.

4   Luke 24:21,22; Mark 16:14

5   John 21:3

Chapter 27 The Witnesses

1   Acts 2:24-31

2   v.32

3   Matthew 28:5-10, 16-17; Luke 24:36-48; John 20:19-29; 21:4-13; 1 Corinthians 15:6

4   Acts 1:3 (The book of Acts is attributed to Luke.)

5   Matthew 28:17; Luke 24:10,11

6   Luke 24:13-31

7   Cited by Wilbur M Smith, in article, "Twentieth Century Scientists and the Resurrection of Christ", *Christianity Today*, April 15, 1957

8   Gray, Jonathan, private files

Chapter 28 Legal Opinion

I   Smith, Wilbur M.A. *A Great Certainty in This Hour of World Crises.* Wheaton: Van Kampen Press, 1951,p.14

2   Smith, Wilbur M. *Therefore Stand: Christian Apologetics.* Grand Rapids: Baker Book House, 1965, pp..425,426

3   Ibid., pp.425,584

4   Greenleaf, Simon *Testimony of the Evangelists, Examined by the Rules of Evidence Administered in Courts of Justice.* Grand Rapids: Baker Book House, 1965, pp.28-30 (reprinted from 1847 edition)

5   Green, Michael *Man Alive.* Downers Grove: Inter-Varsity Press, 1968, pp.53,54

6   Psalm 16:10; Hosea 6:2

7   Romans 1:4; Acts 13:30

8   Romans 1:4; John 10:17,18

9   1 Corinthians 15:14

10   Acts 17:31

11   1 Thessalonians 4:14,16-18

12   Based on Matthew 28:2-4. See also Ellen White's *Desire of Ages* . Silver Springs, Md.: Better Living Publications, 1990, pp. 456, 457. The curator of the religious book section of the Library of Congress in Washington, DC, the largest library in the world, declared: "The book, 'Desire of Ages' by Ellen G. White, is the most beautifully written book on the life of Christ in the Library of Congress."

Chapter 29 Joseph - A Marked Man

1   Acts 4:19,20, NEB

2   v.12, NEB

3   Herodotus, 3.115

4   Creasy, Sir Edward *History of England*

5   Siculus, Diodorus, Roman historian, born in Sicily, first century BC Author of *Historical Library* in 40 books, of which only volumes 1 - 5, and 11 - 20, are extant

6   Camden, William *Brittania* Vol. 1, first published in 1586; republished 1808

7   Strabo *Geography*, in 17 volumes, describing Europe, Asia, Egypt and Libya

8   St. Augustine *Epistolae ad Gregorium Papam*, 600 A.D

9   Gildas *De Exidio Brittanniae, a history of Britain from earliest times*

10   Tertullian (full name: Quintus Septimus Florens Tertullianus), of Carthage 155 - 222 A.D *Tertullian Defensor Fidei* (page 179 of the printed edition)

11   Eedle, Arthur and Rosalind *The Prophetic Telegraph*. Alford, Lincs., England, No.76 (December 1995), p.5

12   Archbishop Ussher, Roman Catholic Archbishop of Armagh in Northern Ireland *Brittannicarum Ecclesiarum Antiquitates*. Wrote a Scheme of Biblical Chronology, which eventually found its way into the margins of almost all Authorised Version Bibles

13   Eedle, p.5

14   Maelgwyn of Llandaff *Historia de Rebus Britannicis*, c.450 A.D

15   Vergil, Polydor *Anglicae Historiae Libri*, Liber II (i.e. Vol.2)

16   *Digest*, xlviii.24, 'De cadav. punit'

17   Matthew 27:57

18   *Onomasticon,* 225.12

19   Mistral, Frederic *Mireio*

20   Maurus, Rabanus *Acts of Magdalen*. The author (776 - 856 A.D) was a Frankish theologian, scholar and teacher and Archbishop of Mayence (Mainz). The manuscript used to be in the Magdalen College Library at Oxford, but is now housed in the Bodleian Library.

21   Isidore *Historia*. The author was Archbishop of Seville from 600 to 636 A.D

22   Baronius *Ecclesiastical Annals*. Cardinal Baronius, an eminent historian of the Roman Catholic church, became Curator of the Vatican Library in 1597.

23   Capgrave, John *De Sancto Joseph ab Aramathea* This English chronicler and hagiologist, an Augustinian hermit, lived most of his life in friary at King's Lynn, Norfolk. The manuscript he quoted was translated from the Latin.

Chapter 30 The Obstructive Bishop

No references or notes

Chapter 31 Secret Chamber

1   Gray, Jonathan *The Ark Conspiracy*. Adelaide, South Australia: P.O. Box 3370, Rundle Mall 5000, 1996, pp.146-151

2   Job 26:9

3   Proverbs 25:2

4   1 Samuel 22:10

5   Exodus 25:17-21

Chapter 32 "There's Nothing Down There"

1   Genesis 3:24

Chapter 33 The "Man" Who Knew

No references or notes

Chapter 34 No Turning Back

1   John 10:15-18

Chapter 35 The Execution Begins

1   Matthew 27:34

2   Luke 23:34

3   Mark 15:25

4   From a medical doctor's description printed in *South East Christian Witness*. Mount Gambier, South Australia: April 1996

5   Mark 15:24

6   Luke 23:35

7   Matthew 27:43

8   Psalm 22:7,8

Chapter 36 Two Thieves

1   Luke 23:41

2   Matthew 5:3

3   Luke 23:43

4   Isaiah 53:12

5   John 19:26

6   v.27

Chapter 37 Act of Love

1   Pines, Shlomo, Professor of Philosophy at Hebrew University, Jerusalem ; David Flusser, professor at Hebrew University, New York Times press release, Feb.12, 1972, carried by *Palm Beach Post-Times,* Feb.13, 1972, "CHRIST DOCUMENTATION: Israeli Scholars Find Ancient Document They Feel Confirms the Existence of Jesus."

2   Zechariah 3:1,2; Job 1:6-12; 2:1-7; Jude 9; Revelation 20:7,8

3   John 3:13; 6:33,41; Micah 5:2; John 17:5; 8:58

4   Isaiah 14:12-17; Revelation 12:9-12; Luke 10:18

5   John 8:44

6   Daniel 6:8

7   Romans 3:31; Matthew 5:17,18; James 2:10-12

8   Philippians 2:5-8

9   John 1:1-3,14; Hebrews 1:2; Colossians 1:16

10   Vandeman, George E. *The Cry of a Lonely Planet.* Mountain View, Ca..: Pacific Press Publishing Association, 1983, pp.255,256

Chapter 38 Black Noon

1   Luke 23:44

2   Bruce, F.F. *The New Testament Documents: Are They Reliable?* 5th revised ed. Downers Grove, Ill.: Inter Varsity Press, 1972, p.113

3   Elgin Moyer, *Who Was Who in Church History.* Chicago: Moody Press, 1968, IIB, sect. 256 B16, p.1165

4   Felix Jacoby, *Die Fragmente der Griechischen Historiker.* Berlin: Wiedmann, 1923,IIB, sect.257 fl6, c.p.1165

5   Daniel 9:26, margin (according to some Bible translations)

6   Matthew 27:46

7   John 17:5;1:2

8   Matthew 27:48; John 19:29,30

9   Vandeman, George E. *The Cry of a Lonely Planet.* Mountain View, California: Pacific Press Publishing Association, 1983, p.20

Chapter 39 Startling Predictions

1   Genesis 22:18

2   ch.26:4; 17:19

3   ch.28:13,14

4   ch.49:8-11

5   Isaiah 11:1,10

6   Jeremiah 23:5,6; 2 Samuel ch.7

7   Micah 5:2

8   See note II for Chapter 19

9   Haggai 2:9

10   Malachi 3:1

11   Psalm 41:9; Zechariah 11:12,13

12   Psalm 22:16

13   "Hanging on a gibbet" was later permitted, not as a death penalty, but rather as a
      degrading punishment after death for idolaters and blasphemers who already had been
      stoned to death.

14   Psalm 22:18

15   John 19:23.24

16   Justin Martyr *Apology* 1.48

17   Psalm 34:20. Not one bone of the Passover lamb (which was a symbol of the coming
      Messiah) was to be broken - Exodus 12:43,46; Numbers 9:12.

18   John 19:33

19   Isaiah 53:9 For the Hebrew word in this sense, or "after death", see Leviticus 11:31; 1
      Kings 13:31; Esther 2:7, where it is before the Infinitive.

20   Stoner, Peter W. *Science Speaks*. Chicago: Moody Press, 1963, pp.100-107

21   Stoner, in the Foreword to his book (No.20)

22   2 Timothy 1:12 ML

Chapter 40 Surprise Under Skull Hill

1   Matthew 27:51

2   John 19:30

3   1 Peter 1:19,20; Revelation 13:8

4   Luke 23:46

5   Matthew 27:51

6   John 19:32,33

7   vv.34-37

8   Matthew 27:50

9   Kiehl, Erich H. *The Passion of our Lord*, Baker Book House, 1990, p.146

10   Sava, A.F. "The Wound in the Side of Christ," *Catholic Biblical Quarterly* 19 (1957): 346

11   Kiehl, pp. 146,147

12   Davis, C. Truman "The Crucifixion of Jesus," *Arizona Medicine,* pp.185,186

13   Cook, Frederick Charles (ed.) *Commentary on the Holy Bible.*London: John Murray,
      1878, pp..349,350

14   Luke 22:44

15   Mark 4:22

16   Matthew 10:26

17   Psalm 85:11

18   Genesis 22:2 NIV

19   v.14 NIV The King James Version says, 'IN the mount of the Lord it shall be seen."

      When Ron Wyatt went searching for the original Mount Sinai (Horeb) he extracted a clue
      from Deuteronomy 1:6- "The Lord spake unto us in Horeb, saying, Ye have dwelt long
      enough IN this mount." The description indicates that the people were "in" a mountain
      range - protected within its borders. When Wyatt went searching for a mountain in the
      correct region which would fit this description, there was only one candidate, in his
      opinion - Jebel el Lawz. An aerial map showed this mountain to be in an almost
      semi-circular shape, enclosing an area of 5,000 acres - certainly quite large enough to
      accommodate several million people and their herds. Jebel el Lawz was the perfect
      candidate. On-site exploration confirmed that it still contained the remains of

structures described in the biblical account. A crucial clue to finding the site had been the expression "IN this mount."

Interestingly, in referring to Mount Moriah, where Jesus was crucified, the King James rendering of Genesis 22:14 uses the same word "IN". Could one infer from this passage that we here have a prophecy stating that "IN the mount" known as Moriah the blood of the Messiah's sacrifice "shall be seen"? As we know, the find was made inside the mountain.

20   John 8:56

21   Deuteronomy 16:5-7

22   John 19:20; Hebrews 13:11-13

23   Hebrews 10:20

24   ch.13:20

25   Exodus 18:5; 19:18

26   Genesis 22:14

27   Psalm 85:10

28   2 Corinthians 5:21

Chapter 41 Questions

1   Genesis 4:10,11 *Modern Language* (emphasis added)

2   Hebrews 12:24 *Modern Language*

3   ch.11:4

4   Bullinger, E.W. *Number in Scripture*. Grand Rapids, Mi.: Kregel Publications, 1967, p.60

5   Daniel 9:24

6   Leviticus 16:21 Compare Exodus 34:7

7   John 1:29

8   Hebrews 9:26

9   Isaiah 53:6

10   2 Corinthians 5:19 Compare Colossians 1:20,22: Ephesians 2:16; Hebrews 2:17

11   Isaiah 53:11

12   Jeremiah 23:6

13   Romans 5:17-21

14   One interpretation of this statement (held since the days of the early Church Fathers) has applied it to the anointing of Jesus Christ as the Messiah. This interpretation, however, runs contrary to the way **qodesh qadashim** ("holy of holies", "most holy") is used in the Old Testament. Outside of Daniel this phrase occurs more than 40 times in the O.T. In every instance it refers to the sanctuary or something connected with it. (The only possible exception is 1 Chronicles 23:13, but this is debatable. It is most likely that even in this passage the expression refers to the sanctuary as well.)

15   At its dedication, the tabernacle and all that it contained was sprinkled with anointing oil **and** blood (Leviticus 8:10,11,30; Hebrews 9:18-21). Oil is symbolic of the Holy Spirit. At his baptism Jesus was anointed with the Holy Spirit. At his death the Anointed One anointed the Mercy Seat with his blood.

587

Chapter 42 Vicious Men

1   My gratitude to Philip Adams, Australian newspaper columnist, for this excellent insight

2   1 Corinthians 1:26-29

3   Jeremiah 16:19-21

4   White, E. MB 33, 1896. Quoted in *Sons and Daughters of God* Washington, DC: Review and Herald Publishing Association, 1983, p.261

Chapter 43 The Ambush

No references or notes.

Chapter 44 On a Knife Edge

1   On his fourth entry into the cavern, Ron Wyatt met four "young men" in there. Apparently they were "guarding" the sacred Ark. The back wall was aglow. The cave had been cleaned up.

   Ron had told me of this experience quite some time ago, and although there was no longer any doubt in my mind that this experience occurred, I had decided not to tell anyone. Not until January 3, 1997, when I received a phone call from a friend in Queensland, Vada Kum Yuen. Her husband Darryl had come across a statement in a very old book. Its author, a writer on biblical history, had revealed a most amazing fact:

   "Four heavenly angels always accompanied the Ark of God in all its journeyings, to guard it from all dangers, and to fulfil any mission required of them in connection with the Ark." *Spirit of Prophecy, Vol.1,p.399*

   On the **very same day** another friend, Denis Stanley, rang, quoting a statement to the same effect, from another book *Spiritual Gifts, Vol.4,p.102*

2   Mecca and Medina are the first two.

3   *U.S. News and World Report,* October 7, 1996, p.45

4   Barala, John *Today the Bible and You.* Tulsa, Okl.: August 1996, Editorial

5   Ibid.

6. *The Jewish Press,* Week of April 14 to April 20, 1995; Nisan 14 5755, "Peres Tells Pope Jerusalem Should be Under Vatican Control". Emphasis supplied

7   White, Rev. Bill *A Special Place.* Grantham, Lincolnshire, England: The Stanborough Press Limited, 1989, p.16

8   Ben-Dov, Meir *In the Shadow of the Temple: The Discovery of Ancient Jerusalem.* New York: Harper and Row, 1985, pp.19,20 (discussing a different excavation project from ours)

9   Ibid.

10 Wigoder, Geoffrey (ed.) *The Encyclopedia of Judaism*, pp.695 and 481-483

Chapter 45 Blood Battle

1   Jones, Steve *The Language of Genes*. Harper Collins Publishers, 1993, p.44

2   Ibid., p.21

3   Ibid., p.24

4   Deuteronomy 29:3,5

5   Luke 18:27

6   Mark 10:27

7   Psalm 16:10

8   Acts 2:27

9   1 John 5:8

10   Genesis 18:14

11   Jeremiah 32:27

12   Wyatt, Mary Nell *Wyatt Archaeological Research Newsletter,* July 1995,p.23. Nashville, TN.

13   Matthew 1:21-23

14   ch.22:29

Chapter 46 What Now?

1   Exodus 25:8

2   Hebrews 9:23

3   *Jerusalem Post* (weekend magazine), October 5, 1991, p.13

4   Jeremiah 3:16

5   Daniel 9:27

6   Revelation 11:18

7   vv.15-17

8   v.19

9   Acts 17:31 Matthew 16:27

10   Romans 14:10; 2 Corinthians 5:10; 1 Peter 4:17

11   James 2:10-12; Ecclesiastes 12:13,14

12   Hershon, Paul Isaac *Treasures of the Talmud,* p.97- Quoted by Sanford Ross Howard in *L'Chayim (To Life).* Thorsby, Al.: SAN Enterprises Inc., 1995, p.346. Compare Leviticus 23:29 - "Whatsoever soul it be that shall not be afflicted in that same day, he shall be cut off from among his people."

13   Prayer Book for the Day of Atonement, translated by Dr. A Th. Philips, revised and enlarged. New York: Hebrew Publishing Co., 1933

14   Revelation 11:15; 17:14; 19:16

15   ch.11:19 LB

16   ch. 16:16,17 LB

Chapter 47 The Final Showdown

1   Luke 21:24 (see Appendix H)

2   See Appendix G

3   *Time,* February 24, 1992

4   Martin, Malachi *The Keys of This Blood.* New York, NY: Simon and Schuster, 1990. Martin is a former Jesuit, a professor at the Vatican's Pontifical Biblical Institute and a prolific author. The book is subtitled "The Struggle for World Dominion between Pope John Paul II, Mikhail Gorbachev and the Capitalist West. The publisher describes it: "It presents a compelling array of daring blueprints for global power and one of them is the portrait of our near future as individuals and citizens of nations."

5   See Appendix I

6   Nexus, April-May 1995

7   Deuteronomy 12:32; Ecclesiastes 3:14

8   The sacrificial laws, however, were canceled by the death of Jesus, who "abolished in his flesh (=fulfillment of the animal flesh symbol) the law of commandments contained in ordinances." (Ephesians 2:15) The sacrifice of the FLESH of Jesus puts a stop to the sacrifice of the FLESH of animals. It might be noted that not once in Scripture is the word "ordinance" ever used specifically for any one of the Ten Commandments.

9   *Operation Vampire Killer*. Phoenix, Ai.: Police Against the New World Order, 1992, p.20

10   Dalvalle, P.A., president of the American Constitution, reported in the magazine Die Botsachaft Vom Reich, art. "One Step Nearer"; reported also in NEWSWATCH, Nov-Dec.,1994

11   Rabbi Leibel Reznick *The Holy Temple Revisited*

12   Micah 4:2

13   Psalm 119:126

14   Exodus 34: 28

15   1 Chronicles 28:2

16   Psalm 89:34

17   ch.. 111: 9

18   Matthew 5:17,18

19   Ecclesiastes 9: 5,6,10

20   Job 14:12,21; 7:9,10; Psalm 115:17; 146:4

21   John 5:28,29; Acts 2:29,34; Job 17:13

22   Ephesians 6:11,12; Mark 1:23-26; Deuteronomy 18:11; Luke 4:33-36

23   Revelation 16:14. Miracles, therefore, are not necessarily an evidence of God's power.. Satan and his ministers can pose as messengers of light (2 Corinthians 11:14,15) .

24   Matthew 24: 23-28 LB

25   Marrs, Texe *Dark Secrets of the New Age*, pp.68,69

26   Revelation 1:7; Matthew 24:27,30,31; 1 Thesealonians 4:16,17

27   Isaiah 33:14-17; 41:17,18; 32:18,19; 4: 5,6; Psalms 91 and 46

28   Daniel 12:1

29   Revelation chs. 21 and 22; Isaiah 35; 65:17-25; 66:22,23; 1 Corinthians 2:9; Psalm 16:11

Index

Abel 428,429
Abraham 55-58,234,404
Africa 70,87,88,98,105,193
Amazon 9,49,101,107
Americas
  95,98,99,116-119,127,195,196
Amorites 542,543
Aqaba, Gulf of 103 See also Red Sea
Arabia 71,105,106,110,112,438,560
Arabs 56,228,469-471,477,496,524
Ark of Covenant
  description 79,341-343
  size 21
  gold of 11
  origin of name 81,125,512
  battery theory 12
  considered holy 11–15
  symbolism 79-83
  contents 84,125
  a blessing 13
  brought disaster 10,12,13,85-87
  Shekinah glory over 24,27
  disappearance 27,28,134,135,231,569
  not taken to Babylon 133,134,433
  not in Second Temple 27,35,134,433
  prophecies concerning 134,135,498-501
  future role 495-501,550
  significance to Jews 411,474,475,497
  search and discovery 228-275,323-343
  possible replicas 22,25,118
  heavenly original 35,83,499-501
Asia 70,87,105,193,196
Atlantic 96-98,106
Atonement, Day of See Yom Kippur
Australia 106,110-112
Abel 51 See also Tower of Babel
Babylon 44,132-135, 137,223,231
Bethlehem 34,161,163,404

Blood 47,49,50,82,83,332,415-419,
  421,423,424,426,428,429,431,432,
  477,479-492,496,519,550-552,554
  See also Sacrificial system
Brazil 101,102,107,195
Britain 62,97,l24,199,313-318
Calvary See Skull Hill
Canaanites 57,87-89,118
Canada 106
Candlestick, 7-branched See
  Lampstand
Cannibalism 53,116,202,203
Carthage 98,315
Ceylon 97
China 92,105,195
Chivim 116,127
Christ See Jesus Christ; Messiah
Cornwall See Britain
Covenant, everlasting
  47,81,155,156,182,200,
  216,421,512,564
  See also Ten Commandments
Crucifixion
  procedure 239,241,243,258,373,382
  site 239-258
Cubit 21,425,560,561
Daniel 137,217,399
Darkness 398-401,413,415
David 10,11,15,93,103,125,247,404
Economy 506,507,547-549
Egypt 40,44,51,60,61,63-69,76,92,
  183,221,562
Ethiopia 12,22-25
Europe 70,87,504
Exodus 63-68
Ezion-geber 102,103,105-107,119
Fiji 54
France See Gaul
Gades 97,104
Garden Tomb 235,263-275
Gaul (France) 62,193,317,321,322
Gentiles 208,227,541-549
Germany 63,193,225
Gethsemane 280,366-368,370
Gibraltar 97,106,315
Golgotha See Skull Hill
Gordon, General 265,409
Greece 57,92,119,193
Haiti 101
Hebrews 65,69,89,118 See also Israel
Hezekiah's Tunnel 31
India 105,193,195

591

I know Jonathan personally and we conducted a UK tour together. Jonathan is more than a sincere man, he is a faithful Christian, and he is either lying or telling the truth. There can be no middle ground.

M. Biant, Derby, United Kingdom

I was very skeptical about the work that Jonathan has done when I first heard his report in New Zealand. When he asked me to make a video for him, I consented. Dr. David Wagner, a dentist and avid geology scientist from this area, went with me to confirm the finding. After the trip, both Dr. Wagner and I were convinced of the accuracy of Jonathan's findings.

Dane Griffin, Hot Springs, NC., United States

When I first heard of the claims made by Gray and Wyatt I was quite frankly dubious about it all... but I resolved to check as carefully as I could on this matter. A trusted friend also started checking. My friend decided to get directly into contact with Gray and Wyatt, which he did, entering into correspondence with them on these issues. He tells me that the replies which he received were satisfactory, not only in basic substance, but were expressed in such a manner as to indicate a genuinely right and Christian spirit in these men. It would seem that they had "gone through the mill" at the hands of those who chose to oppose them. Both passed his critical examination. My friend then turned to examine the criticism made against Gray and Wyatt and found that in many instances the opposition was based on **opinion** rather than solidly proven fact. It would seem that much criticism came down to a "we don't like it" point of view, or... "Why should these men find things when our archaeologists haven't?"but this is not fact... it is more like sour grapes or even like vitriol and much of it does not seem to have been issued in a genuinely Christian spirit.

J. Armitage B.Sc.(Hons)., M.Sc., F.G.S., F.R.A.S., F.R.Met. S., F.B.I.S., Cannock, Staffs, United Kingdom

Having been part of the archaeological teams, I can testify that the remains do exist.

Peter Mutton, NSW, Australia

I have known Jonathan personally many years and have carefully discussed and checked the facts reported in the discoveries of the sites. Also I have visited Jonathan's home to go over the large amount of material, including artifacts, and film, some of which goes back a long time. I have also checked with others who have been to and can confirm the existence of some of the sites, including three Jewish teachers ex Israeli army. I have spoken to several of the diving team who were at Nuweiba and a brother at Perth who put his money where his mouth is and went overseas to see for himself and is fully convinced of the authenticity of the discoveries. They are humble Christians true to the message and God is blessing their efforts wonderfully.

John Paige, Victoria, Australia

I decided with my background in Middle East linguistics and geography, plus my contacts with Senior U.S. Air Force linguistics to put (Wyatt, Gray and colleagues) to the test.... I became fully convinced about their findings in all of the areas.

Larry Hartman, Arabic Cryptologic Linguist Craftsman, Senior Airman, USAF, North Augusta, SC., United States

JONATHAN GRAY'S RECENT EXPEDITIONS IN THE MIDDLE EAST

1993	Israel:	Sodom & Gomorrah
		Jerusalem
	Egypt:	Red Sea
	Turkey:	Noah's Ark
1994	Israel:	Jerusalem
		Sodom & Gomorrah
	Egypt:	Red Sea
	Israel:	Kadesh Barnea & Mount Hor
	Egypt:	Sakkara region
1995	Turkey:	Noah's Ark
	Israel:	Jerusalem
		Sodom & Gomorrah
	Egypt:	Sakkara region
		Red Sea

*Since the above, which appeared in the first three editions, excavations continue.

Rene Noorbergen	Red Sea
Dr Nathan Myer	AOC, Noah's Ark
Bob Murrell	AOC, Sodom & Gomorrah, Red Sea
Dane Griffin	Red Sea/Sodom & Gomorrah/Sakkara region
Brett Murray	Red Sea/Sodom & Gomorrah/Sakkara region
Dr Salih Bayraktutan	Noah's Ark
Dr David Wagner	Red Sea/Sodom & Gomorrah
Richard Rives	S/G, Kadesh Barnea, Noah's Ark
Marty Plott	S/G, Red Sea, Kadesh Barnea
Dr Ali Hassan	Egypt projects

Men who have worked with Ron and/or Jonathan. And there are many others.

1. DEAD MEN'S SECRETS • Hardcover, 373 pages
SURPRISING DISCOVERIES IN LOST CITIES OF THE DEAD   Seafloor, jungle and desert sands give up a thousand FORGOTTEN SECRETS. Technology that vanished - what wiped it out? Did the ancients know too much? Who mapped Australia thousands of years before Australia was "discovered"?

2. THE ARK CONSPIRACY • Paperback, 192 pages
COVER-UPS, BETRAYALS AND MIRACLES   The cloak-and-dagger story behind the discovery of Noah's Ark; attempts to suppress the news. Why some people reject the discovery. And the solid evidence that this is the real thing. A true-life thriller: archaeology at its most exciting.

3. STING OF THE SCORPION * Paperback, 118 pages
ASTROLOGY EXPOSED - THE TRUTH BEHIND STAR NAMES AND SIGNS   Ancient civilisations believed that a serpent - which represented the devil - took control of the world. They believed a virgin's baby would fight the serpent, defeat him and bring peace, life and happiness back to mankind. The pictures on the sky map were used to describe the story and NOT to tell people's fortunes through the stars. The NAMES of the stars, as well as the star sign PICTURES told that story.

4. CURSE OF THE HATANA GODS • Paperback, 96 pages
A STUNNING REAL-LIFE ADVENTURE   One of the most isolated islands on earth is Rotuma, ancient home to a race of GIANTS. But Rotuma shielded a sinister secret, for which there was no scientific explanation. They called it THE CURSE OF HATANA. The evidence for the ANCIENT GIANTS - and the incredible story of a face to face encounter with the CURSE.

. NEWSLETTER BOOKS (back issues)
3 SPIRAL-BOUND BOOKS OF ISSUES OF UPDATE 1-10, 11-20, 21-30.   Covers all discoveries in which Jonathan Gray and his associates are involved, with extra information, as well as ancient giants, dinosaurs, mysteries of ancient South America, surprises in the Grand Canyon, and more. Scores of photos, maps, diagrams.

. REGULAR NEWSLETTER
QUARTERLY UPDATE INTERNATIONAL NEWSLETTER SUBSCRIPTION   All recent developments and new materials are announced in here. Plus other significant archaeological finds around the world, and news of other important world developments relating to the coming New World Order.

. SINAI'S EXCITING SECRETS
Things are happening at Mt Sinai in Arabia ... A new top secret radar base; Bedoins digging up graves. New information and photos can now be revealed to the world. A compilation of data. Spiral bound. 76 pages.

. DISCOVERIES: QUESTIONS ANSWERED
Did Wyatt lie about the blood? Did Gray "seriously edit" an Amiralty Letter to prove a Red Sea land bridge? What's behind the "answers in Genesis" – Standish attack on the discoveries? Did scientists prove "Noah's Ark" to be a fake?   Over 280 questions. Certificates, private letters and facts never before revealed. Input by numerous people. Our most explosive publication ever! Spiral bound. 340 pages.

9. SURPRISING DISCOVERIES 1 * by Jonathan Gray - 2 hours
    Part 1 - Has Noah's Ark Been Found? (THE NOAH'S ARK STORY)
    Part 2 - Lost Secrets of the Ancients (ANCIENT TECHNOLOGY)
    Part 3 - Into the Forbidden Valley (TRIP TO NOAH'S GRAVE SITE)

10. SURPRISING DISCOVERIES 2 * by Jonathan Gray - 2¹/₂ hours
    Part 1 - The Lost Cities of Sodom and Gomorrah (DEAD SEA SITES)
    Part 2 - In Search of Egypt's Lost Army (RED SEA CROSSING)
    Part 3 - Smuggled Out of the Desert (THE REAL MT. SINAI - footage)

11. SURPRISING DISCOVERIES 3 * by Jonathan Gray - 2¹/₂ hours
    THE ARK OF THE COVENANT.   The search for this golden chest which enshrined the Ten Commandmen
    The legend they have to hide!

12. SURPRISING DISCOVERIES 4 * by Jonathan Gray - 75 minutes
    STRANGE SIGNS IN THE SKY. The truth behind star signs.

13. SURPRISING DISCOVERIES 5 * by Jonathan Gray - 1 hour
    SECRETS OF ANCIENT SOUTH AMERICA.   See what happens when a high civilization turns it back on divine law ... and more!

14. SURPRISING DISCOVERIES 6 * by Jonathan Gray - 81 minutes
    IN A COFFIN IN EGYPT.   Mysteries and wonders of ancient Egypt.

15. DISCOVERED: SODOM AND GOMORRAH * by Ron Wyatt. 45 mins
    Gripping ... unique ... eerie ... 4,000 year old buildings, still partly standing, totally turned into ash - a
    peppered with millions of balls of burnt sulphur. Ron Wyatt's probes of the ruins.

16. DISCOVERED: NOAH'S ARK. * by Ron Wyatt. 110 minutes
    Actual footage of all aspects of the field work: graphics explaining the process which preserved the remai
    scientific testing, and much, much more, some never before made public.

17. DISCOVERED: THE EXODUS * by Ron Wyatt. 96 minutes
    A complete documentary of the discovery and evidences of the Red Sea crossing, the REAL Mt Sinai in Arabia, and more.

18. 6 MAJOR DISCOVERIES * by Ron Wyatt. 75 minutes
    Noah's Ark, Sodom and Gomorrah, Red Sea crossing, Mt Sinai, Ark of the Covenant, and how the pyramids were built. Includes questio
    answered live from the audience.

ORDERING COUPON

BOOKS

Dead Men's Secrets	$30	
Ark of the Covenant	$25	
The Ark of Conspiracy	$15	
Sting of the Scorpion	$10	
Curse of the Hatana Gods	$10	
Newsletter (Issues 1-10)	$35	
Newsletter (Issues 11-20)	$35	
Newsletter (Issues 21-30)	$35	
Sinai's Exciting Secrets	$15	
Discov'. Questions Answered	$30	

NEWSLETTER

Per Year – 4 issues ....$25 .....PostPd.

VIDEOS

Surprising Discoveries 1	$30	
Surprising Discoveries 2	$30	
Surprising Discoveries 3	$30	
Surprising Discoveries 4	$30	
Surprising Discoveries 5	$30	
Surprising Discoveries 6	$30	
Discovered: Sodom/Gomorrah	$30	
Discovered: Noah's Ark	$30	
Discovered: The Exodus	$30	
Six Major Discoveries	$30	

CD ROM

The Ark of the Covenant ....$55 ....

....**Sub Total** ....

Post and Pack <u>within</u> Australia-
Orders up to $60, add 20%..
Orders over $60, add 15% ....

....**TOTAL** ....

OVERSEAS INQUIRIES WELCOME

Name ....
Address ....
....P/C ....

Post this coupon to:
Mr. Jonathan Gray
P.O. Box 3370, Rundle Mall
Adelaide. Sth. Australia. 5000
Tel/Fax: +61 8 8388 8072
Email: rev14@hyper.net.au

New Zealand
Surprising Discoveries
P.O. Box 785, Thames.
Tel: +64 7 866 7525